D1592532

Economic Crises and the Breakdown of Authoritarian Regimes
Indonesia and Malaysia in Comparative Perspective

Why do some authoritarian regimes topple during financial crises, whereas others steer through financial crises relatively unscathed? In this book, Thomas B. Pepinsky uses the experiences of Indonesia and Malaysia and the analytical tools of open economy macroeconomics to answer this question. Focusing on the economic interests of authoritarian regimes' supporters, Pepinsky shows that differences in cross-border asset specificity produce dramatically different outcomes in regimes facing financial crises. When supporters are divided by the mobility of their capital assets, as in Indonesia, they desire mutually incompatible adjustment policies, yielding incoherent adjustment policy followed by regime collapse. When coalitions are not divided by the mobility of their assets, as in Malaysia, regimes adopt radical adjustment measures that enable them to survive financial crises. Combining rich qualitative evidence from Southeast Asia with cross-national time-series data and comparative case studies of Latin American autocracies, Pepinsky reveals the power of coalitions and capital mobility to explain how financial crises produce regime change.

Thomas B. Pepinsky is Assistant Professor of Government and a faculty affiliate of the Southeast Asia Program at Cornell University. His research appears in *World Politics, European Journal of International Relations, Journal of East Asian Studies, Journal of Democracy, Studies in Comparative International Development,* and several edited volumes. He received his Ph.D. from Yale University and taught at the University of Colorado at Boulder from 2007 to 2008. He held a Fulbright-Hays Doctoral Dissertation Research Abroad Fellowship in Indonesia and Malaysia from 2004 to 2005.

Economic Crises and the Breakdown of Authoritarian Regimes

Indonesia and Malaysia in Comparative Perspective

THOMAS B. PEPINSKY

Cornell University

CAMBRIDGE UNIVERSITY PRESS
Cambridge, New York, Melbourne, Madrid, Cape Town, Singapore, São Paulo, Delhi

Cambridge University Press
32 Avenue of the Americas, New York, NY 10013-2473, USA

www.cambridge.org
Information on this title: www.cambridge.org/9780521744386

First published 2009

Printed in the United States of America

A catalog record for this publication is available from the British Library.

Library of Congress Cataloging in Publication Data

Pepinsky, Thomas B., 1979–
    Economic crises and the breakdown of authoritarian regimes : Indonesia and Malaysia in
    comparative perspective / Thomas B. Pepinsky.
        p. cm.
    Includes bibliographical references and index.
    ISBN 978-0-521-76793-4 (hardback) – ISBN 978-0-521-74438-6 (pbk.)
        1. Indonesia – Politics and government – 20th century. 2. Authoritarianism – Indonesia.
    3. Indonesia – Economic policy – 20th century. 4. Indonesia – Economic conditions – 20th
    century. 5. Malaysia – Politics and government – 20th century. 6. Authoritarianism –
    Malaysia. 7. Malaysia – Economic policy – 20th century. 8. Malaysia – Economic
    conditions – 20th century. I. Title.
    JQ776.P42 2009
    959.505′4 – dc22   2008055952

ISBN 978-0-521-76793-4 hardback
ISBN 978-0-521-74438-6 paperback

If the fields are ruined, then the city too will be short of
    sustenance.
If there are no subjects, then clearly there will be other islands
    that come to take us by surprise.
Therefore let them be cared for so that both will be stable; this
    is the benefit of my words to you.

    – Mpu Prapañca, the *Nāgarakṛtāgama*

Many are the places and lands which have been destroyed by
    the depredations of the young scions of the ruling house,
    whose rapacious hands can no longer be tolerated by the
    people.

  – Abdullah bin Abdul Kadir Munsyi, *Hikayat Abdullah*

Contents

List of Tables

List of Figures

Acknowledgments

I am grateful to many people for their encouragement and criticism over the many years that this project has taken me to complete. At Yale, Frances Rosenbluth went far beyond the call of duty in giving prompt, critical responses to my endless questions. Stathis Kalyvas and Zé Cheibub made me articulate how my research would be interesting to someone who does not study financial politics in Southeast Asia, and the book is far stronger for it. The three of them together made me turn the product of my field research from a story to an argument. Keith Darden, Justin Fox, Pierre Landry, Ellen Lust-Okar, Nikolay Marinov, Gus Ranis, Ken Scheve, Sue Stokes, Mariano Tommasi, and Jim Vreeland each at various points helped me to think about the wider implications of my argument, both theoretically and empirically. Indriyo Sukmono is a great friend and a language teacher *yang tak ternilai dukungannya*. My graduate school friends Katie Galvin, Steve Kosack, and Tarek Masoud oversaw the first tentative steps in the project, and Rafaela Dancygier and Steve Kaplan gave me valuable feedback as it neared completion.

I also owe a debt of gratitude to my "external coalition" for reading and commenting on portions of the project at various stages, in particular Andy Baker, Carew Boulding, Alasdair Bowie, David Brown, Jason Brownlee, Bill Case, Don Emmerson, Gustavo Flores-Macías, Jeff Frieden, Ken Greene, Steph Haggard, Allen Hicken, Jomo K. S., Joe Jupille, Peter Katzenstein, Jonathan Kirshner, Ehito Kimura, David Leblang, Bill Liddle, Andrew MacIntyre, Rizal Mallarangeng, David Patel, Ken Roberts, Michael Ross, Shanker Satyanath, Dan Slater, Ben Smith, David Waldner, and Sean Yom. What to them probably seemed like forgettable, throwaway comments were for me key criticisms, sometimes devastating ones, that suggested important refinements to the argument and occasionally kept me up at night. Any errors that remain in the book are, of course, my own.

To my many informants in both countries who continue to struggle for reform, good governance, and justice, and hence cannot be cited by name, I give you my thanks.

The bulk of the fieldwork was sponsored by a Fulbright-Hays International Dissertation Research Abroad Fellowship from the United States Department of Education. Language training was sponsored by a Foreign Language and Area Studies Grant from the Department of Education. I was fortunate to receive repeated research grants from both the Leitner Program on International and Comparative Political Economy and the Center for Southeast Asian Studies at Yale. In Indonesia, I benefited from an affiliation with the Freedom Institute in Jakarta, and in Malaysia, from affiliations with the Faculty of Social Sciences and Humanities at Universiti Kebangsaan Malaysia and the Institute for Strategic and International Studies in Kuala Lumpur. In Indonesia, I am grateful to Saiful Mujani, Ahmad Sahal, Sugianto Tandra, Nong Darol Mahmada, Anis, and Tata at Freedom for all of their help, support, and friendship. In Malaysia, I owe special thanks to Nik Anuar Nik Mahmud and Ahmad Nidzammuddin Sulaiman at UKM and to Haji Mohamed Md. Ibrahim and Dato' Seri Mohamad Jawhar Hassan at ISIS-Malaysia. Thanks also to Nelly Paliama at the American Indonesian Exchange Foundation and Don McCloud and Meena Ponnusamy at the Malaysian-American Commission on Educational Exchange for all sorts of visa help.

Lew Bateman and Emily Spangler at Cambridge University Press deserve special praise for dealing with a first-time author. Their patience and professionalism helped make the editorial process smooth and easy.

Parts of Chapters 2, 4, and 5 previously appeared as "Capital Mobility and Coalitional Politics: Authoritarian Regimes and Economic Adjustment in Southeast Asia," *World Politics* 60 (3) (2008): 438–74.

In the end, this book is for Julie. She tolerated a year plus of fieldwork, helped me to track down materials, gave valuable feedback as I worked through the theory, took me out for local cuisine and beer, and kept me very happy at the same time.

Terms and Abbreviations

ABIM	Angkatan Belia Islam Malaysia (Malaysian Islamic Youth Movement)
ABRI	Angkatan Bersenjata Republik Indonesia (Armed Forces of Indonesia)
Apkindo	Asosiasi Panel Kayu Indonesia (Wood Panel Association of Indonesia)
ASB	Amanah Saham Bumiputra (Bumiputra Unit Trust)
ASN	Amanah Saham Nasional (National Unit Trust)
BA	Barisan Alternatif (Alternative Front)
Bais	Badan Intelijen Strategis (Strategic Intelligence Agency)
Bakin	Badan Kordinasi Intelijen Negara (Coordinating Agency for State Intelligence)
balatkom	*bahaya laten komunisme* (latent danger of communism)
Berdikari	Berdiri di Atas Kaki Sendiri (Indonesia's government-owned trading firm; literally, "stand on one's own feet")
Berhad	Limited Liability Corporation (Malaysia)
BI	Bank Indonesia (Central Bank of Indonesia)
BLBI	Bantuan Likuiditas Bank Indonesia (Bank Indonesia Liquidity Support)
BN	Barisan Nasional (National Front)
BNM	Bank Negara Malaysia (Central Bank of Malaysia)

BPPC	Badan Penyangga dan Pemasaran Cengkeh (Clove Marketing Board)
Bulog	Badan Urusan Logistik (Bureau of Logistical Affairs)
bumiputra	Malaysian not of Indian or Chinese ancestry; includes Austronesian peoples of Malaysian Borneo (Bidayuh, Iban, Kadazandusun, etc.) and non-Malay indigenous peoples of the Malayan Peninsula (*orang asli*); also includes by law Thais and Eurasians
CBS	Currency Board System
CDRC	Corporate Debt Restructuring Committee
CLOB	Central Limit Order Book
Danaharta	Pengurusan Danaharta Nasional Berhad (Malaysia government vehicle for purchasing nonperforming loans)
Danamodal	Danamodal Nasional Berhad (Malaysian government body that recapitalized Malaysian banks)
DAP	Democratic Action Party
DPR	Dewan Perwakilan Rakyat (People's Representative Council, Indonesian House of Representatives)
DR	Dewan Rakyat (People's Council, Malaysian Parliament, Lower House)
FELDA	Federal Land Development Authority
Gerakan	Gerakan Rakyat Malaysia (Malaysian People's Movement)
Golkar	Golongan Karya (Party of Functional Groups)
IBRA	Indonesian Bank Restructuring Agency
ICMI	Ikatan Cendikiawan Muslim se-Indonesia (All-Indonesian Association of Muslim Intellectuals)
IMF	International Monetary Fund
ISA	Internal Security Act
Kadin	Kamar Dagang dan Industri (Indonesian Chamber of Commerce)
KeADILan	Parti Keadilan Nasional (National JUSTice Party)

KKN	*korupsi, kronisme, nepotisme* or *korupsi, kolusi, nepotisme* (corruption, cronyism/collusion, nepotism)
Kopassus	Komando Pasukan Khusus (Special Forces Command of the Armed Forces of Indonesia)
Kostrad	Komando Candangan Strategi Tentara Negara Indonesia Angkatan Darat (Strategic Reserve Command of the Armed Forces of Indonesia)
MARA	Majlis Amanah Rakyat (Council of Trust for Indigenous People)
MCA	Malaysian Chinese Association
MIC	Malaysian Indian Congress
MPR	Majelis Permusyawaratan Rakyat (People's Consultative Assembly)
NEAC	National Economic Action Council
NEP	New Economic Policy
NGO	nongovernmental organization
NPL	nonperforming loan
Pancasila	"Five Principles," the governing philosophy underlying the New Order regime
PAS	Parti Islam Se-Malaysia (Pan-Malaysian Islamic Party)
PDI	Partai Demokrasi Indonesia (Indonesian Democratic Party)
peranakan	"descendant," refers to Chinese Malaysians descended from immigrants to Malacca or Penang in the 1800s; also refers to Chinese Indonesians who have assimilated to Indonesian culture
Pernas	Perbadanan Nasional Berhad (National Agency Limited)
Pertamina	Perusahaan Pertambangan Minyak Negara (National Oil Mining Corporation, Indonesia's petroleum parastatal)
Petronas	Petroliam Nasional Berhad (National Petroleum Limited, Malaysia's petroleum parastatal)
PKI	Partai Komunis Indonesia (Indonesian Communist Party)

PNB	Permodalan Nasional Berhad (National Equity Corporation)
PPP	Partai Persatuan Pembangunan (United Development Party)
PRI	Institutional Revolutionary Party of Mexico
pribumi	Indonesian not of Chinese or other nonarchipelagic ancestry; normally includes Indonesians of Arab ancestry
PRM	Parti Rakyat Malaysia (Malaysian People's Party)
Proton	Perusahaan Otomobil Nasional (National Automobile Corporation)
PT	Perusahaan Terbatas (Limited Liability Corporation, Indonesia)
SBI	Sertifikat Bank Indonesia (the standard debt vehicle employed by Bank Indonesia)
SBPU	Surat Berharga Pasar Uang (Bank Indonesia's short-term money market instrument)
Semangat '46	Spirit of 1946
UMNO	United Malays National Organisation
yayasan	literally "foundation," refers to a number of off-budget, unmonitored funding bodies in New Order Indonesia
Yayasan Pelaburan Bumiputera	Bumiputra Investment Foundation

1

Crises, Adjustment, and Transitions

Two Countries, Two Trajectories

On the morning of July 14, 1997, citizens of Jakarta and Kuala Lumpur awoke to a new world. The difference from the previous day was seemingly minor and distant – several hundred miles to the north, the government of Thailand had abandoned its long-standing informal currency peg of the baht to the American dollar. Few would have believed that this decision was the first in a chain of events that would fundamentally remake the political economy of Southeast Asia. Even as foreign investors turned their eyes toward other Asian countries, reconsidering the health of their financial systems, political and economic upheaval seemed unlikely. Indonesia and Malaysia had long embraced the world economy. They were competently run economies with popular leaders who had engineered decades of impressive economic growth. Despite their excesses, authoritarian rule in each country bred stability, prosperity, and development.

A year later, Indonesia and Malaysia were in turmoil. Sustained capital outflows and currency speculation had led to massive depreciation of the rupiah and ringgit and heavy losses in each country's stock market. Economic growth, which for a decade had been among the highest in the world, became economic collapse – GDP contracted nearly 8 percent in Malaysia and more than 13 percent in Indonesia during 1998. In each country, thousands of borrowers in the business community were unable to service their debts. Financial upheaval forced both countries to seek emergency funds from foreign donors to keep their once-buoyant economies afloat. In Indonesia, simmering ethnic animosity that overlay long-standing economic inequality had boiled over into violence. In Malaysia, the prospect of such violence once again appeared.

Despite sharp economic contraction in each country, policies and politics varied widely between them. Previously one of the world's most durable authoritarian regimes, Indonesia was almost unrecognizable in July 1998. For ten months, the regime's adjustment policies shifted wildly: tight monetary policy followed by loose monetary policy, promises of fiscal and trade reform made and then broken, subsidies protected and then cut, bailouts offered and then denounced. President Soeharto resigned from office amid mass urban violence that drove many of his ethnic Chinese cronies overseas and divided his military backers. His successor, B. J. Habibie, had no natural constituency and presided over a largely peaceful transition to democracy while quietly accepting a deeply unpopular adjustment package from the International Monetary Fund.

Malaysia, by contrast, was in July 1998 preparing for one of the most controversial economic policy choices taken by an emerging market economy in the post–Bretton Woods era. A brash critic of the International Monetary Fund's recommendations for Asia, Malaysia's Prime Minister Mahathir Mohamad consistently resisted tight monetary policies and subsidy cuts for poor Malaysians and allowed crony interests to use public funds to forestall their own bankruptcy. In early September, Malaysia imposed extensive capital account restrictions, loosened monetary policies still further, and expanded public spending. At the same time, with the country's security forces firmly behind him, Mahathir ousted his popular deputy prime minister and finance minister Anwar Ibrahim and crushed Malaysia's first truly panethnic democracy movement. Coercion and economic recovery allowed Mahathir and his regime to survive Malaysia's worst-ever economic crisis relatively unscathed.

This book is about the struggles of authoritarian regimes to contain economic crises. The questions that inspire it arise from the diverging experiences of Indonesia and Malaysia during these tumultuous years. Why do authoritarian regimes respond to crises with different policies? Why do adjustment policies within one country vacillate so wildly? What drives protestors into the streets during economic crises? When can authoritarian regimes successfully crack down on their opponents? When do economic crises lead to authoritarian breakdowns?

I answer all of these questions by focusing on political coalitions and their economic interests. I show that during economic crises, authoritarian regimes face powerful pressures from their supporters to enact policies that minimize the burden of adjustment that they face. Regimes enact policies that shift the costs of adjustment away from their political supporters. Across countries, different coalitions of regime supporters therefore produce different political trajectories, both in the adjustment policies that regimes adopt and in the nature of political conflict that the regime faces. When supporters have mutually incompatible preferences over adjustment policies, adjustment policies appear incoherent, and political coalitions are fundamentally unsustainable. When preferences are compatible, regimes adopt their supporters' favored policies, crush their opponents, and survive.

The argument therefore focuses tightly on the causal role of coalitions and economic interests in shaping the dynamics of economic reform and political survival in authoritarian regimes. During economic crises, struggles over adjustment policy and regime survival are fundamentally intertwined. This framework illuminates how the economic shock of the Asian Financial Crisis produced such dramatically different political outcomes in Indonesia and Malaysia. For reasons that I detail in this book, the coalition of supporters that backed Soeharto's New Order regime – ethnic Chinese business groups with extensive holdings of mobile capital, and military-linked firms and a new class of indigenous entrepreneurs whose capital assets were rooted in Indonesia – had contradictory preferences over adjustment. Both sought bailouts from the regime, but the latter demanded that Soeharto close the capital account, whereas the former demanded continual capital account openness as a condition for supporting the regime. Sharp vacillations in adjustment policy during 1997–98 reflect these struggles. This political conflict amid financial meltdown ultimately brought down the regime, leading to a political collapse marked by anti-Chinese violence and the mass exodus of ethnic Chinese Indonesians.

Malaysia's regime, supported by a coalition of the ethnic Malay masses and a newly ascendant coterie of Malay entrepreneurs with fixed investments, faced no such contradictory demands over adjustment policy. Neither group had substantial mobile assets to redeploy overseas, so both demanded that Mahathir ban capital outflows to enable expansionary policies. The seemingly idiosyncratic nature of Malaysia's adjustment measures – consistently resisting austere stabilization policies and maintaining extensive redistributive programs – reflects the demands of this coalition of supporters. Without a fundamental cleavage in its supporters' preferences, the Malaysian regime was able to steer through financial meltdown by adopting its supporters' preferred policies, ensuring that only the regime's opponents bore the costs of adjustment and allowing the regime to survive intact. Differing coalitions therefore explain different adjustment policies and regime outcomes in Indonesia and Malaysia.

The coalitional approach, by examining trajectories of adjustment policy and regime survival in Indonesia and Malaysia, brings a fresh perspective to a topic that has been well studied by area specialists. To be sure, many have noted political resistance to economic reform in both countries, as well as the role of economic crises in motivating antiincumbent protest in the face of recalcitrant authoritarians. But these accounts are incomplete. Studies of resistance to reform in each country, and of regime collapse in Indonesia and regime survival in Malaysia, have neglected the critical interrelationship of antiregime protest and pressures for economic reform. Actors protest against regimes *because* they do not receive favorable policies. The coalitional theory not only provides a unified account of how interest groups pressure regimes for favorable policies but also considers the impact of these pressures on subsequent political trajectories.

Understanding Adjustment and Authoritarian Breakdowns

My theory of crises, adjustment, and regime survival rests on the analytical tools of positive political economy and open economy macroeconomics. By carefully examining the nature of the economic meltdown in each country, I uncover the consequences of different economic policy choices, detailing how these choices spread the costs of adjustment across different citizens in an economy. Assuming a simple behavioral strategy, that actors pressure regimes to enact policies that fulfill their interests, I then derive predictions of policy choices given different kinds of constituencies. I assume here that no policy is "off the table": clients will turn on their patrons if their patrons do not supply them with favorable policies, and regimes will adopt policies that are deeply unpopular to regime opponents and the international community if it is in their supporters' interests to do so. With these tools in hand, I am able to understand policy choices that can seem illogical or irrational (as in Indonesia) or radical (as in Malaysia). This approach also allows me to make wider generalizations on the basis of the experiences of these two countries. Across the world, when authoritarian regimes face economic crises, coalitional pressures dominate struggles over adjustment policy and regime survival.

I am also careful, though, to ensure that theories and assumptions are borne out by the experiences of the two countries. Against the reductionist claim that economic interests alone condition policy responses, I emphasize that political coalitions are the key variable that explains why regimes favor particular interest groups. The adjustment story is inherently political. To show this, I bring a wealth of new data on regime behavior and interest group preferences to the large existing body of literature on crisis politics in each country. In doing so, I have attempted to combine the theoretical precision of positive political economy with the nuance and substance of the area specialist. The experiences of the two countries do reveal that many simple predictions from standard economic models do not obtain. For example, for various reasons that I detail later, rapid currency depreciation in each country did not lead to an export boom, despite the improvement of exporters' terms of trade. Deep study of the countries' economies and political systems was critical for allowing me to test such predictions against the experiences of each.

By linking international economic crises to political regime change through economic adjustment, this book spans two research paradigms in comparative politics and international political economy. The first is the politics of economic adjustment. Political scientists have recognized that economic adjustment has important distributional implications and, hence, that politicians enacting reform will tailor their reform packages to minimize the costs borne by their political supporters. In varying ways, authors ask why governments choose particular economic policies, or why governments fail to enact needed policy reforms, and answer these questions by looking at the preferences that actors within a country have over these policies and at the struggles between the winners and losers from economic reform.[1] Governments enact policies because they fulfill the demands of a politically influential group within the population. Failure to enact necessary reform packages is the result of entrenched opposition from some group with privileged links to the government. Within this positive political economy approach, governments do not arbitrate neutrally among possible reform choices, choosing policies that maximize collective welfare or future economic growth. Instead, governments fulfill particularistic demands for political purposes, with the result that in countries facing similar needs for economic adjustment, policies enacted will vary according to the profile of powerful interest groups within those countries.

---

[1] Alesina and Drazen 1991; Gourevitch 1986; Hellman 1998; Martinelli and Tommasi 1997; Rodrik 1996; Schamis 1999.

A wide literature has asked, given this model of policy formation, what interest groups actually demand in terms of international and domestic economic policies. Interest group approaches have outlined how sectors with differing trade orientations will prefer different exchange rate settings given a world of highly mobile capital.[2] Different levels of asset mobility across sectors influenced the types of political conflicts that arose during Latin America's debt crisis of the early 1980s.[3] In industrialized economies, coalitions of different economic interests influence government responses to international economic crises.[4] A rich literature has followed these works, exploring how differing institutional configurations, collective action costs, and levels of intersectoral factor mobility shape the types of distributional conflicts that arise and the coalitions that form in open economies.[5]

While sharing this analytical tradition, my coalitional approach differs in important ways. Most broadly, economic interests are vital for my theory of adjustment and transition, for they illuminate the dimensions along which policy conflict unfolds during economic crises. But coalitions, not interests, are the decisive factor. Interests do not translate directly into political outcomes absent some organized method of articulation; in short, interests need politics to become policy. In authoritarian regimes, coalitions are the stuff of politics, and they determine which interest groups a regime will favor – given the same menu of interest groups in two countries, different coalitions will produce different policy outcomes. Systematic attention to the coalitional bases of authoritarian rule provides an intuitive framework for understanding the link between economic interests and political outcomes.[6] Other recent work has neglected coalitions, instead favoring reductive assumptions about the class basis of authoritarian rule or ignoring interests entirely.

I also uncover new axes of policy conflict. Building on work on the domestic politics of international monetary relations, I not only study preferences over both interest rates and exchange rates but examine when groups prefer capital account closure as an adjustment policy option. In addition, I focus on financial sector weaknesses, showing how the impact of international adjustment measures on financial sector viability gives

---

[2] Frieden 1991b.
[3] Frieden 1991a.
[4] Gourevitch 1986.
[5] See, e.g., Alt et al. 1996; Alt and Gilligan 1994; Broz and Frieden 2001; Hiscox 2002; Schambaugh 2004.
[6] Pepinsky 2008a.

regimes an impetus to cut links between themselves and the international economy. Finally, I study preferences of three types of actors: labor, fixed capital, and mobile capital. I show that, when currency depreciation exposes banking sector fragility, the dominant cleavages are not among land, labor, and capital or between export-competitive and import-competitive sectors, but between factions of capital based on their cross-border asset specificity, with labor aligning with holders of fixed capital. By implication, I find that the level of conflict among sectors and factors varies according to economic conditions.

Of course, the coalitional approach to the politics of economic adjustment does not exist in isolation. Other explanations for adjustment policy include pressures from international lending institutions, ideology, institutional configurations, cognitive biases, political will, and technocratic competence, among others.[7] In this book, I treat each of these perspectives as alternative explanations, which I examine in light of events in Indonesia, Malaysia, and elsewhere. In revealing how each is incomplete, I demonstrate the power of my coalitional approach.

In the context of Asia's recent financial crises, institutions have received the most attention. Authors have argued that different institutional arrangements affected Asian countries' abilities to commit to creating good economic policies before and during the crisis,[8] and that institutional arrangements affect the course of postcrisis recovery and economic growth.[9] Although these authors do not address explicitly the choice of particular policies, they do suggest how institutions may have constrained the abilities of policy makers to enact policies. The coalitional story, which takes seriously preferences over adjustment policy, makes predictions that institutions alone cannot. Institutions are important, but as they are analytically secondary to an understanding of what groups within a society demand from the government, they alone are as incomplete as a purely economic explanation. Whereas Andrew MacIntyre's institutional approach allows him to study "broad patterns of policy management" in Southeast Asia,[10] coalitions tell us about specific policies and why they were enacted. Coalitions are the political link that mediates how economic interests translate into adjustment policies.

[7] Bates and Krueger 1993; Haggard 2000a; Haggard and Kaufman 1992; Haggard, Lafay, and Morrisson 1995; Haggard and Webb 1994; Krueger 1993; 2000; Manzetti 2003; Nelson 1989; 1990; Remmer 1986; Tommasi 2005; Vreeland 2003; Weyland 2002.
[8] Haggard 2000b; MacIntyre 2001; Satyanath 2006.
[9] Hicken, Satyanath, and Sergenti 2005; Montinola 2003; Pepinsky 2008b.
[10] MacIntyre 2003b, 55.

This book, though, is about more than economic adjustment. It shows how political conflict over adjustment policy affects the ability of authoritarian regimes to survive economic crises. Departing from the usual practice of studying adjustment and regime survival in isolation, my argument links interest cleavages over adjustment policies directly to the question of authoritarian regime survival.

The literature on crises and authoritarian breakdowns has recently turned away from earlier arguments about preferences, coalitions, and elite factionalism in explaining authoritarian regime trajectories.[11] The new scholarship has focused instead on crisis severity and the institutional bases of authoritarian rule. There is some evidence that inflationary crises and recessionary crises have different impacts on the likelihood of democratic transitions.[12] Institutionalists have suggested that military regimes are more likely to break down during economic crises than party-based or civilian authoritarian regimes.[13] Alternatively, authoritarian regimes with political institutions such as elections, parties, and legislatures survive longer than other authoritarian regimes,[14] or just until their dominant parties are unable to marshal the resources that keep the masses supporting authoritarian rule.[15]

My argument challenges the ability of institutions and crisis severity to explain why and how authoritarian regimes break down during economic crises. Coalitional politics during crises is too rich to ignore. Regimes take steps to minimize the impact of crises on their supporters, meaning that crisis severity should not be treated as an exogenous causal variable in the study of authoritarian breakdowns. Institutional perspectives begin with the political structures in place and make predictions based on them, but they ignore how regime leaders and opponents alike assault the political institutions so often held to constrain leaders' authority and their opponents' mobilizational capacity. Adjustment policy and institutional manipulation are both endogenous responses by authoritarian regimes to economic crises. These responses matter; they reveal the contours of political conflict during economic crises, and they allow us to understand just why an economic crisis can unseat an authoritarian regime. It is here that coalitions and economic interests have a powerful story to tell,

---

[11] On these earlier statements, see Bratton and van de Walle 1994; Higley and Burton 1989; O'Donnell and Schmitter 1986.
[12] Gasiorowski 1995.
[13] Geddes 2003, 44–86.
[14] Brownlee 2007; Gandhi and Przeworski 2006.
[15] Greene 2007; Magaloni 2006.

broadening the causal story to explain when – and, more critically, *why* and *how* – economic shocks lead to authoritarian breakdowns.

Data and Methods

The coalitional theory explains policy choice and regime outcomes in terms of strategic interactions among regimes and interest groups. I approach the Indonesian and Malaysian cases, which form the backbone of the empirical work in this book, committed to an argument that is both *internally parsimonious* and *generalizable*. The internal parsimony of the account depends on how well it explains many different types of adjustment across policy domains and on how well it explains various features of regime survival in Malaysia and regime collapse in Indonesia. In assessing internal parsimony, I recognize that the topics of adjustment and regime survival in the two cases are well trodden. I judge my argument to be more internally parsimonious than its competitors when, in comparison with others, it leaves fewer aspects of adjustment and transition unexplained and, in particular, when pieces of evidence are consistent with my account but inconsistent with others.

The cases of Indonesia and Malaysia give some initial leverage for the coalitional argument, as they are similar on many other important dimensions. Both had very open economies dominated by exports and highly open to international financial flows, but with widespread government favoritism in the distribution of fiscal expenditures and extensive political influence in the allocation of credit. Fully convertible currencies made speculation against the rupiah and the ringgit feasible, and managed exchange rate regimes in each allowed speculators to bet against what they believed to be unsustainable currency targets. Both countries entered the crisis with relatively strong foreign reserves. Neither country had an independent central bank capable of vetoing adjustment policy decisions. Leaders in each country were avowed nationalists and maintained extensive personal control over the formation of economic policy. If economic characteristics or institutions alone drive outcomes, then variation between the countries is still more puzzling. Consideration of the political coalitions in both countries is needed to complete the story.

Studying coalitions requires deep, case-specific knowledge. I garnered this information through interviews, local and regional newspapers, opposition publications, reports from nongovernmental organizations (NGOs), national and international statistical sources, and a wide variety of published secondary sources. Newspapers and statistical sources together give a very accurate description of adjustment policy measures as they unfolded over time. Interviewees included key decision makers such as former government ministers and bureaucrats, opposition politicians, activists, local academics, journalists, and employees at international development institutions. Opposition publications and NGO reports give important context to the events and decisions.

It is important not to underestimate the sensitivity of this research, even today, ten years after the onset of the crisis. In both countries, the amounts of money at stake for key individuals reach occasionally into the billions of dollars. In Indonesia, thousands of people died as an indirect result of the political manipulation of that country's economy in 1997 to 1998, and many of the most important individuals have fled Indonesia and are today in hiding. Ongoing investigations mean that many ill-gotten fortunes are still at risk and that actions taken during the crisis may still have legal implications. In Malaysia, where the regime survived the crisis, many interested parties remain close to those in power and are reluctant to discuss their actions during the crisis. Moreover, in Malaysia, freedom of the press remains circumscribed, and many laws discourage open criticism of the regime. On several occasions in each country, I faced interviewees who openly lied about their actions during the crisis. For these reasons, my use of interview data is judicious: I corroborate all statements with other sources or other interviewees. Moreover, anonymity for many interviewees is a paramount concern. For some interviewees and on some topics I operate on strict journalistic "background" rules, where I do not attribute findings to particular individuals, even anonymously by reference to their profession or the date of the interview. When interviewees have explicitly consented, I include as much information as they view to be appropriate.

The drawback of a paired comparison of Indonesia and Malaysia is the potential that other influences on adjustment policy choice and regime survival outweigh the influences of coalitional preferences. I rely on two comparative methods to assess the plausibility of alternative hypotheses and to demonstrate the internal validity of my own theory. First, I examine explanatory variables both contemporaneously across countries and in the context of each country's political history. Second, I trace out the observable implications of several alternative explanations, finding that they misrepresent how the crises actually unfolded in each country.

The generalizability of my account depends on how well the argument explaining Indonesia and Malaysia in the 1990s can travel to other countries during other periods of time. Close attention to the historical record was instrumental for understanding coalitional alignments, preferences over adjustment policies, and struggles over regime survival. Rigorous attention to hypothesis testing ensures that the theory explains both Indonesia and Malaysia correctly. But to show how my argument travels outside of Southeast Asia during the Asian Financial Crisis, I investigate a number of other cases around the world. I judge my argument to be generalizable when I find the same patterns of interest group pressures for adjustment yielding the same types of adjustment policies and the same trajectories of regime survival in similar cases around the world. Looking outside of Southeast Asia also allows me to control more systematically for nagging confounding variables – in particular, authoritarian political institutions and crisis severity. Using this additional evidence, I show that my argument about Indonesia and Malaysia contributes to our understanding of the politics of economic adjustment, authoritarian rule, and regime transitions across the world.

My strategy of inquiry is accordingly eclectic. I use economic theory to derive predictions about policy choices, qualitative research to uncover coalitional alignments and to probe causal linkages between coalitions and adjustment decisions, and statistical analysis to establish cross-national patterns in political outcomes. I see no reason to insist that one method of inquiry is superior to others. Rather, I demand the precise opposite: economic predictions must be borne out by preferences and strategies as articulated by actual actors to fulfill my goal of internal parsimony, and cross-national patterns must reflect my argument's logic in diverse cases to fulfill my goal of generalizability. Bringing together different types of evidence in this way allows different methods to reinforce one another, strengthening the evidence I can bring to bear in favor of my argument.

The Plan of the Book

Chapter 2 lays out the coalitional theory of adjustment and regime survival. It proposes a model of reform under authoritarian rule and derives prediction about adjustment policy demands from three ideal-typical groups: mobile capital, fixed capital, and labor. It also details the argument's global context with data on financial crises from across the developing world. Chapter 3 turns to the cases of Indonesia and Malaysia, specifying the coalitions that support each country's authoritarian regime and mapping these coalitions to the ideal types. In describing the logic of political stability under each regime, this chapter outlines the mechanisms through which each coalition was embedded in each regime's policies and institutions. Chapter 3 also considers the broad area studies literature on each country's regime in a wider theoretical context, foreshadowing the subsequent analyses of alternative political explanations for adjustment and authoritarian breakdowns. Chapters 4 and 5 study each country's economic adjustment in depth, demonstrating how the coalitional theory explains adjustment better than alternative explanations for adjustment policy. Chapters 6 and 7 perform the same task for the question of authoritarian breakdown, again demonstrating that coalitional theory's attention to economic interests and economic adjustment is superior to alternative explanations of authoritarian breakdown and stability. Throughout these empirical chapters, I demonstrate how many aspects of crisis politics in Indonesia and Malaysia are inconsistent with alternative hypotheses but consistent with my own.

Chapter 8 expands the empirical focus of the argument beyond Southeast Asia in the 1990s. I present several quantitative tests of my argument to demonstrate that, consistent with a key implication of my theory, authoritarian regimes that impose capital account restrictions during financial crises are more likely to survive crises than those regimes which do not. I rely on additional case studies to demonstrate how my causal logic applies to these cases – in other words, that my theory explains *why* we observe this regularity. I consider financial crises in the early 1980s in four Latin America autocracies – Argentina, Chile, Mexico, and Uruguay. Two of these countries experienced authoritarian breakdowns (Argentina and Uruguay), while two did not (Mexico and Chile). I argue that adjustment measures adopted in each country are instrumental in explaining this variation in regime survival, and I show how coalitional politics determined these adjustment strategies. I then turn to a subsequent financial crisis in Mexico, the Tequila Crisis of 1994–95. This is a crucial case: the same regime faced another crisis and adopted different adjustment measures. I argue that changes in the regime's support coalition between 1985 and 1990 account for this variation and that contradictory demands over adjustment policy caused the subsequent breakdown of the Mexican regime that began with the Institutional Revolutionary Party's legislative defeat in 1997 and culminated with its loss in the 2000 presidential elections.

Chapter 9 concludes the book with a discussion of its implications. Some of these implications involve the way that political scientists study authoritarianism, economic adjustment, and regime transitions. I argue that political scientists should rethink the nature of authoritarian stability, focusing less on unfettered class conflict or dominant parties and more on how various types of social actors can form coalitions that support authoritarian rule. For studies of open economy politics, I emphasize how domestic financial sector fragility is a crucial variable in understanding macroeconomic vulnerability, international monetary relations, and the politics of economic adjustment. I also argue that studies of the politics of authoritarian breakdowns should pay closer attention to the specific character of economic crises and the particular demands for adjustment policy that they produce.

Other implications from this argument are normative in nature. Disastrous economic adjustment drove Soeharto from power and led the Indonesian state to the brink of collapse, but Indonesia is now a fully functioning democracy. Successful economic adjustment led Malaysia to quicker economic recovery, but it is still as authoritarian as ever. My argument is consistent with the controversial views of some development economists that capital controls can be welfare-enhancing during times of severe economic distress, but it also raises the uncomfortable possibility that the judicious use of capital controls to facilitate economic recovery may come at the expense of basic civil liberties and other political reforms.

2

Coalitional Sources of Adjustment and Regime Survival

The literature on economic crises is replete with stories of divided authoritarian regimes and hotly contested adjustment strategies. Crises often prompt reform and at the same time can provide openings for regime change. Few images are more powerful than the People's Power movement in the Philippines, which arose amid economic crisis and political intransigence to push Ferdinand Marcos from power. Financial collapse in Mexico under Ernesto Zedillo foreshadowed the end of one of the world's most durable and highly institutionalized authoritarian regimes. But for every Marcos there is a Pinochet, for every Zedillo a Mugabe and a Mubarak: an authoritarian ruler whose regime clamps down on its political challengers, breaks from the international economic consensus with radical policies, and survives. These failures of reform and political liberalization are normally treated as missed opportunities, nothing more. Yet these cases hold the keys to understanding the links between crises, adjustment, and regime collapse, for they illuminate why crises have one impact in some countries and a different impact in others.

This chapter introduces my argument of how authoritarian regimes grapple with economic crises. The theory holds that, during such crises, coalitional preferences determine adjustment policy and that conflict over adjustment policy determines the likelihood of regime survival. Specifically, when currency and banking crises co-occur, regimes whose support coalitions include both mobile and fixed capital face contradictory demands over adjustment policy, and as a result authoritarian regimes are likely to break down across this political cleavage. Regimes whose support coalitions include fixed capital and labor (or either one but not both) choose heterodox adjustment policies and are subsequently likely to survive the crisis. Figure 2.1 summarizes the argument, in which arrows represent causal relationships; all are sufficient but not necessary. Regimes may adopt heterodox economic policies in many situations outside of the argument's scope, and authoritarian regimes may break down for a number of reasons outside of the argument's scope.

The argument in this chapter unfolds in several steps. It begins with a broad description of the adjustment problem for any authoritarian regime and then narrows to target the specific problem of adjustment for regimes facing twin banking and currency crises. Along the way, I introduce the key concept of cross-border asset specificity and derive predictions of actors' preferences over adjustment and predictions over the link between adjustment and regime survival. To set the scope for the remainder of the inquiry in this book, I then broaden the focus once more. Charting the global patterns of financial crises and political transitions from throughout the developing world, I indicate where outside of Southeast Asia the coalitional foundations of authoritarian rule will explain economic adjustment and authoritarian breakdowns.

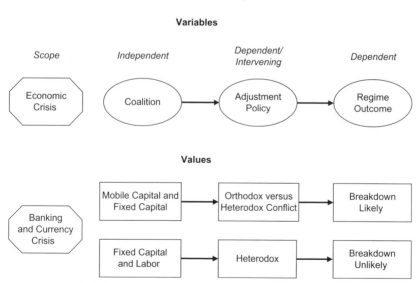

FIGURE 2.1. The Theory.

The Reform Game

I capture economic reform as a strategic interaction between a political regime and a set of constituents. The game relies on several assumptions. First, authoritarian regimes are led by office seekers who depend on some group of "constituents," enacting policies that fulfill their interests. Even authoritarian regimes depend on some social support, and nearly all analyses of authoritarianism currently assume that authoritarian regimes have some sort of constituency. But I do not assume that authoritarian regimes necessarily depend on the interests of a capitalist class or even upon a subset of individuals whose mean income is higher than that of the constituents of a hypothetical democratic government in the same country.[1] As I show later in the case of Malaysia, authoritarian regimes can take advantage of ethnic cleavages within society, relying on a cross-class alliance among members of one ethnic group. Even without ethnic cleavages, we observe across the world a number of inclusive or otherwise "populist" authoritarian regimes – participation is distinct from contestation.[2] Other cases of populist authoritarian regimes include Mexico under the Institutional Revolutionary Party (PRI), Zimbabwe under Robert Mugabe, and by some accounts Egypt under Hosni Mubarak, the Soviet Union under Brezhnev, and Cameroon under Paul Biya. Without its constituents' support, a regime cannot continue to rule. Coalitional politics thereby constrains authoritarian regimes.

During an economic crisis, regimes are unlikely to change their support coalitions. Coalitions are endogenous in the long run but exogenous in the short run. In the long run, authoritarian regimes do adjust their support coalitions, bringing in new supporters to shore up political weaknesses and marginalizing groups that threaten political stability. But in the short run, such adjustments are unlikely, primarily because, as a strategy for maintaining political power amid economic collapse, they are not credible. If a regime can change constituents at will during an economic crisis, then any one constituent – or potential constituent – will expect that the regime will not protect its interests during future upheavals. A potential constituent who believes that the regime will not protect it in the future will probably not support the regime ex ante. Knowing this, the regime will refrain from changing its existing constituents, for other potential constituents will not find the regime's promise to protect their

---

[1] Contrast to Acemoglu and Robinson 2006.
[2] Dahl 1971.

interests credible. In fact, both authoritarian rulers and their constituents will likely create mechanisms – perhaps formal institutions or informal ties such as patronage and exchange – that make defection from the existing political arrangement costly.

Besides the difficulty of credible commitment, startup costs make switching constituents costly. Consider a decision by the leader of a military junta to free himself from officer support. If he wishes to establish a mass political party, he must delegate the tasks of mobilization, organization, and agitation to loyal subordinates. The costs of building a viable political institution for mass support are likely to be high, and doing so will take time. Even if we assume away commitment problems, officers observing his attempt to change constituencies will have an incentive to overthrow him before he neutralizes their own power. Likewise, a patrimonial regime depending on a thick web of patron-client ties, yet wishing to free itself of these ties in favor of others, will face considerable costs in establishing new patron-client relationships. These costs will be particularly high in the short run, making attempts to switch constituencies during economic crises still more unlikely, because attempts to switch are still more unlikely to be successful. If we do observe attempts by regimes to switch constituents and co-opt members of the opposition, this is likely to be a result of the regime already having lost its existing support.[3]

Although coalitions are exogenous for my causal account of adjustment and regime survival, their formation and persistence are certainly interesting. While I do not offer a complete theory of the origins of coalitions, cases from East Asia and Latin America suggest that factional alignments and economic conditions preceding the rise of an authoritarian regime determine the character of its support coalition. In countries such as Indonesia (1965–66), Argentina (1976), and Uruguay (1973), military leaders with personal ties to mobile financiers and facing inflationary crises mounted coups that produced coalitions among the military, industry, and the financial sector. In countries such as Malaysia (1957) and Mexico (1917), which faced neither an inflationary crisis nor a military coup, populist coalitions emerged. In Chile (1973), which faced an inflationary crisis but where the military leaders had no personal or business links to the financial sector, a capitalist coalition without financial sector ties emerged. Parallels to the Mexican and Malaysian experiences include Robert Mugabe's regime in Zimbabwe and Gamal

---

[3] A formal treatment of this argument can be found in Bertocchi and Spagat 2001.

Abdel Nasser's regime in Egypt; Park Chung-hee's regime in South Korea and the shah's regime in Iran parallel Pinochet's Chile. This story obscures many aspects of coalition formation under authoritarianism – the role of politicized ethnicity in Southeast Asia, the co-optation of organized labor in Mexico, the outward focus of probusiness development policies in Chile, and American influence in South Korea and Iran. It nevertheless suggests how initial conditions affect the formation of coalitions, which subsequently shape authoritarian rule. I explore this more fully in the cases of Indonesia and Malaysia.

The role of ideology here is marginal: ideology is a means to an end. Ideology largely reflects the preferences of the regime's supporters and cements coalitions that have emerged. Much as how a populist authoritarian regime facing a crisis does not attempt to shift its support coalition, that regime does not announce a new ideological position.[4] That said, ideological positions constrain the general goals of policy decisions rather than the policy decisions themselves. A regime may announce that particular policies once viewed as unlikely to protect its supporters are now needed to fulfill that same goal. One example may be exchange rate management. Whereas at one time the regime may claim that a floating exchange rate best protects the interests of the masses, it may later claim that a fixed exchange rate best protects their interests. The ideology of the regime – protecting the interests of the masses – remains the same, but the policy requirements to fulfill its goals differ.

Finally, during economic crises, regime supporters are keenly suspicious of bargains that trade present hardship for future benefits. Such bargains suffer from intertemporal commitment problems. When adjustment costs are borne by one constituent disproportionately, other constituents are unable to commit not to use this advantage to reshape the ruling coalition to exclude the disadvantaged constituent from future spoils. Realizing this, constituents avoid bargains wherein they assume the burden of adjustment in exchange for payoffs accruing in future periods. Such commitment problems are a defining feature of politics.[5]

With these assumptions, the game is straightforward (for a complete exposition, see the Appendix to this chapter). In equilibrium, a regime facing a crisis chooses an adjustment policy that maximizes its utility, subject to the constraint that it will not choose policies that cause a constituent to defect. Facing multiple constituents, the regime must choose

---

[4] Hinich and Munger 1994.
[5] Powell 2004.

adjustment policies that fulfill the demands of multiple constituents. What makes adjustment policy contentious in the face of multiple constituents is the possibility that each will demand different policies. With compatible adjustment policy pressures from multiple constituents, the regime adopts their preferred policy. With the regime adopting their preferred policy, constituents continue to support the regime, which survives the crisis. With incompatible preferences, the regime faces incompatible adjustment policy demands. Searching for policies that are acceptable to both constituents prolongs and deepens the crisis until the coalition becomes unsustainable.[6] Ultimately, such a regime is likely to break down – and to break down across the cleavage of adjustment policy preferences, rather than across an alternative cleavage.

This model of crises and transitions differs from existing models in the literature. Barbara Geddes models regime survival in authoritarian regimes by assuming that members of professional militaries have corporate interests distinct from their personal interests, whereas the constituents of other types of authoritarian regimes do not.[7] Military corporate interests generate unique dynamics of rule for military regimes, making military regimes more likely to return to the barracks during economic crises than nonmilitary regimes because of the value that officers place on the unity of their institution. As Geddes recognizes, however, such dynamics depend on the assumptions that officers have neither competing interests nor alternative technologies for policing factional squabbles. Where officers have direct economic interests and where party institutions complement military hierarchies, the importance of a military corporate identity fades, as do predictions based upon this assumption.

The model also differs from Beatriz Magaloni's model of "equilibrium party hegemony," where dominant-party regimes offer economic inducements to constituents who support them.[8] These regimes withhold inducements from those constituents who do not support them, and coordination problems prevent a country's constituents from all choosing to reject the incumbent regime they face. This model has an equilibrium where constituents unhappy with illiberal regimes nevertheless actively support them because the consequences of not doing so are worse. While Magaloni's model is presented in the context of a voter's decision calculus, its core insights are compatible with mine. But her model relies on at

---

[6] See also Alesina and Drazen 1991.
[7] Geddes 2003, 44–86.
[8] Magaloni 2006.

least one of two simplifying assumptions: either all economic incentives are of a single type, or all constituents are, or both. By relaxing these assumptions, we can see how substantive policy conflicts matter in the game of authoritarian regime survival.

My model of crises, coalitions, adjustment, and regime survival can apply in principle to any crisis. To be useful in concrete cases, though, I need an understanding of what adjustment policy choices are and why different actors might care about them. I begin by specifying the nature of the financial crises in Southeast Asia and then explore the distributional impacts of different adjustment policies.

Financial Crises and the Problem of Adjustment

The Asian Financial Crisis and the subsequent crises in Russia, Turkey, and Latin America in the late 1990s are but the most recent examples of a phenomenon that has existed at least since the 1600s.[9] These crises are known as "twin crises." Twin crises refer to simultaneous and causally interrelated currency and banking crises. In a currency crisis – sometimes called a balance-of-payments crisis – demand for a country's currency in foreign exchange markets falls to a level that makes a country's existing exchange rate target unsustainable. The country's central bank must then sell its foreign currency reserves to stimulate demand for its own currency or stop trying to influence its currency's exchange rate. If the government chooses not to defend its currency, the currency devalues. Because unanticipated currency devaluation can wreak havoc on investors who have assumed a predictable exchange rate or on actors accustomed to a particular price for imported goods, dramatic currency devaluations in many cases lead to economic crises.

Banking crises are crises within a country's financial sector. In a banking crisis, a country's financial sector suffers from systemic illiquidity or insolvency. An illiquid bank faces temporary problems in meeting demands for cash from its creditors (depositors), whereas an insolvent bank has a long-term inability to meet those demands. Systemic illiquidity or insolvency in a country's financial sector has serious consequences, as depositors will be reluctant to lend their savings to banks, and high interest rates offered to attract depositors discourage business activity. On its own, either banking or currency crises can have severe consequences; together, as twin crises, they can be devastating.

---

[9] Kindleberger 2000.

The economic literature on twin crises is extensive, most of it studying the causal linkages between currency and banking crises.[10] There are straightforward arguments for why a currency crisis might lead to a banking crisis, or vice versa. Currency crises can cause banking crises when domestic borrowers hold foreign exchange debt under a managed exchange rate regime. In the absence of prudential financial regulation, borrowers, believing that the government will protect the exchange rate peg, borrow in foreign currencies without hedging their debt against exchange rate fluctuations.[11] An exogenous speculative attack that leads to depreciation then squeezes borrowers, whose costs of debt service have increased without a commensurate increase in revenues. Indebted financial institutions must similarly use their assets to pay down their debts rather than lending them to the domestic market for profit. Domestic borrowers may then fall delinquent in their domestic debt, contributing to further deterioration of the balance sheets of domestic financial institutions and tightening the credit market further. The ultimate effect is to turn a currency crisis into a banking crisis.

The logic that leads from a banking crisis to a currency crisis is similar. If foreign currency traders view financial sector health as an important macroeconomic indicator, an exogenous bank run may signal to them that the economy is unhealthy. As a result, individual traders may update their prior beliefs about financial sector health, leading to a self-fulfilling currency crisis as investors exit in search of quality.[12] Under a fixed exchange rate regime, the problem is more concrete. The very policy measures to combat a banking crisis – for example, emergency liquidity support – may be inconsistent with the government's commitment to a currency peg. Under such conditions, speculators, anticipating that the government will float the exchange rate, will launch a speculative attack that ensures that it does.

All of this means that decisions to manage currency crises must take into account the effects of policy instruments on the domestic financial system. Similarly, decisions on how to manage a banking crisis must take into account the effects of policy instruments on a country's international monetary position. The crises can be self-reinforcing: a deteriorating domestic financial system can lead to exchange rate depreciation, which

---

[10] Chinn and Kletzer 2000; Edwards and Végh 1997; Kaminsky and Reinhart 1999; Lahiri and Végh 2005; Miller 1998; Schneider and Tornell 2000.
[11] McKinnon and Pill 1997; 1998.
[12] Goldfajn and Valdés 1997.

in turn exacerbates the original financial sector problems. Economic models of currency and banking crises stemming from these macroeconomic imbalances and moral hazard are now well established in the economic literature.[13]

Solutions

Two solutions, which I term orthodox and heterodox adjustment strategies, are generally applicable across all twin crises. The names I give them are immaterial – one might call them the "Washington Consensus" and "pragmatic economist" views or the "financial openness" and "financial protectionism" views. Each solution involves making a series of potentially costly decisions to break out of the vicious cycle of currency and financial collapse and return to the healthy cycle of investment and financial stability. In broad terms, the strategies of Indonesia and Malaysia (post–August 1998) followed these two kinds of solutions.

Orthodox solutions received the most attention in the early months of the crises and have since been the subject of extensive debate. The essence of the orthodox solution – one advocated most consistently by the International Monetary Fund (IMF) – is macroeconomic discipline and short-term financial sacrifice in the interest of long-term recovery. In the face of a rapidly depreciating currency, central banks should tighten monetary policy to attract investors back into domestic banks. Interest rates should rise to encourage deposits in the local currency. To the extent that domestic banks and firms cannot meet their foreign currency obligations, the government should allow them to fail. Governments should supply emergency liquidity support to banks only in the case that liquidity support prevents wholesale economic collapse. The government should also implement macroeconomic reforms to increase economic efficiency and should trim budgets to eliminate wasteful and costly fiscal expenditures. Under such an adjustment policy, macroeconomic reform and austerity would themselves attract capital back into the country, protecting the exchange rate and injecting needed capital into the financial system. They would also signal the government's resolve to create good policies, instilling confidence in foreign investors concerned with excessive rent seeking and poor monetary management. Bank and corporate failures would be expected, if not welcomed. Only mismanaged firms would succumb to the crisis, rewarding good corporate governance, improving efficiency, and eliminating moral hazard from costly bailouts.

---

[13] Corsetti, Pesenti, and Roubini 1999; Irwin and Vines 1999; Krugman 1998c.

The orthodox solution, despite its support from IMF officials, quickly came under fire because of the high short-term costs that it imposed on national economies. Bank closures led to systemic bank runs that punished all banks, not only poorly managed ones. The ability of interest rate hikes to protect exchange rates depends on the interest elasticity of demand for domestic savings, and in a period of widespread financial turmoil, this demand was highly inelastic. The Asian Financial Crisis hit economies that were not running large budget deficits (as in earlier models of currency crises), so many argued that fiscal restraint placed undue burdens on countries' economies. Finally, IMF conditionality on relatively minor regulatory reforms was seen as inappropriate in the context of almost total financial collapse.

In August 1998 Paul Krugman suggested an alternative policy for economic adjustment.[14] His solution reflected the discontent many economists held with the IMF[15] and mirrored proposals being debated in many Asian policy circles, but it was the best-known articulation of an alternative plan. The basis of Krugman's strategy was capital controls and an exchange rate peg, cutting the link between interest and exchange rates and freeing national governments to enact discretionary macroeconomic policy. Instead of tightening money policy, governments should *loosen* monetary policy to encourage real economic activity. Banks would be free to offer low, less punitive interest rates, as domestic depositors would not be tempted to seek more attractive global interest rates. With an exchange rate peg, industries in the tradable sector – a large group in the affected Asian economies – could anchor their expectations of future import and export costs. Domestic firms with foreign currency debt could settle their debts at a more favorable rate without fearing continuing currency depreciation. Stock markets would be free from unproductive foreign speculators. Governments should also take the opportunity to push through much needed microeconomic reforms to speed a healthy economic recovery. But mandating microeconomic reforms to combat a crisis more related to financial market imperfections was counterproductive, amounting to a punishment whose policy goals were orthogonal to the nature of the crime.

Orthodox and heterodox recovery measures accordingly advocated contradictory policy prescriptions. The IMF stipulated monetary tightening, fiscal cutbacks, and unconditional maintenance of capital account

[14] Krugman 1998a; 1998b.
[15] See, e.g., Corden 1999; Montes 1998.

openness; Krugman and others argued for monetary loosening, tentative fiscal restructuring, and capital account restrictions to make these policies feasible. Both policy prescriptions recognized the Mundell-Fleming trilemma, where governments cannot simultaneously maintain open capital accounts, targeted exchange rates, and discretionary macroeconomic policy.[16] Both also recognized the dilemmas of bank bailouts. A healthy banking system without bank runs is an important public good, so the government should guarantee deposits. Yet during financial turmoil, providing liquidity support to failing banks increases money supply, leading to inflation and counteracting high interest rates while encouraging moral hazard in banking. Allowing bad banks to fail is critical for establishing a healthy financial system, but bank failures, especially during times of financial distress, can themselves lead to financial panics.[17]

Players and Policies

While all members of an economy can expect to experience some economic hardship during financial crises, hardship is distributed unevenly across society. My argument relies on a key concept that appears in various guises elsewhere: cross-border asset specificity, which I frequently gloss as capital mobility. This concept, though, is rarely distinguished from related concepts such as capital liquidity. While terms like liquidity and mobility are deeply related, they are distinct.

I define mobile capital as capital assets that owners can move across national borders. Such assets can take many forms, but what makes them unique is their cross-border mobility. The archetypical example of mobile capital is money. Money can be exchanged for goods and services nearly anywhere in the world, so long as one converts it into the proper national currency. Besides money, other examples of mobile assets may include gold or other precious materials, as well as an individual's skills and expertise. By contrast, fixed capital comprises assets that owners will not move across national borders, either because it is impossible to do so or because they value the ownership of physical stock rather than its liquidation into cash. The customary example of fixed capital is land, which owners simply cannot move; other examples include industrial assets such as factories or equipment.

Here, the distinction between mobility and liquidity becomes important. In modern economies, all assets are potentially liquid. The owner of

[16] Mundell 1963.
[17] Allen and Gale 2000; Chen 1999; Peck and Shell 2003.

a cement processing plant can sell that plant, in effect converting her physical assets into liquid assets. Likewise, many publicly traded companies are controlled not through personal ownership of a firm's assets but rather through share ownership, meaning that the effective owners of fixed capital stock may be able to liquidate them. Thus, while money is the archetype of mobile capital, all potentially liquid assets (i.e., shares) are not mobile capital; and, though all assets are potentially liquefiable, not all assets are mobile. This distinction becomes particularly important when discussing the behavior of majority shareholders of industrial firms in Malaysia, whose ownership of shares gives them effective ownership of fixed assets and leads them to behave accordingly. This contrast between mobile and fixed capital accordingly mirrors the distinction often made between "financial capital" and "industrial capital," although these terms are rarely defined in a rigorous fashion.[18] Note also that the concept of cross-border asset specificity differs from the concepts of asset specificity and intersectoral factor mobility as used in literatures on industrial organization and international trade.[19]

Throughout the book, when referring to political actors I refer to "holders of mobile capital" and "holders of fixed capital." What distinguishes the two types of actors is the cross-border mobility of the majority of their asset holdings. Clearly, some actors may have some of each type of asset, but in almost every case actors fall primarily into one class or the other. Industrial conglomerates, for instance, may have cash reserves or investment arms or even banking subsidiaries, but these are ancillary to the firms' primary industrial activities. It is necessary to inspect both sectoral characteristics and behavioral investment strategies to distinguish fixed from mobile capital empirically. While sectors provide some clues, they are themselves not determinant. Within the same sector, some capital owners may be fixed, whereas others are mobile, as in the contrast between property developers and property speculators. It is also possible in the case of joint ventures or publicly traded corporations for one company to have owners who fall into each group. In New Order Indonesia, many ethnic Chinese owners of mobile capital entered into joint ventures by providing investment funds to military-controlled corporations, whose assets are physical ownership of fixed capital stock. In Malaysia, foreign portfolio investors (whose assets are highly

---

[18] For a review of studies of *Finanzkapital*, from Hilferding through the 1990s, see Winters 1994.
[19] See Alt et al. 1996.

mobile) invest directly into Malay- or government-controlled firms trading on the Kuala Lumpur Stock Exchange, becoming minority shareholders in industrial firms whose majority shareholders are fixed in Malaysia.

We can see the differential impact of orthodox and heterodox strategies on capital owners, even as both promised long-term economic recovery. In particular, the IMF's policy of macroeconomic tightening harms domestic industry and holders of fixed capital through macroeconomic austerity, whereas the heterodox alternative harms mobile capital, both domestic and foreign. Table 2.1 distinguishes capital owners by the cross-border mobility of their capital assets and lists adjustment policy preferences given foreign debt exposure and trade orientation.

To see how capital mobility affects preferences over adjustment policy, imagine a small open economy that maintains a fixed (or quasi-fixed) exchange rate regime between its currency and a benchmark world currency. The country faces a substantial exogenous decrease in its currency's value vis-à-vis the world currency's value – a currency crisis. Its government must now choose between floating its exchange rate to protect its foreign currency reserves and maintaining the currency peg.

Producers in export-oriented sectors (groups A, B, E, and F in Table 2.1) benefit from exchange rate depreciation because their goods become relatively less expensive for foreign consumers. But debt exposure also conditions exchange rate preferences. Consider a domestic firm that borrows in the foreign currency (groups A, B, C, and D). With an exchange rate float, holders of unhedged debt in the foreign currency but whose assets or cash flows are denominated in the local currency will face a heavier debt burden. Such firms prefer an appreciated exchange rate because it lessens their foreign currency debt burden. The net effect for groups A and B is indeterminate; firm preferences depend on their precise mixes of debt and export exposure. Preferences over exchange rate level are also indeterminate for groups G and H, but this is because they suffer from neither foreign debt nor export exposure. But whatever the level that groups demand, all prefer a fixed exchange rate, either to reduce volatility or to stave off the depreciation associated with a completely unmanaged currency. Unlike the standard account of the politics of exchange rate management, where distributional coalitions form along axes of export orientation and import competition,[20] when facing twin crises, distributional coalitions regarding exchange rate management also include the

[20] Broz and Frieden 2001; Frieden 1991b.

TABLE 2.1. *Cross-Border Asset Mobility: Adjustment Policy Preferences*

Trade orientation	High Debt Exposure		Low Debt Exposure	
	High Mobility	**Low Mobility**	**High Mobility**	**Low Mobility**
Exporting	**Group A** Capital account: Open Monetary policy: Indeterminate Exchange rate regime: Fix Exchange rate level: Indeterminate Bank bailouts: Yes Targeted spending: Yes	**Group B** Capital account: Closed Monetary policy: Loose Exchange rate regime: Fix Exchange rate level: Indeterminate Bank bailouts: Yes Targeting spending: Yes	**Group E** Capital account: Open Monetary policy: Loose Exchange rate regime: Fix Exchange rate level: Low Bank bailouts: Yes Targeting spending: Yes	**Group F** Capital account: Closed Monetary policy: Loose Exchange rate regime: Fix Exchange rate level: Low Bank bailouts: Yes Targeting spending: Yes
Nontradable	**Group C** Capital account: Open Monetary policy: Tight Exchange rate regime: Fix Exchange rate level: High Bank bailouts: Yes Targeting spending: Yes	**Group D** Capital account: Closed Monetary policy: Loose Exchange rate regime: Fix Exchange rate level: High Bank bailouts: Yes Targeting spending: Yes	**Group G** Capital account: Open Monetary policy: Loose Exchange rate regime: Fix Exchange rate level: Indeterminate Bank bailouts: Yes Targeting spending: Yes	**Group H** Capital account: Closed Monetary policy: Loose Exchange rate regime: Fix Exchange rate level: Indeterminate Bank bailouts: Yes Targeting spending: Yes

expected debt burden under depreciating exchange rate. Note that for simplicity, I have assumed that no borrowers have hedged their foreign debt, because lax financial regulation and implicit government guarantees led firms before the Asian Financial Crisis to believe that governments would never abandon their currency pegs. And even if some firms purchase hedging instruments, such instruments are costly. Risk-taking firms that succeed in the short term despite imprudent borrowing may outcompete prudential firms, forcing prudential firms to adopt the risky, no-hedging policy.[21]

When currency crises spill over into the domestic financial sector to become twin crises, the government may also intervene to cushion the economy against the currency shock. If it maintains an open capital account, the government can tighten monetary policy, raising the domestic real interest rate greater than the world real interest rate in order to attract foreign capital back into the country. The increase in demand for local currency will itself lead to appreciation. In equilibrium, these values will shift so that foreign and local interest rates reach parity. But tightening monetary policy has the other, familiar effect of depressing real economic activity, encouraging domestic savings, and discouraging spending. No groups will support tight monetary policies on their own because of these balance sheet effects.[22] Higher interest rates even harm domestic banks if their debtors cannot earn enough money to pay down their debt. Indebted nonbank firms may find that appreciation decreases their foreign debt burden but that their cash flows decrease more quickly under the deflationary effects of tight monetary policy. Loose monetary policy leads to capital flight, currency depreciation, and inflation; however, it also decreases the value of savings and prompts real economic activity.

These effects, though, depend on free capital mobility. Controls on capital outflows allow the government to implement expansionary policies without the threat of capital flight, making a fixed exchange rate feasible. This benefits an indebted firm or bank for precisely the foregoing logic, where firms with unhedged foreign debt preferred to maintain the fixed exchange rate rather than floating in the face of downward currency pressure. It likewise, as noted, eases the burden on banks holding deposits from domestic firms and consumers. Ideally, these moves will save the financial sector and initiate recovery of the real economy.

---

[21] See Krugman 1998c.
[22] Walter 2008; Woodruff 2005.

But a move toward capital account closure has costs. Both foreign and domestic currency and stock traders will oppose restrictions on cross-border capital flows, as these remove their ability to short currencies and restrict their ability to speculate freely on stock prices. In fact, any actor who believes that it may wish to convert domestic currency assets to foreign currency will oppose capital account closure. Furthermore, restrictions on capital outflows can discourage capital inflows even if statutory regulations explicitly welcome them. International investors will be wary of making investments if restrictions on capital outflows mean they cannot recoup their investments for some period of time. Expected investment profitability depends largely in this case on economic recovery. So long as investors have optimistic beliefs about the prospects for economic recovery under capital and exchange rate restrictions, barriers on capital outflow will not hamper an international investment-driven recovery. However, investors may be unwilling to bet on the country's investment profitability without the ability to cut their losses.

These considerations together entail that holders of mobile capital (groups A, C, E, and G) favor an open capital account, whereas holders of fixed capital (groups B, D, F, and H) favor capital account closure. Preferences for capital account closure are indirect, originating not in any fundamental opposition to capital mobility but rather in the desire to make feasible expansionary monetary policy, which B, D, F, and H all favor. Holders of mobile capital favor capital mobility because of the simple fact that they can divest and flee overseas in response to unprofitable or volatile economic conditions. For this reason, they have more complex preferences over macroeconomic policy. All may support expansionary monetary policy to stimulate the economy, but exporters (groups A and E) also benefit from loose monetary policy to support a depreciated exchange rate, whereas debtors (groups A and C) benefit from tighter monetary policy to support an appreciated exchange rate. So among mobile capital, indebted producers of nontradable goods (C) will support tighter monetary policy more than indebted producers of export goods (A), who will support tighter monetary policies more than holders of mobile capital without debt (E and G). Group A's precise preferences over monetary policies are indeterminate, depending on firms' mix of debt exposure versus export competitiveness. Favorable balance sheet effects from monetary loosening, though, will dampen A's, C's, and G's support for tighter monetary policy (not captured in Table 2.1).

Note that all groups support two additional adjustment policies: bank bailouts and targeted spending. A strong financial system is a public good, and bank runs can undermine a country's entire financial system. To avoid such problems, monetary authorities can provide emergency liquidity support to insolvent banks. Illiquid financial institutions will prefer liquidity support that keeps them afloat, and sound financial institutions will prefer that illiquid financial institutions receive liquidity support to ward off panic and contagion. Liquidity support does increase the supply of money, thus contradicting high nominal interest rates and tight monetary policy. But in countries facing financial meltdown, liquidity support to insolvent banks will be encouraged by all groups, albeit begrudgingly by many. Governments may also make targeted spending cuts to signal fiscal prudence. These will be opposed by the beneficiaries of such spending. Even if connected firms prefer a fiscal stance that is contractionary overall, they may prefer different mixes of spending cuts; *ceteris paribus*, crony-controlled conglomerates will prefer cuts in basic goods' subsidies, whereas poor consumers will prefer cuts in wasteful infrastructure development projects.

Thus far, my discussion has focused on the interests of firms – or, read differently, on the interests of the owners of capital. What of the interests of labor? There are two possible approaches. One is to assume that each individual worker's preferences for adjustment flow from his or her employer's preferences. The more realistic alternative is to recognize that workers employed by holders of mobile capital are relatively immobile. Capital owners in an investment conglomerate may enjoy a high level of cross-border asset mobility, but aside from perhaps some firm managers, their employees do not. Workers favor policies that protect employment and targeted spending while avoiding inflation. Accordingly, labor, like fixed capital, will prefer capital account closure to enable expansionary policy, bank support that protects cash savings, and a fixed exchange rate that decreases exchange rate volatility. Labor will also prefer targeted spending on redistributive subsidies and will even support spending measures benefiting owners of fixed capital so long as such spending guards employment.

Predictions

The reform game introduced earlier predicts that given these different adjustment policy options, the regime will choose policies that protect the interests of its supporters. During twin crises, a regime supported by firms with heavy foreign debt burdens will try to tighten monetary policy to stem exchange rate depreciation, closing the capital account if firms also demand low interest rates. A regime that depends on the support of urban wage laborers will avoid cutting subsidies that benefit them. A regime that depends on the support of bankers with liquidity problems will supply liquidity support to those troubled banks. A regime that depends on the support of a group of financiers with large pools of mobile investment capital will not choose to restrict capital outflows. And so on. During twin crises, these considerations will determine how regimes choose adjustment policies.

But there are some policy choices that are mutually incompatible. Incompatibility stems from the dilemmas of liquidity support, the interest rate–exchange rate nexus, and capital account management. During twin crises, indebted banks and domestic firms regardless of trade orientation prefer to minimize currency depreciation to minimize debt exposure and also to loosen macroeconomic policy to revive business and protect revenue streams. This is feasible only with restrictions on capital outflows, which groups B and D (fixed capital) will support. In this book, the preferences of groups with low debt exposure (E, F, G, and H) are largely irrelevant, for nearly all politically relevant firms suffer from such debt problems. But mobile capital (groups A and C) will demand that the government ensures capital mobility during the course of the crisis, as they will demand the ability to exit in search of higher rates of return overseas. This irreconcilable contradiction will prevent the regime from adopting a coherent basket of adjustment policies. The regime may attempt to repeg the exchange rate without closing the capital account, benefiting holders of unhedged foreign-denominated debt, but leading to renewed downward currency pressure. The regime's inability to implement coherent adjustment policy will render the coalition unsustainable in the face of continued economic collapse.

A coalition between fixed capital (groups B and D) and labor faces no such irreconcilable policy demands. "Labor" here is a broad term that may capture organized labor under a corporatist arrangement (the Mexican model under the PRI) or a mass base empowered through periodic elections but whose official union representation is weak and politically subordinate (the Malaysian model). Indebted banks and domestic firms will have a natural ally in such working-class constituents, for they will prefer subsidies and expansionary policies that protect employment. Fixed capital will also prefer expansionary macroeconomic policies. Because neither of these policies requires capital mobility, both will favor sacrificing capital account openness in order to stimulate the economy. So a regime that leads a fixed capital–labor coalition during twin crises will retreat from financial openness in order to protect the interests of its supporters. Because its supporters obtain the best possible policy from the regime, they will continue to support it, making a regime breakdown unlikely.

This discussion of capital account management represents just one of the many adjustment policy decisions that arise during twin crises. Yet the logic of adjustment policy choice is identical across other adjustment policy domains. A regime leading a fixed capital and labor coalition will restrict subsidies just until its labor prefers to defect, and it will remain in power just as long as business groups still prefer to support the regime, given that level of subsidies. Faced with the same problem, a fixed capital–mobile capital alliance will reduce subsidies to a much greater extent, for neither of its supporters benefit from them. What all adjustment policy decisions will have in common is that they externalize the costs of adjustment to groups not within the coalition. The distributional implications of twin crises, though, lead mobile capital and both fixed capital and labor toward diametrically opposed adjustment policy demands. A regime that depends on an alliance between fixed capital and mobile capital cannot adopt a policy that prevents defection, whereas a regime that depends on a fixed capital–labor alliance can.

Concretely, the theory predicts that in countries such as Indonesia, where holders of mobile and fixed capital compose the regime's support coalition, we will observe conflict over capital account restrictions and exchange rate settings. The regime will rigorously implement adjustment measures such as subsidy cuts that hurt only labor. Ultimately, however, the regime's support coalition will fracture between holders of mobile capital and of fixed capital, and the regime will collapse on the basis of this policy conflict. In countries such as Malaysia, where both the Malay masses and fixed capital support the regime, we will observe regimes that refuse to cut subsidies benefiting labor, loosen monetary policy, and protect spending programs that target fixed capital. The regime should, though, impose controls on capital outflows to enable it to pursue these expansionary policies. With their preferred policies adopted, the regime's supporters will remain united behind it.

The Global Scope of the Argument

If this argument applied only to Indonesia and Malaysia, it would be an explanation for a historical puzzle – unique in its attention to the logic of adjustment but empirically limited. But the theory also suggests how to understand economic crises, adjustment, and regime survival outside of Southeast Asia. Looking at other twin crises, from the Southern Cone to

TABLE 2.2. *Twin Crises, 1975–1997*

Country	Year	Country	Year
Argentina	1982–1983, 1989–1991	Lao PDR	1995, 1997
Bolivia	1986–1988	Madagascar	1988
Botswana	1996	Malaysia	1986–1988, 1997
Brazil	1990–1991, 1995–1997	Mexico	1982–1987, 1995–1997
Burundi	1997	Mozambique	1993–1997
Cameroon	1994–1996	Nepal	1988, 1991–1995
Chile	1985	New Zealand	1987–1991
Colombia	1985–1987	Nicaragua	1993–1995
Ecuador	1982–1983	Nigeria	1993–1994
Egypt	1980–1981, 1991–1993	Norway	1987–1988, 1992–1993
El Salvador	1990	Peru	1983–1990
Ethiopia	1994	Philippines	1983–1987, 1997
Finland	1991–1994	Romania	1990–1993
Ghana	1983–1989	Sierra Leone	1990–1992, 1997
Guatemala	1991–1992	South Africa	1978, 1985–1986
Guinea-Bissau	1996–1997	Spain	1977–1979, 1982–1984
Guyana	1993	Sweden	1992–1993
Hungary	1991, 1994–1995	Thailand	1983–1986, 1997
Iceland	1985–1986, 1993	Trinidad and Tobago	1985–1990, 1993
India	1993–1997	Tunisia	1993–1995
Indonesia	1997	Turkey	1982, 1994–1995
Italy	1992–1994, 1995	United Kingdom	1976, 1984, 1986
Jamaica	1994	Uruguay	1982–1984
Japan	1992	Venezuela	1984–1986, 1994–1997
Jordan	1989–1990, 1992		
Kenya	1985–1987, 1993–1997	Zambia	1995
Korea, South	1997	Zimbabwe	1995–1997

Source: Compiled from Glick and Hutchison 1999.

Egypt and Cameroon to Nepal, coalitions should determine adjustment strategies and the likelihood of regime survival.

To see just how widely this argument can apply, Table 2.2 shows all countries that experienced twin crises during the period from 1975 to 1997, using data from Reuven Glick and Michael Hutchison.[23] The tabulations include all country-years where there is a currency (banking)

[23] Glick and Hutchison 1999.

TABLE 2.3. *Twin Crises and Authoritarian Breakdowns*

	Breakdown	
	No	Yes (%)
Crisis		
No	874	13 (1.5)
Yes	27	9 (25.0)

crisis preceded by a banking (currency) crisis in the previous two years. The sample includes all industrialized economies, transition economies, and a number of other developing economies. Many countries experienced more than one set of twin crises, and crises often last for years. Moreover, twin crises are not unique to developing countries or poorly run autocracies but occur also in transition economies and advanced industrial democracies.

The consequences of these crises can be severe. In Russia (not listed in the table), twin crises during 1998 led to a 5 percent contraction in GDP in a country that already faced chronically weak growth. In Mexico, twin crises led to a 1 percent GDP contraction in 1982 followed by a 3 percent GDP contraction in 1983, and twin crises in the mid-1990s led to a 6 percent contraction in GDP. Jordan's economy contracted 13 percent during twin crises in 1989. In 1998, during Southeast Asia's twin crises, Malaysia's economy contracted by nearly 8 percent, while Indonesia's economy contracted by almost 14 percent. As twin crises spread from Asia to elsewhere in the developing world, global economic growth declined from 4 percent in 1997 to 2 percent in 1998, the largest change in global growth rates in decades.[24]

The cases in Table 2.2 serve later as the sample of countries whose experiences test the arguments I develop here. But to place some of the puzzles of this book in their cross-national context, Table 2.3 reports some basic results of the link between twin crises and authoritarian breakdowns, using all authoritarian regimes for which Glick and Hutchison have data.[25]

Crises are multiyear events, and so the units along the second row of Table 2.3 are crises, not years. The first row captures country-years without crises. The data show that the unconditional probability of

---

[24] All of these figures come from the World Bank's *World Development Indicators*, available online at http://devdata.worldbank.org/dataonline/.

[25] Data on regime types and political transitions come from Cheibub and Gandhi 2004.

authoritarian breakdown is higher during crises. This result is consistent with simple intuitions, as well as with existing perspectives that link shrinking economic resources to authoritarian collapse.[26] But, perhaps surprisingly, the unconditional probability of experiencing an authoritarian breakdown given twin crises remains quite low, at one in four. The economic crisis of 1997–98 clearly caused the breakdown of Indonesia's New Order regime, but the data show this case to be rather exceptional among its cross-national counterparts. This motivates the quest for a more complete causal linkage between crises and transitions, something that a focus on coalitions and adjustment provides.

Conclusion

Understanding the link between economic crises and regime change requires nuance. We observe simple correlations between crises and regime change, but to understand the mechanisms that link economic hardship to successful political liberalization, we must delve deeper into the intricate politics of authoritarian regime maintenance. We need to investigate just how an economic crisis distributes economic hardship across members of society. We need to understand what type of regime faces the crisis: who its constituents are, and what their economic profiles are. Most important, we need to discern what these supporters demand as policy remedies to economic crises and the compatibility of these demands across the different groups that have the ear of authoritarian regimes. This chapter provides the tools for doing just this, focusing on the financial meltdowns that have periodically swept the global economy since the 1970s.

Twin currency and banking crises place difficult demands on authoritarian regimes. There are no easy solutions to the problem of an insolvent banking sector, nor are there simple ways to convince foreign investors to pump money back into a fragile economy. But regimes do choose among broadly orthodox and broadly heterodox adjustment strategies, and they do so because their supporters demand protection from financial meltdowns. As these adjustment policies may fulfill the demands of powerful constituents, so may adjustment policies divide them. Adjustment policies may especially divide those constituents who demand capital account openness to enable them to seek safe investments overseas from those constituents whose inability to move assets abroad makes them lobby

---

[26] Greene 2007.

for domestic protection from the vagaries of financial markets. This dilemma drives some regimes, those who depend on both mobile and fixed capital for political support, to break down during twin crises. When regimes depend on supporters with fixed capital assets – capitalists in alliance with labor or capitalists alone – they can adopt heterodox adjustment strategies that allow them to survive the crises. Political coalitions in authoritarian regimes hold the key for understanding how financial crises drive adjustment policy choices and, in turn, regime survival.

This concludes the theoretical portion of this book. In the next six chapters, I put the theory to work. I begin by detailing the origins of political coalitions in Indonesia and Malaysia, the key variable that affects battles over economic adjustment and political survival in the two countries during the Asian Financial Crisis.

Appendix

The reform game begins with two players, the regime (R) and the constituent (C). For expository purposes, I treat each player as a unitary agent. R is the Stackelberg leader, so that, when facing an economic crisis, R has a choice of economic policy reform. It can adopt policy reform or remain with the status quo. C, in turn, upon observing R's strategy, can choose to support the regime or defect from it. R prefers remaining in power to losing power, and C prefers the status quo to reform. To make the story concrete, imagine that policy reform in question is the elimination of a particular subsidy that C enjoys. If R chooses reform, then C loses the subsidy, making it strictly worse off. By construction, C may believe that after reform, there is some other political arrangement that will make it better off than continuing under the existing regime R.

Figure 2.2 shows the reform game graphically. I normalize R's payoffs for remaining in power under the status quo to one and for losing power through defection as zero. I similarly normalize C's payoffs to retaining subsidies under the status quo to one and for losing subsidies but supporting the regime to zero. The variable a captures the expected benefit that R receives after reform if C does not defect. The variable b captures the expected benefit that C receives if it defects after reform.

If R continues providing subsidies, C prefers supporting the regime to defecting. If R adopts economic reform and eliminates subsidies, then C chooses whether to continue to support the regime. In this setup, C's payoff b from defecting from the regime is larger than zero, so that C prefers defection to reform under R. Under these circumstances, R

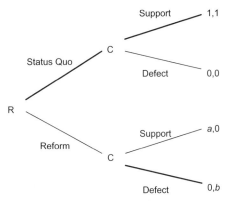

FIGURE 2.2. The Reform Game, $b > 0$ (bold lines represent players' dominant strategies).

foresees that it will lose power if it eliminates subsidies and so chooses to protect the status quo.

This initial setup describes the intuitive problem of economic reform under authoritarianism: autocrats will avoid reforms that threaten the interests of their constituents if their constituents might then defect. Defection is the threat that supporters of an authoritarian regime wield over that regime.

So far, the game simplifies the possibilities of reform. The choices for economic reform are rarely ever binary, for a regime will adopt incremental and targeted measures to balance the benefits it receives from reform and the costs that its constituents pay. In the framework of the game, we can say that, for each possible basket of economic reform, there are different associated values of a and b. We must also vary the costs that C incurs from reform without defection, before assumed to be zero but now captured with the variable c. Figure 2.3 allows for three possible paths of economic reform and ignores the case of status quo preservation.

As shown in Figure 2.3 $c_1, c_2 > b > c_3$ and $a_3 > a_1 > a_2$. Thus, there are some reform measures (Reform 1 and Reform 2) where C still prefers to support the regime rather than to defect. For simplicity, I assume that the costs of defection are uniform regardless of the reform action taken. To determine the reform measure adopted, R compares its benefits from the different reforms. Even though $a_3 > a_1, a_2$, R will not choose Reform 3 because it will cause C to defect; hence, R's payoff will be zero. In the game that Figure 2.3 captures, $a_1 > a_2$; hence, we observe Reform 1.

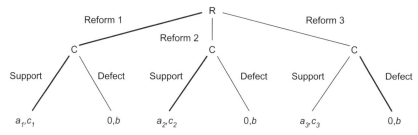

FIGURE 2.3. The Reform Game with Multiple Reform Possibilities (bold lines represent players' dominant strategies).

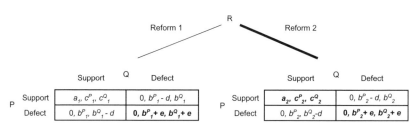

FIGURE 2.4. The Reform Game with Two Constituents (bold lines represent players' dominant strategies).

To complete the game, suppose that there are two constituents, P and Q, who given R's choice then choose simultaneously whether they will support the regime or defect.[27] By construction, R cannot survive in office unless neither P nor Q defects, so R must adopt policies that make neither constituent worse off than each constituent would be under an alternative political arrangement. Figure 2.4 illustrates such a situation, with R choosing between two reforms.

P prefers to support R under either reform, but Q will support R only if it adopts Reform 2. Some extra terminology is necessary. P and Q receive their payoffs b_i^P and b_i^Q if either one of them defects; their values vary depending on the reform decision i taken by R. There is a penalty d (the sucker's punishment) that P or Q can receive if it chooses to support R while its counterpart does not. There is also a benefit e that both P and Q receive if they both defect; its function is to produce only pure-strategy Nash equilibria. For this reason e can be vanishingly small, so long as it is

---

[27] It is straightforward to construct a game where either P or Q moves first, but the results change only trivially.

greater than zero.[28] Here, $c_2^Q > b_2^Q + e$, but $b_1^Q > c_1^Q$, so Q defects if R chooses Reform 1. $c_1^P, c_2^P > b_1^P, b_2^P$, so P prefers to support R regardless of the reform measures adopted. Because Reform 1 leads Q to defect, R will choose Reform 2 and receive payoff a_2. The subgame between P and Q given Reform 2, because of the existence of $e > 0$, is a standard coordination game. There are two pure-strategy Nash equilibria to this subgame – both *P* and *Q* support the regime or both defect from the regime. Given Reform 2, Support-Support yields a Pareto-superior outcome to Defect-Defect. I assume that communication between P and Q allows them to coordinate on this outcome.

Note the interesting possibility of $b_1^Q > c_1^Q$ and $b_2^Q > c_2^Q$, in which case one constituent will strictly prefer to defect regardless of what choice R makes. Thus, regardless of the reform strategy, R receives zero, and the regime collapses. This outcome is inefficient for all players, yet is the equilibrium given their preferences and the commitment problem that prevents players from agreeing that one bears the costs of adjustment in the short term in exchange for some reward in the future.

The observable implications from this simple game are straightforward. Facing a crisis, a regime adopts the policies that its supporters demand. When there are multiple reform possibilities, the regime chooses only among reforms that do not cause its supporters to defect. When supporters have mutually incompatible preferences for adjustment policies, the regime faces an unavoidable choice among policies, one of which will ultimately cause a supporter to defect. This defection brings down the regime.

---

[28] Without *d* or *e*, additional mixed-strategy Nash equilibria exist, but they do not affect the intuition of the game.

3

Authoritarian Support Coalitions

Comparing Indonesia and Malaysia

This chapter shows the development and logic of the different coalitions supporting authoritarian regimes in Indonesia and Malaysia. Indonesia's New Order rested on an alliance between the military and a small coterie of ethnic Chinese Indonesian entrepreneurs. Malaysia's Barisan Nasional coalition depended on (and still continues to depend on) an alliance between the Malay masses and a class of Malay entrepreneurs. These systems were stable and predictable. Each regime used largely informal exchange relationships to regularize mutual reward for leaders and supporters and also to systematize the threat of repression and violence for members of the polity outside of the support coalition. This stability enabled each regime to engineer rapid economic growth at rates nearly unparalleled in the developing world while embedding these support coalitions directly into the apparatus of political rule.

In the terms of the model of an economy introduced in Chapter 2, Indonesia's coalition was one between mobile and fixed capital, whereas Malaysia's coalition is one between fixed capital and labor. The broad actor categories – mobile capital, fixed capital, and labor – are theoretical ideal types, but in this chapter I link each ideal type to a concrete group with clear political allegiances. These mappings reveal the importance of the country-specific histories in understanding political coalitions and their economic interests. In the case of Malaysia, for instance, the regime depends not on "labor" writ large but specifically on the unorganized Malay masses. In Indonesia, fixed capital comprised both military-linked businesses and new *pribumi* (roughly, "indigenous")[1] entrepreneurs.

---

[1] In Indonesian political discourse, "indigenous" citizens are those without Chinese ancestry.

40

These specifics matter for understanding how ideal-typical interest groups operate in specific national contexts, giving context to the general theory proposed in Chapter 2.

Support coalitions in each country developed in line with the conditions that produced authoritarian rule. In Indonesia, the military coup of 1965 ousted the authoritarian regime of President Sukarno, whose ineffective economic management spurred massive inflation. Personal connections between key military figures and ethnic Chinese financiers led the new regime of President Soeharto to embrace holders of mobile capital and to form an alliance with them to engineer economic recovery. Authoritarian rule in Malaysia, by contrast, arose in the wake of peaceful decolonization, with ethnic cleavages overlaying marked disparities in wealth. Successive authoritarian rulers have defined themselves as defenders of Malay economic and social welfare, marginalizing politically both ethnic Chinese and foreign holders of mobile capital in favor of Malay fixed capital and the Malay masses.

Although the problems of authoritarian governance are common across regimes, the specific strategies through which regimes rule vary. Country-specific characteristics such as politicized ethnic cleavages, military professionalism, and initial factor and resource endowments create different kinds of authoritarian regimes. For Indonesia and Malaysia, I rely on a brief historical narrative to chart the development of stable authoritarian political systems that existed by the late 1990s. The narrative emphasizes the role of initial macroeconomic conditions and pre-authoritarian factional alignments, but I leave it for future research to determine whether these cases can instead be understood as the outcomes of political dynamics generalizable across time and space.

Because my theory emphasizes coalitions, I spend some time describing the alternative frameworks – personality, ideology, institutions, and regime "types" – that analysts have employed to understand authoritarianism in each country. Many of these are in fact epiphenomenal on the coalitions that I identify. Ideologies legitimize, albeit often in complex and fascinating ways, existing political arrangements. Likewise, regimes create political institutions that reflect power dynamics at the moment of regime consolidation. In these ways, coalitional interests are embedded in the very structure of authority. In turn, regimes themselves reproduce coalitions by enacting policies that privilege them, strengthening the regime's constituents vis-à-vis other members of society. Typologies of authoritarian governance vary in their aims and scope, but few propose an explicit logic of self-perpetuation. It is for this reason that analysts of authoritarian rule in Southeast Asia and elsewhere have spilled so much ink disagreeing among proper regime classifications – bureaucratic authoritarianism, feudalism, praetorianism, sultanism, competitive authoritarianism, defective democracy, and others – without reaching anything resembling a consensus for either country. While not denying the roles of personality, ideology, and formal institutions for a complete understanding of the intricacies of political life under authoritarianism, I focus here on interests, coalitions, and coercion as the basis of authoritarian politics in Indonesia and Malaysia.

The New Order

Indonesia's New Order arose in the late 1960s following Major General Soeharto's seizure of power in 1966. The previous regime under Sukarno had for a decade struck a delicate balance between two competing sources of political power, the Communist Party of Indonesia (PKI) and the Armed Forces of Indonesia (ABRI). PKI commanded a large, if not overwhelming, following throughout the archipelago. The officers of ABRI, by contrast, were mostly anticommunist, and their control over the state's security apparatus gave them substantial political power. Following the murder of six ABRI generals on September 30, 1965, by supposed PKI followers – the infamous Gestapu (Gerakan Tiga Puluh September, or September 30 Movement) – Soeharto as the commander of the Army's Strategic Reserve Command (Kostrad) in Jakarta launched a brutal anti-PKI offensive.[2] With the PKI crushed and Sukarno under severe pressure from ABRI, on March 11, 1966, Sukarno signed a document known as the Supersemar (Surat Perintah Sebelas Maret, Executive Order of March 11) that gave Soeharto supreme authority to take any actions necessary to maintain the order and safety of the Indonesian people. The following year the People's Provisional Consultative Assembly named Soeharto president, a position he would hold for the next thirty-two years.[3]

In consolidating his personal power and eliminating any opposition, Soeharto was ruthless. Beginning in late October 1965 and continuing for more than a year, Soeharto's allies in ABRI carried out mass executions of PKI members and suspected communist sympathizers.[4] Hundreds of

[2] Sundhaussen 1982, 192–254.
[3] The events of Gestapu and its aftermath remain the topic of endless speculation: see van der Kroef 1971. On the ensuing anti-PKI massacres, see Cribb 1990.
[4] See Anderson and McVey 1971, 60–65.

thousands of Indonesians were killed on the islands of Java and Bali, both in operations carried out by official security forces and in unsanctioned massacres. Among the targets of this violence were many ethnic Chinese Indonesians, suspected by many of harboring sympathies with the People's Republic of China.[5] Despite the heavy price paid among ethnic Chinese Indonesians, the killings cut across ethnic boundaries, often motivated by personal grievances. The use of the Indonesian military to repress forcibly groups suspected of threatening the New Order status quo would become a recurring theme under Soeharto.

Amid widespread violence against PKI members and their suspected affiliates, Soeharto also focused on economic recovery. Indonesia's economy had ground to a standstill by 1965, with approximately 600 percent annual inflation and economic growth nonexistent. From the beginning, the New Order based its legitimating ideology on its ability to provide stable economic growth, with Soeharto enlisting the advice of a group of Berkeley-trained economists who later became known as the "Berkeley Mafia." Especially during the early years of the New Order, members of the Berkeley Mafia had unprecedented personal access to Soeharto and were instrumental in orchestrating Indonesia's economic recovery (Figure 3.1). Within two years of Soeharto's seizure of power, hyperinflation had abated. By contrast, real economic growth began its steady rise that would persist almost uninterrupted until 1997.

Early on, however, the technocrats ran against another ideological camp among policy planners, the "nationalists" (sometimes referred to as "technologs" or "engineers").[6] Although many Indonesian economists favored government intervention in the economy to stimulate economic development, nationalists set their sights on much larger projects. They favored big-ticket development projects, a "big push" requiring government intervention and protectionism to shield infant industries from competitive pressures. The New Order went to great lengths to incorporate statist development principles into its ideology of Pancasila, and it painted *ekonomi Pancasila* (Pancasila economics) as different from Western liberal economics.[7] Influential nationalists included such figures as B. J. Habibie, Soeharto's minister of research and technology from 1978 until 1998, an

[5] Rakindo 1975.
[6] Bresnan 1993; Liddle 1991, 417–422; Mackie and MacIntyre 1994, 35–37; Robison 1988.
[7] Bowen 1986; McCawley 1982; Mubyarto 1987.

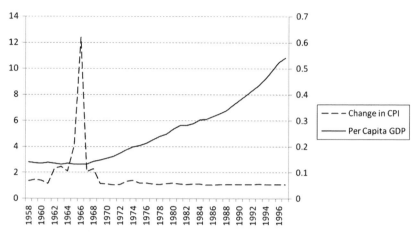

FIGURE 3.1. Indonesian Inflation and GDP, 1958–1997. The Consumer Price Index (CPI) is from seventeen provincial capitals around the archipelago. Per capita GDP comes from an index of GDP by volume with 2000 equivalent to 100, divided by yearly estimated population. *Source:* Calculated from International Monetary Fund 2007.

aeronautic engineer who headed Indonesia's ill-fated domestic airplane corporation.[8]

These ideological battles between technocrats and nationalists masked the political logic of economic policy, which consistently rewarded political supporters in ABRI and a clique of well-connected ethnic Chinese businessmen, later followed by a nascent class of indigenous entrepreneurs. The relationship among Soeharto, the Indonesian military, and ethnic Chinese businessmen relied on a set of exchanges, reinforced by credible threats of violence. In exchange for privileged access to business opportunities, ABRI generals and their subordinates enforced the New Order status quo against domestic challengers. In exchange for physical protection from the near-constant threat of anti-Chinese violence and expropriation, ethnic Chinese *konglomerat* (conglomerates) funneled patronage through the New Order economy. Other members of the New Order political elite benefited from the loyalty of the country's security apparatus and from rents that accrued toward the regime's center. ABRI leaders enjoyed extensive opportunities for personal enrichment. They were joined in the 1980s by a new class of *pribumi* entrepreneurs, who, like ABRI leaders, remained highly dependent on the state for access

[8] On his nationalist ideological orientations, see, e.g., Habibie 1995.

to contracts and rents. Ethnic Chinese *konglomerat* enjoyed protection, favoritism, and a relatively free hand in managing their business empires.

At the heart of this system of exchange lay Soeharto himself, whom Ross McLeod has likened to a discriminating franchiser overseeing a complex net of exchange relationships that exploited economic rents for political power.[9] The "franchisees" (lower-level military figures, ethnic Chinese business groups, and their own subordinates) participated in these exchanges because they accrued benefits from doing so. The centralized organization of patronage minimized the potential for truly unbridled rent seeking that might have plagued a less organized political system.[10] Soeharto was the New Order's sole veto player,[11] and only through personal access to Soeharto were the technocrats able to influence policy: technocratic influence existed only with Soeharto's blessing and only to the extent that it did not interfere with the demands of the regime's other political supporters. Selective patronage combined with repression – often only threatened but still widespread enough to be credible – provided incentives for all players to perpetuate the New Order status quo.

Fixed Capital: ABRI and the Pribumi Entrepreneurs

That Soeharto rose from within the ranks of ABRI makes it understandable that the New Order rested at least in part on a firm basis of military support. But it is not self-evident that this should be so: Soeharto could not simply assume the continued support of ABRI members without fearing the possibility of a coup.[12] Under the New Order, rather, Soeharto constantly nurtured the support of senior military officers while manipulating personnel decisions to prevent the accrual of any significant opposition within ABRI's ranks. ABRI's ranks were the basis upon which indigenous holders of fixed capital grew in Indonesia. Especially before the 1980s but thereafter as well, its ability to repress challengers to the regime placed it at the center of the New Order political economy.

The distribution of economic rents attracted the support of ABRI's generals and their subordinates through off-budget financing, the practice of using quasi-state or even private enterprises to fund ABRI units and line the pockets of military figures. The forms that such relationships took

---

[9] McLeod 2000.
[10] See also Crouch 1979; Imawan 1991; MacIntyre 2003a; Mackie 1993; Mackie and MacIntyre 1994; Shidiq 2003; Shleifer and Vishny 1993.
[11] MacIntyre 1999a; 1999b.
[12] McVey 1982, 90.

varied – from appointing military figures to head state-owned corporations (BUMN), to funneling patronage through development foundations
(*yayasan*), to using military coercion to secure favorable contracts for
business enterprises in exchange for a cut of the profits, or to simple
protection rackets.[13] Moreover, when older generals retired from ABRI,
they could expect to retain influence through their appointment to boards
of directors in large government-linked firms.[14] In creating this system of
privilege that extended from an officer's time in the military ranks
through his retirement to the private sector, the Soeharto regime institutionalized a system of regime self-reproduction that proved remarkably
adept at rewarding subordinates for their loyalty to the regime. The relationship between the military and business is most clear in three BUMNs:
Pertamina (National Oil Mining Corporation), the Indonesian national
oil company; Bulog (Bureau of Logistical Affairs), the government's
commodities board; and Berdikari, a government-owned trading firm.
Each illustrates the mechanisms through which state institutions embedded the military's business interests directly into the mechanism of regime
perpetuation.

The oil boom of the early 1970s created windfall profits for Pertamina,
headed by Lieutenant General Ibnu Sutowo. Ibnu used his position to
enrich himself, while running Pertamina into the ground by 1974 through
overexpansion and imprudent borrowing. Yet he never faced sanction
from Soeharto for this blatant mismanagement and was dismissed with
honor in 1976.[15] Later appointments included a number of figures with
close personal and professional links to General Ibnu.[16] Although never
an efficiently run firm, throughout the New Order Pertamina provided
resource rents, channeled both up toward Soeharto and down as investment for ventures owned by military subordinates.[17]

Bulog and Berdikari performed similar functions. Bulog's primary task
was to ensure stable rice prices despite seasonal and yearly fluctuations
in production by maintaining excess stocks to be released during periods
of rice shortages and purchasing excess rice during periods of excess
production.[18] Profits generated by Bulog, originally run by Lieutenant
General Achmad Tirtosudiro, were distributed toward military-run

---

[13] See Crouch 1975–1976; 1978, 275–293; Lowry 1996; Samego et al. 1998, 67–97.
[14] See, e.g., Bresnan 1993, 107; Haseman 1986, 896.
[15] Glassburner 1976, 1099–1103.
[16] Khong 1986, 164–72.
[17] Prawiro 1998, 101–23.
[18] Prawiro 1998, 127–34; Timmer 1993, 156.

investment companies. The trading firm Berdikari's first head was General Suhardiman, who fell directly under Soeharto's command. While the organization fell into disrepute after some trading debacles in the late 1960s, it later emerged as a major government-linked corporation with interests in logistics, cattle farming, and insurance, in addition to trading.

The business empires built up by ABRI figures focused mainly on specific fixed capital investments, including sectors such as construction, real estate, and forestry (Table 3.1). Included here are only the largest military business ventures. Other state-owned firms maintained fixed capital investments without overt military participation[19] but were privatized under the direction of cronies in the late 1980s.

These ties between the military and big business placed ABRI at the center of the New Order political economy. Equally important for embedding the military in the country's economic life was ABRI's territorial presence. ABRI's doctrine of *dwifungsi* (dual function) stipulated that the Indonesian military was both responsible for national defense and active as a sociopolitical force.[20] On the national level, ABRI maintained an extensive infrastructure for monitoring society and ensuring order. But the doctrine of *dwifungsi* also provided the ideological cover for ABRI's penetration of everyday life at the local level. Throughout the archipelago, in parallel to the traditional positions held by provincial governors, mayors, regents, and village heads, a system of territorial commands placed military figures in regional offices through which they represented the local face of the national security apparatus. Relatively autonomous from the center on quotidian matters, these officials engaged in their own business activities in concert with local business elites.[21] As was the case with large military-run parastatals, smaller business ventures in the periphery enriched local military leaders, who in turn provided protection for their business partners. Because the local holders of power (*penguasa*) and business entrepreneurs (*pengusaha*) both profited from such exchanges, both had an interest in perpetuating them. Those at the highest echelons of the New Order also enjoyed a steady stream of rents that accrued from the periphery toward the center and the stability that their subordinates' penetration of local businesses afforded.

But a well-funded subordinate could always use his access to rents to build up a competing base within the military through which to challenge

---

[19] See Shin 1989, 173–74.
[20] Crouch 1978, 344–48; Djiwandono 1988; Soebijono et al. 1997.
[21] Crouch 1975–76, 523–24; 2001a, 175.

TABLE 3.1. *Ten Largest Military-Linked Business Groups*

Group Name (No. of Companies)	Holding Company and/or Major Companies	Main Business Areas	Backers
Tri Usaha Bhakti (25)	Tri Usaha Bhakti Asuransi Purwadjasa, Sepati Air Transpor	Trade, forestry, contracting, construction, transportation, insurance	Ministry of Defense
Propelat (20)	Propelat	Banking, contracting, freight forwarding	Siliwangi Military Command
Berdikari (19)	PP Berdikari Bank Duta, Berdikari Sari Utama Flour Mill	Banking, insurance, leasing, flour mills, trade, freight forwarding	Bulog, Soeharto
CMC (16)	Capitol Mutual Corp.	Trade, contracting, consulting, architecture, liquified petroleum gas distribution	PT Pembangunan Jaya/ Jakarta Metropolitan Government
Admiral (Yala Trade) (13)	Yala Trade, Admiral Lines	Shipping, forestry	Navy
Bhirwara (11)	Bhirwara Development Corp.	Contracting, trade, real estate, forestry, slaughterhouse	Briwijaya Military Command

Elmi (11)	Kosgoro, Wisma Kosgoro	Real estate, trade, tourism, hotel, contracting	Veterans' Cooperative
Yayasan Dharma Putera (10)	Dharma Kencana Sakti, Mandala Airlines, Garuda Mataram	Airliner, auto assembly	Kostrad
Hanurata	Hanurata Co. Ltd, Hotel and Theater Kartika Chandra	Plywood, hotel, bulk carrier	Yayasan Harapan Kita, Tien Soeharto
Induk Koperasi Angkatan Darat (Inkopad)	Wisma Kartika Plaza	Hotels, fishery	Army

Source: Adapted from Shin 1989, 127.

Soeharto, in order to access the more extensive perquisites that Soeharto and his family enjoyed. To counter this threat, Soeharto constantly manipulated the advancement and succession of ABRI personnel. This enabled him to build up multiple independent bases of support within ABRI, which he could favor or marginalize depending on the severity of the challenge they could present. Although within-ABRI factionalism was most threatening during the 1970s and early 1980s, Soeharto's eventual emergence at the pinnacle of ABRI by the mid-1980s – and ABRI's gradual decline as the dominant player in Indonesia's political economy that began thereafter – did not mean that factionalism disappeared. Indeed, the most important factional struggles were over the gradual institutionalization of ABRI's role in the New Order political economy, pitting ABRI's more professional members against Soeharto and his close associates.

Riots in Jakarta on January 15, 1974, during the visit of Japanese prime minister Kakuei Tanaka, revealed an initial resistance of several more professional members of ABRI to the military's increasing penetration of business and society.[22] Several ABRI members, led by General Sumitro, had in late 1973 begun to take up the cause of university students who demanded greater public accountability from Soeharto and other generals. Besides Soeharto, a major target of Sumitro's ire was Major General Ali Murtopo, head of the special intelligence body Opsus (Special Operations) and an adviser to Soeharto. Prime Minister Tanaka's visit occasioned large protests against what students viewed as unjust crony linkages between military figures and foreign and domestic capital. Hoping to discredit those generals with business connections, Sumitro did not take firm action to stop the protests or the two-day riots that followed them. But Sumitro overestimated his position and was dismissed by Soeharto shortly thereafter. Soeharto used this opportunity to consolidate his control over the state intelligence apparatus, appointing loyalists to key positions and enacting tighter restrictions on student and press activities.

These early personnel shake-ups put Soeharto loyalists – including Ali Murtopo – into the highest levels of the New Order's security apparatus. When Murtopo became minister of information in 1978, another Soeharto loyalist, Lieutenant General Leonardus Benyamin ("Benny") Murdani, took his position as the deputy head of the Coordinating Agency for State Intelligence (Bakin). At the same time that Murdani held this post at Bakin, he headed the Strategic Intelligence Agency (Bais),

[22] Crouch 1978, 314–16; Hansen 1975.

Bakin's counterpart in the Ministry of Defense.[23] Murdani gradually consolidated his position within the armed forces throughout the 1980s, expanding the influence of Bais and rising to the positions of ABRI commander from 1983 to 1988 and minister of defense from 1988 to 1993. Yet by the 1990s, Murdani's reputation for professionalism rather than business put him in conflict with Soeharto, with Murdani and his allies criticizing Soeharto's children's increasing involvement in the corporate world.[24] This proved to be his undoing. Soeharto dismissed Murdani as minister of defense in 1993 and subsequently tore down Murdani's institutional support within ABRI by dismantling Bais and rotating Murdani loyalists toward retirement.[25]

Murdani's marginalization also reflected what some analysts have called a cleavage between nationalist ("red-and-white," referring to the Indonesian flag) and Islamist ("green") factions within ABRI.[26] Murdani, a Catholic, embodied the former group; generals such as Feisal Tanjung (commander of ABRI from 1993) and Raden Hartono (army chief of staff from 1993) represented the latter. The rise of Tanjung and Hartono suggested a turn toward Islam in New Order politics in the 1990s, especially with the continued influence of B. J. Habibie as a Muslim nationalist intellectual. However, it is almost certainly more accurate to view the rise of Islamists as a strategic move by Soeharto to neutralize Murdani's influence, as evinced by the simultaneous advancement of other officers in ABRI without Islamist credentials.[27] For example, General Wiranto, with links to the nationalist camp, advanced from his position as Soeharto's personal assistant to Kostrad commander in 1995. Major General Prabowo Subianto, Soeharto's son-in-law, became commander of the army's Special Forces Command (Kopassus) in 1995. While occasionally linked to the Islamists, Prabowo owed his position and hence his allegiance to Soeharto rather than any members of the Islamist faction.

Personnel shake-ups within ABRI reveal the extent to which military business interests had become embedded in the New Order's political hierarchy by the early 1990s. Extensive opportunities for personal enrichment through business placated many potential challengers to Soeharto, but when such enticements were unsuccessful or insufficient, strong-arm

[23] Editors 1982.
[24] Bertrand 1996, 327; Said 2001, 64–65; 2002, 133–43.
[25] Honna 1999, 93–94; Liddle 1996a, 60–61; Editors 1994, 90.
[26] See Editors 1997.
[27] Liddle 1996a, 61; Said 2001, 73–76; Sulistiyo 2001, 298–300.

tactics and personnel manipulations were necessary. In addition to helping Soeharto maintain his control over the New Order's security apparatus, officer rotations also kept younger officers from becoming disillusioned and moved loyal older officers into lucrative retirement opportunities. It is not possible to understand ABRI's functioning and organizational development under the New Order, or its factionalism and institutional reproduction, without reference to business interests. This mix of co-option and coercion had by the 1980s created the first component of the New Order's support coalition: a military establishment with heavy fixed capital investments, which Soeharto could reliably use to challenge opponents.

However influential ABRI remained for the New Order political economy after the mid-1980s, observers noted by this time the blossoming of a new group of fixed capital holders, the *pribumi* entrepreneurs.[28] ("Entrepreneur" here is something of a misnomer, for in this context it refers to individuals whose greatest business assets are political connections.) This group of fixed capital holders is distinct from ABRI, originating not from the ranks of the military but from elsewhere, most frequently from the regime's official political organ Golkar or from connections to high-ranking Golkar members or the military.[29] The classic example is Soeharto's own family, whose business interests ranged from toll roads to airlines to clove marketing. But other *pribumi* business groups emerged in the 1980s as well, associated with groups such as the Association of Indigenous Indonesian Entrepreneurs, the Association of Young Indonesian Entrepreneurs, and the Chamber of Commerce and Industry (Kadin).[30]

Still, like ABRI's business interests, the majority of the investments and assets of the new *pribumi* entrepreneurs were rooted in Indonesia, in particular in ventures that depended on state infrastructural spending, the access to which was guaranteed by political favoritism.[31] While the growth of the new *pribumi* entrepreneurs in the late 1980s and early 1990s allowed them to join ABRI-affiliated business as the two primary engines of non-Chinese capital accumulation in Indonesia, the most important characteristic uniting them with ABRI was that their capital assets, too, were rooted in Indonesia.

[28] See Robison 1986, 342–67; Winters 1996, 184–90.
[29] Robison and Hadiz 2004, 58–60.
[30] Eklöf 2002, 223–25; MacIntyre 1994.
[31] Winters 1996, 187.

Mobile Capital: *The* Konglomerat

Chinese Indonesian financiers supported the New Order regime because of the physical protection that they received from Soeharto's allies within ABRI. With the protection of ABRI, a small number of well-placed ethnic Chinese businessmen developed giant corporate empires, known as *konglomerat*, with diversified interests and large pools of investment capital. In exchange for this protection, ethnic Chinese *konglomerat* gave military figures a cut of their profits and used their business connections to facilitate the entry of ABRI figures into business. Long-standing anti-Chinese discrimination meant that the comparatively wealthy ethnic Chinese minority could not threaten the New Order's political authority and gave aspiring ethnic Chinese businessmen an incentive to cultivate close personal ties with the regime. From the New Order's first years, officials seized the opportunity to employ ethnic Chinese financiers for political gain.[32] The political arrangement that subsequently arose between ethnic Chinese financiers and the New Order reproduced this system of exchange: the regime institutionalized "Chineseness" as a cleavage in Indonesian politics at the same time as it adopted economic policies that favored the *konglomerat*.[33] This arrangement had important downstream consequences. Largely constrained by their dependence on indigenous patrons, ethnic Chinese entrepreneurs concentrated on short-term business ventures and financial sector dealings and diversified against the risks inherent in long-term joint investments.[34]

Chinese Indonesians' preference for protection from ABRI was a consequence of their vulnerable position within Indonesian society. This vulnerability has a basis in Indonesia's colonial history. Since Dutch colonial times, ethnic Chinese living in Indonesia have occupied the peculiar position of a "merchant" or "pariah" minority – akin to Lebanese in West Africa, Indians in East Africa, and Jews in prewar Europe. Under the Dutch East India Company's rule, the Chinese in Indonesia – along with Indians and Arabs – were considered *vreemde Oosterlingen* (foreign Easterners), subject to a different set of legal codes than *pribumi* Indonesians (Inlanders) and given special economic rights.[35] This system placed ethnic Chinese living in Indonesia in the middle rung of the colonial economic hierarchy, below Dutch colonial rulers but above *pribumis*.

[32] King 2000, 610–11; Liddle 1999b, 51–52; Mackie and MacIntyre 1994, 39; McLeod 2000, 157.
[33] Chua 2008, 28–63.
[34] Mackie 1992.
[35] See Setiono 2003.

The result of Dutch colonial policies was economic stratification across ethnic lines and, consequently, anti-Chinese prejudice and discrimination. As is the case elsewhere in Southeast Asia, ethnic Chinese constitute a disproportionate percentage of traders and merchants in Indonesia, and like many economically dominant minorities, Chinese Indonesians face charges that they have divided political loyalties, that they discriminate against *pribumis* in business affairs, that they are politically opportunistic, and so forth.[36] Contributing to this view has been the fact that relatively few Chinese Indonesians have converted to Islam. Of course, the vast majority of ethnic Chinese Indonesians are not wealthy, and most Chinese Indonesians know no other home than Indonesia and speak Bahasa Indonesia as their first or only language. In parts of Kalimantan (Indonesian Borneo), the majority of ethnic Chinese Indonesians are farmers rather than traders. The existence of negative stereotypes, however untrue, and the vulnerability of ethnic Chinese Indonesians to violence or expropriation by dissatisfied *pribumis*, has throughout Indonesia's history made it attractive for aspiring Chinese entrepreneurs to forge alliances with the holders of power in return for physical protection. Even before Soeharto's seizure of power, close links between power holders and ethnic Chinese Indonesians were prevalent, and they only grew under Soeharto.

An oft-repeated assertion during the New Order stated that Chinese Indonesians compose approximately 3 percent of the country's population, yet control approximately 70 percent of the country's wealth. It is impossible to ascertain the truth of this statement – definitions of wealth vary, as do definitions of Chineseness – but the penetration of the New Order economy by ethnic Chinese *konglomerat* was apparent by the 1970s and grew further in the 1980s and 1990s (Table 3.2).

Beyond the heavy domination of ethnic Chinese Indonesians, a striking observation from this list in Table 3.2 is the identity of those non-Chinese figures. Among the top ten Indonesian business figures, the only non-Chinese are Bambang Trihatmodjo and Indra Rukmana, Soeharto's second son and his son-in-law. The first private *pribumi* businessman to enter the list is Aburizal Bakrie – but Bakrie & Brothers was founded in the 1940s and prospered as well under Sukarno's rule. Although ethnic Chinese *konglomerat* were a vanishingly small fraction of all Chinese Indonesians, their influence in the New Order's political economy was enormous.

[36] Coppel 1983, 3–29.

TABLE 3.2. *Twenty-five Leading* Konglomerat *in 1997*

Conglomerate Name	Primary Owner	Ethnicity
Salim	Liem Sioe Liong (Sudono Salim)	Chinese
Astra International	Prajogo Pangestu (Phang Dju Phin)	Chinese
	Bob Hasan (The Kian Seng)	Chinese
Sinar Mas	Eka Tjipta Widjaja (Oei Ek Tjhong)	Chinese
Gudang Garam	Rachman Halim (Tjoa To Hing)	Chinese
Lippo	Mochtar Riady (Lee Mo Tie)	Chinese
Bimantara	Bambang Trihatmodjo	*Pribumi* (Soeharto's son)
	Indra Rukmana	*Pribumi* (Soeharto's son-in-law)
Gajah Tunggal	Sjamsul Nursalim (Liem Tjoen Ho)	Chinese
Ongko	Kaharudin Ongko (Ong Ka Huat)	Chinese
Djarum	Robert Budi Hartono (Oei Hwie Tjhong)	Chinese
	Michael Bambang Hartono (Oei Hwie Siang)	Chinese
Rodamas	Tan Siong Kie (Hanafi)	Chinese
Nusamba	Bob Hasan (The Kian Seng)	Chinese
	Sigit Harjojudanto	*Pribumi* (Soeharto's son)
Kalbe Farma	Boenyamin Setiawan (Khouw Lip Boen)	Chinese
Dharmala	Soehargo Gondokusumo (Go Ha Kim)	Chinese
Argo Manunggal	The Ning King	Chinese
Barito Pacific	Prajogo Pangestu (Phang Dju Phin)	Chinese
Maspion	Alim Husin (Lim Wen Kwang)	Chinese
Bakrie & Brothers	Aburizal Bakrie	*Pribumi*
Humpuss	Hutomo Mandala Putra	*Pribumi* (Soeharto's son)
Danamon	Usman Admadjaja (Njauw Jauw Woe)	Chinese

(continued)

TABLE 3.2 *(continued)*

Conglomerate Name	Primary Owner	Ethnicity
Cipta Cakra Murdaya	Murdaya Widyawimarta (Poo Tjie Gwan)	Chinese
Panin	Mu'min Ali Gunawan (Lie Moek Ming)	Chinese
Jan Darmadi	Jan Darmadi (Jauw Jan Foek)	Chinese
Pembangunan Jaya	Jakarta Government Ciputra (Tjie Tjin Hoan)	n/a Chinese
Sampurna	Putera Sampurna (Liem Tien Pao)	Chinese
Raja Garuda Mas	Sukanto Tanoto (Lim Sui Hang)	Chinese

Source: Adapted from *Warta Ekonomi*, November 24, 1997; Sato 2003; Shin 1989, 213–16. Spelling of Chinese names varies among sources.

In nearly all high-profile cases of business partnerships between ABRI figures and ethnic Chinese *konglomerat*, the *konglomerat* used their access to investment capital to facilitate ABRI business ventures. Several examples illustrate how New Order figures employed Chinese Indonesian businessmen as *cukongs*, or financiers, to support their forays into business.[37] Liem Sioe Liong, an immigrant from Fujian province in China and the New Order's wealthiest private citizen, established connections with the military during the 1950s when he earned a supply concession for ABRI's Diponegoro division, then headed at that time by Soeharto himself. By the 1990s, Liem's Salim Group had invested in flour milling, cement production, and many other business areas, each done through the exploitation of close links to Soeharto and the military. PT Bogasari, for instance, jointly owned by the Salim Group and Soeharto's cousin Sudwikatmono, held a monopoly on flour milling that it preserved by contributing profits to Kostrad's Yayasan Dharma Putera.[38] William Soeryadjaya (Tjia Kian Liong) founded PT Astra International in the late 1950s, and the group benefited under the New Order from relations with Ibnu Sutowo. PT Astra International rose to prominence in the 1970s and

[37] It is a daunting task to trace exhaustively all of the specific business relationships between ABRI figures and *konglomerat*, particularly in regional commands. Some good sources are Mackie 1992; Schwarz 1994; Shin 1989; Vatikiotis 1998.
[38] Eklöf 2002, 217; Sato 2003, 16–17.

1980s on the back of its subsidiary PT Toyota–Astra Motor, which held the sole license to import and distribute Toyota automobiles. It suffered a setback in 1992 when its subsidiary Bank Summa collapsed, despite continued government favoritism.[39] Sofyan Wanandi (Liem Bian Koen) was a former student activist whose brother Jusuf (Liem Bian Kie) helped with Ali Murtopo to found the influential nationalist policy think tank, the Centre for Strategic and International Studies. Sofyan served as a manager for the Ministry of Defense's holding company Tri Usaha Bhakti in addition to heading his own Gemala Group.

The vulnerability of Chinese Indonesians served the New Order regime well. To ensure this vulnerability and thereby to minimize ethnic Chinese entrepreneurs' political threat, the New Order regime pursued a number of cultural policies that reinforced the distinctions between *pribumi* and Chinese Indonesians.[40] Chinese Indonesians, unlike *pribumis*, had their ethnic identity ("Chinese") stamped on their identity cards. In interactions with the Indonesian bureaucracy, Chinese Indonesians often faced hurdles rarely faced by *pribumis*, such as demands that they prove their Indonesian citizenship. Meanwhile, the New Order regime's policy of assimilation banned Chinese-language publications, Chinese-inspired cultural practices, and Chinese New Year celebrations and directed Chinese Indonesians to adopt Indonesian names to replace their Chinese names. Wealthy *konglomerat* had political influence through their business connections, but their participation in formal New Order politics was almost nonexistent. Only a few Chinese Indonesians ever served as members of the Indonesian Parliament (DPR), and not a single Chinese Indonesian served in a New Order cabinet until Soeharto's final term, when he nominated Muhammad "Bob" Hasan as minister of trade and industry.

Christian Chua has written extensively on how New Order cultural policies reproduced the peculiar symbiosis between *konglomerat* and regime, making Chinese Indonesians at once "pariahs" and "partners."[41] He underscores an important point: New Order cultural policies had an instrumental logic that buttressed the regime's stability. Such policies were not an outgrowth of simple racism – although racism explained their origin and mass appeal – but rather a tool for reproducing the regime. By eradicating Chinese cultural symbols while preserving the essential distinction between Chinese and *pribumi* Indonesians,

---

[39] MacIntyre and Sjahrir 1993, 13–15; Shin 1989, 256–57.
[40] Chua 2004; Heryanto 1998, 100–4; Liem 2000.
[41] Chua 2008, 37–61.

the regime perpetuated the stereotypes so necessary to maintain the New Order status quo.

The creation of social policies that discriminated against Chinese Indonesians, along with the threat of violence and expropriation, makes it appear that ethnic Chinese business figures were the weak party under the New Order. But this ignores the vast wealth that *konglomerat* were able to extract in return for the services they provided. In return for funneling their investments toward industries of strategic political importance, *konglomerat* received monopoly privileges, tariff protection, closed-bid tenders, resource rents, and a vast array of other targeted benefits and inducements. It was through these connections that ethnic Chinese *konglomerat* grew so quickly to dominate the New Order economy.

The *konglomerat*, though, retained an important source of leverage against the potential for expropriation. Scholars have long noted the high cross-border mobility of ethnic Chinese cronies' assets, concentrated in liquid investment capital and ready to funnel abroad at the first sign of political turmoil.[42] As holders of mobile investment capital, ethnic Chinese Indonesians retained the ability to vote with their feet by moving their capital assets offshore or channeling their investments to foreign markets. The New Order maintained a very open capital account beginning in the late 1960s, allowing foreign investors to deploy their assets in the Indonesian market but also to remove them in the event of an economic downturn. In the same manner, capital openness also allowed ethnic Chinese Indonesians to move their investment capital overseas in the event that their political situation took a turn for the worse. The "Chineseness" of ethnic Chinese *konglomerat* helped to make this possible: close personal, dialect group, and financial linkages to the overseas Chinese business community (in Southeast Asia and beyond) provided *konglomerat* with a ready network for the redeployment of capital assets overseas.[43] This potential for exit contained the potentially rapacious instincts of military leaders and *pribumi* entrepreneurs, who might have tired of the benefits conferred upon ethnic Chinese cronies. Indonesia's open capital account policy accordingly made credible the exchange relationships between the New Order regime and its ethnic Chinese supporters at the same time that it shaped Indonesia's economic relations with the rest of the world.

---

[42] Chua 2008; MacIntyre 2003a; Winters 1996.
[43] Mackie 1999.

One high-profile case of the New Order regime turning against a former crony illustrates such dynamics. After his conviction in 1996 for
defrauding the state-owned bank Bapindo (Development Bank of Indonesia), Eddy Tansil (Tan Tjoe Hong) escaped from a lavish cell in Jakarta's
Cipinang prison by bribing prison officials. In searching for Tansil, officials immediately concentrated on his offshore assets in Singapore and
Hong Kong. An Indonesian corruption watchdog group later placed him
in Fujian, in southern China.[44] Tansil's case demonstrates how Chinese
Indonesian *konglomerat*, as holders of politically valuable financial capital, could use the mobility of their assets in order to hedge against domestic political troubles. In fact, his brother Hendra Rahardja (Tan Tjoe Hin)
later made news himself during Indonesia's crisis by fleeing overseas to
escape prosecution.

The observation that so many ethnic Chinese *konglomerat* held mobile
investment capital creates one important inferential difficulty. How can
we assess whether "Chineseness" or capital mobility is the key causal
factor that explains differences between them and holders of fixed capital? Here it is important to recognize that not all ethnic Chinese Indonesian cronies were financiers. A few gained possession of fixed assets, in
particular in the forestry sector. Prajogo Pangestu, born Phang Dju Phin in
Kalimantan, earned a reputation as one of Indonesia's timber barons and
rose to prominence with his *konglomerat* Barito Pacific. Bob Hasan,
born The Kian Seng in Semarang and one of only a few high-profile
konglomerat to embrace Islam, like Liem Sioe Liong had connections
to the Diponegoro division dating to the 1950s.[45] By the 1990s, in addition to his control over the forestry sector, Hasan was co-owner with
ABRI and Soeharto's son Hutomo Mandala Putra ("Tommy") of PT
Sempati, the first passenger airline to "compete" with Indonesia's flag
carrier Garuda Indonesia.[46] Prajogo and Hasan, in fact, worked together
to rescue PT Astra International in the early 1990s. Prajogo and Hasan's
possession of forestry concessions – fixed assets – becomes of critical
importance during the authoritarian breakdown of the 1990s, for unlike
the vast majority of other ethnic Chinese cronies, they did not flee the
country and take their mobile assets with them.

The New Order regime hence rested on coalition between ethnic
Chinese businessmen, on one hand, and the Indonesian military and

[44] *Far Eastern Economic Review*, May 23, 1996; *Jakarta Post*, December 29, 1998.
[45] Barr 1998.
[46] Lowry 1996, 143.

pribumi entrepreneurs, on the other. Although Chinese entrepreneurs feared expropriation, and ABRI figures and some *pribumi* entrepreneurs lamented the domination of the Indonesian economy by a group that it saw as opportunistic, the groups each found that mutual exchange was an attractive road to personal enrichment. Regime behavior and public policy both illustrate how the coalitions were embedded in the very fabric of the New Order political economy. While an open capital account was the *konglomerat*'s hedge against political vulnerability, social policy kept them vulnerable and encouraged the direct links between *konglomerat* and *pribumi* entrepreneurs (both ABRI-linked and private) that proved mutually enriching for both. While ABRI-linked businesses funneled cash to the military, they also tied Soeharto's subordinates to the reproduction of the regime and represented lucrative opportunities for pensioners. It is through these mechanisms that coalitional interests were articulated and represented, following a logic of rule that enabled capital accumulation while reproducing the coalitional alignments at its core.

It is important to emphasize just how mutually beneficial the relationships between holders of fixed and mobile capital were before the onset of the Asian Financial Crisis. On most policy issues, and for most of the 1980s and early 1990s, differences in cross-border asset specificity did not divide ABRI businessmen and *pribumi* entrepreneurs from ethnic Chinese *konglomerat*. As Jeffrey Winters notes, much like ethnic Chinese *konglomerat*, *pribumi* entrepreneurs by the 1990s "support market-regulated access *as government policy* but do everything they can *as individuals* to gain an advantage over their competitors. In other words, they act like every other capitalist in the world."[47] And, in similar ways, Indonesia's halting steps toward liberalization in the late 1980s benefited ethnic Chinese *konglomerat*, ABRI business figures, and the new *pribumi* entrepreneurs, each of whom employed private access to the regime to secure valuable contracts and licenses.[48] Yet owing to their political vulnerability, ethnic Chinese Indonesians never entered into the same kinds of "complex patterns of intertwined share-holdings in overlapping groups of companies" with indigenous entrepreneurs, as found in countries such as Thailand.[49] Mutually beneficial exchange relationships served as the basis of the New Order political economy through the 1990s. But the differences between the *konglomerat*, who provided investment capital

---

[47] Winters 1996, 189 (emphasis in original). See also Robison 1986, 364–65.
[48] McLeod 2000; Rosser 2002.
[49] Mackie 1990, 85.

but whose assets remained highly mobile as a hedge against domestic political turmoil, and *pribumi* and ABRI-linked businesses, whose capital investments were largely fixed in Indonesia, are of critical importance for understanding each group's reaction to the financial and currency turmoil that would envelope Indonesia in 1997–98.

Mahathir's Malaysia

The Malaysian political system rests on an explicit cross-class alliance between the Malay masses and a group of wealthy Malay elites with extensive involvement in both the corporate world and politics. Like Indonesia, Malaysia has an economically dominant Chinese minority, but, unlike the case in Indonesia, these wealthy Chinese Malaysian business figures with mobile capital assets have largely been left out of the ruling coalition. Instead, since independence from Britain in 1957, the Malaysian regime has promoted institutions and policies that favor Malays at the expense of non-Malays.

Ethnicity is the dominant political cleavage in Malaysia. Malaysia's population is just over 50 percent ethnic Malay, with Chinese Malaysians composing almost 24 percent and Indian Malaysians another 7 percent. The balance of the population is a mix of relatively small non-Malay indigenous groups that reside in Malaysian Borneo and even smaller numbers of Eurasians and Thais. The terms "Chinese" and "Indian" obscure what are in reality very diverse communities. Chinese Malaysians include both long-settled *peranakan* Chinese and the larger group of immigrants that arrived in the 1800s and early 1900s, which can be divided still further among different provincial or dialect groups and groups with varying attachment to overseas Chinese affairs.[50] The Indian community, though largely Tamil, contains significant numbers of Telugu and Malayalam speakers in addition to Punjabi, Sikh, and Indian Muslim minorities. It is plain that the identities of many Malaysians are fluid and situational, in particular among non-Malay Muslims. Yet in Malaysian politics, differences within ethnic communities pale in comparison to the dominant cleavage between *bumiputras* (Malays and non-Malay indigenous communities)[51] and non-*bumiputras*. Government policies almost always officially target *bumiputras*, but the fact that Malays constitute

---

[50] Tan 2000; Wang 1970.
[51] By law, *bumiputras* include Malays, Thais, Eurasians, hill peoples in the Malay Peninsula (known as *orang asli*), and indigenous Borneans (i.e., Dayak, Kadazandusun, and many others). It excludes only Malaysians of Chinese or Indian descent.

the majority of all *bumiputras*, along with the geographic isolation and cross-cutting ethnic and religious cleavages of non-Malay *bumiputras*, means that these policies in effect target Malays.

The ruling coalition in Malaysia is the Barisan Nasional (BN, National Front), whose dominant member is the United Malays National Organisation (UMNO), a strictly Malay party. Other parties in the BN include a Chinese party (the Malaysian Chinese Association, MCA) and an Indian party (the Malaysian Indian Congress, MIC), a small noncommunal but largely Chinese party (Gerakan Rakyat Malaysia, or Gerakan), a tiny People's Progressive Party, and a fluid mix of small parties based in the East Malaysian states of Sabah and Sarawak. Opposition parties are also de facto ethnically based. The Democratic Action Party (DAP) is predominantly Chinese, despite an officially multiculturalist social democratic platform. Competing for Malay votes is the Pan-Malaysian Islamic Party (PAS), which advocates the creation of an Islamic state in Malaysia, and the multiethnic People's Justice Party (PKR), whose predecessor KeADILan formed in 1999. In East Malaysia, parties are predominantly either ethnically based or panethnic but religiously based.

The origins of a political system that reflects ethnic and communal tensions lie in the British colonial experience. The British found in Malaya a low land-labor ratio, but abundant tin and rubber. The colonial administration therefore welcomed the immigration of Chinese and Indian laborers, the former employed primarily in tin mines and the latter on rubber estates. As immigrant labor communities in Malaya grew, coethnics followed to work in the trading and service sectors, both in urban areas where Chinese came to dominate and in rural areas. Under the British, upper-class Malays entered some areas of colonial administration, but Malays otherwise received little attention from the colonial regime and remained rooted in the traditional sector.[52] The economic divisions between Malays and Chinese and Indian immigrant communities – along with no small amount of British prejudice against the Malays as "lazy natives" – contributed to growing and increasingly politicized interethnic wealth disparities.[53] The long-settled descendants of immigrant communities, especially urban Chinese, came to control the vast majority of domestic capital, with the remainder dominated by British and other foreign capital.[54] Malays and other *bumiputras*, by contrast, found

---

[52] Faaland, Parkinson, and Saniman 2003, 5–7; Fisk 1982, 21.
[53] Abraham 1997; Hua 1983, 53–61; Syed Hussein 1977.
[54] Jomo 1986, 208–9.

themselves far poorer, despite outnumbering Chinese and Indians by a considerable margin.

Political organization in Malaysia began in earnest by the late 1930s and continued after the Second World War, during which the Japanese occupation force had discriminated heavily against ethnic Chinese residents of Malaya and spawned the predominantly Chinese-based Malayan Communist Party (MCP). UMNO arose in opposition to a British decolonization scheme known as the Malayan Union, which appeared to many Malays to have sacrificed too many rights to non-Malays.[55] The MCA was created as a British-sponsored competitor to the MCP, and the MIC as a similar organization that agitated for Indian rights.[56] Shortly before independence in 1957, the three parties came together to form the Alliance, an elite interethnic coalition that gave UMNO political superiority in exchange for noninterference in Chinese business affairs.[57]

This bargain was successful for more than a decade, until Malay dissatisfaction at continued interethnic disparities and a growing Chinese political movement opposing the MCA's subservience to UMNO led to a comparatively poor showing for the Alliance in the 1969 elections. Alliance parties retained a majority in Parliament, but no longer commanded the two-thirds majority necessary to amend the Malaysian constitution. Shortly thereafter, ethnic rioting broke out in Kuala Lumpur, leading Prime Minister Tunku Abdul Rahman to suspend Parliament and declare a state of emergency.[58] From 1969 until 1971, the country was under the rule of an unelected National Operations Council, which allowed Parliament to re-form in 1971 on the condition that it adopt far-ranging legislation that entrenched UMNO domination of politics. The BN subsequently superseded the Alliance, signifying the onset of overtly Malay-dominated politics that has persisted in Malaysia until today.

To observe that UMNO dominates the BN, and that the BN dominates Malaysian politics, is to underestimate the extent to which questions of ethnic identity pervade political and economic life in Malaysia. The regime has created an impressive number of institutions whose primary task is redistributing wealth to Malays in order to raise their economic status to that of Chinese and Indian Malaysians. These institutions embed ethnic favoritism directly into Malaysia's political economy, and ensure

---

[55] Stockwell 1977.
[56] Arasaratnam 1979, 99, 113–14; Heng 1988, 54–59.
[57] Mauzy 1983, 16–20; von Vorys 1975.
[58] Comber 1983; Funston 1980, 211–40; Goh 1971; von Vorys 1975, 259–390.

that both ordinary Malays and the new Malay rich have an incentive to perpetuate the status quo. The regime, in turn, uses selective repression to combat threats to the status quo from panethnic challengers (labor movements, civil society) as well as Malay-based challengers (most notably PAS). Violence is not nearly as prevalent in Malaysia as in Indonesia, but the domination of Malaysian security organs by Malays both reflects Malay political ascendance and reinforces the political status quo.

The Malay Masses

The Malay masses benefit directly from the many political and economic benefits that they receive from the regime. In turn, they support the holders of power by voting for UMNO and BN candidates at elections and remaining relatively quiescent otherwise. The numerical dominance of the Malaysian polity by Malays means that no government can hope to win an election without a substantial proportion of the Malay vote. But in a political system where elections serve more to legitimate the regime than as true arenas of national electoral contestation, the support of the Malay masses is a critical check against potential opposition movements of a nonelectoral sort. For this reason, especially since 1971, the government has considered the distributional implications of all public policies. Successive UMNO governments have openly targeted *bumiputras* (read: Malays) with direct and indirect subsidies and supports, to the exclusion of Chinese and Indian Malaysians and in particular the non-Malay poor. Elections link the regime to ordinary Malays, legitimizing the regime and reproducing its method of rule.

The basic tools of interethnic redistribution arose under the New Economic Policy (NEP). Promulgated in 1971 with the reconvening of Parliament, the NEP adopted as its targets the elimination of "hard-core" poverty throughout the country as well as the elimination of interethnic income and wealth disparities. Policies stressed open government involvement in the economy, ending the previous, relatively laissez-faire economic system judged to have "failed" Malays.[59] Its best-known target was that, by 1990, *bumiputras* would control 30 percent of the Malaysian economy in terms of equity or ownership. When in 1990 this target had yet to be reached, the government announced the National Development Policy, which adopted much of the same language and targets as the NEP. Public emphasis on the NEP's goal of improving interethnic redistribution provides a continual reminder to the Malay masses that they owe many of

---

[59] Faaland, Parkinson, and Saniman 2003, 7–48; Jomo and Gomez 1996.

their present benefits to the regime in power. Yet these policies do indeed reward the Malay masses, illustrating how public policy articulates their demands.

The first instruments of pro-Malay redistribution were agricultural and rural development policies, many of which actually preceded the NEP. The Rural and Industrial Development Authority targeted rural Malays for small-scale rural development schemes and helped to foster small-scale entrepreneurs. Faced with poor results, in 1966 the authority was reorganized as MARA (Council of Trust for Indigenous People) under the Ministry of Entrepreneurship and Cooperative Development. Its expanded task was to nurture small *bumiputra* businesses, especially in rural areas, through development grants and training.[60] Since then, MARA has expanded into tertiary education, with its training institute developing into a technological university and brought under the Ministry of Education. The Federal Land Development Authority (FELDA), which settles landless peasants and operates in the oil and rubber plantation sectors, is another key rural development organ. While it does not have a statutory obligation to favor Malays, in practice it does, in fact distributing patronage to UMNO loyalists.[61] Under Mahathir, development grants to the rural and agricultural sectors ensured political stability, with the effect that rural Malays constituted the main supporters of UMNO.[62]

Despite the focus on rural development to lift the Malay poor out of poverty, the regime has also attempted, especially since the 1980s, to nurture *bumiputra* ownership of corporate wealth on a mass scale. Mechanisms to accomplish this goal include favorable university entrance requirements, hiring guidelines, state-run development banks, lending rules, restrictions on corporate equity ownership, discounted stock allocations, government tenders, and many others. The regime also created numerous government-owned industrial firms, most notably the national oil company Petronas (National Petroleum Limited) in the 1970s and the national automobile corporation Proton (Malaysian Automobile Corporation) in the 1980s. The regime also established several government-linked investment trusts through which it distributes corporate equity to *bumiputras*. The main investment firm is Pernas (National Agency Limited, now known as PNS), responsible with making strategic

---

[60] Gale 1981, 45–56.
[61] Scott 1985.
[62] Abdul Aziz 1994; Gomez and Jomo 1999a, 231; Jomo and Gomez 2000, 284. This began to change in the 2008 general elections.

investments to support *bumiputra* companies and increase equity ownership. It has also created politically linked favorites.[63]

Government-sponsored unit trusts are managed by PNB (National
Equity Corporation), a subsidiary of Yayasan Pelaburan Bumiputera
(Bumiputra Investment Foundation), itself headed by the prime minister.
The regime founded PNB in the late 1970s out of concern that Malays
receiving discounted share offers were simply reselling them to Chinese
Malaysian investors at a higher price and pocketing the difference.[64] PNB
created Amanah Saham Nasional (ASN, National Unit Trust) in 1981,
enabling ordinary *bumiputras* to purchase units at a fixed price of one
ringgit per unit. In 1990 PNB freed ASN's unit prices but transferred all
existing shares to a new unit trust, Amanah Saham Bumiputra (ASB,
Bumiputra Unit Trust), which operates under ASN's previous fixed-price
scheme, unless investors specifically asked to remain with ASN. Two
additional *bumiputra*-only unit trusts were created in 2000 and 2001.
PNB also manages four unit trusts open to all Malaysians, but reserves a
portion of these for *bumiputras*. All unit trust schemes have heavy sub-
scription from *bumiputras*, and they consistently offer high returns that
far exceed traditional forms of savings. Another high-performing unit
trust scheme is the Armed Forces Provident Fund, which serves the
Malay-dominated military. Because the regime manages these unit trusts
in exchange for political support, the regime has an interest in their
profitability and, hence, in the performance of stocks in which they
invest.

Pro-*bumiputra* social policies reinforce the economic policies. While
the favoritism in social policies granted toward Malays was apparent
even before 1969, Malay supremacy became a fact of Malaysian politics
with the NEP. Malay is the country's national language, despite the fact
that a substantial proportion of Malaysians do not speak Malay at home,
and Islam is the national religion, despite the fact that a large minority of
Malaysians are not Muslims. The constitution explicitly recognizes these
and other Malay rights, colloquially referred to as *ketuanan Melayu*
(Malay supremacy).

The point of these policies is not simply that they favor Malays. Rather,
the economic blandishments that they offer encourage ordinary Malays
to support the regime, and social policies reinforce ethnic identification
while providing the ideological backing for them. The bargain, in other

[63] Gale 1981, 86–108; Gomez 1990, 12–13; Searle 1999, 62.
[64] Gomez 1994, 56; Gomez and Jomo 1999b, 34–38; Searle 1999, 62–63.

words, forms a constitutive part of the BN regime and, in turn, bolsters the alliance between the Malay masses and the BN regime.

But embedding the bargain in public policy is itself insufficient to ensure regime stability. Just as important to the exchange relationship between the Malay masses and the regime are the threats that each group wields. In the electoral arena, Malays could punish the regime by throwing their vote behind one of the country's opposition parties, one of which (DAP) offers a coherent social democratic platform and another (PAS) the promise of Islamic law. Nonelectoral threats to the regime are possible as well and are credible because of Malay dominance of the police and armed forces.[65] The regime's consistently pro-Malay policies ensure that these threats have not come to pass.

The regime has its own strategies to preserve the status quo. It systematically manipulates both the electoral system and the conduct of elections, ensuring that UMNO and the BN prevail in elections with comfortable two-thirds majorities in the Dewan Rakyat (the lower house of Parliament), enough to amend the constitution at will. In reality, before the 2008 elections the BN has held closer to a five-sixths majority in the Dewan Rakyat. The regime openly "campaigns" before the official date of elections, gerrymanders constituencies to minimize the number of non-Malay majority seats, and criminalizes opposition campaigning.[66] During elections, there are regular problems with registration, vote counting and vote secrecy, military postal balloting, vote buying and money politics, and even occasions of election violence.[67] Malaysian elections are seldom instances of truly blatant fraud or intimidation, but they are also neither free nor fair at a basic level, and even less so when the regime believes that it may lose its two-thirds majority.

Outside of the conduct of elections, the regime's repressive legislation operates regularly against opponents, real and potential. The Internal Security Act (ISA), for instance, provides for detention without trial at the discretion of the home minister. While designed to facilitate state security against communist insurgents, administrations have more often employed the ISA to silence political opposition during times of political crisis. Examples include "Operasi Mayang" against student demonstrators in 1974 and "Operasi Lalang" against opposition politicians in 1987,[68] as well as the detention of Anwar Ibrahim and his associates in

---

[65] Alagappa 1988, 29–31; Enloe 1978, 273–74; Jeshurun 1988, 260–63.
[66] Crouch 1996, 61–62; Gomez 1998, 266; Lim 2003; Rachagan 1987.
[67] Election Watch 1995; Gomez 1998; Rachagan 1993.
[68] Committee Against Repression in the Pacific and Asia 1988; Crouch 1996, 84.

1998. The Official Secrets Act and the Sedition Act criminalize the most basic forms of government criticism either in public or in Parliament, proscribing even questioning the premise of Malay special rights.[69] The Printing Presses and Publications Act restricts media reporting, and BN constituent parties control all national print and broadcast media in English, Malay, Chinese, and Tamil.[70] The Universities and University Colleges Act criminalizes student political participation.[71] The Societies Act requires that all organizations be approved by the Home Affairs Ministry, which has revoked licenses from and denied licenses to politically unpalatable groups.[72] Since 1971, the regime has employed these and other laws to infiltrate, co-opt, regulate, and/or criminalize all challengers, from student organizations to NGOs, societies, and Islamists.[73]

Unions and other labor organizations are special targets, as they present natural (class-based) competitors for the loyalties of the Malay masses. Jomo K. S. and Patricia Todd characterize industrial relations in Malaysia using the term "hollow corporatism," where organized labor exists but operates under tight restrictions on organizing and activism.[74] This is important because it gives character to the ideal type of a group called "labor" in my theory of adjustment and regime survival (see Chapter 2). In Malaysia, the regime depends on the support of the Malay masses, whose interests align with this ideal type but who should not be understood as an organized labor movement that pressures the regime as such. Consequently, in the substantive discussion of Malaysia's adjustment and transition, I avoid using the term "labor" when referring to the Malay masses.

The product of these institutions is a set of policies that reward the Malay masses for supporting the existing political arrangement while selectively employing intimidation and repression to deter potential challengers. In return, the Malay masses permit the regime to rule, and they enjoy a stunning array of social and development programs that explicitly target them, regardless of need. These policies help to reproduce the BN's system of rule and fundamentally shape its policy choices. But in addition to this, they have also created a coterie of newly wealthy Malays who owe their livelihood to the protection and favoritism granted under the regime.

---

[69] Crouch 1994, 18; Means 1991, 122.
[70] Gomez 1994, 66; Mustafa 2002, 149–50; Zaharom 2002.
[71] Means 1991, 35–38; Muzaffar 1986, 11–14, 142–43.
[72] Barraclough 1984; Muzaffar 1986, 231–35.
[73] Camroux 1996; Jomo and Todd 1994, 75–77; Lee 1988.
[74] Jomo and Todd 1994. See also Ramasamy 1994.

Fixed Capital: New Malay Entrepreneurs

The new Malay rich are the second pillar of the Malaysian regime's support coalition. Like the Malay masses, they benefit directly from political patronage and pro-*bumiputra* economic policies. But the new Malay rich constitute a far smaller group whose fortunes have expanded dramatically under the NEP. Their investments are largely fixed in Malaysia and their wealth is dependent on political favoritism rather than economic expertise, giving them little hope of creating wealth outside of the country and thus a keen interest in preserving the political status quo within the country. The new, politically connected Malay rich do so by contributing to UMNO and the BN and rewarding politicians with corporate positions and contracts. In exchange, ruling politicians continue to adopt policies that favor them. In these regards, the new Malay entrepreneurs parallel the *pribumi* entrepreneurs in Indonesia; but in Malaysia, fixed capital's coalition is with the Malay masses. Like the Malay masses, its alliance with the regime shaped public policy and embedded its interests into the BN's system of rule.

The growth of the new Malay rich proceeded closely alongside government intervention in the economy. As noted previously, government enterprises such as Petronas and Proton were political projects that reserved jobs and opportunities for Malays. Other companies rose alongside them, especially between the mid-1970s and mid-1980s as Mahathir and other political elites attempted a "big push" much along the same lines as that favored by nationalists in Indonesia.[75] Each project gave new opportunities for Malays to take positions as managers or corporate directors. The regime's new involvement in business also attracted members of political and administrative classes to business ventures, enough so that already by 1983 half of all Malay directors of listed firms had political or administrative backgrounds, versus a figure of just 6 percent for non-Malay directors.[76] Starting in the mid-1980s, the regime reversed course, embarking on a major privatization initiative in order to arrest an economic slowdown – again, similar to that adopted by the New Order around the same time. Yet, as in Indonesia, political considerations hamstrung privatization in Malaysia.[77] Problems included undervalued share prices, closed tenders, opaque decision making, and "two-ringgit" holding companies that helped to shield beneficiaries' identities from public scrutiny.

---

[75] Bowie 1991, 93–125.
[76] Lim 1983, 70.
[77] Jomo 1995.

By the 1990s, it was clear that obtaining political patronage from an UMNO figure – Mahathir, his close ally and former finance minister Daim Zainuddin, and/or Anwar Ibrahim – was a key strategy for building a business empire (Table 3.3, from Gomez 2002, 87–90). Notable in this list are the business investments of many of these figures, in businesses specific to Malaysia such as construction (Halim Saad), air transportation (Tajudin Ramli), automobile distribution and heavy industry (Yahya Ahmad), while only a minority (e.g., the government-linked MBf Holdings) had any external capital investments.

The rise of Daim Zainuddin and his protégés illustrates the links between the regime and the new Malay entrepreneurs.[78] Formerly a lawyer, in the 1970s Daim was offered the position of chairman of Peremba, a holding company of the Ministry of Finance–run Urban Development Authority. At Peremba, Daim oversaw the advancement of Malay managers (among them, Halim Saad and Tajudin Ramli) who later became strong UMNO partisans in the 1980s and 1990s. Daim's wealth grew through the use of the regime's resources to engineer buyouts, mergers, and takeovers. This continued after Mahathir named him head of Fleet Holdings, a UMNO holding company, and later after he became finance minister in 1984, a position that he held until his official retirement in 1991. For example, in 1986 Daim used Peremba's funds to purchase his own stake in United Malayan Banking Corporation at a price far beyond its market value.[79] In 1990 Peremba was privatized, along with several other government-linked firms purchased by UMNO loyalists at deflated prices. In 1984 his former employees Halim and Annuar Othman were appointed as directors of Hatibudi, another UMNO-linked investment corporation. In 1990–91 a move to delink UMNO's party investments from formal party control placed them in the hands of Daim's protégés.[80] After his retirement in 1991, Daim remained a close "special adviser" to Mahathir, and he reentered politics as one of Mahathir's key allies during Malaysia's financial crisis in 1998.

Nurtured by the regime, Daim and other entrepreneurs found that close links with the UMNO machine were advantageous. Not only did a close association with UMNO create its own immediate benefits from patronage, but it increased a firm's standing vis-à-vis unconnected firms,

---

[78] For comprehensive surveys of political favoritism enjoyed by Malays in the corporate world, see Cheong 1993; Gomez 1990; 1991; 1994; 2002; Gomez and Jomo 1999b; Searle 1999.

[79] Cheong 1993, 75–76.

[80] Gomez 1994, 42.

TABLE 3.3. *Party-Linked Malay Business Leaders in Malaysia*

Name	Listed Companies	Political Links
Halim Saad	Renong, United Engineers (M), Kinta Kellas, Time Engineering, Ho Hup Construction, Faber Group, FCW Holdings, Park May, Crest Petroleum	Daim Zainuddin
Tajudin Ramli	Malaysia Airlines, Malaysian Helicopter Services, Technology Resources Industries	Daim Zainuddin
Wan Azmi Wan Hamzah	RJ Reynolds, Land & General, Rohas-Euco Industries, Bell & Order, Systematic Education Group	Daim Zainuddin
Samsudin Abu Hassan	Granite Industries, Austral Amalgamated, Dataprep Holdings	Daim Zainuddin
Ahmad Sebi Abu Bakar	Advance Synergy, Prime Utilities, United Merchant Group, Ban Hin Lee Bank	Daim Zainuddin and Anwar Ibrahim
Tunku Abdullah	Malaysian Assurance Alliance, Melewar Corporation, George Town Holdings, Aokam Perdana, Malayan Cement, MBf Holdings Bhd	Former UMNO MP; Mahathir Mohamad
Yahya Ahmad	HICOM Holdings, Diversified Resources Gadek, Gadek Capital, Edaran Otomobil Nasional (EON), Proton, Kedah Cement Holdings, Cycle & Carriage Bintang, Golden Pharos, Uniphoenix Corporation	Mahathir Mohamad and Anwar Ibrahim

(continued)

TABLE 3.3 *(continued)*

Name	Listed Companies	Political Links
Tengku Adnan Mansor	Star Publications, Berjaya Group, Berjaya Singer, Berjaya Industrial, EMC Logistics, Minho, Dunham-Bush (M)	Former UMNO Youth Treasurer and Supreme Council member
Rashid Hussain	Rashid Hussain, DCB Bank, Kwong Yik Bank	Daim Zainuddin and Anwar Ibrahim
A. Kadir Jasin Nazri Abdullah Mohd Noor Mutalib Khalid Ahmad	New Straits Times, TV3, Malaysian Resources Corp, Malakoff Commerce Asset-Holdings	Anwar Ibrahim
Abdul Mulok Damit	Pengkalen Industrial Holdings, Construction & Supplies House	UMNO MP; Daim Zainuddin
Ishak Ismail	KFC Holdings (M), Idris Hydraulic, Golden Plus Holdings, Ayamas Food Corporation, Best World Land, Promet Pintaras Jaya, Scientex Incorporated, Gemtech Resources	Anwar Ibrahim
Mohamed Sarit Yusoh	KFC Holdings (M), Ayamas Food Corporation, Golden Plus Holdings, Malayawata Steel, Khee San, Goh Ban Huat	Anwar Ibrahim
Amin Shah Omar Shah	PSC Industries Setron (M), Atacorp Holdings, Kedah Cement Holdings, Daibochi Plastic & Packaging Industry	Daim Zainuddin

Name	Listed Companies	Political Links
Basir Ismail	Cycle & Carriage Ltd, Cycle & Carriage Bintang, Cold Storage, United Plantations, Fima Corporation	Mahathir Mohamad
Mohd Noor Yusof	Datuk Keramat Holdings, George Town Holdings	Mahathir Mohamad
Kamaruddin Jaffar	Sabah Shipyard, Wing Teik Holdings, Westmont Industries, Inch Kenneth, Kajang Rubber, Mercury Industries	UMNO leader in Kelantan; Anwar Ibrahim
Kamaruddin Mohamad Nor	Eastern & Oriental, Dialog Group	UMNO leader in Kelantan; Anwar Ibrahim
Shuaib Lazim	Ekran, George Town Holdings	Former UMNO state representative; Mahathir Mohamad and Daim Zainuddin
Annuar Othman	Konsortium Perkapalan	Daim Zainuddin and Anwar Ibrahim
Hassan Abas	Cycle & Carriage Bintang	Daim Zainuddin
Shamsuddin Kadir	Sapura Holdings, Uniphone Telecommunications	Mahathir Mohamad
Azman Hashim	AAMB Holdings, Arab-Malaysian Corporation, Arab-Malaysian Finance, Arab-Malaysian First Property Trust, Arab-Malaysian Development, South Peninsular Industries	UMNO member
Ibrahim Mohamed	Uniphoenix Corporation, Damansara Realty	Mahathir Mohamad
Ibrahim Abdul Rahman	Industrial Oxygen Inc.	Father of Anwar Ibrahim

(continued)

TABLE 3.3 *(continued)*

Name	Listed Companies	Political Links
Mirzan Mahathir	Mamee-Double Decker, Lion Corporation, Dataprep Holdings, Konsortium Holdings, KIG Glass Industrial, Sunway Building Technology, Worldwide Holdings, Artwright Holdings	First son of Mahathir Mohamad
Mokhzani Mahathir	Tongkah Holdings, Technology Resources Industries, Parkway Holdings, Pantai Hospital, UCM Industrial Corporation	Second son of Mahathir Mohamad
Mukhriz Mahathir	Reliance Pacific	Third son of Mahathir Mohamad
Ahmad Zahid Hamidi	Hamidi Kretam Holdings	Anwar Ibrahim

Source: Adapted from Gomez 2002, 87–90, table 3.2.

making it easier for connected firms to obtain credit. This, in turn, had a transformative effect on UMNO's membership. By the time Mahathir had risen to the post of prime minister, the core UMNO membership profile had begun to change from teachers and civil servants to upwardly mobile businessmen. For as access to patronage increased up the UMNO party hierarchy, so did the value of obtaining a position in UMNO. In the 1990s, evidence emerged of enormous sums of money spent by candidates hoping to win a divisional nomination and thereafter a seat in the Dewan Rakyat.[81] In a related strategy to cement the close relationships between UMNO officeholders and the highest echelons of the Malaysian security forces, prominent military retirees could expect appointments on company boards, stock deals, and other blandishments.[82]

What happened to the Chinese Malaysian business community? In the early years of the Alliance, Chinese business had worked closely with

---

[81] Gomez 1996.
[82] Case 1996, 174–75; Searle 1999, 83; Sieh 1992, 124.

UMNO, with MCA president Tan Siew Sin heading the powerful Ministry of Finance from 1959 until 1969, and then again until 1974. This history notwithstanding, Chinese enterprise and the non-Malay poor were the biggest losers in an explicitly pro-Malay political system. Yet the regime was careful not to discriminate them out of existence. Chinese businesses still penetrated the economy, and a quiescent business community was still valuable for fostering economic growth.

Chinese Malaysian business groups adopted a number of strategies in response to the BN's open pro-Malay policies. They neatly parallel the concepts of exit, voice, and loyalty proposed by Albert Hirschman.[83] One strategy ("voice") followed by some ethnic Chinese business groups in Malaysia was to compete with Malay enterprise, pooling resources under the MCA's Multi-Purpose Holdings Berhad (MPHB), which mimicked UMNO's party-held investments in the 1970s and early 1980s. While some had limited success, MPHB foundered in the early 1980s as it came into conflict with UMNO-linked investments and as the MCA's political strength waned.[84]

More important were the two alternatives to this strategy. One alternative ("exit") was to retreat from active involvement in politics and diversify. Such firms extended capital investments abroad and focused domestically on activities such as finance and property speculation that gave high profits with quick turnarounds.[85] Malaysia's richest man, Robert Kuok Hock Nien, with diversified trading interests across Asia and who currently resides in Hong Kong, is emblematic of this strategy. Engaging in high-risk, short-term speculative ventures and diversifying overseas, this group mirrored the behavior of ethnic Chinese Indonesians with mobile capital assets but without their political favoritism. While such firms continued to operate in Malaysia, they (again like Indonesian *konglomerat*) never entered into truly "complex patterns of intertwined share-holdings in overlapping groups of companies" with Malay entrepreneurs.[86]

The other alternative adopted by Chinese business leaders was to mimic the new Malay rich by forging close business relationships with UMNO leaders. These ethnic Chinese firms in Malaysia did form tight links with Malay entrepreneurs through interlocking directorates and

---

[83] Hirschman 1970.

[84] Gale 1985; Gomez 1994, 180–228; Jesudason 1990, 155–58; Searle 1999, 178–82.

[85] Chin and Jomo 2001, 97; Crouch 1996, 208–11; Heng 1992, 143; Jesudason 1990, 147–52; Searle 1999, 190.

[86] Mackie 1990, 85.

corporate cross-holdings. In doing so, they bypassed the MCA entirely.[87]
Among the most important of the business figures adopting this strategy
were Vincent Tan Chee Yioun of Berjaya Group, with interests in property and gambling, and Ting Pek Khiing, of the property and industrial
development group Ekran Berhad. As Peter Searle notes, such ethnic
Chinese firms with fixed capital interests have formed tight alliances with
Malay firms as well as direct alliances with UMNO.[88] The key point
about these firms – one that will later help to distinguish the effects of
capital specificity on policy choice from the effects of ethnicity – is their
cross-border asset specificity. Both Tan and Ting, for instance, were fixed
capital holders and key UMNO favorites who were important players
during Mahathir's struggle to adjust out of Malaysia's financial crisis.
On Malaysian Borneo, a slightly different outcome obtained. There, ethnic Chinese businesses with fixed capital investments such as property
development and plantation farming have overtaken majority ethnic
Chinese regional parties, such as the Sarawak United People's Party,
and brought them into the BN as regional component parties.[89]

The logic of exchange among the new Malay rich and the BN-led
regime is clear and persists today. UMNO politicians reward loyalty to
the party with favorable access to business opportunities, distributed
through tenders, privatization, stock offers, and party-held corporations.
The threat of withholding government favoritism keeps cronies loyal to
the regime. In reverse, the threat of directing funds away from the party
and toward political competitors ensures that the regime follows through
with patronage. Although the Malay business community has never forsaken UMNO as a whole, competition within the party in the past has
had important consequences for the Malay corporate world as factional
alignments evolve. The fortunes of the allies of former minister of finance
Tengku Razaleigh, who challenged Mahathir for UMNO's presidency in
1987 and for the office of prime minister in 1990, are instructive.[90] The
regime cut Razaleigh's corporate allies off from contracts and loans,
favoring instead new corporate allies tied to Anwar and established ones
linked to Daim and Mahathir.[91]

---

[87] Gomez 1998, 260; Gomez and Jomo 1999b, 44, 47–49; Heng 1992; Jesudason 1997,
128; Searle 1999, 190–221.
[88] Searle 1999, 190–221.
[89] Chin 1997.
[90] On Razaleigh's challenge and its political fallout, see Khong 1991; Means 1991, 200–57;
Milne and Mauzy 1999, 39–48.
[91] Gomez 1998, 240–43.

In sum, the Malaysian regime since the early 1970s has relied on two groups, each of which receives benefits from the regime in exchange for political support. Favoritism in economic and social policy ensures support from ordinary Malays; favoritism in corporate and financial policy ties the new Malay rich to the regime. The strategic use of ethnicity is the key to the continual maintenance of this system of exchange and support across classes, for it demonstrates how regime institutions embedded each group's economic interests directly into the system of rule. Wealth does not unite the new Malay rich with Chinese Malaysians, because the new Malay rich differ from most wealthy non-Malays in Malaysia in terms of cross-border asset specificity. The Malay rich have capital investments that are fixed in Malaysia, whereas most wealthy Chinese Malaysians' capital assets are far more mobile. As in Indonesia, it does not follow that *all* Chinese Malaysians have mobile capital: those Chinese Malaysian businessmen wishing to exploit fixed investment opportunities have in fact aped the new Malay rich, forgoing political alliances with the MCA and seeking direct connections with UMNO and the BN. The coalitional alignments between ordinary Malays and the new Malay rich are instrumental for understanding adjustment policy during Malaysia's currency and banking crises from 1997 to 1998.

Discussion: Alternative Models of Authoritarian Politics

There are many alternative accounts of politics in each country with different theoretical foundations, but striking among them is their agreement on the broad characterization of politics that I offer here. Analysts of New Order politics agreed that ethnic Chinese Indonesian cronies developed strong ties with ABRI and that this relationship held mutual benefits for both. Analysts disagreed only about the durability of this relationship, the role of political institutions or ideology, the growth of Soeharto's personal authority, the capability of other members of the Indonesian polity to influence New Order politics, and the theoretical model or regime type of which Indonesia was an exemplar. Likewise, analysts of Malaysian politics under Mahathir agreed that the regime relies on an explicit system of Malay favoritism targeting ordinary Malays and rewarding wealthy Malay cronies with extensive fixed investments. Analysts disagreed only about the residual political influence of Chinese Malaysian business, the extent to which institutions are vulnerable to executive interference, the role of Islam versus ethnicity, the future salience of ethnic identities in a country with a rapidly growing middle class, and how authoritarian Malaysia is in the comparative context. My approach places me firmly with other scholars who understand politics in Indonesia and Malaysia by studying the economic interests of powerful social actors in each country.[92]

I note here two alternative ways that authors have conceived of politics in each country as a basis for the alternative hypotheses for adjustment policy and regime breakdown that I explore later. I focus on the political institutions of authoritarianism and the depth of authoritarianism as the most important alternative ways to differentiate between Indonesian politics under Soeharto and Malaysian politics under Mahathir.

Regime typologies and theoretical models of New Order politics abound. In the 1970s and early 1980s, observers often placed the country's vast bureaucratic apparatus, in alliance with ABRI, at the center of the regime.[93] Benedict Anderson argued for the maximal interpretation of bureaucratic-military dominance, with the New Order as the "state *qua* state."[94] Others pushed the dominance of the military still further into Amos Perlmutter's "ruler-type" praetorianism.[95] Neo-Marxist scholars, by contrast, focused on capitalist accumulation under the New Order, noting the informal alliance between ethnic Chinese entrepreneurs and "politico-bureaucrats."[96] This approach has clear links to other work on neopatrimonialism in the Indonesian military,[97] but adds the bureaucracy as an independent locus of power. Later studies of New Order politics focused on additional groups, such as rural producers and business associations, finding that in some cases they were able to exert influence over policy making.[98] On the basis of these cases and the complex factional alignments within ABRI, the bureaucracy, and the business community, several authors proposed what might be termed "pluralism with adjectives" to describe Indonesian politics: "constrained pluralism," "managed pluralism," and "limited pluralism."[99]

Other researcher target the New Order's political institutions. Noting that the New Order retained democratic institutions such as a legislature

---

[92] In Indonesia, this perspective is represented by, among others, MacIntyre 1991; Robison 1986; Robison and Hadiz 2004; Winters 1996. In Malaysia, this perspective is represented by, among others, Gomez and Jomo 1999b; Jomo 1986; Searle 1999.
[93] Girling 1981; Jackson 1978; King 1982; McVey 1982.
[94] Anderson 1983.
[95] Jenkins 1984; Perlmutter 1969.
[96] Robison 1982.
[97] Crouch 1979.
[98] Liddle 1987; MacIntyre 1991.
[99] Bresnan 1993; King 1995–96; Soesastro and Drysdale 1990.

and regular elections, some place the regime somewhere between full authoritarianism and full democracy, terming it a "pseudo-democracy."[100] The New Order did severely limit Indonesia's party system. The regime permitted only two competitors to the dominant Golkar after the forced merger of opposition parties in 1975: the nationalist-tinged Indonesian Democratic Party (PDI) and the Islamist-tinged United Development Party (PPP). Soeharto and his allies had effective veto power over most party platforms espoused by each, as well as influence over personnel decisions. By contrast, the corporatist organ Golkar had maintained a close relationship with ABRI since the 1950s, and this relationship evolved under the New Order such that Golkar as a political organ became a member of the Greater Functional Groups Family (Keluarga Besar Golongan Karya) along with ABRI and the Indonesian Civil Servants' Corps (Korpri).[101]

The strain of scholarship that classifies Malaysia's regime as democratic is much stronger. Until the breakdown of the Alliance in 1969, the consociational model of elite bargaining[102] was an attractive way to view the interelite accommodation practiced by UMNO, MCA, and MIC leaders. But since 1971, under the BN, it has been impossible to view the regime as consociational, for UMNO and Malays are clearly dominant, and democratic practices have been superseded by authoritarian control.[103]

Analysts who focus on Malaysia's political institutions, such as regular elections and a Parliament that functions, struggle to make sense of post-1971 Malaysian politics. The most common conclusion is that Malaysia inhabits a middle ground between full democracy and full authoritarianism, where democratic institutions cannot be eliminated, but where they do not make government turnover possible, instead lending the regime legitimacy and encouraging some political responsiveness. Terms used to reflect this system include "quasi-democracy," "controlled democracy," "semi-democracy," "pseudo-democracy," "semi-authoritarian democracy," "soft authoritarianism," a "semi-authoritarian" regime, and "authoritarian populism."[104] Yet even among these works, there is a sense that these institutions are somehow disguising or reflecting a more fundamentally authoritarian system of rule. Others are agnostic about the framework under which to classify Malaysia but note that,

---

[100] Case 2002, 8–9, 29–63.
[101] Reeve 1985.
[102] Lijphart 1969.
[103] Chee 1991; Milne and Mauzy 1999, 17–18; Mohammad Agus 1992.
[104] Case 2001a; 2004; Crouch 1994, 14; Lee 2003, 37–38; Means 1996; Munro-Kua 1996; Muzaffar 1986, 297; Zakaria 1989.

under Mahathir, the country's political system became progressively more authoritarian over time.[105]

The preceding reviews show that understanding authoritarian institutions in each country is far from straightforward. Forced to make a choice, the most glaring differences between authoritarian institutions in Indonesia and Malaysia seem to lie in Malaysia's more robust party system in contrast to Indonesia's more restricted party system, and in Indonesia's open military involvement in politics versus Malaysia's civilian regime. In cross-national classifications of authoritarian regimes, Indonesia's New Order is considered a military or hybrid military-civilian regime, whereas Malaysia's is a civilian or party-based authoritarian regime. This then suggests a straightforward hypothesis: variation in regime behavior is the product of variation in political institutions.

A related but conceptually distinct issue is the depth of authoritarianism in each country. Cross-national indicators of regime types and civil liberties consistently find Indonesia under Soeharto to be more authoritarian than Malaysia.[106] The differences reflect restrictions on party formation and more overt political repression in Indonesia. Thus, while both countries were authoritarian, Indonesia under Soeharto was "more authoritarian" than Malaysia under Mahathir. If so, the comparison between Indonesia and Malaysia is unhelpful or misleading, more fruitfully conceived as a comparison between a "competitive authoritarian" or "electoral authoritarian" regime and a dictatorship.[107] Similar to the case with authoritarian institutions, an alternative explanation for regime behavior in each country is that more authoritarian regimes behave differently than less authoritarian regimes.

While authoritarian institutions vary between Indonesia and Malaysia, there are powerful reasons why we should not dismiss the comparison between Malaysia and Indonesia as indeterminate. Differences in level of authoritarianism and authoritarian institutions yield indeterminate hypotheses about adjustment policy responses and regime transitions. UMNO was less hegemonic than Golkar, but this does not explain why Indonesia would adopt the adjustment policies that Indonesia did, nor does it explain why Malaysia's policies varied so strikingly. Recent research has argued that political institutions facilitate policy

---

[105] Khoo and Loh 2002; H. Singh 2000.
[106] Freedom House 2006; Polity IV Project 2006.
[107] Levitsky and Way 2002; Schedler 2002.

coordination in countries like Malaysia.[108] But this predicts policy coordination only on *some* policy; it cannot explain why factions coordinated specifically on capital account closure, an exchange rate peg, expansionary monetary policy, additional redistributive subsidies, and corporate bailouts. Likewise, if Indonesia's political institutions failed, this cannot explain the specific character of policy conflict, whether that conflict is over capital outflows and the interest rate–exchange rate nexus or over some policy schism, from which there are many to choose in the Indonesian context. An institutionalist argument here is too reductive to explain substantive politics. To understand this, preferences of regime supporters are still essential.

With regard to political transitions, in the context of the near collapse of the economies in the two countries, the political centralization and sheer brutality of the New Order regime should have made Indonesia more likely to crush its domestic opposition and steer through the crisis. To quote Jeffrey Frankel, "How is it that a strong ruler like Indonesia's Suharto can easily weather 32 years of political, military, ethnic, and environmental challenges," to which we might add several petroleum crises and other economic shocks, "only to succumb to a currency crisis?"[109] It seems reasonable that Malaysia's "more democratic" regime should have succumbed to popular demands for leadership turnover, as happened under the democratic regimes in the Philippines, South Korea, and Thailand. If economic crises lead militaries to turn against patrons, then what explains the timing of this decision (in May 1998 rather than some other time), why has the military remained united in the wake of the New Order,[110] and why has Soeharto escaped prosecution in the ten years since his resignation?

All of these questions arise when one probes the relationships between authoritarian institutions and depth of authoritarianism, on the one hand, and adjustment policies and regime transitions, on the other. They suggest that there is still an incomplete account of preferences – why groups agitate for particular policies, and why governments fulfill the demands of some of their constituents at the expense of others. These are the holes that an understanding of the coalitional bases of authoritarian rule fills. In the next four chapters, I detail the importance of coalitional politics for the politics of adjustment and authoritarian breakdown. When I move to a broader sample of countries in Chapter 8, I return to these alternative explanations as well.

---

[108] Brownlee 2007.
[109] Frankel 2004, 5.
[110] Kammen and Chandra 1999.

4

Adjustment Policy in Indonesia, June 1997–May 1998

On October 13, 1997, the World Bank's representative in Jakarta, Dennis de Tray, remarked that "Indonesia is not Thailand."[1] The comment was supposed to inspire confidence in Indonesia's ability to manage the crisis sweeping through East Asian financial markets, drawing a sharp contrast between the rigidity of Thailand's political institutions and the flexibility of Indonesia's centralized political structure. Indonesia was in negotiations with the IMF, which would provide Indonesia with emergency funds and reassure foreign investors of the government's resolve to bring the economic troubles to a quick end. International media characterized Soeharto's decision to seek IMF aid as a positive, proactive step. Foreign governments worried about the Soeharto family's involvement in inefficient enterprises that the IMF sought to eliminate, but they remained optimistic that the agreement would help Indonesia, with its history of "sensible macroeconomic policies," to return to healthy growth.[2]

Indonesia completed the IMF agreement (IMF I) on October 31, 1997. Yet within weeks, troubling signs had emerged that suggested that the New Order would resist many of the conditions upon which the IMF and other foreign governments had insisted. Bank Indonesia (BI), the Indonesian central bank, raised interest rates sharply but shortly thereafter reduced them again. It further undercut its high interest rate policy by providing emergency liquidity support to troubled banks. In a bid to increase efficiency and without explicit deposit insurance, the Finance Ministry announced closures of sixteen small and troubled banks, but

---

[1] *The Australian*, October 14, 1997.
[2] *Financial Times*, October 13, 1998.

later allowed one to reopen under a new name. Two months later, the government announced a blanket guarantee on all demand deposits and vowed not to close any financial institutions in the future. Soeharto announced the deferral of a number of costly spending projects, later reinstated them, and still later deferred them again. In each of the three successive IMF agreements signed under Soeharto, in November 1997, January 1998 (IMF II), and April 1998 (IMF III), Soeharto pledged to adopt measures to liberalize trade, reform corporate and financial sector governance, cut subsidies, and eliminate monopolies. The government reneged on almost all of these pledges at the implementation stage.

The tight centralization of Indonesia's political structure under Soeharto permitted these policy fluctuations. Amid extensive reshuffling of economic advisers, all policies that Soeharto mandated were implemented.[3] In this chapter, I show that across policy areas, the New Order regime chose policies that shifted the burden of adjustment onto the shoulders of poor Indonesians. Policy vacillation represented distributional conflicts between the holders of mobile and fixed capital, both of whom were supporters of the New Order regime. The test of my theory comes not only from the decisions that the regime took during the crisis but also from the preferences for crisis management expressed by groups both within and outside of the regime's support coalition. The theory uncovers the implicit logic behind what most observers have seen as altogether incoherent policy responses. I summarize the findings in Table 4.1. The first column contains specific policies, grouped by policy type. The second column lists the losers from each adjustment policy – those who bear the burden of each specific adjustment policy. The third column gives an assessment of the policy's implementation. Policies given the label "poor" were either not implemented or implemented and then reversed. Policies given the label "fair" were implemented with a middle level of success, meaning that the government resisted some parts of them, failed to implement them fully, or used other policies that contradicted them. Policies given the label "good" were implemented fully, with little or no resistance.

Note here that many policies do not have real "winners," only groups that avoid bearing the majority of adjustment costs. An example in

---

[3] Interview with an official in an international development agency, March 2006; interview with Emil Salim, economist and former state minister for population and environment, March 6, 2006.

TABLE 4.1. *Economic Adjustment in Indonesia: Policies, Losers,*
Implementation

Policy Measure	Losers	Implementation
Fiscal and trade policy		
Suspension of 15		
megaprojects	Connected firms	Poor
Corporate reform	Connected firms	Poor
Decreases in tariffs	Diffuse	Fair
Cuts in subsidies	Labor/poor Indonesians	Good
Monetary and financial policies		
Increases in interest rates	Business	Fair
Slow growth in money		
supply	Connected banks	Poor
Financial sector reform	Connected banks	Poor
Foreign economic policy		
Free floating exchange rate	Fixed and mobile capital	Fair
Open capital account	Fixed capital	Good

the Indonesian banking sector is emergency liquidity support. Highly
indebted banks facing bank runs and loan-gearing problems do not thrive
on the basis of emergency liquidity support – their profit margins still
contract severely, resulting in overall losses for bank owners. But these
banks do better than they would have with two alternative policies, one
that would allow these uneconomical banks to go under and one that
would have resulted in punishingly high interest rates.

The conclusion from Table 4.1 is broad support for the coalitional
approach. These policies together meant that, as Soeharto's New Order
combated Indonesia's twin crises, poor Indonesians bore the burden of
adjustment costs. In addition, Indonesia's coalition between fixed and
mobile capital – represented by the military and *pribumi* entrepreneurs
and ethnic Chinese cronies – created contradictory demands for adjustment policies. Policy conflicts arose over capital account and exchange
rate management, with all regime supporters agitating for a rupiah peg
but ethnic Chinese cronies resisting capital account closure. I show in
Chapter 6 that in addition to generating the adjustment policy struggles
detailed here, these contradictory preferences over adjustment policy ultimately led to the breakdown of the New Order.

Crisis Onset

At its basis, the crisis in Indonesia originated in regional currency contagion.[4] The crisis began in Thailand, where a property investment boom
and an overvalued exchange rate fed speculative pressure that eventually
forced the Thai government to devalue the baht. International investors
subsequently began to reappraise the macroeconomic fundamentals of
other countries in the region. As investors' confidence in countries such
as in Indonesia evaporated, capital inflows slowed, eventually becoming
capital outflows. Currency speculators capitalized on these outflows by
betting against national currencies, driving currencies down still further
and exposing further macroeconomic vulnerabilities. In this way, a
change in investor beliefs about Indonesia's economic prospects prompted a massive financial meltdown.[5]

While external events determined the onset of Indonesia's crisis, poor
economic fundamentals certainly contributed to Indonesia's financial
collapse. Analysts had raised concerns for at least two years about non-
performing loans (NPLs) and inconsistent macroeconomic policies in the
context of massive capital inflows.[6] Furthermore, with foreign interest
rates significantly lower than domestic interest rates, both banks and
nonbank firms borrowed abroad. Foreign borrowing is not itself risky,
but the government's crawling-peg exchange rate regime implied a guarantee that encouraged firms not to hedge their foreign debts against
exchange rate fluctuations. By the eve of the crisis, in early 1997, analysts
have estimated that only 30 percent of Indonesian foreign debtors had
adequately hedged their foreign currency borrowings.[7]

Unhedged foreign debt was only part of the problem. By 1997 the
majority of foreign debt had a maturity window of a year or less. With
debtors' income streams dependent on long-term growth, this implied a
mismatch between assets and liabilities in firms' balance sheets. In turn,
when domestic borrowers lost their ability to repay banks, banks were
unable to pay back their own foreign debts.[8] Moreover, credit to Indonesian borrowers had flowed largely to unproductive activities such as

---

[4] McLeod 1998a, 916.
[5] Corbett and Vines 1999, 166–67; Garnaut 1998, 5; Goldstein 1998, 17–19.
[6] See, e.g., Feridhanusetyawan 1997, 24–25; Manning and Jayasuriya 1996, 11; Usman
1997, 96.
[7] Hill 1999, 59–60. On unhedged foreign debt in Indonesia's crisis, see Djiwandono 2001b,
44–47; Goldstein 1998, 11; Haggard 2000b, 18; Kenward 1999, 85; McLeod 1998a, 921;
Nasution 1999, 82; 2000, 148–49; Soesastro and Basri 1998, 6.
[8] Frécaut 2004, 39.

TABLE 4.2. *Selected Indonesian Debt Indicators, in Millions of U.S. Dollars and as a Percentage of Total Foreign Debt*

Period	Total	Bank Debt (%)	Nonbank Private Debt (%)	Short-Term Debt (%)[a]
1990	26,369	5,014 (19.01)	12,279 (46.57)	13,440 (50.97)
1991	28,887	5,804 (20.09)	14,437 (49.98)	15,091 (52.24)
1992	30,055	6,507 (21.65)	15,300 (50.91)	17,184 (57.18)
1993	32,918	7,578 (23.02)	16,633 (50.53)	18,796 (57.10)
1994	37,505	7,829 (20.87)	20,167 (53.77)	21,291 (56.77)
1995	48,116	8,948 (18.60)	28,841 (59.94)	27,578 (57.32)
1996	59,602	11,788 (19.78)	36,759 (61.67)	34,248 (57.46)
1997 Q2	63,507	12,400 (19.53)	39,742 (62.58)	34,667 (54.59)
1997 Q4	64,217	12,445 (19.38)	39,714 (61.84)	35,104 (54.66)
1998 Q2	52,738	7,274 (13.79)	34,234 (64.91)	26,189 (49.66)
1998 Q4	49,551	5,935 (11.98)	32,999 (66.60)	23,702 (47.83)

[a] As a percentage of total debt.
Source: Bank for International Settlements.

real estate speculation, activities that would not perform in the event of an economic contraction.[9] Table 4.2 captures this foreign debt boom in the Indonesian financial and corporate sectors, showing the consistent rapid growth in foreign borrowing.

Debt grew by more than 20 percent per annum by 1994–96, far outpacing GDP growth. Short-term debt consistently composed slightly more than half of all borrowing, and private-sector debt (both bank and nonbank) by 1997 was more than 80 percent of all borrowing. Because these data represent only reported debt from banks reporting to the Bank of International Settlements, they likely underestimate the true amount of foreign debt, in particular the most dangerous type – short-term unhedged private debt.

The crawling-peg exchange regime had encouraged borrowers not to hedge their foreign debt through a classic problem of moral hazard. Well-connected firms simply believed that the regime would not permit a devaluation of the exchange rate. Even in the event of rupiah devaluation, both debtors and their foreign creditors believed that the government would somehow ease their debt burdens. This belief encouraged banks and firms to make excessively risky lending decisions by discounting the possibility of a currency readjustment.[10] Indonesia's poor state of

[9] Goldstein 1998, 7–9; Kartasasmita 2000, 10; Nasution 1999, 76.
[10] Wilson 2000.

financial regulation allowed this expansion of imprudent borrowing,[11] which grew in the wake of financial sector liberalization in the early 1990s absent a suitable regulatory apparatus.[12]

These factors together constitute the "technical factors" that led to Indonesia's twin crises: a weak financial sector, a quasi-fixed exchange rate, and high levels of unhedged short-term debt.[13] After the float of the Thai baht drew foreign investors' attention to these vulnerabilities, Indonesia moved from robust growth to economic crisis in the space of several months. The New Order regime responded by turning to economic policy levers to soften the economy's landing and to regain the confidence of international investors.

Fiscal and Trade Policy

The IMF mandated extensive structural reforms to increase efficiency, lower tariff barriers, and eliminate corruption. In the first IMF agreement signed on October 31, 1997, the government pledged to reduce tariffs on cement, steel, chemicals, rattan, wheat, soybeans, and garlic.[14] Moreover, it also vowed to press forward with privatization and deregulation efforts and promised to delay expensive "megaprojects" in order to decrease fiscal expenditures for the upcoming several years. IMF II took these measures further.[15] It pledged elimination of electricity subsidies beginning on April 1, 1998, to be accompanied by elimination of subsidies on all fuel except for kerosene and gasoline, and the imposition of a 5 percent local tax on fuel. It also planned to eliminate the Clove Marketing Board (BPPC) by June 1, 1998, to restrict the monopoly on rice held by Bulog, to break up the plywood monopoly held by the Indonesian Wood Panel Association (Apkindo), and to replace export taxes on timber and forest products with rent taxes. Finally, the government agreed to discontinue public expenditure on megaprojects and to eliminate public subsidies for the Indonesian National Car (PT Timor Putra Nasional) and on the Indonesian National Aircraft (IPTN). IMF III mandated yet more reforms, stipulating immediate price rises for sugar, wheat flour, and corn,

[11] Djiwandono 2001a, 32; 2001b, 11; Enoch, Frécaut, and Kovanen 2003, 76; Goldstein 1998, 12; Haggard 2000b, 32–38; Kenward 1999, 81–87; Lindgren et al. 1999, 15, 55–57; Nasution 1999, 84–86; Pangestu and Habir 2002, 6–7.
[12] Haggard 2000b, 19; Kartasasmita 2000, 11; Nasution 2000, 149; World Bank 1998, 4.
[13] Hill 1998, 96–97; 1999, 59–60.
[14] Government of Indonesia 1997.
[15] Government of Indonesia 1998b.

as well as future elimination of subsidies for soybeans, which the government matched with decreased subsidies on kerosene and electricity.[16] Related public-sector corporate reforms included the privatization of a number of public enterprises, the inclusion of all nonbudget funds in the official budget, and increased transfers of profits from public enterprises to the government's official budget. All three IMF agreements also sought to tighten macroeconomic policy through budget cutbacks, calling for a sharp contraction in fiscal policy in order to draw capital back into the country, which the IMF later relaxed to permit very modest budget deficits.

The primary concern from the perspective of the New Order regime, however, was that each of these reforms threatened the business interests of key members of the regime's capitalist coalition. So government pledges notwithstanding, measures to reform trade policy and fiscal policy proceeded in fits and starts, with backtracks and refusals. Predictably, the regime's obstructionism centered on those reforms that threatened the interests of the regime's closest supporters. The fifteen megaprojects postponed in September had restarted by mid-November, and all of them had links to the regime's supporters.[17] These included *pribumi* entrepreneurs behind clearly uneconomical ventures such as a new power plant (Tanjung Jati-C) for the already overburdened state-owned electricity monopoly, and Indonesia's first domestic petroleum refining plant. During the second IMF agreement, the government vowed again to repostpone or reconsider a number of these same megaprojects. Yet even then, the regime kept the megaprojects alive through renewed "feasibility studies" and promises of only temporary delays.[18]

State enterprise privatization also ran into snags, with the stakeholders in well-connected companies resisting implementation through political channels. The cases of Apkindo and BPPC illustrate how connected firms avoided IMF restructuring. Bob Hasan's Apkindo had held a monopoly over the manufacture and marketing of plywood since the 1980s. IMF II specifically targeted Apkindo's plywood monopoly as an example of an inefficient government-sanctioned monopoly. Minister of Industry and Trade Tungky Aribowo ended the monopoly in early February 1998, but this administrative move had little effect on Hasan's overall control of the plywood industry. Apkindo recommended to the Ministry of

[16] Government of Indonesia 1998a.
[17] Soesastro and Basri 1998, 20.
[18] *Far Eastern Economic Review*, March 19, 1998; April 9, 1998.

Industry and Trade that shipments of plywood go through another Indonesian government board, the Indonesian Association of Shipping, in effect reproducing the plywood marketing cartel under a different government body.[19] A month later, Hasan replaced Aribowo as minister of industry and trade, gaining with that portfolio the ability to impose export restrictions on certain key commodities. Several weeks before the collapse of the New Order, Hasan placed such restrictions on plywood, allowing him to direct again which firms received favorable treatment.[20] As late at early May 1998, Hasan decreed that members of Apkindo could impose limits on exports, allowing him once again to control the supply and the price of plywood.[21]

The BPPC saga was similar. Created in 1991 and since then under the control of Tommy Soeharto, BPPC held a trade monopoly in cloves. As well as being a significant export good, cloves are also a key ingredient in Indonesia's multibillion dollar domestic clove cigarette industry. BPPC paid artificially low prices for all cloves produced and charged artificially high prices when reselling them. It compounded these distortions through its intervention in the global clove market: it was the sole licensed importer of cloves from other countries, which it priced so as not to compete with its own stock. While IMF II mandated the dissolution of BPPC, the organization arose again under a new partnership system between BPPC and several small cooperatives.[22] In fact, in mid-March, the new vice president B. J. Habibie claimed during a meeting with Japanese prime minister Ryutaro Hashimoto that eliminating BPPC's monopoly on cloves – as well as eliminating Bulog's monopoly on nonrice foodstuffs – would contradict the Indonesian constitution.[23] IMF III finally dismantled BPPC, but Tommy created a new company from which *kretek* manufacturers had to purchase cloves in order to fulfill customs and excise requirements. At the end of April 1998, under Tommy's continued monopoly, Indonesia's backlog of surplus cloves had reached 167,000 tons.[24]

Such manipulation of IMF structural reform conditions to protect the narrow interests of fixed capital in Indonesia is unsurprising given the

---

[19] *Asian Wall Street Journal*, February 10, 1998.

[20] Barr 1998, 35.

[21] *Asian Wall Street Journal*, May 8, 1998.

[22] *Straits Times*, March 25, 1998.

[23] *Suara Pembaruan*, March 19, 1998.

[24] *Asian Wall Street Journal*, April 27, 1998; *Australian Financial Review*, April 28, 1998; Colin Johnson 1998, 33.

TABLE 4.3. *Wholesale Price Inflation, Forty-four Largest Cities,
December 1997–May 1998*

Component	Percent Change
Food	52.17
Prepared food, beverages, and tobacco products	46.29
Housing	27.03
Clothing	59.17
Health	47.19
Education, recreation, and sports	18.27
Transportation and communication	39.99
GENERAL INDEX	40.06

Source: Badan Pusat Statistik 1999, 4–5.

New Order's history. Resistance among the beneficiaries of the regime's enormous public expenditures is also consistent with this history. The secondary literature has chronicled these struggles well. Ignored, though, are fiscal reform measures that the government *did* implement: increases in excise taxes for alcohol and tobacco, and price rises for fuel, electricity, sugar, wheat flour, corn, soybean meal, and fishmeal.[25] Common to all these policy measures is the group that bears the burden of adjustment: poor Indonesians. In the longer term, the increase in distributional efficiency coming from careful, systematic reform of Indonesian tariffs and subsidies would undoubtedly benefit most Indonesians, but the short-term decisions most quickly and faithfully agreed upon by the New Order government are those just described. Price rises proposed had an immediate negative impact on poor households, especially in the urban areas where rising unemployment eroded labor's ability to consume and where individuals could not compensate for higher prices by producing food for consumption (as many rural poor could).[26]

To illustrate the impact of the crisis on the urban poor in Indonesia, Table 4.3 shows the distribution of inflation across commodities for urban Indonesians. The data show dramatic price increases in just six months, with the largest gains accruing to food and clothing. These became central themes for labor organizers and working-class protestors in the spring of 1998 (see Chapter 6). Even the IMF appears to have had more concern for Indonesian labor than the New Order: while IMF III mandated *increases* in food subsidies, the government failed to implement

[25] Government of Indonesia 1998a.
[26] Booth 2000; Friedman and Levinsohn 2002; Haggard 2000b.

them. The scheduled rise in fuel and electricity prices had yet to take place at the date that IMF III was signed, but the sudden move on May 4 to implement them – made ahead of even the IMF's optimistic schedule – demonstrates one of the regime's final attempts to shift the burden of fiscal adjustment away from its supporters among holders of fixed and mobile capital.

Monetary Policy

Along with a contractionary budget, the IMF mandated monetary policy tightening through interest rate hikes. I specifically address exchange rate and finance policies in subsequent sections, so I bracket the implications of monetary policy on financial institutions and demand for the rupiah in this section. Instead, I concentrate here primarily on the determinants of the level and variance of interest rates, understanding the implications of these policies for the arguments I make later. Figure 4.1 plots the nominal interest rate using Indonesia's interbank overnight call rates from January 1, 1997, to June 30, 1998. Two characteristics of these interest rate movements are noteworthy: the upward trend beginning in early August 1997 and lasting throughout the period, and the wide variance accompanying this upward trend. The upward trend in interest rates reflects the regime's attempt to contract the economy and discourage capital flight, but the rapid swings in interest rates reflect distributional conflicts within the New Order regime regarding proper monetary policy settings.

The decision to raise interest rates beginning in August 1997 was part of a concerted effort by the government to protect the rupiah. During the previous month and a half, from the beginning of pressure on the rupiah, the government had defended the currency against speculators using BI's foreign reserves. But as currency speculation continued, BI changed course to avoid depleting these reserves. On August 6, BI raised interest rates on Bank Indonesia Certificates (SBIs) from 11 to 15 percent, and several days later it moved funds from state-run corporations (BUMNs) to the central bank's accounts. Additionally, BI and the Ministry of Finance transferred Rp12 billion from the accounts of several BUMNs and *yayasan* into the central bank's coffers. This sum constituted around 45 percent of the total funds held by BUMNs and was designed to complement interest rate hikes by tightening liquidity.[27] Despite these policy

---

[27] Budisusilo 2001, 17; Djiwandono 2001b, 49–50; Nasution 1999, 93.

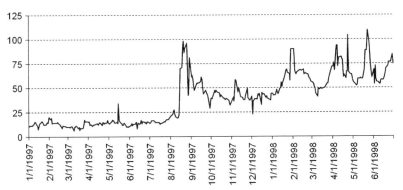

FIGURE 4.1. Indonesian Interbank Overnight Call Rates. *Source:* Thomson Datastream 2006a.

changes, the government remained unable to keep the rupiah within its target zone of depreciation. The government allowed the rupiah to float on August 14 and immediately thereafter raised domestic interest rates sharply in order to keep a lid on inflation, control speculation, and discourage capital flight.[28] This shows up in Figure 4.1 as the first large interest rate spike during the end of August.

Shortly thereafter, however, the data show a marked decrease in the nominal interest rate, to around 50 percent during the month of September and decreasing to around 40 percent during October. What explains this shift? Officials such as BI governor Soedradjad Djiwandono have argued that the interest rate defense of late August was excessive, constituting an overshoot that shocked the domestic financial sector.[29] This is no doubt the case – the interest rate hike exposed the highly leveraged domestic financial sector and was at any rate insufficient to combat foreign investors' perceptions about the rupiah's value. But the decision to reverse the interest rate hike was not a purely technical decision; rather, it was the product of a calculated political decision coming directly from Soeharto, at the behest of his business allies and likely also his children, to ease liquidity conditions immediately in order to protect their firms' balance sheets.[30] Soeharto himself demanded that BI ease interest rates, not

[28] Budisusilo 2001, 17; Djiwandono 2000, 52; McLeod 1998b, 39; Pincus and Ramli 1998, 726; Soesastro and Basri 1998, 7.
[29] Djiwandono 2004.
[30] Interview with an economist at an international development institution and former adviser to the Indonesian government, March 17, 2006; interview with M. Chatib Basri, economist and director of Lembaga Penyelidikan Ekonomi dan Masyarakat, March 17, 2006; Soesastro 2000, 132.

only in private but also in public statements on the government's plan for crisis adjustment.[31]

While the technocrats of BI had never enjoyed political independence from Soeharto,[32] political involvement in central bank decision making reached a peak as the technocrats in BI attempted to find a mix of policies that would avoid economic collapse.[33] Here, corporate profitability directly influenced politics. Both fixed capital and mobile capital suffered from high interest rates, but only high interest rates could encourage the resumption of capital inflows. On several occasions, high-ranking officials in BI and the Ministry of Finance came into open conflict with Soeharto and his relatives over finance and exchange rate policies, and both Minister of Finance Mar'ie Muhammad and Governor Soedradjad Djiwandono of BI found themselves replaced by more pliable Soeharto allies in the early months of 1998 because of their opposition to government policies. Demands from the corporate and financial sectors for monetary loosening were a constant pressure on the government during the crisis.[34]

Thus began the struggles between the policy of using interest rate hikes to curb inflation and capital flight and demands from the regime's supporters to lower interest rates to less punitive levels. Figure 4.1 reveals three additional interest rate spikes before Soeharto's resignation – one each in early November, late January to early February, and mid-April. These correspond to each of the IMF agreements, and the subsequent decreases represent policy slippage following complaints from connected businesses and banks about tight liquidity. In particular, *konglomerat* such as Sofyan Wanandi and *pribumi* entrepreneurs such as Aburizal Bakrie both urged the government to lower interest rates; other corporate and political figures publicly echoed these sentiments.[35] The predictable consequence of this looser monetary policy stance was inflation. Figure 4.2 plots consumer prices and wholesale producer prices in seventeen provincial capitals.

This rapid inflation, like the subsidy cuts discussed previously, hurt urban wage laborers and other poor Indonesian workers the most. It was most apparent in the prices of basic goods[36] – which compounded

[31] *Bisnis Indonesia*, August 30, 1997.
[32] Ali et al. 2003; Rahardjo 2000.
[33] Cole and Slade 1998; Malley 1998; Sjahrir 1999.
[34] See, e.g., Soesastro and Basri 1998, 42.
[35] *Jakarta Post*, November 19, 1997; November 21, 1997; March 27, 1998; Mann 1998, 76.
[36] Booth 2000; Bullard, Bello, and Malhotra 1998; de Brouwer 2003.

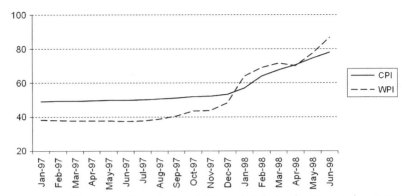

FIGURE 4.2. Consumer Price Index (CPI) and Wholesale Price Index (WPI), January 1997–June 1998 (2000 = 100). *Source:* International Monetary Fund 2007.

the increase in the domestic costs of imported goods as a result of rupiah depreciation

But lower-than-necessary interest rates were not alone in causing inflation. An additional source, with much more severe consequences in terms of prompting inflation, was growth in the money supply. All three IMF agreements signed under Soeharto called for low base money growth and very slow broad money growth in order to rein in inflation. As Figure 4.3 shows, however, monetary aggregates grew throughout the crisis months. This money supply growth was the product largely of liquidity support provided to banks and financial institutions. Because the solutions continued questionable loans and emergency liquidity support had consequences for money supply, this provides a convenient segue into a discussion of financial policy.

Finance and Corporate Policy

The government's singular failure to restrain money supply growth and raise interest rates to levels high enough to protect the rupiah exchange rate was the product of demands from connected firms to ease tight liquidity conditions. Finance policy and corporate policy during the crisis centered on the difficulties of keeping banks and other firms afloat with a floating exchange rate. BI and the Ministry of Finance faced a familiar dilemma. Responsible for managing the supply of rupiah, they sought to minimize inflation that arose from monetary expansion and exchange rate depreciation. But because they were also responsible for ensuring

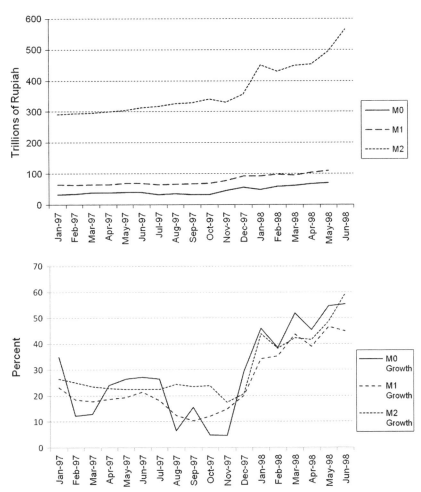

FIGURE 4.3. Money Supply, January 1997–June 1998. Trillions of Rupiah (*top*) and Percent Growth, Annualized and Seasonally Adjusted (*bottom*). *Source:* International Monetary Fund 2007.

the stability of the domestic banking sector, they sought to prevent bank failures from undermining confidence in the Indonesian economy as a whole. Most monetary authorities perform this function through guaranteeing at least a portion of all deposits in the financial sector, but before 1997 there was no such guarantee in Indonesia aside from the widely held belief that the government would not allow banks to fail.

As previously noted, banks immediately complained to the government that high interest rates harmed their ability to lend for profit.

Already by August 27, more than fifty domestic banks were unable to meet their 5 percent statutory reserve requirements, and the effects of monetary tightening were widely acknowledged.[37] Fixed capital's voice appeared strong, as a number of businesses welcomed the news of monetary loosening after the initial interest rate hikes, claiming that this would prevent Indonesia from slipping into recession.[38] In easing interest rates, BI also began to provide liquidity support to troubled banks to keep them afloat. These instructions came specifically from Soeharto in the form of several Presidential Instructions issued to BI in early September.[39] This liquidity support continued throughout the final year of Soeharto's rule.

Liquidity support by BI has been the target of criticism since the fall of Soeharto, mostly because of allegations of favoritism and cronyism. The great majority of liquidity support went to banks connected to the first family or to holders of mobile capital.[40] The amount of liquidity support that connected banks obtained was truly staggering, with a number of them (Table 4.4) receiving funds in excess of 500 percent of equity and 75 percent of assets. The percentage breakdown of liquidity support offered to nonviable, crony-controlled banks as opposed to properly governed but temporarily illiquid banks is impossible to ascertain. However, the amount of liquidity support doled out by BI totaled Rp141.9 trillion, and many of the banks in Table 4.4 received tens of trillions of rupiah. More than Rp52 trillion went to Bank Central Asia alone.[41]

Bank Indonesia's liquidity support program (BLBI) helped distressed banks in two ways. First, with BI's deposit guarantee, it nationalized the extensive debt problems of the *konglomerat* – now, liabilities incurred by the *konglomerat* would be the responsibility of all Indonesians. Second and more pernicious, the manner through which BI provided support allowed indebted bankers to access BI's funds continuously for purposes unrelated to banking problems. At the end of every business day, BI automatically provided cash to banks with an outstanding deficit to the central bank. Bankers realized that by *creating* deficits in their accounts at BI, they could receive funds from BI at their own demand. Bank owners took these funds and used them to bail out their own troubled firms.

---

[37] Djiwandono 2000, 52.
[38] *Kompas*, September 10, 1997.
[39] Djiwandono 2004, 63.
[40] Haggard 2000b, 67; Radelet and Woo 2000, 173.
[41] *Bisnis Indonesia*, September 22, 1998; Sato 2003, 39.

TABLE 4.4. *Some Beneficiaries of Liquidity Support in Excess of 500 Percent Equity*

Bank Name	Group and/or Owner	Connection
Bank Central Asia	Salim Group (Liem Sioe Liong)	*Konglomerat*
Bank Centris	Andri Tedjadharma	*Konglomerat*
Bank Dagang Nasional Indonesia	Gajah Tunggal (Sjamsul Nursalim)	*Konglomerat*
Bank Danamon	Danamon (Usman Atmadjaja) and Bank Central Asia	*Konglomerat*
Bank Hokindo	Hokindo Group (Hokianto)	*Konglomerat*
Bank Kredit Asia	Hashim Djojohadikusumo	Brother of Prabowo Subianto
Bank Modern	Samadikun Hartono	*Konglomerat*
Bank PDFCI	Bahana Investa Argha (Sudjiono Timan)	*Konglomerat*
Bank Pelita	Hashim Djojohadikusumo	Brother of Prabowo Subianto
Bank Subendra	Sudwikatmono	Soeharto's cousin
Bank Surya	Sudwikatmono	Soeharto's cousin
Bank Tiara Asia	Ometraco (Ferry Teguh Santosa)	*Konglomerat*
Bank Umum Nasional	Bob Hasan	*Konglomerat*

Sources: Jakarta Post, April 5, 1998; September 23, 1998; Sato 2003.

Holders of mobile capital simply exchanged them for dollars and parked them in overseas accounts.[42]

Liquidity support to banks was not the only way that the government used hard cash to bail out cronies. Lower interest rates directly benefited both mobile and fixed capital. Within days of the interest rate hikes

[42] Interview with Fuad Bawazier, former director general of taxation and minister of finance (1998), March 6, 2006; interview with M. Chatib Basri; interview with Sjahril Sabirin, former governor of Bank Indonesia, March 17, 2006; interview with Sri Adiningsih, economist and former ombudswoman at the Indonesian Bank Restructuring Committee, March 9, 2006; interview with an economist at an international development institution and former adviser to the Indonesian government, March 2006.

following the rupiah float on August 14, business leaders such as Aburizal Bakrie were agitating for looser policies to ensure business profitability.[43] The Indonesian Chamber of Commerce (Kadin) was divided, with individual business figures agitating for lower interest rates even as the organization tried to support the government's higher interest rate policy.[44] Members of other trade organizations strongly opposed high interest rates as well.[45] Likewise, cash injections benefited connected firms. The government pledged in late November that state banks and other public firms would inject Rp40 trillion in liquidity into the Indonesian economy in the form of emergency loans to private companies, particularly those in the export sector.[46] In a move that sharply illustrates the degree to which labor's interests were subordinated to those of fixed and mobile capital, a good portion of this sum came from PT Jamsostek, the government-owned workers' insurance firm, attracting popular criticism from labor leaders and regime critics despite Soeharto's assurance that he would personally oversee the use of these funds.[47]

Furthermore, as part of the government's corporate lending drive, during the early months of the crisis several crony-held firms obtained huge loans from state banks. The total amount disbursed through government directed loans to nonbank firms is even more difficult to estimate than liquidity support to banks, but at least one case stands out, that of Soeharto associate and ethnic Tamil Indonesian businessman Marimutu Sinivasan. Soeharto directed the state-owned Bank Negara Indonesia to provide U.S.$754 million (in addition to approximately Rp1.9 trillion – $260 million at the prevailing exchange rate) to Sinivasan's Texmaco group during the peak of the rupiah's freefall between November 1997 and April 1998.[48] Incredibly, during this period Texmaco also received more than U.S.$1 billion in loans from other state-owned banks.[49] This sum stands out not only because of its sheer size but because it illustrates the ease with which connected firms could obtain favorable loans from the government even during times of financial turmoil.[50] Not only was Texmaco's fitness as a borrower questionable, but the total amount lent

[43] *Jakarta Post*, August 17, 1997.
[44] Interview with Aburizal Bakrie, former head of Kadin, March 14, 2006.
[45] Interview with Zulhefi Sikumbang, head of Gabungan Pengusaha Ekspor Indonesia, March 13, 2006.
[46] *Jakarta Post*, November 25, 1997.
[47] *Jakarta Post*, December 8, 1998.
[48] King 2000, 617.
[49] *Asiaweek*, December 24, 1999.
[50] *Bisnis Indonesia*, December 1, 1999.

surpassed statutory lending limits. Texmaco used these funds to shore up other short-term obligations and expand the textile conglomerate's facilities, in direct contradiction of the loan's terms.[51] Even Soedradjad Djiwandono, who was the BI governor at the time and denies that crony connections influenced the provision of liquidity support, admits that Texmaco abused state loans in order to stay afloat.[52]

Liquidity support and loan facilities during the Indonesian crisis directly contradicted the government's stated goal of tightening monetary policy. Figure 4.3 shows the growth of broad money as a result of liquidity injections and imprudent loans. Between November 1997 and January 1998, for example, M2 grew by a sum roughly equal to the total amount of M1. So despite nominal interest rate hikes throughout the crisis, increases in money circulation contradicted these policies by suppressing necessary rises in *real* interest rates.[53] Not only was an interest rate defense of the rupiah impossible with depressed real interest rates, but price inflation increased rapidly as a result of this lending (see Figure 4.2).

Other policies complemented emergency loans and liquidity support in assisting troubled banks. On October 21, BI lowered the foreign reserve requirements for commercial banks from 5 to 3 percent.[54] By freeing up foreign currency from BI and returning it to domestic banks' accounts, this decision helped to increase liquidity. Also, in late October, BI chose to reintroduce its short-term money market instruments (SBPUs), allowing it to provide even more liquidity for banks eager to borrow funds over the short term.[55] As argued previously, this monetary expansion combined with cuts in subsidies and rapid exchange rate depreciation fueled the inflation that so burdened poor Indonesians.

But even as the regime quietly offered liquidity support to mobile and fixed capital, it simultaneously sought to project resolve to international financial markets. To this end, the regime announced on November 1 the closure of sixteen small, troubled domestic financial institutions. While initial press reactions described the decision as a positive, proactive step toward prudent financial policies,[56] uncertainty about the criteria for bank closures fed into popular concern about the health of the banking

[51] *Asiaweek*, December 24, 1999.
[52] *Jakarta Post*, December 8, 1999.
[53] Boorman et al. 2000, 39; Fane 2000; Grenville 2000; McLeod 2004.
[54] *Kompas*, October 21, 1997.
[55] *Jakarta Post*, October 21, 1997.
[56] *Kompas*, November 2, 1997; *Suara Pembaruan*, November 2, 1997.

sector as a whole. In what retrospectively appears to be a predictable response, depositors – unaware of any explicit deposit guarantee from BI and uncertain whether other financial institutions would survive any future round of closures – panicked. The ensuing bank runs affected all banks, not just those closed by the government.[57] While the government did offer to guarantee the deposits of all small depositors with savings of less than Rp20 million, these guarantees were not enough to assuage worried depositors.[58] The guarantees were at any rate not clearly articulated in the domestic press, and it was difficult for ordinary Indonesians to access their guaranteed funds.[59]

Contributing to the banking panic in early November 1997 was the perception that political maneuvering from Soeharto and his associates had affected the choice of bank closures. Some economists believed that the affected banks were too small and were offered as a sacrifice to international financial observers, while the truly guilty banks, such as Liem Sioe Liong's Bank Central Asia and others listed in Table 4.4, remained protected.[60] By contrast, some bank owners complained that closures were politically motivated by anti-Soeharto factions within BI and the Ministry of Finance.

Two bank owners stand out in this second group: Soeharto's second son Bambang Trihatmodjo and Soeharto's half brother Probosutedjo. Bambang, after first accepting the rulings of the minister of finance, several days later announced that he would challenge the decision to close his Bank Andromeda in court. In comments to the press, he blamed the closures on a conspiracy by unnamed elements to "tarnish the family name" or even to "bring down the family."[61] His sister Siti Hardiyanti Rukmana (Tutut), herself a partner in innumerable government projects, supported Bambang in his quest to protect his banks, calling it a quest for "justice."[62] Probosutedjo, owner of Bank Jakarta, challenged the Ministry of Finance as well. Rumors suggested that Finance Minister Mar'ie Muhammad might retire to avoid continued political problems.[63] In the end, BI and the Ministry of Finance avoided a showdown with Bambang by permitting

---

[57] *Media Indonesia*, November 3, 1997; *Suara Karya*, November 3, 1997.
[58] *Kompas*, November 2, 1997.
[59] Hill 2000, 129.
[60] Interview with Arief Budisusilo, deputy chief editor of *Bisnis Indonesia*, March 5, 2006; interview with Thee Kian Wie, economist at Lembaga Ilmu Pengetahuan Indonesia, October 11, 2004.
[61] *Republika*, November 5, 1997.
[62] *Media Indonesia*, November 7, 1997; *Suara Karya*, November 7, 1997.
[63] *Merdeka*, November 7, 1997.

the reopening of Bank Andromeda as Bank Alfa. This decision came directly from Soeharto in a phone call placed to Soedradjad.[64] The new bank retained its predecessor's financial interests, as well as its employees, changing only the name on its letterhead. Probosutedjo's case against the Ministry of Finance continued for several more weeks.[65]

Not all participants agree that there was political interference in bank closures. Soedradjad Djiwandono has argued in several memoirs that the sixteen banks were clearly uneconomical, thus warranting closure.[66] Indeed, all of these banks had questionable balance sheets, and many of them were involved in high-level official corruption. The managing director of Bank Pacific, Endang Utari Mokodompit – daughter of Ibnu Sutowo, the corrupt former head of Pertamina – had racked up more than Rp2 trillion in debt in 1995, requiring a bailout from BI but incurring no punishment.[67] Nonetheless, the government did not close the banks with the most extensive financial improprieties, because they were closest to Soeharto. Furthermore, the government levied no fines or punishments against any of these bankers as long as Soeharto was in power. And in the cases of Bank Andromeda and Bank Jakarta, the government allowed bankers to avoid closing their banks. Protecting political supporters undermined bank closures that were meant to convey that the "Soeharto stamp" would no longer influence the banking sector.[68]

In response to the market's negative reaction to these bank closures, in late November Soeharto and the minister of finance now announced that BI would no longer close troubled banks. But this announcement placed BI and the Ministry of Finance in a new bind: if the government refused to close insolvent banks, how would they deal with insolvent banks or future bank runs? Faced with bank runs but refusing to close banks, monetary authorities' only options are to declare a moratorium on withdrawals (technically equivalent to closing banks), to sacrifice the central bank's deposit guarantee, or to provide liquidity support to keep banks afloat. BI still had no policy explicitly guaranteeing deposits at this time, so it responded with liquidity. The result was that by insuring the deposits of all depositors, including small ones, the government contributed to inflation, undermining especially the value of small depositors' savings.

[64] Interview with Emil Salim.
[65] *Jakarta Post*, November 26, 1997.
[66] Djiwandono 2000, 62; 2001b, 126.
[67] *Inside Indonesia*, October–December 1997.
[68] Interview with Emil Salim.

As several authors have argued, either consistently much higher interest rates[69] or sterilization measures through the vigorous sale of SBIs (Bank Indonesia's standard debt vehicle)[70] would have capped inflation during this period.

By early January 1998, the situation had yet to improve. Saddled with foreign debts, which steadily increased in cost because of exchange rate depreciation, owners of fixed and mobile capital began to advocate a temporary debt moratorium under the auspices of BI.[71] As early as November, Mar'ie Muhammad traveled to Japan to negotiate a debt roll-over from Japanese creditors, but these efforts only delayed loan repayments.[72] Under IMF II, the Ministry of Finance created the Indonesian Bank Restructuring Agency (IBRA). IBRA's task was to identify troubled banks and merge them with healthy banks, restructure their loans, and/or bring their assets and liabilities under BI's direct control. In addition to helping navigate the technical problems of heavy debt exposure, IBRA would signal the government's resolve in managing foreign and domestic debts. It was by design an independent body, free from political oversight and interference; IMF II mandated that both BI and IBRA were to be independent from Indonesia's executive branch.[73]

These promises of political independence of monetary and financial authorities were empty ones. IMF officials complimented IBRA's institutional design and praised its statutory ability to make difficult decisions to save Indonesia's financial sector. But the regime kept IBRA's workings secret throughout Soeharto's final months in office, and politics interfered in IBRA's personnel decisions.[74] IBRA's first head, Bambang Subianto, lasted just over a month, with Soeharto ordering that he be replaced on March 6 by Iwan Prawiranata, with no explanation save for that "many people did not like his approach."[75] This shake-up was accompanied by the dismissal of Boediono from his position as BI director and followed several weeks after Soedradjad Djiwandono's replacement by Sjahril Sabirin as governor of BI. Prawiranata had strong personal connections to the banking industry, having previously held positions as president of three state-owned banks. His personal conflicts of interest were

[69] Fane 2000.
[70] Grenville 2000.
[71] *Kompas*, January 2, 1998.
[72] *Bisnis Indonesia*, December 3, 1997.
[73] *Jakarta Post*, February 3, 1998.
[74] Enoch, Frécaut, and Kovanen 2003, 79–80; Lindgren et al. 1999, 59–60.
[75] *Jakarta Post*, March 7, 1998.

representative of the status of many members of IBRA who had personal stakes in the performance of banks facing intervention from IBRA.[76]

IBRA's task mirrored other efforts by the private sector to find solutions to problems in the financial and corporate sectors from February 1998 until Soeharto's resignation. In these efforts, holders of mobile and fixed capital worked together to minimize the troubles befalling them. Shortly after the formation of IBRA, Soeharto announced the formation of a private-sector corporate debt task force in consultation with The Ning King and Anthony Salim, the former a close Soeharto associate and the latter the son of Liem Sioe Liong.[77] Two weeks later, this became the Corporate Foreign Debt Restructuring Committee, headed by the economist and longtime Soeharto associate Radius Prawiro.[78] Its "contact committee," in addition to The and Salim, included an A-list of business figures and cronies and even Tommy Soeharto.[79] Throughout the remaining months of the crisis, Prawiro and Salim negotiated with foreign creditors in an effort to solve the problem of tight domestic liquidity and heavy foreign debt burdens. By the end of April, negotiators had reached an agreement in principle with American, German, and Japanese creditors in which the Indonesian government would serve as an intermediary between domestic debtors and foreign creditors, itself bearing the burden of continued foreign exchange depreciation.[80] These negotiations continued until the very end of Soeharto's rule, as the negotiators hammered out details of when Indonesia would repay its debts and what rupiah-dollar exchange rate the government would adopt as its baseline.

Meanwhile, as Prawiro's team attempted to settle foreign debt issues, mobile capital continued to push for increased liquidity. Widigdo Sukarman, head of the Association of State-Owned Banks, and Subowo, head of the National Association of Private Banks (Perbanas), suggested an agreement among bankers to voluntarily lower their interest rates without waiting for BI, which continued with its policy of higher interest rates to defend the rupiah.[81] Calls for lower interest rates from BI continued throughout the remainder of the crisis, even as IBRA funneled emergency funds to banks. In a new bid to keep many of these banks afloat, the new

[76] *Jakarta Post*, April 22, 1998; April 25, 1998.
[77] *Jakarta Post*, January 28, 1998.
[78] *Merdeka*, February 10, 1998.
[79] *Jakarta Post*, February 14, 1998.
[80] *Bisnis Indonesia*, April 18, 1998.
[81] *Jakarta Post*, March 27, 1998.

minister of finance in the Seventh Development Cabinet, Fuad Bawazier, on April 10 slashed the government's requirement for minimal bank capital from Rp1 trillion to Rp250 billion.[82] This decision allowed many deeply troubled banks to use newly freed funds to pay down their debts.

In April 1998, shortly before signing IMF III and in an apparent show of due diligence in reforming Indonesia's financial sector, IBRA announced what became its final push under Soeharto. On April 4 the government froze seven bank licenses and placed seven others under the management of IBRA. These included all of the banks listed in Table 4.4, excluding the Salim Group's Bank Central Asia, but including the state-owned Bank Ekspor Impor and the private Bank Deka. Attempting to avoid the punishing bank runs of early November 1997, this time the Finance Ministry made explicit the government's deposit guarantee. Initial responses from the affected bankers were unclear, but Bob Hasan – newly installed as minister of trade and industry, and with a controlling stake in Bank Umum Nasional – claimed to accept IBRA's move.[83] Domestic reactions were more positive, with economist and frequent critic Kwik Kian Gie demanding an investigation into liquidity provisions.[84] This did not come to pass under Soeharto. Instead, the IBRA deputy chief Rini Soewandi announced that IBRA would continue to support the seven banks that had been brought under IBRA management without having their licenses frozen, arguing that they were a vital part of Indonesia's banking industry.[85] In fact, the six private banks in this group were among the heaviest users of BLBI funds. Between the end of March 1998 and April 17, only three weeks later and *after* IBRA took control of what it had labeled the fourteen most troubled banks, total BI liquidity increased from Rp80 trillion to Rp103 trillion.[86] The total reached Rp119 trillion by Soeharto's resignation.[87]

In the years since Soeharto's resignation, Indonesian authorities have investigated what has become known as the "BLBI scam," trying to uncover just why so many insolvent banks were able to obtain so much liquidity credit that disappeared into dollar-denominated accounts overseas. The answer, predictably, lies in the extensive business and personal connections between mobile capital and economic managers and political

---

[82] *Jakarta Post*, April 11, 1998.
[83] *Asian Wall Street Journal*, April 6, 1998.
[84] Agence France-Presse, April 7, 1998.
[85] *Bisnis Indonesia*, April 22, 1998.
[86] *Bisnis Indonesia*, May 5, 1998.
[87] *Kompas*, March 8, 2000.

authorities. In March 2000, almost two years after Soeharto's resignation, investigators announced the names of fifty-seven individuals from BI, the Ministry of Finance, IBRA, and private banks.[88] All were alleged to have committed conspiracy to defraud the government of Indonesia through their liquidity provisions. Moreover, assets seized by the government to pay back BLBI debts after Soeharto's resignation were overvalued by government auditors, reducing the debt burdens of BLBI's largest beneficiaries.[89] Despite these allegations, few have been convicted.

Exchange Rate and Capital Account Policy

The discussion thus far has focused mainly on domestic economic policy. The crisis started, however, because of regional currency contagion, and Indonesia's foreign economic policies remained a key adjustment policy lever. Of course, domestic macroeconomic policies affect foreign economic policies. With the rupiah rapidly depreciating from approximately Rp2,000 to the dollar to more than Rp10,000 to the dollar in the space of only half a year, highly leveraged owners of fixed and mobile capital faced stark choices about their management of Indonesia's capital account and exchange rate policies – especially given the existing struggles over macroeconomic and sectoral policies.

Figure 4.4 plots the nominal exchange rate between the rupiah and the U.S. dollar from January 1, 1997, to June 30, 1998. As in the case of interest rates, apparent in the data is a sharp upward trend, with several spikes corresponding to policy decisions and political events. The first hints of rupiah depreciation begin in July 1997 and become more severe after BI allowed the rupiah to float freely on August 14 of that year. Spikes in January and March 1998 reflect international perceptions of Soeharto's recalcitrance in implementing IMF reforms, and improvements thereafter reflect optimism after the signing of IMF II and IMF III. Riots and Soeharto's resignation prompted massive capital flight, reflected in additional spikes in rupiah depreciation in May and June 1998.

The initial decision to float the rupiah represented a departure from the New Order's thirty years of managed exchange rates. Since 1986, in theory, BI had pegged the rupiah to a weighted basket of currencies reflecting Indonesia's major trading partners, but in reality the dollar

---

[88] *Kompas*, March 8, 2000.
[89] Interview with Hery Trianto, reporter for *Bisnis Indonesia*, March 2, 2006; interview with Yosef Ardi, reporter for *Bisnis Indonesia*, March 6, 2006.

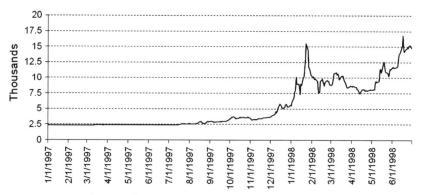

FIGURE 4.4. Daily Rupiah–U.S. Dollar Exchange Rate, January 1997–June 1998.
Source: Thomson Datastream 2006b.

dominated this basket – by most estimates, more than 99 percent.[90] BI permitted the rupiah to depreciate at a predictable level versus the dollar rather than maintaining a strict peg, a system known as a "crawling" peg. When the currency pushed on the top or bottom of an intervention band (8 percent of the target rate by January 1997), BI intervened to correct the rupiah's value. The rupiah's depreciation had for years approximated a constant real rupiah–U.S. dollar exchange rate.[91]

The first signs of currency trouble for Indonesia arose following the baht's devaluation. BI widened its intervention band to 12 percent on July 11, with little impact on currency outflows and speculation, so between July 20 and August 14, BI spent approximately U.S.$1.5 billion of its foreign reserves to keep the rupiah within its 12 percent band.[92] By August 14 BI concluded that the rupiah's intervention band itself caused speculation by giving traders a benchmark value against which to short the rupiah. Governor Soedradjad Djiwandono reports that he and other BI officials studied various exchange rate policy options for combating speculation but that BI officials viewed an exchange rate float as a way to preserve Indonesia's currency reserves, especially after having witnessed Thailand's expensive and ultimately ineffective defense of the baht earlier that summer.[93]

[90] Rajan 2002, 140.
[91] Hill 1999, 59.
[92] Soesastro and Basri 1998, 7.
[93] Djiwandono 2000, 52; 2001b, 39–43. See also Budisusilo 2001, 21; Djiwandono 2001b, 47; Nasution 2002, 38–39.

Yet floating the rupiah did not mean that BI and the Indonesian government no longer attempted to influence the value of the rupiah. In fact, the
opposite is true – in the subsequent months, BI used various policies to
combat the rupiah's depreciation in order to protect firms' balance sheets.
These policies fell into three varieties: policies that changed the legal
ability of foreign investors to trade in rupiah, policies that changed the
supply (and hence price) of the rupiah, and policies that attempted to
persuade currency traders that Indonesian economic conditions were
improving. BI's experience with the first variety was short. On August
29 BI announced a limit on forward rupiah transactions at U.S.\$5 million
per investor in order to prevent rupiah speculation.[94] Yet this legal limit
had little practical bite, as currency traders could avoid it by taking forward positions at multiple banks. Coordinating Minister for Politics and
Security Soesilo Soedarman suggested using antisubversion laws to arrest
speculators, but the regime ignored this.[95]

At the same time, BI adopted a complementary strategy of using
monetary policy to influence global demand for rupiah. It began with
interest rate hikes to dissuade currency traders from divesting from
Indonesia, the logic being that high interest rates would make rupiah
deposits attractive, discouraging capital outflow and hence protecting
the exchange rate by mediating rupiah holders' demand for foreign
exchange. The negative consequences for the highly leveraged Indonesian financial and corporate sectors ultimately derailed high interest
rates. BI quickly regretted this decision to float the rupiah, taken without
knowledge of the financial sector's fragility.[96] Governor Soedradjad
Djiwandono's memoir includes a poignant example of domestic reaction
to the rupiah float, recorded in early September of 1997. Faced with
unexpected rupiah depreciation, a number of business and financial leaders met with BI officials to register their complaints about the increased
debt burdens they now faced. They claimed that they had become accustomed to a predictable rate of depreciation and hence had "of course"
not hedged their foreign debt.[97] By the end of September, BI officials were
defending tight money policies to protect the rupiah while acknowledg-
ing the need for loose money policies to protect economic growth, as

---

[94] Budisusilo 2001, 17; Nasution 1999, 88; Sharma 2001, 90–91; Sjahrir 1999, 42.
[95] *Kompas*, August 29, 1997.
[96] Interview with Djisman Simandjuntak, economist and former chairman of the CSIS
(Centre for Strategic and International Studies, Jakarta) Foundation, March 15, 2006;
interview with M. Chatib Basri.
[97] Djiwandono 2001b.

demands for preventing deterioration of the rupiah exchange rate joined with demands for maintaining loose monetary policy.[98] BI also intervened in the rupiah market, spending an unknown quantity of its remaining foreign reserves to combat rupiah depreciation.[99]

Not all members of the Indonesian corporate sector should have opposed rupiah depreciation. Exporters with rupiah-denominated inputs should have found that currency depreciation increased global demand for their products, now comparatively cheaper in the world market. A number of small, debt-free, export-oriented industries with rupiah-denominated inputs did indeed benefit from the rupiah's depreciation.[100] In general, though, the benefits for exporters given rupiah depreciation were mixed, for three main reasons.[101] Many Indonesian industries producing for export markets relied on imported goods for production, later exported as finished goods. For example, the large Indonesian textile industry produced goods for the export market but relied on dollar-denominated inputs such as cotton.[102] Increased production costs hence erased much of the increase in global competitiveness on finished exports.[103] A second problem was the simultaneous depreciation of other regional currencies. The Indonesian palm oil industry serves as an illustration. While Indonesian palm oil became less expensive than it had been previously, Malaysian palm oil became less expensive as well because of ringgit depreciation, eroding Indonesia's positive terms-of-trade shock vis-à-vis other palm oil exporters. Most of Indonesia's main exports – manufactured goods, textiles, and agricultural goods – faced competition from other countries with depreciating currencies. Third, the banking crisis in Indonesia made it nearly impossible for exporters to obtain trade credits from their foreign partners.[104] Together, these three factors eliminated much of the windfall benefits that export-oriented industries might have expected from rapid currency depreciation.

Officials quite rightly blamed the lack of an export boom in the wake of the rupiah's depreciation on financial and corporate sector problems, along with the rising costs of imported goods.[105] Table 4.5 makes clear

[98] *Bisnis Indonesia*, September 27, 1997.
[99] Gill 1998, 150–51; Simandjuntak 1999, 173.
[100] See, e.g., Sandee, Andadari, and Sulandjari 2000 on small-scale furniture industry in Jepara, Central Java.
[101] Interview with Zulhefi Sikumbang.
[102] Colin Johnson 1998, 19.
[103] Simandjuntak 1999, 175.
[104] Interview with Zulhefi Sikumbang; Corden 2001, 55.
[105] *Kompas*, February 27, 1998.

TABLE 4.5. *Exports by Commodity Type, January–April 1997 and January–April 1998*

	Gross Tonnage			Value[a]		
	1997	1998	Percent Change	1997	1998	Percent Change
Primary commodities	67,092,355	74,807,097	11.50	8,090,577	6,114,504	−24.42
Foodstuffs	2,207,356	1,991,323	−9.79	1,704,787	1,458,487	−14.45
Unrefined goods	1,029,364	1,489,665	44.72	842,813	863,775	2.49
Fertilizers, ores, metals, and other minerals	23,423,600	32,697,962	39.59	607,333	365,592	−39.80
Fuels	40,342,229	38,521,571	−4.51	4,720,791	3,231,403	−31.55
Non-iron ores	89,806	106,576	18.67	214,853	225,246	4.84
Secondary commodities	5,526,649	6,974,715	26.20	8,442,896	7,192,989	−14.80
Steel	235,154	567,782	141.45	98,092	191,665	95.39
Chemicals	1,228,377	2,090,879	70.21	636,808	789,751	24.02
Agricultural products	2,347,789	2,708,792	15.38	1,440,895	854,973	−40.66
Transportation and other industrial products	937,518	1,141,364	21.74	2,061,562	2,014,715	−2.27
Textiles	233,723	239,126	2.31	1,017,578	813,070	−20.10
Clothing	83,753	56,242	−32.85	1,131,359	758,246	−32.98
Other consumption goods	460,335	170,531	−62.96	2,056,602	1,770,569	−13.91
Unclassified	42,239	5,135,679	12058.62	101,883	2,830,598	2678.28
TOTAL	72,661,243	86,917,491	19.62	16,635,356	16,168,091	−2.81

[a] In thousands of U.S. dollars, F.O.B.
Source: Badan Pusat Statistik 1998, 45.

the impact of rupiah depreciation on Indonesian exporters. Altogether, the value of Indonesian exports in the first four months of 1998 shrank by 2.8 percent in comparison to the same period in 1997. In the cases of textiles, agricultural products, and minerals, export volumes increased even as export values decreased. In the case of steel and non-iron ores, the value of exports increased, but the rate of increases in value lagged behind increases in gross tonnage. Although it is difficult from aggregate figures to judge the effects of export contraction on specific firms, in no case did an increase in the value of exports match or exceed its increase in volume.

The data show that rupiah depreciation in the context of Indonesia's financial meltdown hurt most exporters rather than helping them. Combined with increased foreign debt burdens, this gave most Indonesian firms a preference for minimizing exchange rate depreciation and volatility. So while BI tried to protect the rupiah's value by manipulating the global rupiah supply, this was unsuccessful because of domestic policy backtracking – interest rates not high enough and excessive money supply growth. Herd behavior among currency speculators and international investors reinforced the difficulties facing Indonesian policy makers. Even if rupiah holdings seemed attractive to some foreign investors, enough of these investors believed that the rupiah remained overvalued to discourage individual investors about the rupiah's short-term prospects. After only several months, the debate in Indonesia and elsewhere shifted to questions of investors' perceptions about Indonesia's economic prospects, as the government sought to inspire enough confidence among foreign investors that they would resume the capital inflows that had sponsored past economic growth.

Indonesian authorities and international lending agencies did so through promises of economic reform. By implementing economic reforms widely viewed by outsiders as needed to eliminate distortions in the economy, Indonesian officials believed that they would attract capital inflows that would stabilize the rupiah.[106] And, indeed, as the exchange rate data in Figure 4.4 show, the rupiah-dollar exchange rate did improve temporarily after each successive IMF agreement under Soeharto. But these exchange rate improvements did not last long, primarily because of failures and reversals in implementing the IMF's specific adjustment plans. The overall effect of IMF reforms as signaling devices,

---

[106] Djiwandono 2000, 53; Mann 1998, 50; Soesastro 2000, 132; Soesastro and Basri 1998, 10; Thee 2003, 184.

TABLE 4.6. *"Love Indonesia Campaign" Donations*

Donations Recorded on	Gold (kilograms)	Rupiah (trillions)	Foreign Currency (U.S. dollars)
March 4, 1998	194.9	5.9	418,233
May 11, 1998	248.1	10.5	446,472

Sources: Suara Pembaruan, March 5, 1998; *BusinessNews*, May 13, 1998.

designed to improve foreign investors' perceptions of Indonesia's long-term economic viability, was accordingly minimal.

With efforts to change the perceptions of currency traders and international investors failing, Soeharto turned to moral suasion. Specifically, the government, through its "Love the Rupiah Movement" headed by Soeharto's daughter Tutut, tried to convince Indonesians to convert their currency holdings to rupiah and to donate cash and precious metals to BI in order to replenish the central bank's dwindling foreign reserves.[107] Tutut also spearheaded additional efforts launched in early January to limit unnecessary imports, with names like the "Love Domestic Production" and the "Love Saving and Living Simply."[108] In each of these cases, the goal was to increase domestic demand for rupiah and minimize the use of rupiah to purchase imports. In fact, the issue of converting the largely dollar-denominated assets of large *konglomerat* to rupiah became a divisive political issue, with the Muslim arm of the New Order establishment declaring currency speculation to be *haram* (forbidden) and Chinese Indonesians under intense scrutiny regarding their willingness to support the government. The Love the Rupiah Movement – later to become known as the "Love Indonesia Movement" (Gerakan Cinta Indonesia) – had little real impact on the rupiah's depreciation, despite the modest sum of donations recorded between January and May 1998 (see Table 4.6).

A final attempt by the government to stabilize the exchange rate was its proposed currency board arrangement. Under a currency board system (CBS), a country commits to a fixed exchange rate by delegating the authority for currency management to a "currency board" bound by law to maintain a specified exchange rate. The first signs of this plan appeared in the first week of February, after a series of secret meetings between Steve Hanke, an American professor with some success in

[107] *Bisnis Indonesia*, January 9, 1998; *Media Indonesia*, January 9, 1998.
[108] *Suara Pembaruan*, January 10, 1998.

implementing currency boards in other emerging markets, and New Order officials including Widjojo Nitisastro, Mar'ie Muhammad, Soedradjad Djiwandono, Fuad Bawazier, and Soeharto himself. Reports indicated that Soeharto had called the meeting because of his frustration with currency speculators driving down the rupiah, and he was searching for a way to "kill them" with policy.[109] Yet members of Kadin, as well as Bimantara Group CEO Peter Gontha, are known to have introduced Soeharto to this idea.[110] By February 6 the Indonesian media had learned of the proposal, with politicians cautiously describing it as a potential solution to the depreciating exchange rate and perhaps to the country's economic problems with a hard peg of Rp5,000 to the U.S. dollar.[111]

A currency peg was popular among holders of both mobile and fixed capital. Among holders of fixed capital assets, in particular the new *pribumi* entrepreneurs, Kadin chair Aburizal Bakrie claimed that the CBS was a costly but necessary step to restore financial sector health.[112] Peter Gontha argued that currency stability would give investors an incentive to bring capital back into Indonesia.[113] Habibie, state minister for research and technology and by then the leading candidate for vice president in the Seventh Development Cabinet, pledged his support for the plan.[114] Exporter organizations supported the CBS as a tool to achieve currency stability.[115] Mobile capital supported the plan as well. James T. Riady of Lippo Group echoed Bakrie's words of support.[116] Other *konglomerat* supported the CBS because it would allow them to exchange their rupiah holdings for dollars at more favorable exchange rates and then park these assets overseas.[117] Soeharto's immediate family also strongly supported the CBS proposal.[118] Later media reports claimed that small-business owners eager for currency stability had begun to pressure BI to implement the CBS as well.[119]

---

[109] *Jakarta Post*, February 10, 1998.
[110] Interview with Arief Budisusilo.
[111] *Media Indonesia*, February 6, 1998.
[112] *Kompas*, February 19, 1998. Bakrie has since claimed that he never supported the CBS proposal; interview, March 14, 2006.
[113] *Bisnis Indonesia*, February 21, 1998.
[114] *Asian Wall Street Journal*, February 19, 1998.
[115] Interview with Zulhefi Sikumbang.
[116] *Kompas*, February 19, 1998.
[117] Bullard, Bello, and Malhotra 1998, 99; Robison and Hadiz 2004, 158; Robison and Rosser 1998, 1603; Sharma 2001, 103.
[118] Interview with Emil Salim.
[119] *Media Indonesia*, March 5, 1998.

The proposed rupiah peg at Rp5,000 to the U.S. dollar was a large improvement over the prevailing rate, with the rupiah trading around 9,000 to the U.S. dollar in February (see Figure 4.4). The benefits were clear for importers, who would find foreign goods less expensive, and the statements of business leaders also suggest that domestic businesses valued currency predictability. But almost immediately, economists began to question the appropriateness of a CBS. Sri Adiningsih, for example, warned that absent capital controls, a fixed rupiah would eliminate macroeconomic policy autonomy.[120] Others argued that without capital controls, high interest rates to support the rupiah peg would punish poor Indonesians.[121] Privately, technocrats advised Soeharto that the country had insufficient reserves to make the CBS feasible.[122] On February 19 Soeharto dismissed BI governor Soedradjad Djiwandono, replacing him with the relatively unknown Sjahril Sabirin. Official government sources did not name a reason for Djiwandono's dismissal, but political observers agree that his opposition to the CBS was responsible.[123] International reactions against the CBS proposal were swift and negative. Shortly after announcing the plan, Soeharto received phone calls from foreign leaders and ratings agency officials who urged him to reconsider the plan.[124] IMF officials registered their strong opposition as well and met with Soeharto to dissuade him from following through with the CBS.[125] Ultimately intense international pressure prevailed, and the government tabled the CBS proposal. The new minister of finance, Fuad Bawazier, announced on March 14 that the government had decided to delay implementation of the CBS while it studied other options.[126] Suggestions for a new exchange rate regime continued to float around policy circles, including the idea of returning to the rupiah's intervention band.[127] But, for the remainder of Soeharto's rule, the government confined itself to using monetary policy and foreign exchange intervention to prevent the rupiah's continued slide.

Bank Indonesia and Soeharto never implemented capital controls to break the links between macroeconomic policy and the exchange rate. While fixed capital and mobile capital both supported a rupiah peg,

[120] *Bisnis Indonesia*, February 7, 1998.
[121] *Kontan*, February 16, 1998; *Jakarta Post*, February 20, 1998.
[122] Interview with Emil Salim.
[123] *Suara Karya*, February 20, 1998. Sjahril Sabirin has stated that he never supported the CBS proposal; interview, March 17, 2006.
[124] *Jakarta Post*, February 20, 1998; *Bisnis Indonesia*, February 24, 1998.
[125] *Asian Wall Street Journal*, February 19, 1998.
[126] *Republika*, March 16, 1998.
[127] *Bisnis Indonesia*, March 25, 1998; *Bisnis Indonesia*, April 2, 1998.

capital account policy divided them. Mobile capitalists demanded the ability to move capital abroad, a fact consonant with Indonesia's long history of capital account openness.[128] In fact, the crisis itself heightened the *konglomerats'* demand for capital account openness. Facing a domestic economic meltdown, in January 1998 they began to move vast sums of capital overseas in search of a less volatile and more credible store of value than the rupiah.[129] This furthered the rupiah's collapse, creating a self-fulfilling dynamic in which the rupiah's declining value justified the need to move capital overseas. Loose monetary policy designed to keep businesses afloat, and the general lack of transparency in financial oversight, contributed further to the exodus of mobile capital.

In fact, despite the recognition by Soeharto's economic advisers that a CBS would make macroeconomic policy ineffective without restrictions on cross-border capital flows, the government was in the process of making it *easier* for Indonesians to move currency abroad. In early February the government lifted the limits on Indonesians moving hard rupiah currency abroad from Rp50,000 to Rp5,000,000, and simplified the process of moving larger sums abroad – with no set limit on the total amount that Indonesians could expatriate.[130] In reality, such laws regarding rupiah movements had historically had little bite, but this policy confirms the regime's commitment to preserving capital openness in the interest of mobile capital. Also reflecting mobile capital's preferences, BI reiterated in early February that it would not limit the ownership of foreign currency or its movement over national borders, despite pleas from Tutut and fixed capitalists for the *konglomerat* to convert foreign currency holdings into rupiah, and the imposition of foreign currency deposit ceilings in domestic banks.[131] Estimates of the total sum of liquid capital channeled overseas by the *konglomerat* range from U.S.$80 billion to U.S.$165 billion.[132]

Could policy makers have been simply ideologically opposed to capital controls, reflecting Indonesia's long adherence to the "Washington Consensus" of liberalized capital markets and free trade? Almost certainly not – recall from the preceding discussion that, at the same time, New Order officials were in the process of reneging on a whole host of other liberal

---

[128] Interview with Emil Salim; interview with a Chinese Indonesian political observer, February 2006; interview with Sri Adiningsih.
[129] Chua 2008, 70.
[130] *Bisnis Indonesia*, February 5, 1998; *Kompas*, February 5, 1998.
[131] *Republika*, February 4, 1998.
[132] Chua 2008, 88.

economic policies, as well as attempting to impose a CBS amid fierce international opposition. Moreover, politicians did consider seriously the possibility of capital controls because of heavy pressure from holders of fixed capital. Syarifuddin Harahap, a DPR member from PPP, suggested that a combination of a CBS and capital controls would punish the foreign speculators.[133] Fuad Bawazier, appointed as minister of finance in March 1998, strongly recommended complementing the CBS with capital account restrictions. He also urged Soeharto to jail businessmen found to have moved their funds overseas.[134] Moreover, two Australian economists wrote a prominent article advocating temporary capital controls in order to prevent the rupiah's free fall, and foreign observers openly speculated that Soeharto would impose capital controls in addition to implementing the CBS.[135] Members of the domestic economic policy community and the domestic media debated the concept of capital controls throughout this period.[136]

Despite this active debate, the Indonesian government refused to implement capital controls that would have freed macroeconomic policy under a currency peg. Free movement of capital across Indonesia's borders had long rested at the foundation of New Order political economy, and mobile capital required an open capital account as a condition for supporting the regime. This forced the regime to combat the crisis using contradictory macroeconomic policy measures, with policies designed to shore up the exchange rate leading to tight liquidity and measures to loosen liquidity, further weakening the rupiah. As was the case with the other policy measures discussed in this chapter, the fate of the majority of Indonesians figured only tangentially into the regime's adjustment policy decisions. As we see in Chapter 6, conflict among Soeharto's supporters over exchange rate management and capital movement ultimately caused the New Order's collapse.

Alternative Explanations?

This chapter has shown that adjustment policies consistently favored connected firms in particular, but mobile and fixed capital in general, to the detriment of poor Indonesians. Only subsidy cuts – whose costs were

---

[133] *Republika*, February 16, 1998.
[134] Interview, March 6, 2006.
[135] *Straits Times*, February 19, 1998; Agence France-Presse, March 9, 1998; *Asian Wall Street Journal*, March 10, 1998; *Jakarta Post*, March 16, 1998.
[136] Interview with Arief Budisusilo; interview with Djisman Simandjuntak.

borne disproportionately by the poor – were implemented consistently; the Soeharto regime resisted, backtracked on, or ignored other IMF-mandated adjustment policies reviewed in this chapter.

But the coalitional theory is not the only possible explanation of adjustment policies in Indonesia. In the literature on Indonesia's crisis, the main alternative explanation of adjustment policy argues that policy decisions during Soeharto's final year in office were actually illogical. Note that this is a subtle articulation of the null hypothesis, that there is no systematic explanation for adjustment policy. Indonesian crisis management in this view is incoherent, a perspective implicit in arguments attributing Indonesia's demise to its weak bureaucracy[137] or to wildly uncontrollable crony capitalism.[138] Neoclassical economists often make a similar point, equating policy vacillation with capricious or myopic policy making.[139] Another perspective, one embraced by many political observers, suggests that wide swings in policy were the result of Soeharto's diminished mental capacity, brought on by age, the death of his wife, sickness, and perhaps senility.[140]

This chapter rejects this null hypothesis. Instead, I have argued that shifts in policy all represented calculated attempts by Soeharto and the New Order regime to protect the interests of their political supporters. Soeharto faced the crisis with full confidence in his own ability to manage it,[141] and I find support for my theory across a number of interrelated adjustment policy measures. Contradictions in adjustment policy demands in the area of capital account management and exchange rate policies, in fact, reflect the very essence of the distributional conflicts at the heart of Indonesia's political economy. Volatility in attempts to find a suitable adjustment policy are evidence in favor of my theory, not support for the interpretation that policy making was incoherent.

The second alternative hypothesis concerns the role of the IMF and is particularly important for a comparative study of Indonesia (which accepted IMF aid) and Malaysia (which did not). Could IMF agreements have determined Indonesia's adjustment policies? Evidence suggests not. At the most fundamental level, Indonesia *did not* implement the IMF's aid conditions. I have shown how the New Order repeatedly backtracked, sidestepped, and ignored IMF policies that did not conform to supporters'

---

[137] Chalmers Johnson 1998; L. Weiss 1999.
[138] Hughes 1999; Robison and Rosser 1998.
[139] Bird and Milne 1999; Hill 2000.
[140] Crouch 2001a, 176–77; Elson 2001, 276–88; Loveard 1999, 333.
[141] Interview with Emil Salim.

preferences. I have also shown that the New Order government *did* implement adjustment measures – primarily eliminating subsidies – that did not hurt its political supporters.

Applying the Indonesian case to the literature on the politics of IMF lending gives a theoretical context for this view. Some governments accept IMF loans with high levels of conditionality in order to push through unpopular reforms, as IMF loans raise the costs of noncompliance.[142] But in the case of Indonesia, IMF agreements were not so much an attempt by Soeharto to raise the costs of noncompliance vis-à-vis domestic supporters, as they were an attempt to restore international investor confidence.[143] Given the linkages between international capital flows and domestic economic conditions, and insofar as confidence lay at the heart of Indonesia's crisis, this was a strategy for restoring growth and investment and hence protecting the regime's supporters. Soeharto's supporters viewed a refusal to implement reforms to be less costly than implementing them.

When IMF reforms contradicted the interests of the New Order's supporters, Soeharto and New Order politicians openly confronted it. In addition to the confrontations noted previously, in early March 1998 Foreign Minister Ali Alatas decried the IMF's demands for reform as too difficult for immediate implementation.[144] Meanwhile, Soeharto began to tout a cryptic plan referred to as "IMF-Plus," although it remains unclear what this plan actually entailed. Harmoko, head of the Golkar faction in the DPR, came out strongly against the IMF's liberal economic reforms that contradicted the "family basis" of the Indonesian economy.[145] Still, in cases when the government did implement IMF reforms that harmed poor Indonesians, the IMF was a convenient scapegoat for Indonesian officials.[146] Director General of Customs and Excise Soehardjo, for instance, blamed sharp rises in cigarette prices on the IMF.[147] Similar statements abound during the final months of Soeharto's rule.

A final possible alternative explanation concerns the technical feasibility of certain adjustment policies. In particular, capital controls are

---

[142] Vreeland 2003.
[143] Interview with M. Chatib Basri; interview with Thee Kian Wee; Djiwandono 2000, 53; Soesastro 2000, 132; Soesastro and Basri 1998, 10; Thee 2003, 64.
[144] *Bisnis Indonesia*, March 7, 1998.
[145] *Kompas*, March 9, 1998.
[146] Interview with an economist at an international development institution, February 2006.
[147] *Bisnis Indonesia*, March 20, 1998.

notoriously difficult to implement effectively. Former BI director I Nyoman Moena noted the difficulty of restricting capital flows as a justification for preserving capital account openness.[148] Other Indonesian and foreign economists, both at the time and since, have noted that capital account restrictions would create opportunities for backroom dealing in Indonesia's notoriously corrupt bureaucracy.[149] Although these technical objections to capital account restrictions are valid, they do not explain the political decision not to implement capital controls. In the following chapter, I discuss how the Malaysian regime struggled with this very same issue, ultimately banning capital outflows despite the possibility of bureaucratic abuse.

In conclusion, the three primary competing hypotheses that explain Indonesia's adjustment policy – random policy decisions, IMF requirements, and technical impossibilities – are less compelling than my argument. In addition, the qualitative evidence reviewed here confirms the logic of this coalitional theory of adjustment policy. Under Soeharto, the coalition of fixed and mobile capital that supported the New Order regime resisted adjustment policies specifically because of the distributional costs associated with them. Next, I demonstrate how a different coalitional structure determined Malaysia's markedly different adjustment policy. Relying on a coalition between the Malay masses and the new Malay rich, Mahathir Mohamad's regime was able to implement capital controls, peg the ringgit, and implement expansionary macroeconomic policies that were ultimately successful in restoring growth and forestalling authoritarian collapse.

---

[148] *Merdeka*, January 24, 1998.
[149] Interview with Emil Salim; interview with M. Chatib Basri; interview with Sjahril Sabirin.

5

Adjustment Policy in Malaysia,
June 1997–December 1999

Malaysians often remarked during the early months of 1998 that every time Prime Minister Mahathir Mohamad opened his mouth, the ringgit depreciated. It was not hard to see why. As the Kuala Lumpur Stock Exchange (KLSE) tumbled and the ringgit depreciated, Mahathir's public demeanor ranged from defiant to vitriolic. He blamed Malaysia's currency and financial crisis on hostile "rogue" factions from George Soros to Western colonialists to the International Monetary Fund to a global Jewish conspiracy. In contrast to the positive reviews of Soeharto's crisis management in the first months of Indonesia's crisis, Mahathir's outbursts earned him condemnation from the foreign investment community. Confronted with what seemed to be an increasingly unhinged autocrat, foreign observers lambasted Mahathir for ignoring his regime's own failures in macroeconomic planning, and for downplaying the policy mismanagement that became ever more apparent as foreign investors took a second look at Malaysia.

Mahathir's public persona hid the regime's struggles over adjustment policy. The government's initial steps were actually encouraging from the IMF's perspective and included a vow to eliminate wasteful public expenditures and pledges of fiscal discipline by Anwar Ibrahim. In his words, these adjustment measures amounted to "IMF without the IMF." Yet the regime's commitment to IMF-style policies was short-lived. Interest rate hikes to encourage capital inflows were temporary and not nearly as sharp as those in other crisis countries. The regime restarted many of the postponed infrastructure projects, using the logic of "strategic investment" to excuse what were clearly uneconomic ventures. While exhorting

Malaysians to spend their money domestically, the government also embarked on redistributive policies that targeted the Malay poor. Finally, at the beginning of September 1998, the regime announced a stunning ban on a wide range of capital outflows, pegged the Malaysian ringgit to the U.S. dollar, and embarked on even more drastic macroeconomic expansion.

This chapter shows how coalitional alignments within the Malaysian regime determine this particular mix of adjustment strategies. As in Indonesia, political centralization without effective veto gates allowed the regime to adapt to the crisis quickly and decisively as it unfolded. But Malaysia's regime enacted policies that fulfilled the demands of both the new Malay rich and the Malay masses. As with the case of Indonesia, the test of my theory comes not only from the final policy decisions enacted by the regime but also from the preferences for adjustment policies articulated by individuals both within and outside of the regime's support coalition. A summary of the findings appears in Table 5.1. Unlike Indonesia's, Malaysia's adjustment strategy not only resisted orthodox policies but also proposed a range of specific policies targeting the regime's key supporters. Table 5.2 summarizes the most important of these policies.

The conclusion from Tables 5.1 and 5.2 is further support for the theory outlined in Chapter 2. Macroeconomic expansion eased the burdens facing holders of fixed capital assets, including Malays in the corporate and industrial sectors, non-Malay fixed capital, and ordinary Malays whose corporate wealth the regime held in trust. Ordinary Malays also benefited from the continued blandishments that had long

TABLE 5.1. *Adjustment Policy in Malaysia: Policies, Losers, Implementation*

Policy Measure	Losers	Implementation
Fiscal and trade policy		
Suspension of megaprojects	Connected firms	Poor
Corporate reform	Connected firms	Poor
Cuts in subsidies	Labor/poor Malaysians	Poor
Monetary and financial policies		
Increases in interest rates	Business	Poor
Slow growth in money supply	Connected banks	Fair
Financial sector reform	Connected banks	Fair
Foreign economic policy		
Free floating exchange rate	Mobile and fixed capital	Poor
Open capital account	Fixed capital	Poor

TABLE 5.2. *Key Policy Measures in Malaysia*

Policy	First Implemented
Targeting Malay masses	
Housing subsidies	October 1997
Stable public utility prices	November 1997
Stable prices for food staples	November 1997
"Fund for Bumiputra Entrepreneurs"	June 1998
Targeting fixed capital	
Share buy-ups	October 1997
Buyouts of postponed projects	November 1997
Countercyclical infrastructure spending	March 1998
Targeting both	
Import cuts	October 1997
Monetary expansion	June 1998
De-internationalization of the ringgit	August 1998
Capital controls	September 1998
Exchange rate peg	September 1998

enticed them to support the regime. The losers in these exercises were holders of mobile capital, both domestic and foreign: financial market speculators, currency and stock traders, marginalized ethnic Chinese financiers, and others. Having never been part of the regime's support coalition, they bore the immediate costs of Malaysia's heterodox adjustment strategy. In Chapter 7, I show that these adjustment policies enacted under Mahathir ultimately allowed Malaysia's regime to survive the crisis.

Crisis Onset

As was the case in Indonesia, the proximate cause of the crisis in Malaysia was regional contagion from the baht's devaluation in Thailand. With regional currency traders reallocating their currency holdings away from strong ringgit positions, capital flowed out of Malaysia, and the ringgit suffered. Ringgit depreciation in turn uncovered Malaysia's own macro-economic vulnerabilities, which a decade of strong growth had masked.[1] An important vulnerability facing Malaysia was the rapid pile-up of foreign loans in the domestic financial sector (Table 5.3).

Debt growth in 1995 and 1996 was 16.7 and 29.6 percent per annum, respectively, an amount far outpacing GDP growth during this period.

---

[1] Rasiah 2001b.

TABLE 5.3. *Selected Malaysian Debt Indicators, in Millions of U.S. Dollars and as a Percentage of Total Foreign Debt*

Period	Total	Bank Debt (%)	Nonbank Private Debt (%)	Short-Term Debt (%)[a]
1990	9,445	1,047 (11.09)	1,658 (17.55)	2,053 (21.74)
1991	10,350	1,980 (19.13)	1,871 (18.08)	2,976 (28.75)
1992	11,895	2,941 (24.72)	2,680 (22.53)	4,074 (34.25)
1993	17,394	5,249 (30.18)	4,405 (25.32)	7,394 (42.51)
1994	17,460	3,865 (22.14)	7,177 (41.11)	6,579 (37.68)
1995	20,979	4,419 (21.06)	10,147 (48.37)	7,895 (37.63)
1996	29,794	6,504 (21.83)	13,732 (46.09)	11,178 (37.52)
1997 Q2	37,437	10,486 (28.01)	16,440 (43.91)	16,249 (43.40)
1997 Q4	34,046	9,904 (29.09)	15,927 (46.78)	14,419 (42.35)
1998 Q2	28,781	7,282 (25.30)	14,280 (49.62)	10,993 (38.20)
1998 Q4	27,948	6,013 (21.51)	13,266 (47.47)	9,310 (33.31)

[a] As a percentage of total debt.
Source: Bank for International Settlements.

Using different sources, Jomo K. S. estimates that during this period the stock of foreign debt held by private banks tripled.[2] By the onset of the crisis, in fact, Malaysia had the highest ratio of loans to GDP in Asia.[3] The ratio of private-sector debt to GDP was 192.5 percent for 1997, whereas comparable figures for Indonesia were only 61.1 percent, with Thailand and South Korea at 116.3 and 141.4 percent, respectively.[4]

There are notable contrasts with Indonesia. For one, short-term foreign debt was lower in Malaysia by 1997, at 43.4 percent of total outstanding debt rather than Indonesia's peak of 57.4 percent. Moreover, bank debt approached 30 percent of all debt, compared to 20 percent in Indonesia. The most important contrast, however, was that the problem of short-term *unhedged* foreign debt – not captured in the figures in Table 5.3 – was far less serious in Malaysia. In Malaysia, a more robust system of financial regulation prevented an excess of short-term foreign debt (hedged or unhedged) in Malaysia.[5] Domestically, though, worrying financial sector developments extended beyond the rapid growth of foreign debt. The 1990s economic expansion led to rapid growth in the

[2] Jomo 1998, 183.
[3] Athukorala 1998b, 284; 2001, 71; Rasiah 2001a, 69.
[4] Athukorala 2001, 49.
[5] Athukorala 2001, 24–25; Bank Negara Malaysia 1999, 286; Chin and Jomo 2001, 113; Jomo 2001c, 13.

property sector, with heavy bank exposure in directed lending toward speculative real estate investments. At the same time, lenders fed the rapid growth of Malaysian equities and securities markets. These patterns of lending led to heavy concentration of domestic portfolios in the property and equity sectors – an estimated 42.6 percent of all domestic loans were to these two sectors.[6] In 1996 and the first half of 1997, portfolio capital inflows in general – beyond direct lending – rose dramatically. Whereas in the early part of the 1990s foreign direct investment constituted the bulk of capital inflows, in the middle of the decade capital inflows shifted in composition to overwhelmingly portfolio investment.[7] One way of measuring this vulnerability is to compare a country's stock of foreign currency reserves with the total stock of mobile capital, meaning both bank lending and portfolio inflows. A ratio of less than one signifies vulnerability to sudden shifts in demand for a country's currency. This "reserves to mobile capital" ratio in Malaysia was .559, not the worst in Asia, but notably worse that Indonesia.[8]

In Indonesia, stock markets have been historically underdeveloped, so firms must rely on bank lending for investment purposes. In Malaysia, the Kuala Lumpur Stock Exchange is relatively mature, so firms can easily raise capital by issuing shares rather than seeking direct loans. The primary explanation for the expansion in capital inflows into the KLSE in the 1990s is political: the regime uses the stock market to reward cronies and to disburse patronage to ordinary Malays who invest in government-run unit trusts. The stock market boom that accompanied economic expansion in the 1990s, and which attracted heavy lending for share purchases from the domestic financial sector, also encouraged the rapid inflow of foreign portfolio capital eager to take advantage of rising stock prices.[9] Such portfolio inflows can be liquidated and repatriated almost instantaneously. And continuing weaknesses in corporate governance meant that in the event of a stock market contraction, foreign investors – almost exclusively minority shareholders – would have an incentive to divest and seek more stable investments overseas. By 1996, buoyed by this inflow of foreign portfolio investment, Malaysian stock market capitalization was more than 227 percent of GDP, the highest such ratio

---

[6] Corsetti, Pesenti, and Roubini 1998, 30. See also Athukorala 1998b, 284; 2001, 48–49; Haggard 2000b, 59–60; Lindgren et al. 1999, 80–81; Ng 2001, 176.

[7] Athukorala 1998b, 283; 2001, 29; Chin and Jomo 2001, 112; Ong 1998, 222.

[8] Athukorala 2001, 47.

[9] Athukorala 1998a, 93–94; 2001, 32–38; Chin and Jomo 2001, 101–8; Jomo 2001b; Rasiah 1998, 362; 2001b, 51.

anywhere in the world.[10] Yet the ringgit's effective peg to the U.S. dollar discouraged portfolio investors from protecting themselves against a sudden currency revaluation, even as capital inflows fed exchange rate overvaluation.[11]

Malaysia's vulnerabilities were accordingly the rapid growth of foreign bank debt, imprudent lending to a booming property sector and share market, a pegged exchange rate, and rapid inflows of portfolio capital into the KLSE. Their antecedents, as in Indonesia, were excessive public investment, state-directed lending, and stock market expansion, each politically motivated[12] and exacerbating the vulnerabilities of a country deregulating its financial sector before having created the proper regulatory apparatus.[13] Mahathir's regular outbursts, moreover, certainly hastened the collapse of stock prices and the ringgit. Politics became paramount as the regime responded to the crisis with adjustment policies meant to restore economic growth.

Fiscal and Trade Policy

Fiscal and trade policy adjustments followed quickly upon the ringgit's float in the summer of 1997. These had far more observable effects than the imposition of capital controls later in 1998 and hence were more contested. As early as August 12, 1997, Anwar Ibrahim suggested that the government would postpone government investment in a series of "lumpy" investments and "noncritical" government projects.[14] Yet, within two days, he reversed himself and vowed to maintain government spending levels, focusing adjustment instead on increasing exports and decreasing imports.[15] This pattern of spending cuts followed by reversals continued as the crisis progressed. Mahathir announced on September 4 that the government would postpone a number of government-linked heavy investment projects. These included among others the massive, highly criticized Bakun Dam, being built in Sarawak by UMNO's Chinese Malaysian patron Ting Pek Khiing, as well as other projects of dubious value such as an international airport for the north of the Malay Peninsula.[16] In

---

[10] Jomo and Hamilton-Hart 2001, 81.

[11] Jomo 1998, 183.

[12] Rasiah 2001b; Rustam 2001; Syed Husin 1998.

[13] Chin and Jomo 2001, 100, 09; Jomo 1998, 183; Rasiah 2001b, 47–58.

[14] *Utusan Malaysia*, August 12, 1997.

[15] Gill 1998, 39, 51.

[16] *Utusan Malaysia*, September 5, 1997; *Asian Wall Street Journal*, September 5, 1997; *New Straits Times*, September 6, 1997.

TABLE 5.4. *Deferred Investment Projects in Malaysia, by Month*

September 1997
  Bakun hydroelectric project
  Putrajaya Administrative Centre Phase II
  Northern Regional International Airport
  Kuala Lumpur Linear City project
  Cameron Highlands–Fraser's Hill–Genting Highlands road project
  Straits of Malacca Malaysia-Indonesia bridge
October 1997
  Johor light rail
  Penang light rail
  Military procurement
  Highway construction

Source: Utusan Malaysia, September 5, 1997; *New Straits Times*, October 18, 1997.

mid-October, in presenting the first draft of Malaysia's 1998 budget, Anwar announced a further round of spending deferments (Table 5.4). The regime designed these cuts to instill confidence in foreign investors of the country's prudent economic management, which would ideally encourage capital inflows.

Yet budget cuts and deferments were deeply unpopular with connected firms that benefited from them. For this reason, UMNO leaders soon effectively reversed spending cuts to these linked firms, either by restarting them or by compensating groups that suffered from spending cuts. Fixed capital was the main winner. Despite having postponed investment in the already wasteful Bakun Dam project, for example, the government announced in late November 1997 that it would take over the Bakun concession from Ting's Ekran Holdings.[17] Other projects that had been deferred earlier in the autumn of 1997, such as transportation and petroleum distribution infrastructure for the northern part of the Malay Peninsula, were restarted as well.[18]

Investor reactions to the deferment of megaprojects and the spending cuts of the draft 1998 budget were disappointing.[19] Shortly after the decision to bail out Ekran Holdings, though, Anwar announced additional spending cuts in an addendum to the 1998 budget proposed in October 1997.[20] The proposed adjustment measures contracted

[17] *New Straits Times*, November 21, 1997; *Utusan Malaysia*, November 21, 1997.
[18] Haggard 2000b, 60–61; Jomo 1998, 190.
[19] Jomo 2003, 186; Ram 1997a.
[20] *New Straits Times,* December 6, 1997; *Utusan Malaysia*, December 6, 1997.

government spending by 18 percent, deferring several additional infrastructure projects and postponing imports for state-run firms. In the
terminology of the time, the orthodox measures in Anwar's budget supplement were "the IMF without the IMF." But in other areas, Anwar's
budget addendum was not as contractionary as international lending
institutions had hoped. The Malay masses' losses were minimal, as
expenditures on myriad social programs were unaffected by spending
cuts.[21] Likewise, despite spending cuts, fixed capital benefited from a
monetary policy that remained loose, with no interest rate hikes to draw
capital back into the country.[22]

On balance, then, Malaysian fiscal policy by the end of 1997 followed
a roughly neutral pattern. Under Anwar's hand, the Ministry of Finance
deferred spending on wasteful investment projects, yet protected spending
on redistributive social spending that targeted the Malay masses.[23] But
because government spending is a method of patronage distribution, the
spending cuts that harmed fixed capital were reversed. Through late
1997, compensation schemes such as that of the Bakun Dam project were
common, but a more fundamental shift in policy was also underway.
Already by November 1997, a move to supersede Anwar's policy-making
autonomy in the Finance Ministry was underway in the formation of
what later became the National Economic Action Council (NEAC). Part
of the Prime Minister's Department, the NEAC's membership included
the heads of all ministries with economic portfolios as well as a host of
private-sector business representatives. Notably, Daim Zainuddin served
as executive director. The NEAC assumed responsibility for forming all
economic policies during the crisis.[24]

The formation of the NEAC in late 1997 both signaled Mahathir's
dissatisfaction with Anwar's budgetary policies, from which he
distanced himself, and represented a channel through which Malay- or
crony-run fixed capital could directly influence policy making.
Throughout the early months of 1998, most of the budgetary cutbacks
stipulated in the fall of 1997 were reversed, protecting the fortunes of
connected firms. Fiscal expansion was already evident by March 1998.[25]
In late June, following a UMNO General Assembly meeting fraught with

[21] Bank Negara Malaysia 1999, 591.
[22] Athukorala 1998b, 285–86.
[23] Interview with Anwar Ibrahim, former deputy prime minister and finance minister of
Malaysia, July 7, 2006.
[24] Mahani 2002, 25–26.
[25] Athukorala 2001, 66; Mahani 2002, 48.

hostility toward Anwar, Mahathir appointed Daim Zainuddin as a minister with special functions in the Prime Minister's Department, signifying the further marginalization of Anwar at the behest of business groups. Just before the assembly, Anwar announced an additional RM7 billion in countercyclical spending, and shortly thereafter he introduced RM5 billion in infrastructure development funds to replace funds not forthcoming from banks.[26] By mid-July, Anwar began to advocate still more spending, urging government agencies to release approved funds to contractors in order to stimulate economic activity.[27] Meanwhile, Mahathir advocated still stronger spending measures. In doing so, he linked spending projects and infrastructural investments to the interests of fixed capital, arguing that these would protect Malay business interests in the spirit of the New Economic Policy.[28]

These expansionary fiscal measures became still stronger after the imposition of capital controls and the ringgit peg of early September 1998. The 1999 budget, tabled on October 23, 1998, included new infrastructural investments, directed tax cuts for "strategic" firms, and enough of a general spending increase to warrant an RM16.66 billion deficit for 1999 when combined with revenue shortfalls.[29] These spending measures had a strong redistributive component that protected the interests of struggling (Malay) fixed capital, while promising to encourage economic growth as a more general set of expansionary policies.

Big-ticket investment projects and expanded discretionary spending thereby protected the interests of fixed capital, in particular Malay fixed capital. The Malay masses also benefited from extensive redistributive measures as part of the fiscal adjustment measures. These, unlike spending on big-ticket investment projects, were never contested between Anwar, as finance minister, and Mahathir and Daim. As early as late June 1997, when commenting on the possibility of spending cuts, Anwar assured citizens that spending on health, education, and rural development would not suffer.[30] These pledges continued as the crisis progressed, becoming distinctly pro-*bumiputra* by October,[31] when significant funding began. In mid-October 1997, the government announced that

[26] *Utusan Malaysia*, June 19, 1998; *Berita Harian*, July 2, 1998.
[27] *Utusan Malaysia*, July 27, 1998.
[28] *Utusan Malaysia*, July 22, 1998; *Utusan Malaysia*, August 21, 1998.
[29] *New Straits Times*, October 24, 1998; *Asian Wall Street Journal*, October 26, 1998; Mahathir 1998b.
[30] *Utusan Malaysia*, July 1, 1997.
[31] *Mingguan Malaysia*, October 5, 1997; *Utusan Malaysia*, July 8, 1998.

the government petroleum company Petronas would purchase an RM1 billion bond from the newly formed government housing company Syarikat Perumahan Negara Berhad to support low-cost housing, later to be supplemented with an additional RM1 billion ringgit in April 1998.[32] In November the government announced to great fanfare that it would not raise mail, telephone, and electricity prices.[33] In March MARA revealed that it would commence work on a technical university dedicated to training *bumiputras*.[34] Additional social spending arrived on March 23, 1998, with a package from the Finance Ministry entitled Measures to Strengthen the Stability of the Malaysian Economy, which pledged RM1 billion in additional aid for poor Malaysians,[35] and in early June, with the formation of the Fund for Bumiputra Entrepreneurs that pledged RM500 million to *bumiputra* small businesses.[36]

Subsidies and basic goods pricing reinforced these measures and reflect the pressure that Malay labor brought to bear on the regime. By early fall, unions and consumer groups began to urge the government to ban price increases for basic goods. Between November 1997 and May 1998, UMNO Youth joined them in protesting price rises for palm cooking oil, toll roads, sugar, chicken, wheat flour, condensed milk, onions, and eggs.[37] Anwar and Mahathir themselves both opposed price rises for goods like wheat flour, refined rice, palm oil, and tolls.[38] While Malay fixed capital might have suffered from lower toll prices, for example, Minister of Works S. Samy Vellu ensured that the regime compensated firms with toll concessions.[39] Where prices on imported goods did rise to reflected new costs associated with ringgit depreciation, Mahathir and Minister of Domestic Trade and Consumer Affairs Megat Junid Megat Ayob demanded investigation into traders that raised prices more than the amount permitted by the government.[40] Moreover, the formerly government-owned power-generating firm Tenaga Nasional Berhad again pledged that it would not raise electricity prices before the end

---

[32] *Business Times* (Malaysia), October 10, 1997; *Utusan Malaysia*, April 28, 1998.
[33] *New Sunday Times*, November 9, 1997.
[34] *Utusan Malaysia*, March 4, 1998.
[35] Anwar 1998b.
[36] *Utusan Malaysia*, June 6, 1998.
[37] See, e.g., *Utusan Malaysia*, November 19, 1997; March 10, 1998; *Mingguan Malaysia*, December 7, 1997.
[38] *Utusan Malaysia*, December 1, 1997; *Business Times* (Malaysia), June 4, 1998.
[39] See, e.g., *Business Times* (Malaysia), May 28, 1998.
[40] *Utusan Malaysia*, December 13, 1997; June 8, 1998.

of 1999, despite having experienced an 88 percent decline in profits in late 1997.[41]

The National Economic Recovery Plan, released in early August 1998, foreshadowed the further expansion of pro-*bumiputra* redistributive measures that took place after a ban on capital outflows in early September of that year. Targeting ordinary Malays, the plan specifically noted the negative impact of the crisis on "household income, employment opportunities, and *bumiputra* equity ownership" and pledged measures to redress these problems.[42] The 1999 budget, which, as noted, expanded investment to ease the fortunes of troubled Malay firms, strongly favored the Malay poor and middle classes as well.[43] For example, the government implemented almost no new taxes to finance the fiscal expansion; the only exceptions were taxes on "sin" goods such as alcohol, gambling, and cigarettes – the first two of which are legally prohibited to Malays. Additionally, small-business development funds specially reserved for *bumiputras* received additional injections.[44] Independent of the 1999 budget, new second finance minister Mustapha Mohamed announced an additional package of at RM2.678 billion in development spending.[45] Thus, when government-controlled mass media referred to the expansionary 1999 budget as a "budget close to the people,"[46] this was not far from the truth.

In the realm of trade policy, Malaysia's anticompetitive efforts were less drastic than Indonesia's. The regime's refusal to accept IMF conditionality meant that it faced little external pressure to lower trade barriers that required clever manipulation of corporate regulations. In fact, the government pursued a standard orthodox adjustment program in adjusting to a terms-of-trade shock: promoting exports (capitalizing on the benefits of ringgit depreciation) and limiting imports (minimizing the costs of ringgit depreciation). This took place through moral suasion in the Buy Malaysia campaign[47] as well as through government directives to replace imports with local products. In these directives, there are hints of protectionism that benefited Malay fixed capital. In October 1997, for example, the government announced that it would no longer import

---

[41] *Utusan Malaysia*, November 8, 1997; August 12, 1998.
[42] National Economic Action Council 1998, 15–16.
[43] Mahathir 1998b.
[44] *New Straits Times*, October 26, 1998.
[45] *Utusan Malaysia*, October 23, 1998.
[46] *Utusan Malaysia*, October 24, 1998.
[47] *New Straits Times*, October 23, 1997; *Utusan Malaysia*, April 1, 1998.

foreign automobiles for use as official government vehicles but instead purchase all vehicles from the national car manufacturer Proton.[48] Insofar as Proton would not be profitable without such protection, this is consistent with the regime favoring politically connected ventures.

Monetary Policy

Expansionary fiscal policies directly supported fixed capital and the Malay masses, but monetary policy was arguably just as important as an adjustment tool. Monetary policy decisions influence finance policy and exchange rate policy, so, as in the discussion of Indonesia, I do not discuss the impact of monetary policy on financial institutions and demand for the ringgit in this section. Instead, I concentrate here primarily on the determinants of the level and variance of interest rates. To illustrate how the regime avoided monetary contraction, Figure 5.1 plots nominal interbank overnight call rates in Malaysia from January 1, 1997, to December 31, 1998. Of interest in this series are three of its features: the very brief interest rate spikes in May and July 1997, the very gradual increase in interest rates between August 1997 and February 1998, and the dip that coincides with the imposition of capital controls and an exchange rate peg in September 1998.

The initial interest rate spikes in early summer of 1997 reflected attempts by Bank Negara Malaysia (BNM) to stem currency depreciation. But in the wake of the ringgit float, instead of sharply raising interest rates to prevent further ringgit devaluation, BNM maintained a far more modest monetary stance because of the extensive local currency debt held by fixed capital. Mahathir, for example, repeatedly pledged that the regime would not allow interest rates to rise unnecessarily.[49] He also challenged the financial sector, warning banks not to raise interest rates any further on their own.[50] Such statements notwithstanding, for the first six months after the ringgit float, BNM did oversee the limited interest rate increases that are represented in Figure 5.1, which were directed at containing capital flight.[51] But even this moderate contraction harmed fixed capital, coming as it did at the same time as contractionary fiscal policies.[52] Nik Mohamed Nik Yaacob of the Sime Darby Group, for example, complained that tight monetary conditions were threatening

[48] *Utusan Malaysia*, October 16, 1997.
[49] *Utusan Malaysia*, October 28, 1997; *Business Times* (Malaysia), January 1, 1998.
[50] *Berita Harian*, December 1, 1997.
[51] Bank Negara Malaysia 1999, 176–77.
[52] Chin and Jomo 2001, 117; Jomo 2003, 188; Ram 1997a.

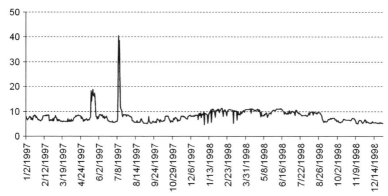

FIGURE 5.1. Malaysian Interbank Overnight Call Rates. *Source:* Bank Negara Malaysia.

the viability of the group's subsidiaries.[53] Similar statements from other business owners and politicians abound.[54]

Because of this opposition from Malay fixed capital, as the crisis progressed the government became increasingly hostile to interest rate hikes that had negative impacts on politically connected business groups. Mahathir consistently criticized high interest rates throughout the spring of 1998, and by June the targets of his criticism included BNM and private financial institutions alike.[55] Other UMNO politicians joined him in urging banks to increase lending and to lower interest rates.[56] Later that month, after Daim rose to the position of Minister with Special Functions, interest rates slowly began to decrease. They became still more expansionary in August 1998, coinciding with the release of the National Economic Recovery Plan that mandated expansionary policies to stimulate the economy. Anwar, Mahathir, and others in the NEAC justified this change in policy by noting the hardships facing fixed capital.[57]

Loose monetary conditions did have opponents among some Malaysian officials, who favored the IMF's policy of monetary contraction to draw capital back into the country. Most notable among them were the governor and deputy governor of BNM, Ahmad Mohd. Don and Fong Weng Phak, who were both privately critical of the NEAC's

---

[53] *Utusan Malaysia*, November 10, 1997.
[54] *New Straits Times*, November 28, 1997; *New Sunday Times*, March 1, 1998.
[55] *Utusan Malaysia*, April 22, 1998; *New Straits Times*, June 6, 1998.
[56] *Utusan Malaysia*, March 16, 1998; *New Straits Times*, June 8, 1998.
[57] *Business Times* (Malaysia), July 1, 1998; *New Straits Times*, August 12, 1998.

adjustment strategy in the summer of 1998. The two tendered their res-
ignations on August 28, publicly stating that they disagreed with lower
interest rate policies.[58] More than likely, the regime forced the pair to
resign because of its displeasure with BNM's monetary management.[59]
Ahmad's replacement, Ali Abul Hassan Sulaiman, was more compliant
with Mahathir and Daim's preferences for loose monetary policy.

Monetary policy loosened still further after the imposition of capital
controls, which Mahathir made clear were designed to enable further
interest rates reductions.[60] Whereas interbank overnight rates averaged
9.16 percent in August, in September they averaged 6.71 percent –
with a drop from 8.47 to 5.52 in the four days between September 1
and September 5. Financial institutions responded quickly to these
looser monetary conditions by increasing lending.[61] These expansionary measures reinforced the fiscal expansion in the 1999 budget and
protected the interests of fixed capital by still further easing economic
conditions.[62]

From the perspective of the Malay masses, consistently loose monetary conditions can have costs. While they can protect employment by
ensuring that firms do not collapse as the result of economic hardship,
another consequence is inflation. Indeed, inflation in Malaysia was a
particular concern for the Malay poor, for whose consumption baskets
imported food composed a large proportion.[63] It is clear from consumer
groups' complaints that inflation was a key concern.[64] Figure 5.2 plots
consumer prices for Peninsular Malaysia along with wholesale producer
prices.

The data show that in contrast to Indonesia, where both indices
increased dramatically during the final months of Soeharto's reign,
Malaysian policy makers avoided rapid inflation. This was accomplished
both through the ringgit peg, which limited imported inflation, and
through aggressive pricing policies. Nevertheless, throughout the crisis,
policy makers recognized the possible inflationary consequences of loose
monetary policy, responded to labor's demands for lower prices, and

[58] *Business Times* (Malaysia), August 29, 1998; *New Straits Times*, August 29, 1998.
[59] See, e.g., Hwang 2003, 304.
[60] *Utusan Malaysia*, September 2, 1998.
[61] *New Straits Times*, November 4, 1998; *Business Times* (Malaysia), November 20, 1998.
[62] Jomo 2003, 151, 90.
[63] Ishak 2003; Jomo and Lee 2001.
[64] *Mingguan Malaysia*, December 7, 1997; *Utusan Malaysia*, March 10, 1998.

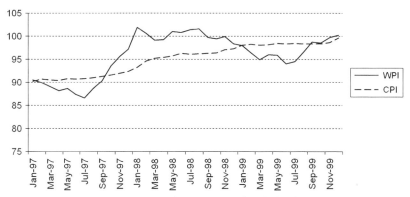

FIGURE 5.2. Consumer Price Index (CPI) and Wholesale Price Index (WPI), January 1997–December 1999 (2000 = 100). *Source:* Calculated from International Monetary Fund 2007.

sought interest rates that gave a sufficient monetary stimulus without an excessive inflationary impact.[65]

Finance and Corporate Policy

Budget allocations, pricing policies, and interest rate levels are vital tools for easing the adjustment costs of connected groups, but they are coarse. Financial and corporate policies adopted during the crisis targeted particular connected firms. As a measure of the financial turmoil in Malaysia during the crisis, Figure 5.3 charts the development of the KLSE Composite Index during the crisis.

The collapse in Malaysian stock prices was swift and severe. Between its peak in late February 1997 and its trough in early September 1998, the index tumbled from 1,271.57 to 262.7, a stunning 79.3 percent decrease. This decrease was the result of the heavy sell-off of Malaysian stocks during the crisis, as well as the stock speculation that so infuriated Mahathir, as investors bet against the KLSE. It is no accident that stock prices bottomed out in late August 1998.

While capital controls did not arrive until early September 1998, already by late summer 1997 the regime had considered measures to protect stock prices. On August 28, 1997, Mahathir announced the "designation" of one hundred heavily traded stocks on the KLSE. Designation prevented speculation by requiring immediate delivery of cash for stock purchases, in return for actual scrip, in contrast to the former practice of

[65] *Utusan Malaysia*, May 5, 1998; *New Straits Times*, October 17, 1998.

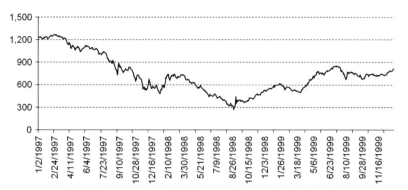

FIGURE 5.3. Kuala Lumpur Stock Exchange Composite Index, January 1997–December 1999. *Source:* Bank Negara Malaysia.

settling accounts at the end of each day. This decision was deeply unpopular with traders, who responded either by simply selling all of their shares or by using the futures market, where such restrictions did not exist.[66] Such tactics forced the authorities to lift this designation the next day.

The regime's next attempt at protecting share prices was even more interventionist. In early September, Mahathir announced that the government's strategic investment arm Khazanah Nasional would marshal RM30 million of public funds to purchase shares in "strategically important" firms from local investors at above-market prices. Among the beneficiaries were government-linked financial institutions such as Maybank Bhd, Arab-Malaysian Merchant Bank Bhd, RHB Bank, and Commerce Asset-Holdings Bhd.[67] An additional RM30 million would come from other state sources, including the state-owned pension fund, the Employees Provident Fund (EPF), and PNB. In doing so, the government hoped to strengthen these firms' financial positions; predictably, many observers considered this move to be a blatant attempt to save politically connected firms from market discipline.[68] The result was a further sell-off in stocks, the result of foreign investors' perceptions growing steadily negative about the regime's desire to address fundamental imbalances in the country's economy.

With the end of capital inflows and subsequent capital outflows came a collapse of the property market, and with it a sharp rise in NPLs. Estimates of the ratio of NPLs to total lending vary, with J. P. Morgan

[66] Gill 1998, 56; MacIntyre 2001, 107; Ram 1997b, 4.
[67] *Utusan Malaysia*, September 20, 1997.
[68] *Asian Wall Street Journal*, September 5, 1997.

estimating 15–25 percent of all loans, Standard and Poor's 20 percent, and others estimating as much as 30 percent.[69] These created a credit squeeze that further harmed all businesses – but, in particular, those with heavy government connections.[70] Most NPLs, for example, arose in government-owned or government-controlled financial institutions, including giants Bank Bumiputra Malaysia Bhd (BBMB), Sime Bank, and Malayan Banking.[71] Banking and corporate difficulties were especially acute for stocks heavily subscribed by *bumiputras*.[72] By summer 1998, among *bumiputra*-owned companies with shares distributed by the Ministry of Trade and Industry – a common method for using the corporate sector to distribute patronage – seventy-six of eighty-two had share prices below their initial public offering.[73]

As with monetary and fiscal policies, the regime's initial responses were consistent with IMF orthodoxy. In October 1997 the regime forbade lending to the property sector, with the exception of low-income housing purchases.[74] Near the end of 1997, the government implemented deposit guarantees to prevent bank runs and a flight from small, vulnerable financial institutions to larger ones.[75] As was the case with Indonesia, though, deposit guarantees during financial panic effectively nationalized the banking sector's difficulties, with the government now forced to bail out vulnerable financial institutions. Finally, starting on January 1, 1998, BNM reclassified NPLs, from six months in arrears to three months.[76] Doing so tightened financial supervision by more accurately reflecting the extent of problem debt. Each move also effectively tightened the country's macroeconomic stance.

Backtracking on these tighter financial regulations began almost immediately, despite Anwar's pledge not to direct any financial institutions to make loans for political purposes and a stern warning to banks to lend only to firms experiencing temporary cash-flow problems.[77] Poor investor reactions to the earlier use of Khazanah funds to bail out connected firms did not prevent the regime from embarking

---

[69] *Far Eastern Economic Review*, March 5, 1998; Berg 1999, 8.
[70] Athukorala 2001, 67–68; Gomez and Jomo 1999b, 195; Navaratnam 1999, 41; Ng 2001, 176–77; Tan 2003; Yap 2001, 51.
[71] Gomez 2002, 102; Gomez and Jomo 1999b, 193; Rustam 2004, 282–84.
[72] Mahani 2002, 90; National Economic Action Council 1998, 111.
[73] *Business Times* (Malaysia), June 22, 1998.
[74] *Utusan Malaysia*, December 22, 1997.
[75] Bank Negara Malaysia 1999, 189.
[76] Bank Negara Malaysia 1999, 202.
[77] *Berita Harian*, November 26, 1997; *Utusan Malaysia*, December 6, 1997.

on a wide range of similar practices in the subsequent year. In fact, allocations of funds from government-owned entities to UMNO-affiliated fixed capital became more open. The best-known transaction involved the use of EPF funds to bolster United Engineers (Malaysia) Berhad (UEM), a firm under the corporate control of Daim's protégé Halim Saad.[78] The deal came through a proposal to purchase a stake in UEM's North-South Highway Project, a wholly owned subsidiary.[79] Earlier, in November 1997, UEM had borrowed heavily to purchase shares of its parent company Renong at far-above market value, paying RM3.24 for shares trading at RM1.90.[80] Renong was widely understood to be the main holding company for UMNO's corporate assets, and additionally the groups that sold the shares at inflated prices themselves had corporate ties to Halim as well.[81] The complex set of maneuvers that allowed UEM to engineer this reverse takeover of Renong violated several investment laws.[82] Just when the outcry over the UEM-Renong purchase had died down, news of UEM's crippling debt became public.

Beyond UEM-Renong, additional EPF funds went to buy shares of Sime Darby, despite a clear conflict of interest where the CEO of its subsidiary Sime Bank sat on the board that made decisions about the entities in which EPF would invest. Sime Bank posted an RM1.8 billion loss in early March 1998.[83] In spring 1998, the government allowed RHB Bank, whose founder Rashid Hussain had strong corporate links to Daim, to take over Sime's troubled banking subsidiary. By late April, when the Sime Bank takeover was complete, EPF had an 11.1 percent stake in RHB Bank's parent company, Rashid Hussain Bhd, despite Anwar's insistence that EPF funds had not been involved in the deal.[84] Additional support for Rashid Hussain Bhd came from another government-run pension fund, Kumpulan Wang Amanah Pencen.[85] Ultimately, the UMNO cooperative Koperasi Usaha Bersatu (KUB) profited disproportionately from the sale

---

[78] Hilley 2001; Lim 1998b; Perkins and Woo 2000, 239.
[79] *Business Times* (Malaysia), March 25, 1998; *Far Eastern Economic Review*, April 30, 1998.
[80] *Asian Wall Street Journal*, November 19, 1997; Lim 1998a, 187.
[81] *Asian Wall Street Journal*, November 28, 1997.
[82] *Straits Times*, November 20, 1997; *Asian Wall Street Journal*, January 12, 1998; Jomo 1998, 187.
[83] Lim 1998b, 6; 1998c; Yap 2001; *Business Times* (Malaysia), March 21, 1998.
[84] *Utusan Malaysia*, March 4, 1998; *New Sunday Times*, April 12, 1998; *Business Times* (Malaysia), April 24, 1998.
[85] *Straits Times*, April 24, 1998.

of Sime Bank, in which KUB had a minority share, and the subsequent discounted purchase of the government-owned Malaysian Mining Corporation.[86] These two moves in one fell swoop eliminated much of KUB's unprofitable liabilities in favor of profitable assets, for the benefit of UMNO.

Bank Bumiputra Malaysia Berhad's mounting debt problem presented another problem for the regime. A government-owned bank founded in 1965 to channel loans and investment toward *bumiputras*, BBMB had been involved in high-profile corporate scandals in the 1980s necessitating bailouts from Petronas.[87] BBMB weathered the political fallout from these bailouts to become Malaysia's second largest bank by 1997, but by early 1998 had run into severe loan gearing problems. To stay afloat, BBMB required a cash injection estimated by the government at RM750 million in early March 1998, but the actual amount eventually reached far higher.[88] Financial sector adjustment packages allowed the government to inject funds into BBMB for its third bailout in fifteen years, but instead of using these new bank recapitalization facilities, the regime adopted a different strategy. First, ignoring BBMB's heavy NPL burden, Khazanah purchased RM400 million of BBMB shares in late August 1998.[89] Second, BBMB merged with Commerce Asset-Holdings Bhd, with CAHB purchasing BBMB stocks and issuing shares directly to Khazanah and the Ministry of Finance. CAHB's major stakeholders included none other than Renong and EPF.[90]

Government-run institutional investors were not the only sources of bailouts. Petronas, the national petroleum firm, purchased and injected cash into other UMNO associates. Perhaps most egregious was the use of Petronas funds to support Konsortium Perkapalan Berhad (KPB), a shipping company that was majority-owned by Mahathir's first son Mirzan, through an indirect set of transactions.[91] Under the leadership of Petronas's president and CEO Hassan Marican, a third party (Malaysian International Shipping Corporation, for whom Hassan also served as chairman) purchased a Petronas subsidiary and used those funds to purchase KPB, thereby relieving Mirzan of the vast majority of KPB's extensive debts.[92]

---

[86] *Business Times* (Malaysia), March 18, 1998.
[87] Jomo and Gomez 2000, 280; Lim 1986, 38.
[88] *Asian Wall Street Journal*, March 4, 1998; *New Straits Times*, March 5, 1998.
[89] *New Straits Times*, September 19, 1998.
[90] *Business Times* (Malaysia), September 21, 1998; *New Straits Times*, September 25, 1998, Gomez 2004a, 164–65.
[91] Lim 1998b.
[92] *New Straits Times*, March 7, 1998; *Asian Wall Street Journal*, March 9, 1998.

Mahathir denied any involvement in the deal even as critics called for an independent valuation of KPB's businesses, but the use of public funds to rescue his son's failing business demonstrated how profits from fixed capital assets (in this case, petroleum) could protect the interests of allied fixed capital.[93]

After having extended RM34 billion to domestic financial institutions without an overall improvement in bank solvency, the NEAC decided upon a more systematic approach to financial sector troubles.[94] In the summer of 1998, the regime created three new bodies to address banking and corporate sector problems.[95] Pengurusan Danaharta Nasional Berhad (Danaharta), under the Ministry of Finance, purchased NPLs from domestic financial institutions and then worked to maximize loan recovery from borrowers. Complementing Danaharta under BNM was Danamodal Nasional Berhad (Danamodal), which injected capital into illiquid or insolvent financial institutions to forestall their collapse. Finally, the Corporate Debt Restructuring Committee (CDRC) provided institutional support for negotiations between creditors and debtors. Initially, the regime attempted to raise U.S.$2 billion in bonds on foreign markets to fund Danaharta and Danamodal but found no subscribers.[96] Yet the regime pushed ahead with the plans, raising money instead through domestic sources such as EPF and Khazanah and planning to raise additional sources through the World Bank and Asian Development Bank. By the end of 2000, Danaharta had taken possession of RM47.5 billion worth of NPLs.[97]

Successful economic recovery has encouraged the regime to promote Danaharta, Danamodal, and the CDRC as prudent managers of the country's financial problems.[98] Yet observers questioned the propriety of these loan purchases and recapitalization exercises given Malaysia's history of political interference in the financial sector.[99] Of the RM47.5 billion in NPLs managed by Danaharta, more than half (RM27.1 billion) came from Sime Bank and BBMB alone.[100] Others are financial

---

[93] Pillay 1998.

[94] Bank Negara Malaysia 1999, 177.

[95] Athukorala 2001, 67; Bank Negara Malaysia 1999, 220–25; Mahani 2002, 147–71.

[96] *Asian Wall Street Journal*, July 27, 1998.

[97] *New Sunday Times*, August 9, 1998; *New Straits Times*, August 22, 1998; Mahani 2002, 150.

[98] See, e.g., Danaharta 2005; Mahani 2002.

[99] Interview with an anonymous Malaysian economist, April 2005; interview with Lim Kit Siang, former secretary-general of the Democratic Action Party, July 12, 2006; *New Straits Times,* July 15, 1998; Gomez and Jomo 1999b, 197.

[100] Mahani 2002, 150.

institutions previously shown to have benefited from government re-sources (BBMB, Sime Bank), as well as those linked to UMNO's corporate allies, such as Tunku Abdullah's MBf Holdings and Azman Hashim's Arab-Malaysian Group. Also questionable were the opaque procedures for deciding which banks would benefit from loan relief and recapital-ization, and the CDRC's negotiation procedures that invited abuse by firms such as Renong.[101]

The use of public funds to bail out fixed capital still facing problems continued after the imposition of capital controls.[102] In early October, the regime issued an RM10.5 billion bond to facilitate Renong and UEM's debt repayments.[103] The following year saw the effective renationaliza-tion of Malaysia Airlines, under the control of another of Daim's pro-tégés, Tajudin Ramli, through a stock purchase that paid RM8 for shares trading at around RM3. The airline company had posted RM669.7 million in losses for the year ending March 31, 1999, and the purchase gave Tajudin a healthy return after the buyout of his 29.09 percent stake.[104] A similar transaction, once again using EPF resources, bought out Halim Saad's stakes in Timedotcom.[105] Also in 1999, Petronas rescued Proton, to the tune of RM1 billion. Proton sales had lagged since 1998, and the deal created some consternation among large minority shareholders in Proton, such as Japan's Mitsubishi Corp.[106] In each of these rescue pack-ages, fixed capital is the beneficiary, and political links to the executive are clear.

Changes in a number of policies concerning financial regulation com-plemented corporate bailouts. In late spring 1998, the regime lifted the legal lending limits for housing (already exempted from previous lending restrictions) and automobiles.[107] Later, in the summer of 1998, the gov-ernment reversed the January initiative on NPLs, returning to the pre-vious standard of six months in arrears.[108] Statutory reserve requirements were lowered steadily from 13.5 to 10.0 percent in February and

---

[101] Felker 2000, 56–57; Yap 2001, 54.
[102] Anonymous interview with a Malaysian journalist, July 2006; anonymous interview with a Chinese Malaysian opposition party worker, July 2006.
[103] *Utusan Malaysia*, October 10, 1998.
[104] *Business Times* (Malaysia), June 9, 1999; *Far Eastern Economic Review*, December 7, 2000.
[105] *Straits Times*, May 23, 2001; *Asian Wall Street Journal*, June 21, 2001; Salazar 2004, 288.
[106] *New Straits Times*, August 26, 1999; *Asian Wall Street Journal*, August 6, 1999.
[107] *Utusan Malaysia*, April 15, 1998.
[108] Bank Negara Malaysia 1999, 203.

ultimately to 4.0 percent by September 16. The regime also increased the .5 percent reserve variability limit to 2 percent.[109] Earlier ceilings on lending for property investment or for stock market purchases were raised, and the regime directed financial institutions to achieve a minimum of 8 percent growth of loans for 1998.[110] These measures boosted liquidity in the financial system while increasing the amount of time that loans could remain in arrears. Several additional campaigns promoted lending toward low-income groups, which had the effect of targeting the Malay poor.[111]

Two other facets of financial and corporate adjustment policy are worth noting. One plan that attracted some attention in 1999 was Mahathir's plan to consolidate the country's many financial institutions into six "anchor" banks.[112] Amid economic recovery and some opposition, nothing came to pass. Another was the temporary relaxation of *bumiputra* equity requirements in the Malaysian corporate sector. With the tight liquidity conditions prevailing in Malaysia by 1998, the regime seized upon the untapped potential of non-Malay investment capital to shore up enterprises that could not raise sufficient financing from Malay sources.[113] It later relaxed temporarily requirements for foreign firms as well in order to encourage capital inflows.[114] Yet, despite this encouraging sign of liberalization, the regime retained tight control over these share issues to non-Malays, ensuring that the primary beneficiaries were in fact Chinese Malaysian holders of fixed capital who had long possessed strong UMNO links.[115]

These corporate and financial sector policies minimized the adjustment costs borne by fixed capital holders and targeted those connected to Mahathir, Daim, and the BN in general. Firms such as UEM, Renong, KPB, Malaysia Airlines, and Proton are industrial enterprises rooted in Malaysia. Unable simply to redeploy capital assets overseas into investments with higher returns, they required the regime's assistance to remain viable. Analyses of share prices in the wake of capital controls and Anwar's sacking, in fact, show that firms with overt connections to

---

[109] *Utusan Malaysia*, May 1, 1998.
[110] *New Straits Times*, September 2, 1998; *Utusan Malaysia*, September 24, 1998; *Asian Wall Street Journal*, September 10, 1998; *Business Times* (Malaysia), September 14, 1998.
[111] Athukorala 2001, 79–80.
[112] Chin and Jomo 2001, 127.
[113] *Asian Wall Street Journal*, February 26, 1998; *Utusan Malaysia*, February 26, 1998.
[114] *Straits Times*, July 24, 1998.
[115] Gomez 2002, 103–4.

Mahathir and Daim systematically outperformed unconnected firms.[116] But this is only part of the story of the regime's corporate and financial policy adjustments. The BN regime relied on the support of the Malay masses in addition to the support of Malay cronies, and the heavy government favoritism shown to corporate leaders could have generated a populist backlash without clear evidence that ordinary Malays profited from the regime's corporate and financial policy maneuvering. For this reason, pressure on the government to protect the Malay masses remained high; factions within UMNO articulated this pressure consistently throughout the crisis.[117]

The primary tool through which corporate and financial policies directly affect ordinary Malays is government-held *bumiputra*-only unit trusts. Returns for the two schemes over the previous fifteen years had averaged around 15 percent, making them an excellent investment for ordinary Malays without large cash savings. Not surprisingly, the value of these pooled stock market investments remained a politically charged topic throughout the crisis.[118] The regime ensured that whatever the state of the country's stock markets, the dividends of the two largest *bumiputra*-only unit trusts, ASN and ASB, remained high. At the onset of the crisis, the regime tapped excess Malay investment power by increasing the amount of funds that each individual could place in either scheme, from RM100,000 to RM200,000.[119] Throughout the crisis, officials such as Deputy Finance Minister Affifudin Omar urged Malays to invest any excess funds in the schemes.[120] By the end of October 1997, ASN traded at below RM1 per share, its lowest price ever, leading to warnings that dividends of 13.75 percent would be impossible.[121] In the end, ASB declared an 11.5 percent payout for 1997, down only 1.75 percent from 1996, which Mahathir stressed was an identical dividend payment (10.25 percent) with a cut only in the fund's yearly bonus. Officials also emphasized that the total cash value of the payment, RM3.3 billion, actually exceeded that of the previous year.[122] ASN's 1997 dividend was 10.5 percent, down from 13.75 percent in 1996. While this was a more

---

[116] Johnson and Mitton 2003.
[117] See, e.g., *Utusan Malaysia*, April 24, 1998.
[118] Anonymous interview with a Malaysian economist, April 2005; *Business Times* (Malaysia), September 8, 1997; *Utusan Malaysia*, November 10, 1997.
[119] *Utusan Malaysia*, September 15, 1997.
[120] *New Straits Times*, December 8, 1997; *Business Times* (Malaysia), July 23, 1998.
[121] *Utusan Malaysia*, November 14, 1997.
[122] *Business Times* (Malaysia), December 13, 1997.

significant drop, the chairman of Permodalan Nasional Berhad (ASN's manager) Ahmad Sarji Abdul Hamid stressed that ASN's dividend represented very healthy returns given the state of the KLSE.[123]

Although both ASN and ASB declared lower returns in 1997, it is important to stress that dividends of more than 10 percent meant that both funds remained excellent investment opportunities for Malays in a period of increasing financial turmoil. Another saving scheme that pooled Malay funds for capital market investments and was designed to help Muslims save for the pilgrimage to Mecca, Tabung Haji, declared a 9.5 percent dividend in 1997, identical to 1996.[124] During the subsequent year, UMNO leaders sought to create still more investment opportunities for Malays, including a fund for women that pooled resources from women in UMNO and other BN component parties.[125] Throughout the rest of 1998, the government urged *bumiputras* to increase their investments in ASN and ASB, as well as to invest further in the panethnic government unit trust Amanah Saham Wawasan 2020 (ASW).[126] ASW announced a 9.8 percent dividend in mid-August 1998, down only slightly from 10.1 percent the previous year.[127] At the close of 1998, ASB announced 10.5 percent total payouts,[128] again representing a very healthy profit in a year where financial sector upheaval caused the country's gross domestic product to contract by more than 8 percent.

The contrast between ASN/ASB's relatively high dividends and the more disappointing performance of EPF savings is instructive and reveals the regime's efforts to target its Malay constituency. EPF invests funds from all Malaysians, not only *bumiputras*, as the ASN/ASB trusts do. As early as October 1997, opposition parties and NGOs complained about the use of EPF funds to bail out cronies, and by March of the following year, DAP head Lim Kit Siang began to rally opposition politicians to question EPF funds being lent to KPB, UEM, Sime, and others.[129] Amid the transactions that funneled EPF funds to vulnerable firms, the regime continually stressed that EPF dividends were safe.[130] When the fund announced only a 6.5 percent dividend in March 1998, Mahathir

---

[123] *New Straits Times*, December 20, 1997.
[124] *Utusan Malaysia*, December 23, 1997.
[125] *New Straits Times*, February 12, 1998; *Business Times* (Malaysia), April 28, 1998.
[126] *Berita Harian*, May 29, 1998; *New Straits Times*, June 3, 1998.
[127] *New Straits Times*, August 15, 1998.
[128] *Berita Harian*, December 11, 1998.
[129] *Utusan Malaysia*, October 17, 1997; *Business Times* (Malaysia), March 24, 1998.
[130] *Berita Harian*, February 2, 1998.

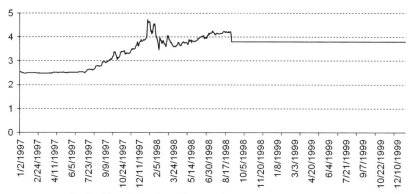

FIGURE 5.4. Daily Ringgit–U.S. Dollar Exchange Rate, January 1997–December 1999. *Source:* Bank Negara Malaysia.

deflected criticism from Lim that the government played favorites with its unit trust schemes, while Anwar assured pension fund holders that their deposits in EPF benefited from the regime's guarantee.[131]

Exchange Rate and Capital Account Policy

With tight liquidity conditions causing hardship for Malaysian firms, demand for expansionary policies was high, but such policies would further ringgit depreciation. Figure 5.4 plots the nominal ringgit–U.S. dollar exchange rate from the beginning of 1997 through 1999. Mirroring the performance of the KLSE, the ringgit's depreciation is steep and sudden. Following the ringgit float on July 14, 1997, its decline continued steadily throughout the rest of 1997, with a temporary spike in depreciation rates in winter 1998 amid the first signs of political strife between Mahathir and Anwar. Thereafter, the ringgit resumed its steady depreciation until the ringgit's peg was at RM3.80 to the U.S. dollar. The ringgit would remain pegged to the U.S. dollar throughout the remainder of the crisis.

Malaysia differed from Indonesia in the intensity of its initial currency defense. The regime initially defended the ringgit by intervening in the foreign exchange market, spending approximately 12 percent of its foreign reserves between June 30 and July 15.[132] The defense proved

[131] *Utusan Malaysia*, March 6, 1998; March 28, 1998; Lim 1998c.
[132] *Asian Wall Street Journal*, July 27, 1997.

unsuccessful, prompting the July 14 decision to float the ringgit. The announcement of a ringgit float did not completely end the use of reserves; not until August 12 did Anwar and Mahathir publicly vow that they would no longer attempt to save the ringgit.[133] Even through early 1998, there were signals that BNM still had a hand in managing the ringgit.[134]

Other policy measures attempted to clamp down on ringgit speculation more directly. On August 3, 1998, BNM limited foreigners' access to the ringgit by banning swap deals unrelated to commercial transactions valued at more than U.S.$2 million. Doing so gave the ringgit a temporary respite, but the interventionist move had negative repercussions in the KLSE. Holders of mobile capital, both domestic and foreign, now unable to employ forward ringgit contracts to hedge their exchange risk, simply divested their holdings.[135] Moreover, the brisk ringgit trade in offshore markets meant that restrictions in Malaysia had little effect on many speculators' daily activities.[136]

Also notable during the initial months of Malaysia's crisis were Mahathir's public outbursts against currency speculators. Unlike Indonesia's Soeharto, who remained out of the public eye throughout the crisis, Mahathir earned widespread condemnation from international observers for his increasingly virulent tirades against what he perceived to be the enemies of Malaysia's economy.[137] For a time, he seized in particular upon George Soros, proclaiming to have "proof" that the American financier had systematically engaged in ringgit manipulation to punish Malaysia for supporting Myanmar's accession to the Association of Southeast Asian Nations.[138] Periodically, Mahathir and other leaders gave cryptic warnings to mobile capital not to sabotage the economy.[139] Most notably, while delivering a keynote speech at a joint World Bank–IMF meeting in Hong Kong on September 20, Mahathir suggested that countries should eliminate capital movements, stating that "currency trading is unnecessary, unproductive, and immoral" and calling for

---

[133] *Asian Wall Street Journal*, August 16, 1997; Gill 1998, 39–40.
[134] *Berita Harian*, January 8, 1998.
[135] *Utusan Malaysia*, August 4, 1997; *Business Times* (Malaysia), August 4, 1997; Gill 1998, 37; Ram 1997b.
[136] *Asian Wall Street Journal*, August 5, 1997.
[137] *Utusan Malaysia*, July 22, 1997; June 13, 1998; *Far Eastern Economic Review*, October 2, 1997.
[138] *Mingguan Malaysia*, July 27, 1997; *Business Times* (Malaysia), November 3, 1997.
[139] *Business Times* (Malaysia), July 30, 1997.

countries to make it illegal.[140] Two weeks later, while addressing the Pacific Economic Cooperation Council in Chile, he suggested that governments should regulate currency trading if they cannot ban it.[141] Mahathir's tirades, however, only pushed the ringgit further down against the dollar.

As in Indonesia, currency depreciation alone could in principle have helped the economy by improving the terms of trade for the country's large export sector. As early as August 1997, though, observers worried that depreciation's trade-enhancing effects might be masked by its other effects. These would include inflation, share price declines, and the foreign exchange losses through increasingly expensive foreign-denominated debt.[142] Data on Malaysia's export performance from 1997 to 1999 make it clear that even the anticipated export boom did not come to pass (Table 5.5).

Overall, Malaysia's export receipts shrank by almost 7 percent in 1998, although in ringgit terms exports grew slightly. The only commodity classification that experienced growth was animal and vegetable oils and fats, driven by the rise in palm oil exports – palm oil being denominated in ringgit rather than dollars, as are other export commodities. The explanations are similar to explanations for Indonesia's poor export performance during the crisis: competitive devaluations in regional competitors, exchange rate uncertainty, decreased foreign and regional demand for Malaysian products, and increased import costs for dollar-denominated inputs to finished exports.[143]

While the ringgit continued to plummet through late 1997 and 1998, Mahathir and other regime leaders embarked on two types of strategies in order to stem the ringgit's fall. The first strategy was a campaign of moral suasion, closely paralleling similar tactics in Indonesia, urging Malaysians to take steps to minimize the ringgit's depreciation. This included calls in Chinese-language dailies for citizens to stop ringgit speculation and later the Love Malaysia campaign, encouraging citizens to buy local products.[144] Fixed capital played a large role in the direction of moral suasion campaigns. The Love Malaysia campaign began on the efforts of Lee Kim

---

[140] Mahathir 1998a, 25.
[141] *Asian Wall Street Journal*, October 2, 1997.
[142] *Asian Wall Street Journal*, August 27, 1997; anonymous interview with a Malaysian economist, July 2006; Pillay 1997.
[143] Athukorala 2001, 68; Bank Negara Malaysia 1999, 578–82; Gomez and Jomo 1999b, 197; Yap 2001, 51.
[144] *Utusan Malaysia*, September 4, 1997; Athukorala 1998a, 96; Mahani 2002, 75.

TABLE 5.5. *Malaysian Exports by Commodity Type, 1997 and 1998*

Commodity Type	Value^a		
	1997	1998	Percent Change
Food	1,885.7	1,580.3	−16.20
Beverages and tobacco	265.5	235.8	−11.19
Crude materials, inedible	3,591.0	2,379.3	−33.74
Mineral fuels, lubricants, etc.	6,378.5	4,503.0	−29.40
Animal and vegetable oils and fats	4,621.1	5,452.9	18.00
Chemicals	2,800.4	2,542.8	−9.20
Manufactured goods	7,063.3	6,079.4	−13.93
Machinery and transport equipment	44,072.3	43,282.9	−1.79
Miscellaneous manufactured articles	6,869.6	6,343.6	−7.66
Miscellaneous transactions and commodities	972.1	697.9	−28.20
TOTAL	78,519.3	73,103.0	−6.90

^{a} Millions of U.S. dollars, F.O.B.
Source: Calculated from Jabatan Perangkaan 1999, 167.

Yew, whose property development firm Country Heights Holdings Bhd had recently opened the luxurious Mines Resort City outside of Kuala Lumpur.[145] The campaign quickly became a government favorite, eventually spawning the Buy Malaysia campaign. In early January 1998, Mahathir requested Malaysians to sell overseas property holdings and repatriate the proceeds while refraining from making currency deposits overseas.[146]

The second strategy involved policy adjustments to encourage capital inflows. With the property sector floundering, the regime lifted the tax on property ownership for foreign individuals, hoping to inject fresh capital into the property market while helping the ringgit.[147] To encourage the return of mobile capital assets to Malaysia, the regime eased taxes on repatriated capital.[148] Similarly, recognizing that ethnic Chinese entrepreneurs composed a large proportion of the country's domestic mobile

[145] *New Straits Times*, December 2, 1997.
[146] *Business Times* (Malaysia), January 10, 1998. Lim 1998a, 51.
[147] *Utusan Malaysia*, August 28, 1997; *Asian Wall Street Journal*, September 8, 1997; Ram 1997b.
[148] *Utusan Malaysia*, May 19, 1998; *Straits Times*, May 21, 1998.

TABLE 5.6. *Quarterly Investment Flows, 1997–1998 (millions of ringgit)*

	Portfolio Investment		Foreign Direct Investment	
	Receipts	Net Inflows	Receipts	Net Inflows
1997 Q1	47,431	5,647	1,180	−750
1997 Q2	41,793	−8,584	1,674	−185
1997 Q3	39,614	−16,000	1,355	−30
1997 Q4	27,317	−5,492	1,739	−246
1998 Q1	27,005	5,596	978	−166
1998 Q2	12,284	−3,275	1,106	−287
1998 Q3	8,918	−3,669	913	−876
1998 Q4	5,652	−717	2,946	−1,797

Source: Jomo 2001b, 139.

capital, temporary suspension of *bumiputra* equity requirements in the corporate sector attempted to entice it back into the country. None of these measures had its desired effect, and the year following September 1997 witnessed massive capital outflows, a large proportion of which flowed across the Johor Strait to Singapore.[149] The figures in Table 5.6, while not capturing the direction of outflows, make apparent the extent of the foreign investment reversal.

The data reveal not only the extent of net capital outflows in 1997 but also the comparative severity of the portfolio investment crunch as compared to the reversal in foreign direct investment. As compared to 1998, the sum of net outflows of portfolio investment in 1997 had declined, but this was due to the smaller total amount available to flow out, captured by dwindling receipts in that year.

The regime was unwilling to contract the economy because of strong pressures from fixed capital and labor – the Malay masses – for accommodating monetary policies. Likewise, spending cuts were deeply unpopular among holders of both fixed and mobile capital. Hence, the regime seized upon international economic policies to facilitate economic recovery. Mahani Zainal Abidin, an economist who served on the NEAC's Working Group, writes in her memoirs that members of the NEAC had considered pegging the currency as early as February 1998, at a period when net outflows of hot money had temporarily ceased, but that for the next seven months the specifics of that plan and the idea of capital account restrictions remained a tightly guarded secret.[150] There were,

[149] Athukorala 2001, 69–71.
[150] Mahani 2002, 109, 21–23.

TABLE 5.7. *Regulations on Capital Account Transactions, September 1, 1998*

Banned	Requires Government Approval	Unaffected
Transport of ringgit currency in excess of RM1,000 by all individuals	Overseas investment greater than RM10,000 by Malaysians	Outflows of dividends and profits from portfolio investment
Transport of foreign currency in excess of RM10,000 by Malaysians	Credit in ringgit from nonresident sources	Inflows of portfolio investment
Outflows of portfolio investment principal (for one year)		Inflows or outflows of foreign direct investment
Domestic ringgit trade by foreign financial institutions		Current account transactions (imports and exports)
Overseas trade in ringgit (effective September 30)		

however, signs in the domestic and international presses that Malaysian policy makers were contemplating radical adjustment measures. KLSE executive chairman Mohd. Azlan Hashim, for instance, had urged the regime to find a way to control speculation and overseas stock trading by mobile capital.[151] By the time of the June UMNO General Assembly meeting, Mahathir was discussing a series of steps (that he would not name) to protect the ringgit and expand the economy, noting that he and the NEAC were deeply troubled by continued capital outflows, which had by then resumed.[152]

The plan ultimately implemented combined a number of particular legal restrictions on capital outflows and overseas ringgit transactions with guarantees and reassurances about transactions that would remain legal.[153] The specifics are important (Table 5.7).

The first component of the capital controls package arrived on August 31, 1998, with the deregistration of the Central Limit Order Book

---

[151] *Utusan Malaysia*, March 23, 1998.
[152] *Business Times* (Malaysia), June 26, 1998; *Mingguan Malaysia*, June 28, 1998.
[153] Athukorala 2001, 76–78; Bank Negara Malaysia 1999, 279–93, 329–31; Haggard 2000b, 73–85; Mahani 2002, 117–21.

(CLOB), a shadow market for Malaysian securities located in Singapore. The status of the CLOB, created in 1990 when stock markets of Malaysia and Singapore formally split, had for years been a source of tension between the two countries. Earlier in August, Malaysia had requested that the Singapore Stock Exchange close the CLOB, with no effect. The freeze in share trading on the CLOB eliminated a lucrative pathway through which stock traders could purchase their shares in Malaysia and sell them in Singapore – collecting the proceeds in Singaporean dollars.[154] Targeting mobile capital, the CLOB's deregistration would, in Mohd. Azlan's words, "bring back Malaysian shares to Malaysia."[155] Without legal recognition of transactions made on the CLOB, traders had no option but to return to the KLSE. Within days, the KLSE showed signs of improvement as overseas holders of Malaysian shares rushed back into Malaysia.[156]

The next step, announced on September 1, 1998, was a selective ban on capital outflows along with an exchange rate peg of RM3.80 to the U.S. dollar. The regime publicly linked the controls to its desire to lower interest rates while combating harmful stock and currency speculation.[157] The ban on capital outflows, however, made no reference to capital *inflows* or current account transactions. Nor did the regime impede foreign direct investment. In fact, the regime explicitly welcomed capital inflows, to stimulate the economy and reflate the stock market. Moreover, because of the de-internationalization of the ringgit, foreign holders of ringgit assets – the majority of them currency traders or speculators – were forced to repatriate their assets. Immediately following the CLOB's deregistration and the ringgit's de-internationalization, RM10 billion flowed back into the country.[158] The regime's policies thus targeted the most mobile types of mobile capital without fundamentally breaking from Malaysia's long history of economic openness.

In the wake of capital controls, and despite widespread fears from international financial institutions that financial repression would harm Malaysia's economy, Malaysia's economy improved. Whether or not

---

[154] *Straits Times*, August 5, 1998; *Utusan Malaysia*, August 6, 1998; *Asian Wall Street Journal*, September 1, 1998.
[155] *New Straits Times*, September 1, 1998.
[156] *Straits Times*, September 4, 1998.
[157] Group interview with a member of the NEAC Secretariat, May 17, 2005; interview with Mohamed Ariff, executive director of the Malaysian Institute for Economic Research, July 10, 2006; *Utusan Malaysia*, September 2, 1998; *New Straits Times*, September 7, 1998.
[158] Ong 1999, 160.

exchange controls and reflationary macroeconomic policy had a causal role in this recovery – the counterfactual is that Malaysia had simply bottomed out by September 1998, so recovery was inevitable – there is no evidence that heterodox policies harmed Malaysia.[159] Indeed, the capital account restrictions and a pegged exchange rate afforded to Malaysian policy makers the autonomy to enact the reflationary monetary and fiscal policies outlined in this chapter. In other words, regardless of the possibility that Malaysia might have recovered absent capital controls, capital controls allowed the regime to oversee economic recovery on its own terms, by continuing to support fixed capital and the Malay masses rather than by enacting politically devastating subsidy cuts and corporate reforms. Content with the economy's turnaround, in February 1999 the regime tweaked the exchange controls, announcing a system of declining levies on the repatriation of portfolio investment principal to replace the complete ban on capital outflows, with levies decreasing as maturity periods increased. In September 1999 the regime adjusted exchange controls still further, adopting a uniform 10 percent levy on all principal outflows. Capital controls were eliminated altogether in May 2001. The ringgit peg lasted several years longer and was finally relaxed in summer 2005.

What of the political foundations of capital controls? Policy choice and implementation in Malaysia followed political exigencies rather than economic logic. There was some clear opposition to capital controls at home. Among owners of mobile capital, reactions from the international investment community were deeply critical, with Malaysia's credit ratings downgraded still further and the KLSE no longer included among regional stock indexes.[160] Foreign investors lambasted the policies as irrational and harmful.[161] In Singapore, outrage at the regime's restrictions on currency trading was particularly virulent by individuals with cross-border holdings.[162]

Domestically, Mahathir had for months attacked mobile capital.[163] UMNO Youth called for investigations into "unpatriotic" firms moving their investments abroad, in particular to Singapore.[164] In May, the multiethnic Gerakan Party joined the effort, criticizing Chinese mobile capital

---

[159] See Kaplan and Rodrik 2001; Krugman 1999. For opposing views, see, e.g., Boorman et al. 2000, 12.
[160] Haggard 2000b, 84.
[161] *Asian Wall Street Journal*, September 2, 1998; *New Straits Times*, September 5, 1998.
[162] *Straits Times*, September 3, 1998.
[163] *Utusan Malaysia*, January 29, 1998.
[164] *Utusan Malaysia*, March 13, 1998.

for parking funds in Singapore.[165] With capital controls, such investors with the inclination to redeploy assets overseas into more profitable investments – mobile capital – suffered.[166] But often overlooked in the wake of the fall 1998 crackdown on domestic political opponents was opposition to capital controls from the DAP, the largely Chinese opposition party, which criticized bans on capital outflows *despite* the DAP's otherwise social democratic political ideology.[167] BNM officials opposed the plan for more ideological reasons, as they represented one outpost of liberal economic orthodoxy within the regime. Yet BNM officials were unable to gainsay the decisions reached by the NEAC, leading Ahmad Mohd. Don and Fong Weng Phak to resign.

Just as important, the imposition of capital controls with the corresponding exchange rate peg was extremely popular among fixed capital holders and the Malay masses. With controls on capital outflows, the regime was able to implement expansionary policies that favored connected business groups and to continue making targeted subsidies to the Malay masses. These policies not only earned Mahathir and the BN nationalist credentials but also protected key networks of political support and patronage.[168] Exporters, unconcerned with outflows of hot money but harmed by ringgit volatility, explicitly welcomed the exchange rate peg.[169] Fixed capital supported capital controls because of the looser macroeconomic conditions that they enabled the regime to implement and the stability that the exchange rate peg brought.[170] Critically, aside from the DAP with its large ethnic Chinese constituency, other opposition parties competing for Malay votes adopted positions that supported the regime's adjustment policies. While campaigning on issues of social justice and economic reform, they actually *supported* capital controls and the expansionary macroeconomic policy that accompanied them.[171] Given that capital controls preceded Mahathir's sacking of Anwar by only one day (see Chapter 7), controls on capital outflows also served a more

---

[165] *Mingguan Malaysia*, May 10, 1998; *Utusan Malaysia*, May 11, 1998.
[166] Interview with Mohamed Ariff; *New Straits Times*, September 3, 1998; *Straits Times*, September 8, 1998.
[167] Interview with Lim Kit Siang.
[168] Haggard 2000b, 73; Jomo 2001a, 215; see also Toyoda 2001, 102–7.
[169] Mahani 2002, 115.
[170] Interview with Mohamed Ariff; interview with Ramon Navaratnam, president of Transparency International Malaysia., July 17, 2006; anonymous interview with a Malaysian economist, July 2006; *Business Times* (Malaysia), September 3, 1998.
[171] Interview with Anwar Ibrahim; interview with Chandra Muzaffar, former deputy chairman of Parti KeADILan Nasional, July 5, 2006.

tactical purpose, eliminating the possibility of further rounds of currency and stock speculation that might have to accompany the subsequent crackdown against the regime's political opponents. In these ways, capital controls with a fixed exchange rate were the final piece of the regime's adjustment strategy.

Alternative Explanations?

This chapter has argued that Malaysia's economic adjustment policies to the Asian Financial Crisis had a straightforward political logic: protecting the interests of fixed capital and Malay labor. Doing so involved protecting the BN's corporate allies in addition to the Malay masses and deflecting the costs of adjustment toward the (largely ethnic Chinese) owners of mobile capital who had never held the ear of the regime in the way that the Malay masses and the overwhelmingly Malay holders of fixed capital had.

Consistent results across policy domains notwithstanding, there are other potential determinants of adjustment policy in Malaysia. I focus on two prominent alternative explanations for the pattern of adjustment policy found in Malaysia. The first holds that Malaysia's crisis was not serious enough to warrant IMF loans and, accordingly, that Malaysia's relative insulation from international policy pressures enabled the regime to adopt its own preferred policies. The second focuses on Malaysia's relatively well-managed financial sector – free of the overwhelming burden of bad loans that plagued Indonesia – and the implication that the Malaysian regime simply did not face the same policy problems that drove the New Order to collapse. At base, both of these claims challenge my contention that the crises in both countries were fundamentally comparable.

Was Malaysia's crisis shallow enough that the country did not require international lending support, or perhaps that it did not qualify for IMF assistance? By any metric, Malaysia's crisis was severe: the economy contracted nearly 8 percent in 1998 as a direct result of a financial sector crisis. The country certainly "qualified" for IMF assistance given the state of its financial sector, and many international investors called upon Malaysia to accept IMF assistance.[172] Moreover, the regime did seek and obtain foreign financial support throughout the crisis. The regime accepted World Bank loans targeting social spending, U.S.$300 million

---

[172] Athukorala 2001, 74; Lim 1998a, 7, 18–30.

during the summer of 1998 and an additional U.S.$400 million in March 1999.[173] These loans were especially noteworthy because the World Bank had previously ceased operations in Malaysia. The regime also sought and accepted U.S.$2.6 billion in recovery aid directly from the government of Japan through the so-called New Miyazawa Initiative.[174] It is therefore simply untrue that Malaysia's crisis was not severe enough to require support from international donors. Malaysia declined to seek IMF loans because its political leaders feared the conditions that the IMF would place upon their disbursement. As was the case with capital controls, many opposition parties supported Mahathir's resistance of IMF conditionality as well, even as they criticized crony dealings in the corporate and financial sectors.[175] Throughout the crisis, Mahathir warned of the higher interest rates, subsidy cuts, and public-sector wage restrictions that the IMF would mandate.[176] Subsequently, speaking in front of the UMNO General Assembly meeting at the height of the crisis in June 1998, he stressed that the IMF would require Malaysia to suspend the NEP.[177] Speaking several years after the crisis, Mahathir himself confirmed that he did not approach the IMF because of the political implications of IMF conditionality: "If I want to go to the IMF, I know that I will be surrendering the control of our economy. In Malaysia this is not possible as we have Bumiputeras and the non-Bumiputeras."[178] Mahathir's own statements reflect the fundamentally political concerns of the regime's leadership with the IMF's orthodox adjustment policies. The decision to resist IMF loans was itself a part of Malaysia's heterodox adjustment strategy.

The second alternative explanation focuses on the relatively sound financial system in Malaysia and its consequences for adjustment policy. Malaysia's burden of NPLs was far smaller than Indonesia's, because of the relatively consistent enforcement of prudential regulations on direct, short-term, unhedged foreign currency borrowing. Did this comparative lack of loan vulnerability correspond to a freer hand to intervene in macroeconomic policy settings and international monetary relations, as some allege?[179] Almost certainly not. Recall that the same regulatory apparatus

---

[173] *Utusan Malaysia*, July 22, 1998; *Times* (Malaysia), April 3, 1999.
[174] Asian Development Bank 1999.
[175] See, e.g., Syed Husin 1998.
[176] *Utusan Malaysia*, November 29, 1997; July 4, 1998.
[177] Mahathir 1999, 45.
[178] Quoted in Mahani 2002, 275.
[179] E.g., Interview with Mohamed Ariff.

that discouraged direct foreign borrowing encouraged rapid inflows of foreign portfolio capital. Malaysia's ratio of mobile capital to GDP actually exceeded Indonesia's, and stock market capitalization as a percentage of GDP in Malaysia was an order of magnitude higher than in Indonesia. Because portfolio capital played such an important role in Malaysia's economy as compared to the situation in Indonesia, this should have made Malaysia even *less* willing than Indonesia to restrict cross-border capital movements. Only by taking into account the political links between fixed capital and the Malaysian regime, and the political marginalization of holders of mobile capital, can one understand why the regime adopted an adjustment strategy that so clearly ran counter to the interests of mobile capitalists.

The two dominant explanations for Malaysia's heterodox adjustment strategy, which explicitly contrast Malaysia's economic conditions to Indonesia's, yield unsatisfactory explanations of the particular mix of adjustment policies that Malaysia's regime adopted in response to the Asian Financial Crisis. I now move to the second puzzle of this book and show how variation in adjustment policy responses produced different regime outcomes in the two countries.

6

Authoritarian Breakdown in Indonesia

Soeharto resigned from the office of president of Indonesia on May 21, 1998, some ten months after the onset of currency speculation against the rupiah. His resignation signaled the end of the New Order regime and the beginning of a period of transition toward democracy. His successor, B. J. Habibie, who had been serving as vice president, was an aeronautical engineer known more for his nationalist economic ideology and loyalty to Soeharto than for any independent political skill. By the end of 1999, Abdurrahman Wahid (Gus Dur) assumed the country's presidency, and Indonesia's transition to democracy was complete. One of the world's most enduring dictatorships became the world's third most populous democracy.

Yet a firm understanding of why the New Order collapsed as it did, when it did, remains elusive. The theory advanced in Chapter 2 shows how political conflict over adjustment policy drove the breakdown of the New Order. The New Order collapsed because mobile capital – in the Indonesian context, ethnic Chinese *konglomerat* – withdrew its support from the regime. This fracture in the New Order's support coalition took place gradually, during the first six months of 1998, during which time Indonesia saw a dramatic upsurge in anti-Chinese violence. It culminated in anti-Chinese riots during May 13–14, 1998, which drove most of the *konglomerat* overseas. Many factional alignments existed in Indonesia along which the regime might have fractured: capital (mobile and fixed) versus labor, or Muslim versus non-Muslim, or even political Islam ("green") versus secular nationalism ("red and white"). But because twin crises ignite contradictory adjustment policy demands that pit mobile capital against fixed capital and labor, the regime's breakdown reflected this coalitional split.

The benefits to this account are threefold. First, it fits the historical record better than the alternatives. Second, it also assumes no fundamental shift in the nature of the New Order regime with the onset of the economic crisis in Southeast Asia. The same regime that was able to engineer an impressive electoral victory in June 1997, and near unanimous elite support in March 1998, was unable to maintain political power in May 1998. Finally, there are no black boxes in this account, no actors without agency, so that unfolding events did not leave any group unable to behave strategically to fulfill its interests. While the crisis changed the constraints facing the actors, actors behaved rationally given these new constraints. In the end, rioting and opposition protest did not convince Soeharto that the regime was unpopular, nor did they threaten his ability to restore order. Rather, riots drove a key faction of Soeharto's supporters from the country. This account thus links economic crisis to authoritarian collapse through the impossibility of reform acceptable to the regime's supporters.

Ex Ante Unlikely, Ex Post Inevitable

I am not the first to examine the collapse of the New Order. But one problem facing existing research is that, at first glance, the breakdown of the regime in May 1998 appears overdetermined. Most potential determinants of regime collapse suggest a high likelihood of political transition. Indonesia's New Order was in the midst of one of the world's worst peacetime economic crises since World War II; corruption and outrageous nepotism plagued the country's economy; students protested in the streets demanding *reformasi*; rioters looted urban Indonesia and thousands of Chinese Indonesians were killed and raped; tensions between Islamist and nationalist military factions appeared high; Soeharto had recently suffered two minor strokes and was reportedly mentally unstable; and policy vacillation suggested an incoherent adjustment plan. This means that for a social scientist interested in explaining the New Order's breakdown, there are plenty of accounts from which to choose. Table 6.1 groups existing explanations according to the direction of causation for transition – from the bottom up, or from the top down – and according to the hypothesized cause – a lack of legitimacy, wholesale collapse, and interests. The entry "coalitional fracture" (top-down, interests) describes the general family of arguments into which my explanation fits.

TABLE 6.1. *Families of Explanations for the New Order's Breakdown*

	Direction of Causation	
	Top-Down: Decisions of the holders of power caused the regime's breakdown	*Bottom-Up:* Decisions of individuals outside of the regime caused the breakdown
Cause		
Legitimacy: Without legitimacy, the New Order regime could no longer rule	Father of development	Illegitimate regime
Collapse: The strategies that kept the New Order in power were no longer feasible	Old man	Structural contradictions
Interests: Dissatisfied individuals or groups pushed the New Order from power	Coalitional fracture	Massive groundswell

Legitimacy

Explanations that explain regime collapse as a consequence of regime illegitimacy come in two versions. The first, glossed as "father of development," suggests that Soeharto's resignation was a voluntary step taken by a benevolent leader. Its advocates include some biographers and New Order apologists. In the wake of the economic crisis and student protests, so the argument runs, Soeharto realized that he no longer commanded the support of the Indonesian people. Fearing that there would be additional student victims after the Trisakti massacre, Soeharto resigned for the good of the nation.[1] Malik Fadjan, minister of religion in Habibie's cabinet, suggests an even more magnanimous interpretation – that Soeharto himself generously followed the will of the Indonesian masses, who were no longer confident in his ability to lead the country.[2]

The legitimacy argument is the easiest explanation to dismiss, for New Order history makes it difficult to entertain this explanation. The level of popular legitimacy that the New Order regime enjoyed was not constant

[1] Luhulima 2001, 15–16; Sulastomo 2001, 72.
[2] Quoted in Luhulima 2001, 22.

throughout the thirty-two years of Soeharto's rule but rather varied roughly in line with economic conditions and across different class and ethnic groups in Indonesian society. Past regime actions suggest that political legitimacy, like democratic institutions such as political parties and elections, was a "useful fiction."[3] That is, political legitimacy was welcome when present and ignored when absent. Even more telling are the regime's responses to potential threats to its legitimacy. It is difficult to imagine that Soeharto was greatly concerned with the legitimacy of his actions when he created a system so efficient at suppressing the expression of antiregime sentiments.

A related argument ("illegitimate regime") suggests that while Soeharto may not have voluntarily stepped down, the New Order collapsed because it was illegitimate. This explanation locates the agency for transition not within Soeharto but outside of the regime, where popular support for the New Order evaporated as the economic crisis worsened. For a regime so wedded to developmentalist ideology, sharp economic contraction during the eleven months from June 1997 to May 1998 led to a crisis of legitimacy. This is a popular argument, one at the basis for most explanations of the New Order's collapse.[4] In either form, the illegitimate regime hypothesis is almost identical to that of the "father of development" hypothesis, but for the view that the lack of legitimacy forced (rather than inspired) Soeharto to resign. But, again, past incidents of economic contraction did not coincide with a regime breakdown. Two examples of economic contraction were the oil shocks of 1982–83 and 1986–87, both of which led to serious economic reversals.

Comparison with the Malaysian experience is instructive as well. Malaysia's regime, too, had long relied on developmentalist legitimacy embodied in more than a decade of strong economic growth. Figure 6.1 plots quarterly GDP growth rates for Indonesia and Malaysia throughout 1997 and 1998.

In terms of quarterly GDP contraction, Malaysia's downturn was worse between the fourth quarter of 1997 and the first quarter of 1998 than Indonesia's at any point before Soeharto's resignation. When comparing the economic effects of the crises in Indonesia and Malaysia, most researchers cite the year-on-year real GDP contraction of 13 percent in Indonesia as evidence of more severe contraction in Indonesia than in Malaysia, which experienced a 7 percent contraction. These figures

---

[3] Liddle 1996b.
[4] Abdul Gafur 2000; May 1998, 233–34; Schwarz 1999, 4; Young 1998, 112. A wrinkle, that social rather than economic conditions drove Soeharto's resignation, is in Aspinall 1998, 139.

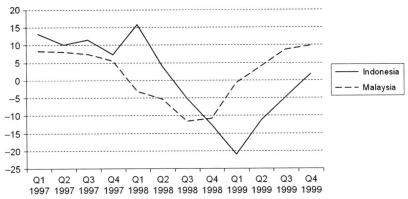

FIGURE 6.1. Indonesia and Malaysia, Annualized Quarterly Real GDP Growth Rate, 1997–1998 (seasonally adjusted). *Source:* Calculated from International Monetary Fund 2007.

obscure the fact that the worst part of 1998's economic contraction occurred *after Soeharto had resigned.* This suggests that crises of legitimacy are at best indirect causes of authoritarian breakdowns, requiring a micrologic that links illegitimacy to regime collapse.

Massive Groundswell of Discontent

To bridge the gap between illegitimacy during economic crises and regime breakdown, a third class of arguments looks to the sustained mass protest of a grand coalition of social forces, which included students, Islamists, housewives, urban wage laborers, and eventually even populist parliamentarians.[5] By May 1998 their demands had congealed around the singular objective of driving Soeharto from office. In these accounts, popular protests drive authoritarian regimes from power. Yet implicitly, when the New Order regime had confronted popular protests in the past, we should have then seen an increased likelihood of authoritarian breakdown. This is plainly not the case. New Order history is replete with examples of large popular protests against the New Order regime, including the Malari riots of 1974 and student protests in 1977–78, along with more recent examples of PDI supporters during the 1996–97 election cycle.[6] Large riots also occurred on several occasions during the New Order, most notably the Tanjung Priok riots of 1984 and the Medan riots of 1994.[7]

---

[5] Aspinall 2005; Haggard 2000b, 116; Vatikiotis 1998, 163–64.
[6] Crouch 1978, 314–16. Aspinall 1995, 30; Eklöf 1997, 1185–86.
[7] Pangestu and Azis 1994, 4; Raillon 1993.

But *reformasi* protests were far larger than any other student-, party-, or worker-led protest under the New Order, which makes it difficult to compare them to previous episodes. Still, other facts are also inconsistent with the hypothesis that protest drove regime collapse. Throughout history, the New Order regime contained popular protest through the credible threat of force, yet there is no evidence of such a breakdown of military capabilities or an unwillingness of security forces to maintain order. While protests began in the early weeks of 1998, before the March 1998 session of the People's Consultative Council (MPR) that gave Soeharto his seventh five-year term as president, the armed forces enforced a complete halt to all protests and violence.[8] Even in the context of the deadly riots of May 13–14, 1998, Commander of the Armed Forces General Wiranto called upon soldiers from West Java to restore order and was wholly successful. Finally, Amien Rais, leader of the mass Islamic organization Muhammadiyah, attempted to organize a massive pro-*reformasi* rally in central Jakarta for May 20, but troops deployed to maintain order led him to call off these rallies for fear of another massacre. These examples show security forces to be *able* to restore order, but they have little to say about the *willingness* of these security forces to maintain order.

The comparison with Malaysia again reinforces the conclusion that protests themselves did not bring down the regime. Malaysia's *reformasi* movement was similarly powerful, bringing together reformist Malays and Chinese and Indian Malaysians for sustained massive protests. These protests, as in Indonesia, attacked Mahathir's management of the crisis and his authoritarian character.[9] Wan Azizah Wan Ismail, wife of deposed Malaysian deputy prime minister Anwar Ibrahim and a central figure in the Malaysian *reformasi* movement, wrote of a "people's movement" in Indonesia that successfully deposed one authoritarian regime, while its sister movement in Malaysia failed in the same endeavor against another.[10] Others have noted that Indonesia's protests were more "symbolic" than actually powerful.[11] While the focus on popular discontent brings us closer to linking economic contraction to regime upheaval, it still cannot itself explain the breakdown of the New Order.

[8] Colin Johnson 1998, 6, 8.
[9] Hilley 2001; M. Weiss 1999; 2005.
[10] Wan Azizah 2001.
[11] B. Singh 2000, 99–100; Young 1998, 104–29.

Irrationality

A number of authors reject attempts to find a purposive logic in Soeharto's actions, instead embracing his apparently illogical behavior and arguing that some combination of personal weakness, sickness, or decreased mental capacity made Soeharto unable to remain in power ("old man"). By March 1998 he had served as president for thirty-two years, a reign unmatched in modern politics with the exception of Fidel Castro. Some also noted that by the mid-1990s Soeharto seemed unconcerned with the immense amount of rents that his children and cronies collected, suggesting that he was "blind" to the limits of his own power.[12] Moreover, Soeharto's health was in decline, with physical infirmities manifest in his speech and gait. Others noted Soeharto's isolation after the death of his wife Tien Soeharto in 1996, speculating on the possible effects of sorrow and loneliness on his rule.[13] Finally, Soeharto suffered two minor strokes in December 1997, precisely when Indonesia's crisis began to reveal itself as more serious than observers had previously thought. Many view Soeharto's political recalcitrance in the face of reformist pressures to be some evidence of his mental incapacity.[14]

Suggestions of Soeharto's mental decline are compelling enough to warrant serious consideration. Yet there is evidence that observers overestimated Soeharto's infirmity. For one, Soeharto lived for almost ten years after his resignation. His behavior during this period suggests a Javanese cultural interpretation of *lengser keprabon, madeg pandito*, a phrase recalling a Javanese sultan who graciously retires as the *raja* and enters a state of spiritual reflection.[15] Soeharto carefully cultivated this image while in office as well as during his retirement. His actions during retirement were, of course, unobservable in the months preceding and following his resignation, when theories of Soeharto's diminished mental capacity were most popular. Only with the benefit of hindsight can we observe behavior that seems more rational than previously thought.

There is, though, a more compelling reason to be wary of explanations of the New Order's breakdown that rely on Soeharto's irrationality. Almost all accounts of the New Order attribute its longevity in a large part to Soeharto's skilled manipulation of competing political factions. During the 1990s, these factions included a growing Islamic movement,

---

[12] Case 2002, 55; Elson 2001, 249; Hill 1999, 77; Radelet and Woo 2000, 171; Sidel 1998, 162.

[13] Crouch 2001b, 148.

[14] Elson 2001, 276; Emmerson 1999b, 42; Editors 1999, 138.

[15] Luhulima 2001; Sulastomo 2001.

intramilitary factionalism between Islamists ("green") and nationalists ("red-and-white") in ABRI, and bureaucratic squabbles between nationalists and technocrats. Although political succession was a topic of scholarly speculation given Soeharto's advanced age,[16] few observers predicted an imminent breakdown of the regime because of Soeharto's personal weaknesses. In fact, what scholarly consensus existed at the time held that the 1997 election cycle in Indonesia was a masterful victory for the New Order.[17] And while secondhand accounts of Soeharto's final year in office often attribute policy vacillation to Soeharto's diminished capabilities, many of Soeharto's associates during this period affirm that he was still mentally sharp.[18]

Structural Contradictions

A final perspective focuses on political institutions and social change in linking economic crisis to authoritarian breakdown in Indonesia. These arguments take many forms, but all share the view that the New Order contained some structural contradiction that made authoritarian breakdown at some point inevitable. One prominent argument holds that Indonesian politics had "no mechanisms to generate mass support and manage opposition," suggesting that when facing high political opposition, authoritarian regimes without a grass-roots, party-based institutional structure face higher costs in containing opposition than those which do possess such structures.[19] Comparing the collapse of New Order Indonesia to the stability of Mahathir's Malaysia seems to reinforce this. But the meaningful difference between UMNO and Golkar is unclear. Both were mass political organizations promoting an organicist ideology of their party as the proper voice for society – colored with appeals to Asian values or Asian-style democracy. Both parties dispensed patronage to win political support and used the machinery of power to circumvent troublesome election laws. The two parties clearly differed in a number of critical dimensions, mostly dealing with their relationship to the larger party system – severely restricted in Indonesia but tolerated in Malaysia. Still, even if Indonesia's severely restricted party system hampered the regime's ability to respond to popular demands for reform, this does not explain

---

[16] See, e.g., Bertrand 1996.
[17] Eklöf 1997, 1195; Gill 1998, 152; Robison and Rosser 1998, 1604–5.
[18] Interview with Emil Salim; interview with Fuad Bawazier; interview with Djisman Simandjuntak; interview with Jakob Oetomo, founder and editor of *Kompas*, March 14, 2006.
[19] Haggard 2000b, 51, 116, 25.

why Malaysia's regime did not face the sort of popular demands for economic reform that the New Order did. And even without reference to Malaysia, an institutional explanation is unconvincing. The observable implications of institutions failing to prevent authoritarian breakdown – uncontrollable mass demonstrations, a security apparatus unwilling to act against demonstrators – are absent in Indonesia.

Another perspective suggests that the New Order's policy history itself caused the regime's collapse, where the Asian Financial Crisis was merely the tremor that brought down the house of cards. Some argue that a faulty political system and perverse development strategy made the regime unsustainable.[20] But this can make little sense of the timing of the regime's collapse. Others note that by opening the country to cross-border capital flows, Soeharto exposed the regime to the vagaries of international markets, which could undermine the existing coalition.[21] But the role of mobile capital in bringing down the Soeharto regime does not explain why the regime did not adopt policies to protect itself – as Malaysia did – or why it took thirty years for such contradictions to manifest themselves.

Others appeal to personnel change within key political institutions, in particular the rise of a younger generation of ABRI leaders with no experience in the independence struggle and hence little personal loyalty to Soeharto.[22] Factionalism within ABRI was certainly present, but subsequent research into post-Soeharto military politics questions its role in bringing down the New Order. Douglas Kammen and Siddharth Chandra make this point clear: "If, as many observers have argued, the Army is deeply divided, then why has it remained united in the face of Soeharto's fall?"[23] Events in the weeks following Soeharto's resignation demonstrate how observers overestimated factional problems. Wiranto engineered the marginalization of his rival, the head of Kostrad and Soeharto's son-in-law, General Prabowo Subianto, with relative ease, suggesting that Prabowo's political influence within ABRI depended on having his father-in-law in office.

A different version of this argument is that the central problem for personnel change lay with Soeharto himself, whose management of subordinates in Golkar and ABRI kept him in power but left unclear the path for succession were Soeharto to retire. Regardless of Soeharto's mental

---

[20] Fatah 2000, 240.
[21] Aspinall and Berger 2001.
[22] Aspinall 1998, 132–34.
[23] Kammen and Chandra 1999, 15.

capacity, which in retrospect seems to have been less fragile than at the time, Soeharto's age and his plan for retirement were a clear concern and had been for some time. When the Asian Financial Crisis hit Indonesia, then, it coincided with an impending *political* crisis, one pitting Soeharto (and his children) against a group of subordinates waiting impatiently for him to resign.

This explanation for the New Order's collapse – that it would have happened anyway, and the economic crisis just accompanied it – is unfalsifiable in its simplest form. But it requires an ad hoc account of its timing. As I detail in this chapter, not until after the *konglomerat* fled Indonesia in May 1998 did loyal Golkar and ABRI figures defect. Had the New Order's collapse been merely a problem of succession, it is curious why they waited so long. Soeharto's strokes in December 1997 would seem to have been the ideal opportunity for subordinates to push him from office. Likewise, the March 1998 MPR session provided a clear opportunity for succession in the event that subordinates truly demanded it. Note that by then, the severity of Indonesia's crisis was clear, and calls for Soeharto's resignation by opposition elites were open and frequent. Yet Soeharto easily won unanimous support for a seventh term in office, forming a cabinet whose membership reflected the interests of fixed capital perhaps more than any previous cabinet had. So, while the problem of succession was obvious, this did not lead to regime change until the coalition between fixed and mobile capital fractured.

A weaker form of this hypothesis is that when the economic crisis hit Indonesia, it highlighted unspoken concerns by loyal subordinates about whether their economic interests would survive in a post-Soeharto New Order regime. The economic crisis accordingly hastened the impending political crisis. Though probably true, this is less a hypothesis than a description of how the crisis played out in Indonesia and, by itself, makes little sense of the contours of policy conflict in the New Order's final months. Whatever their views on the Soeharto family's unending greed and Soeharto's refusal to name a successor, Golkar and ABRI subordinates did not turn on them; they turned on the *konglomerat* over issues of economic management. And these subordinates stuck by Soeharto for months, just until the May riots drove the *konglomerat* and their assets overseas.

Whatever the incompleteness of these "succession crisis hypotheses" in Indonesia, they appear even weaker in the Malaysian context. To explain regime survival in Malaysia using this framework, it must be that Mahathir's regime survived the crisis because leadership succession was no issue, or because a clear party hierarchy and internal procedures for leadership turnover made the succession path more clear, or because subordinates were unconcerned about their economic interests in a post-Mahathir BN regime. As I show in Chapter 7, these suppositions are all incorrect: political succession had been a major concern within the regime, procedures for leadership turnover have always been a subject of intense political jockeying, and subordinates were quite concerned about their economic interests in a post-Mahathir regime.

A final hypothesis proceeds from modernization theory, which notes the rise of a modern, educated Indonesian middle class, perhaps quiescent but with a latent desire for democracy and political reform.[24] If this were true, we should observe a unified push from middle-class Indonesians for democratization in the final months of the New Order. But the idea that economic development created a mass of prodemocracy middle-class Indonesians is only partially true. Economic development under the firm hand of the state also created a dependent middle class, comfortable with the status quo and fearful of what democratization would mean for its economic well-being.[25] In fact, the *reformasi* movement featured a marked lack of united opposition from middle-class representatives and organizations until the final days of Soeharto's rule. Most student demonstrators came from middle-class or even upper-class backgrounds, but their willingness to join ideological forces with retrenched urban workers to demand reform was limited. In late May, for instance, middle-class student protestors beat a hasty retreat to the arms of security forces for fear of *amuk massa* (rioting masses).[26] Muslim organizations remained divided by a traditionalist-versus-modernist cleavage, hindering their participation in the prodemocracy movement,[27] while the Chinese-*pribumi* cleavage remained salient among middle-class protesters.[28] In addition to facing a security apparatus that was still capable of repressing its political opposition, the *reformasi* movement was hardly the coherent, unified movement that could effectively topple a regime. This lack of "cohesive oppositional unity" hamstrung *reformasi*.[29] The mechanisms of patronage and reciprocal clientelism, so important for Soeharto's political

[24] Emmerson 1999b, 39–40.
[25] Liddle 1999b, 59.
[26] Siegel 2001.
[27] Kadir 1999.
[28] Crouch 2001b, 140–41.
[29] Elson 2001, 288.

support, appear to have worked just as planned in dividing the loyalties of the middle class.

Coalitional Fracture

The nature and timing of the New Order's collapse accordingly casts doubt on existing arguments. An explanation *must* account for the institutional continuity of ABRI before and after Soeharto's resignation, Soeharto's subsequent management of his public persona, sharp ideological contradictions within the *reformasi* movement, the New Order's historical resiliency to crises of legitimacy and economic growth, and Soeharto's authority over New Order politics at least as late as March 1998. This account must also explain why Soeharto resigned on May 21, 1998, rather than in December 1997 (during his personal health crises), in January 1998 (when student protests began to escalate), in March 1998 (during the MPR session when he chose B. J. Habibie as vice president), on May 4, 1998 (when he made the unpopular decision to eliminate petroleum and electricity subsidies), or on May 13–14, 1998 (during massive anti-Chinese violence). Similarly, it must describe what made resignation on May 21, 1998, more attractive than clinging to power even longer.

Taking the coalitional fracture hypothesis seriously can be difficult for the simple reason that its predictions are almost trivial. Of course, it is true that some kind of division in the elite led to the New Order's collapse. Viewed this way, describing authoritarian breakdowns as caused by coalitional fractures simply begs a further question: what causes elite fractures? Chapter 2 provides the answer: Indonesia's elite fracture resulted from differing preferences over adjustment policy. The remainder of this chapter demonstrates how these led to the New Order's breakdown.

Late New Order Politics

In May 1997 a breakdown as spectacular as the one seen only a year later seemed unthinkable. General elections dominated Indonesian politics in 1997, as Soeharto stood for his seventh five-year term as president. This decision was never in doubt, as Soeharto had given no indication of any willingness to retire, and had long claimed that he would remain as president as long as the Indonesian people wanted him to occupy that post.[30] Nevertheless, Soeharto's advanced age – he would turn seventy-six before

---

[30] Soeharto 1989, 466–70.

his scheduled inauguration in March 1998 – brought the issue of political succession to the forefront. Political maneuvering hence focused on the position of vice president, as that individual would inherit the presidency if Soeharto died before the elections scheduled for 2002.

The vice president at the time was Try Sutrisno, but Soeharto's predilection for rotating his lieutenants in order to prevent any individual from amassing significant political power made it unlikely that Sutrisno would retain the position. From early on, State Minister of Research and Technology B. J. Habibie was a favorite. In addition to his influential post in the Sixth Development Cabinet, his sponsorship of import-substitution industrialization and heavy industry endeared him to Soeharto and other nationalists in the New Order regime. Protectionism and favoritism for "strategic industries" was especially welcome from companies such as the PT Timor Putra Nasional – manufacturer of Indonesia's national car and under the leadership of Soeharto's son Tommy. Habibie's justification for ISI initiatives also fit well with the New Order's ideological emphasis on the government's proper role in economic planning and development.[31] Moreover, Habibie benefited from the additional support of ICMI, the regime's association of Muslim scholars and intellectuals. These qualifications as a moderate Muslim, a highly educated and capable planner, and an unabashed Soeharto loyalist made him a strong candidate for vice president. Aside from Sutrisno and Habibie, other possible contenders included Soeharto's daughter Tutut and several ministers in the Sixth Development Cabinet.[32]

Although there was speculation about factional alignment inside the regime, threats from outside the regime were minimal. Soeharto loyalists had engineered the ouster of the head of the Indonesian Democratic Party (PDI), Megawati Sukarnoputri, in 1996.[33] As the election approached, civil violence broke out sporadically, including anti-Chinese and anti-Christian violence in Tasikmalaya and continued Madurese-Dayak violence in the province of West Kalimantan, among others.[34] Such violence held little threat for the New Order's survival. As elections in 1997 approached, international investors remained upbeat about Indonesia's economic performance and prospects for growth. The question of Soeharto's successor remained the biggest political issue affecting the investment

[31] Habibie 1995.
[32] B. Singh 2000, 57–58.
[33] Aspinall 2005, 175–201.
[34] Sidel 2006, 68–105.

climate, garnering the attention of fund managers and institutional investors, but the likelihood of dramatic political changes seemed low.

During the campaign itself, the regime was keen to ensure a resounding electoral victory. To do this, it relied on tried-and-true methods of intimidating opposition politicians, regulating the content of the media, and engineering giant "festivals of democracy" to rally voters. Election violence was also more prevalent than in earlier elections. Two hundred sixty Indonesians died in election-related violence, the highest number in Indonesian electoral history.[35] Harmoko, the Golkar chairman and minister of information, responded to increased campaign violence by dismissing it as criminal and warning that the government would deal with it harshly.[36]

In the event, Golkar won a stunning victory, even by New Order standards. Golkar candidates took 74.2 percent of the vote, exceeding by a significant margin what many considered their goal of 70 percent. This total was high enough to lead the United Development Party (PPP) to open complaints – actually quite rare under Soeharto, given the extent of historical campaign irregularities – of electoral fraud. Personnel shifts in the government occurred shortly after the elections. These saw General Raden Hartono taking the position of minister of information from Harmoko, with Harmoko retaining the position of Golkar chairman and now occupying the new position of state minister with special functions. Hartono had previously held the position of army chief of staff, a position newly filled by Wiranto, before then the commander of Kostrad. Political changes and election violence notwithstanding, the position of the New Order regime by mid-1997 was one of strength. The major political issue facing Indonesia was Soeharto's problem of engineering a smooth handoff to a successor upon his eventual retirement. This, though, was nothing new for New Order politics.

From Economic to Political Crisis

By July 1997 the regional economic crisis began to overshadow political maneuvers within the New Order regime. Still, the likelihood of radical turnover seemed low. The regime insisted that the rupiah float was not a sign of weakness, but an indication of the regime's ability to quickly diagnose economic problems and take appropriate remedies. Furthermore, the regime described its experiments with adjustment policies as tentative and

---

[35] McLeod 1997, 5–6; Suryadinata 2002, 32–36.
[36] *Asiaweek*, May 30, 1997.

exploratory, embracing the possibility of future changes as economic conditions developed and the consequences of initial policy measures became clear.[37]

Outside of the public eye, the story was different, as groups with private access to the regime pressured Soeharto to adopt favorable policies. Yet their complaints did not translate into demands for Soeharto's resignation, or even into demands for political reform, but rather into requests that the regime rethink adjustment policy measures. Calls for sensible crisis management continued during the month of November, in the wake of the closure of sixteen banks. Opposition PPP and PDI factions within the House of Representatives (DPR) called for transparency in the determination of bank closures, mirroring general concerns among businesspeople and economists that a lack of transparency had led to bank runs in other, better-managed banks.[38] Well-connected business figures commenting on the closures also expressed reservations about the closures' propriety, with Kadin spokesman Aburizal Bakrie asking that the government consider mergers instead of closures in the future.[39]

We see in the debate on bank closures the first signs of political concerns expressed by mobile and fixed capital. On the whole, though, the regime closed ranks in the wake of the bank closures. The head of the ABRI fraction in the DPR, Syarwan Hamid, reaffirmed that body's support for the bank closures as reflecting the national interest.[40] The government also dispatched police and army troops to ensure order at banks facing deposit runs and reassured the public that it had decided to close the banks only to protect the common good.[41]

The first real shock to Indonesia's political establishment was Soeharto's sudden decision not to attend a meeting of the Organisation of the Islamic Conference in Tehran, scheduled for early December. Upon returning from a twelve-day global trip, Soeharto disappeared into his residence in Jakarta, with aides citing doctors' recommendations that he take a ten-day break from his punishing work schedule.[42] Rumors of his rapidly declining health quickly spread, despite efforts of the regime to downplay the seriousness of his condition. Foreshadowing the possibility that dissatisfied elements might seize the chance to disrupt Soeharto's planned reelection

[37] *Jakarta Post*, September 27, 1997.
[38] *Bisnis Indonesia*, November 4, 1997; *Suara Pembaruan*, November 4, 1997.
[39] *Merdeka*, November 6, 1997.
[40] *Kompas*, November 6, 1997.
[41] *Media Indonesia*, November 7, 1997; *Kompas*, November 8, 1997.
[42] *Straits Times*, December 7, 1997.

as president during the March MPR session, ABRI commander Feisal
Tanjung announced further repressive measures, blaming political unease
on unspecified communist elements.[43] Soeharto's last-minute cancellation
of an ASEAN leaders' conference in Kuala Lumpur about a week later led
to a further round of rumors and speculation about his health.

   This speculation led to the first public discussions of the possibility that
Soeharto might die in office – not at some undefined point in time but in
the near future.[44] Political commentator Christianto Wibisono began to
draw parallels between Soeharto's health crisis and the rumored health
crisis that preceded Sukarno's ouster amid economic crisis some thirty
years before.[45] Amien Rais, by now a frequent regime critic, called for
Soeharto not to stand for another term as president, marking the most
public expression of dissatisfaction with the regime yet. But, despite this
mounting evidence of popular discontent with the economy and the
obvious opportunity that Soeharto's health crisis presented for his subordinates to engineer political change, the regime's supporters remained
allied with the regime.

   Part of the regime's strategy involved eliminating individuals within the
government who might not be willing to implement its favored adjustment
policies, or making token gestures toward political reform that might
alleviate some of its most vocal critics. The latter explanation probably
underlies the murky dismissal of four BI directors on December 22.
Soeharto dismissed the directors – Hendrobudiyanto, Paul Soetopo
Tjokronegoro, Heru Soepraptomo, and Mansjurdin Nurdin – without
providing any explanation for his decision or first consulting with BI
governor Soedradjad Djiwandono.[46] Two of their replacements, Sjahril
Sabirin and Iwan Prawiranata, later proved to be usefully malleable allies.
Rumors subsequently emerged that the decision to replace the four directors was the consequence of their past official corruption.[47] Later events
confirmed these suspicions. On December 26 the media reported the
arrest of Soetopo and Soepraptomo for questioning about their alleged
failure to report banks' liquidity problems to Soedradjad and their possible misuse of liquidity support.[48] On that day, Hendrobudiyanto also

---

[43] *Straits Times*, December 10, 1997.
[44] Soesastro and Basri 1998, 20.
[45] *International Herald Tribune*, December 13, 1997.
[46] *Bisnis Indonesia*, December 23, 1997; *Kompas*, December 23, 1997; *Merdeka*, Decem-
    ber 23, 1997.
[47] *Jakarta Post*, December 24, 1997; *Kompas*, December 24, 1997.
[48] *Media Indonesia*, December 26, 1997; *Merdeka*, December 26, 1997.

returned from abroad to answer questions from investigators, although Mansjurdin Nurdin remained unaccounted for.[49] Yet the case quickly disappeared from public view, despite calls for transparency and accountability in the legal proceedings by increasingly vocal dissidents.[50]

This conflict underlines the increasing importance of adjustment policy in determining how political conflict unfolded, as for the first time financial sector problems led to shake-ups in the regime's personnel. The New Order subsequently stepped up its defense of economic management. Tutut led the charge with her public support of the Love the Rupiah campaign, targeting mobile capital in doing so. Tutut not only asked the *konglomerat* to show patriotism by holding rupiah assets but also pledged that the Soeharto family itself would exchange its foreign currency holdings for rupiahs.[51] Amid some popular speculation that *konglomerat*'s business practices and involvement in currency deals showed their lack of patriotism, the regime began to target the *konglomerat* directly for participation in the Love the Rupiah campaign. These sentiments were particularly acute in the wake of the poor international reaction to the 1998 budget announced on January 5, which led to further rupiah depreciation and saw urban Indonesians beginning to hoard food and other necessary goods. With hoarding came accusations of price gouging from goods traders. Wealthy Indonesians – increasingly viewed by the public as Chinese Indonesians – bore the brunt of popular dissatisfaction in urban areas.[52] The regime designed the Love the Rupiah campaign to present a united front of *pribumi* businessmen, *konglomerat*, and government figures with a firm plan to end economic troubles.[53] For months after the initiation of the Love the Rupiah campaign, Indonesian newspapers printed stories of Indonesians – both rich and poor – spontaneously converting their assets into rupiah.

As the Love the Rupiah campaign proceeded, regime spokespeople also confirmed Soeharto's authority over the country's economy. Quoted in Golkar's newspaper *Suara Karya*, the head of the Golkar's Central Leadership Committee, Abdul Gafur, warned that any demands for Soeharto's resignation were inappropriate, and that Soeharto alone would decide when a leadership transition was proper.[54] However much some

---

[49] *Jakarta Post*, December 27, 1997; *Kompas*, December 27, 1997.
[50] *Kompas*, December 28, 1997.
[51] *Media Indonesia*, January 9, 1998; *Kompas*, January 10, 1998.
[52] *Bisnis Indonesia*, January 10, 1998; *Jakarta Post*, January 10, 1998.
[53] *Jakarta Post*, January 12, 1998.
[54] *Suara Karya*, January 9, 1998.

subordinates might have worried about their fortunes in a post-Soeharto Indonesia, all still threw their support behind the regime. Harmoko similarly warned that complaints of the crisis's impact on national welfare were both untrue and counterproductive.[55]

The Konglomerat *and Chinese Indonesians*

Protests by ordinary Indonesians in response to the crisis began in earnest in early 1998. On January 12, citizens protested against the rise in commodity prices in the East Javanese town of Banyuwangi.[56] In response, East Java's provincial government immediately requested that the central government intervene to arrest those accused of speculating and price gouging.[57] At the same time, the regime announced that currency speculation was not only not patriotic but also subversive – and that the government would prosecute speculators.[58] It became clear during these weeks that protestors were targeting not just wealthy Indonesians or even local traders but specifically Chinese Indonesians. Subsequent developments would reveal that this was not simply a conflict over ethnicity but one between mobile and fixed capital.

The perception of the Love the Rupiah campaign's united front weakened in the following days as a result of complaints about the *konglomerat*'s failure to participate. Specifically, newspapers carried complaints that non-*pribumi* Indonesians had not fully cooperated with the campaign.[59] The specific charges again non-*pribumi* Indonesians reveal the importance of their economic behavior in generating resentment. In an effort to head off any incipient divide between mobile and fixed capital, and to encourage the former to remain loyal, Soedradjad held a closed meeting attended by some of the wealthiest and influential *konglomerat* as well as notable *pribumi* business figures.[60] While the proceedings of the meeting remain secret, it is commonly believed that the two groups confronted one another and discussed what adjustment measures might be mutually acceptable. The role of ABRI in advocating fixed capital's interests also grew. Following Soedradjad's meeting, ABRI leaders phoned several *konglomerat* to "encourage" them to donate funds to the Love the Rupiah campaign. ABRI spokesman General Wahab Mokodongan expressed some frustration with

[55] *Kompas*, January 12, 1998.
[56] *Kompas*, January 13, 1998.
[57] *Suara Karya*, January 13, 1998.
[58] *Republika*, January 13, 1998.
[59] *BusinessNews*, January 14, 1998; *Media Indonesia*, January 14, 1998.
[60] *Media Indonesia*, January 14, 1998; *Republika*, January 14, 1998.

the *konglomerat*'s alleged refusal to show patriotism.[61] For the first time, the split between mobile and fixed capital – reflected here as one between Chinese *konglomerat* and *pribumi* entrepreneurs and ABRI – became visible.

The signing of the second IMF agreement on January 15 overshadowed this potential split between mobile and fixed capital. While foreign researchers have noted the humiliating manner in which Soeharto signed the agreement, the New Order's propaganda machine portrayed the agreement as successful. In a rare media appearance, looking fit and confident, Soeharto asked for patience and claimed that the success of economic reform depended on the entire Indonesian nation.[62] In the following days, ethnic Chinese began more publicly to contribute gold and other valuable items to the Love the Rupiah campaign.[63] Liem Sioe Liong also vowed to bring his foreign currency holdings back into Indonesia as rupiah. Yet data in Table 4.6 reveal these pledges to have been empty; massive amounts of capital fled from Indonesia in 1998, contributions to the Love the Rupiah campaign were minimal, and Liem's own capital remained abroad.

Mass Muslim organizations also joined in the Love the Rupiah campaign and pledged to support the regime. Members of Nahdlatul Ulama, Indonesia's largest Muslim organization, donated gold to Soeharto personally as a show of their loyalty and prayed that Soeharto would retain the office of president in the March MPR elections.[64] During this period, chairman of the Council of Indonesian Ulamas (MUI) Hasan Basri declared currency speculation to be *haram* – forbidden – under Islam. MUI also ruled that every Muslim Indonesian had the duty to support the government in overcoming the economic crisis.[65] Tutut, the public face of the Love the Rupiah movement, donated two kilograms of gold to the government as part of what she now called the Love Indonesia Campaign.[66]

Amid these public attempts at unity within the regime, tensions between mobile and fixed capital continued to escalate. From the latter part of January until mid-February, sporadic riots took place across Java and on

[61] *Jakarta Post*, January 15, 1998; *Merdeka*, January 15, 1998.
[62] *Bisnis Indonesia*, January 16, 1998; *Jakarta Post*, January 16, 1998.
[63] *Kompas*, January 18, 1998.
[64] *Jakarta Post*, January 19, 1998; *Suara Karya*, January 19, 1998.
[65] *Media Indonesia*, January 20, 1998; *Jakarta Post*, January 20, 1998; January 24, 1998; *Suara Karya*, January 24, 1998.
[66] *Kompas*, January 20, 1998; *Media Indonesia*, January 20, 1998.

several of the outer islands.[67] While deteriorating economic conditions were the proximate cause of the riots, the victims were largely ethnic Chinese shopkeepers, and the justifications given by most rioters were grievances against ethnic Chinese economic exploitation. Such sentiments also appeared among members of the New Order establishment, again targeting *konglomerat* as mobile capital. Tutut, for instance, attempted to shame *konglomerat* into making even more contributions to the Love the Rupiah campaign.[68] On January 19 Harmoko made a speech in which he alleged that the economy was plagued with "rats" that had to be brought to justice.[69] Syarwan Hamid reiterated this theme a week later at a pro-government rally at the Sunda Kelapa mosque in Central Jakarta. Again without specifically naming Chinese, he warned that "each rat has the potential to become a traitor."[70] In these two statements, the meaning of "rat" is clearly Chinese, and the source of treason is capital flight.

These statements – and similar ones made by ABRI affiliates in the following weeks – also revealed a degree of ABRI factionalism,[71] a subject that became more relevant in the wake of the MPR session. On one side was Prabowo. On the other was General Wiranto, at that time still Kostrad commander and a firm Soeharto loyalist. Feisal Tanjung and Syarwan Hamid had personal and business links to Prabowo, and their clique of ABRI leaders gradually gained a reputation as hard-liners in supporting Soeharto against students and other members of the *reformasi* movement. Wiranto, Soeharto's former personal adjutant, was no less a supporter of Soeharto, but he and his supporters appeared as soft-liners during the *reformasi* movement. The hard-liners' anti-Chinese statements reflected something other than simple prejudice against Chinese entrepreneurs. Rather, they were a calculated attempt to shift the blame for the economy's decline away from Soeharto and onto the vulnerable Chinese, specifically targeting the issues of capital flight and currency depreciation. This may have been an attempt to lay a foundation for possible future military intervention in politics.

Others in the regime took these comments seriously. Soeharto, for one, met with Protestant leaders to discuss the problem of ethnic and/or religious violence in the near future.[72] Wiranto condemned the anti-Chinese

[67] Colin Johnson 1998, 6, 8; Ocorandi 1998; Soesastro and Basri 1998, 36.
[68] *Bisnis Indonesia*, January 20, 1998.
[69] *Suara Karya*, January 20, 1998.
[70] *Merdeka*, January 28, 1998.
[71] See, e.g., Aspinall 1998, 150–51; Case 2002, 62; Hefner 2000, 201–7; Honna 1999, 121; Sulistiyo 2001, 297–300; Vatikiotis 1998, 161–62.
[72] *Jakarta Post*, January 29, 1998.

statements made by Prabowo's hard-line allies.[73] Sofyan Wanandi, meanwhile, furthered the split between mobile and fixed capital when he announced that he and other *konglomerat* would not participate in the Love the Rupiah campaign but would rather focus on exports.[74] Sofyan later amended this statement to say that these attempts at moral suasion were bound to fail because the combined wealth of all the *konglomerat* would hardly make an impact on the amount of capital fleeing the country.[75] Animosity against mobile capital had by this time spilled onto the larger ethnic Chinese community, leading many ethnic Chinese with sufficient means to consider the necessity of seeking refuge overseas.

Throughout the fall of 1997, debate on possible vice presidential nominees had declined, only to return in early 1998. Even the otherwise critical Amien Rais suggested that the rupiah's continued decline in the wake of the IMF agreement was a result of "political games" meant to unseat the government.[76] Representatives in the DPR echoed these worries, lashing out at reformist groups who were "playing with the people's fate." By now, Amien Rais led the charge by calling for "total reform," even with the high probability that *reformasi* would involve bloodshed.[77] The chief of social and political affairs for the armed forces (Kassospol), General Yunus Yosfiah, similarly denounced the tendency of protestors to link economic problems to the regime's political structure, rejecting any possibility of a leadership change or any types of political reforms that did not follow the constitution.[78] Once again, leaders labeled opposition activities as treachery and promised to protect Indonesia's continued political and economic development at any cost.[79] On February 11 Feisal Tanjung and Minister of Home Affairs Yogi SM warned that ABRI would not tolerate political dissent that would threaten the smooth functioning of the upcoming MPR session.[80]

In mid-February, just as observers began to take seriously rumors about the imposition of a currency board system, thinly veiled complaints about mobile capital arose once again. Syarifuddin Harahap, who had publicly endorsed capital controls, wrote of a conspiracy led by Western

---

[73] Hefner 2000, 202–5.
[74] *Merdeka*, January 20, 1998.
[75] *Media Indonesia*, January 21, 1998.
[76] *Republika*, January 23, 1998.
[77] *Jakarta Post*, February 11, 1998.
[78] *Suara Karya*, January 27, 1998.
[79] *Republika*, January 24, 1998.
[80] *Jakarta Post*, February 12, 1998.

capitalists to overthrow the Soeharto regime. He linked the efforts of westerners, though, to the *konglomerat* who had taken the wealth of the nation for themselves through exploitation of the *pribumi*.[81] The head of the PPP's Central Leadership Committee, Ismail Hasan Matareum, suggested cryptically that *pribumi* Indonesians might "get negative impressions" from the actions of the *konglomerat*, arguing that the economic crisis that had befallen Indonesia would be an opportunity for the people to see for themselves who the real, loyal Indonesians were.[82] While these accusations against *konglomerat* swirled, the *konglomerat* continued to lobby the regime against imposing capital controls, the one policy that might have assuaged such concerns.[83]

Additionally, on at least one occasion a local government attempted to make middle-class Chinese Indonesians accept public responsibility for the crisis. On February 16 a pro-Islamic newspaper reported that the mayor of Surabaya – Indonesia's second largest city and a major economic center – called together some six thousand ethnic Chinese entrepreneurs to meet in a public square.[84] Those called were not *konglomerat* but rather only locally influential ethnic Chinese businessmen, mostly of the middle class. The mayor exhorted these ethnic Chinese to contribute to the Love the Rupiah campaign, but its implications were more disturbing. The decision to target only ethnic Chinese for their lack of patriotism was not new, given the history of the New Order. Furthermore, in the past Soeharto had occasionally gathered together influential *konglomerat* to make specific requests of them. Here, though, a local government was willing to name ordinary Chinese businessmen and traders in a public forum, and link their "lack of patriotism" to the economic crisis. In the event, only around six hundred individuals turned up at the meeting. Wealthier ethnic Chinese businessmen, who largely did not attend, argued that they had not received their notices, suggesting either their fear of media exposure or a purposeful attempt by the local government to inflame anti-Chinese sentiments.

Final Months of Regime Unity
The final months of the New Order were marked by intense political conflict over adjustment policy. Amid speculation about the CBS,

[81] *Republika*, February 16, 1998.
[82] *Republika*, February 16, 1998.
[83] Interview with Emil Salim; interview with a Chinese Indonesian political observer, February 2006; interview with Sri Adiningsih.
[84] *Republika*, February 16, 1998.

Soeharto dismissed BI governor Soedradjad on February 19. At the time, the regime gave no reason for Soedradjad's sudden dismissal, but rumors immediately surfaced that Soedradjad lost Soeharto's favor because of his opposition to the CBS.[85] Soedradjad's replacement was Sjahril Sabirin, the little-known World Bank employee whom Soeharto had appointed as a BI director in December. The market reaction to Sjahril was decidedly negative. Soedradjad's reputation as a liberal technocrat and capable administrator made him relatively popular among foreign economists and the IMF, while Sjahril was considered likely to implement Soeharto's demands without question. But other political developments revealed that, while some factional struggles within the military remained salient, in areas other than adjustment policy the regime remained remarkably united.

Soedradjad's dismissal was the first in a final series of leadership changes that occurred during the March MPR session. In early March, Soeharto dismissed the head of the Indonesian Bank Reconstruction Agency (IBRA), Bambang Subianto, in favor of Iwan Prawiranata. Prawiranata, who like Sjahril had been only recently appointed as a BI director, was also a political unknown without a credible record of economic management. However, Prawiranata's former position as director of Bank Bumi Daya linked him to several corporate empires. Moreover, while head of IBRA, Prawiranata retained his position as managing director of BI, which threatened IBRA's independence from the central bank.[86] These shake-ups in the regime's economic team accompanied new leadership changes in ABRI. Previously, in February, Soeharto had promoted Wiranto to the position of commander of ABRI and installed Prabowo as commander of Kostrad.[87] Position shuffling within ABRI extended far down the ranks of the military leadership, leading to speculation that Soeharto was ensuring that only his most loyal supporters occupied influential positions.[88]

Student demonstrations against the government, triggered by the upcoming MPR session, began during the week of February 19–26 at Depok and Salendra campuses of the University of Indonesia.[89] Security forces contained these protests to campus grounds, minimizing their impact on the conduct of the session.[90] During the MPR session itself, support for Soeharto's seventh term as president was unanimous, but also

[85] *Suara Karya*, February 20, 1998.
[86] Colin Johnson 1998, 47.
[87] Colin Johnson 1998, 5.
[88] Sumarkidjo 2001, 141; Editors 1999.
[89] Aspinall 1999, 215–16.
[90] Soesastro and Basri 1998, 52.

TABLE 6.2. *Key Appointments to the Seventh Development Cabinet*

Name	Cabinet Position
B. J. Habibie	Vice president
General Feisal Tanjung	Coordinating minister of politics and security
Ginandjar Kartasasmita	Coordinating minister of the economy, finance, and industry
General Raden Hartono	Minister of home affairs
Ali Alatas	Minister of foreign affairs
General Wiranto	Minister of defense and security, commander of ABRI
Fuad Bawazier	Minister of finance
Bob Hasan	Minister of trade and industry
Siti Hardiyanti Rukmana ("Tutut")	Minister of social services
Sjahril Sabirin	Governor of Bank Indonesia

notable was the new membership of the Seventh Development Cabinet announced thereafter (Table 6.2).

The Seventh Development Cabinet's membership reflected fixed capital to an unprecedented degree, representing an attempt by Soeharto to shore up his support among these constituents. Ginandjar Kartasasmita, a generally respected economist but a nationalist with links to the mining sector, had ultimate responsibility of reviving the economy. Naming Bob Hasan as minister of trade and industry meant that the first ethnic Chinese Indonesian to occupy a cabinet post was also one of the most corrupt. The new minister of finance, Fuad Bawazier, was a strong supporter of the CBS and (privately) of capital controls. Tutut's only real qualification for minister of social services was her relationship to Soeharto, and this appointment went over especially poorly abroad.[91] Habibie's economic nationalism made him popular among fixed capital but was seen as particularly troubling among foreign observers.[92] Also noteworthy was the decision to grant Soeharto absolute authority to protect Indonesia's national security against all threats.[93] Calls for political reform from opposition leaders and students notwithstanding, the MPR session demonstrated the strength of Soeharto's position among the New Order political establishment.[94]

[91] *Asiaweek*, March 27, 1998.
[92] *Asiaweek*, March 20, 1998; Haggard 2000b, 68–69; Colin Johnson 1998, 5.
[93] Liddle 1999a, 20.
[94] Interview with Emil Salim.

Despite some predictions to the contrary, military factionalism had little significance on the MPR session. ABRI's head representative in the MPR, General Susilo Bambang Yudhoyono, and Indonesian police commander, General Dibyo Widodo, had each expressed strong support for a Soeharto-Habibie ticket during the session.[95] Yudhoyono's ABRI links put him close to Wiranto and other soft-liners. Yet Habibie's Islamist credentials also linked him to members of the hard-line "green" faction. Feisal's post as coordinating minister for politics and security placed him highly in the Seventh Development Cabinet, and Prabowo's appointment as commander of Kostrad gave him his own contingent of troops based in Jakarta. In the end, Habibie emerged as a consensus candidate acceptable to both nationalist and Islamist camps in ABRI, while his nationalism earned him the support of Golkar, fixed capital in general, and Soeharto himself.

After the MPR session, ABRI leaders again warned that the regime would take decisive action to guarantee political stability. Student protestors continually tested the regime on this count, but when the regime demanded a halt to protests, as during the MPR session, security forces easily obliged. The generals did allow limited student protests, though, which suggested a politically consequential Wiranto-Prabowo split.[96] After all, by not repressing students, ABRI allowed their demonstrations to grow; and while ABRI confined the demonstrations to campuses, leaders rarely condemned student actions outright.[97] Moreover, with foreign media keenly interested in the demonstrations, the international costs of employing coercion to halt protests were high. Perhaps concerned about these international costs of crushing the student movement, ABRI did make token attempts to engage with student leaders and other opposition figures.[98]

But this did not mean that ABRI factionalism prevented the organization from halting demonstrations. In April, leaders of student protest organizations began disappearing, with some released after brutal detentions and others never to return. Subsequent investigations revealed that forces loyal to ABRI, and specifically to Prabowo and his allies within Kopassus, carried out these kidnappings and interrogations.[99] Moreover,

---

[95] *Suara Pembaruan*, March 10, 1998.
[96] Honna 1999, 121; Suryadinata 2002, 50.
[97] Aspinall 1999, 216; Shiraishi 1999, 74.
[98] *Asiaweek*, April 17, 1998.
[99] Aspinall 1999, 216; Emmerson 1999a, 307; Colin Johnson 1998, 8; Luhulima 2001, 87–96.

Soeharto himself warned students of the dangerous ground upon which
they tread. In the wake of unsatisfactory dialogues with protestors,
Soeharto directed students to cease demonstrations and return to class
or face the repressive force of the Indonesian military.[100] Some observers
have overestimated Wiranto's moderation during the final months of the
New Order. He was unsympathetic to students' demands for political
reform, warning students that the military would take swift action to deal
with unruly or violent protestors.[101] In early April, the regime banned
students from participating in what it had called "practical politics."[102]
While students could protest on campus, security forces under Wiranto's
command reacted swiftly and effectively to smother protests that moved
into the streets.[103] And in fact, as the anti-Soeharto vitriol of student
protests increased during Soeharto's final weeks in office, Wiranto's pros-
ecurity position hardened notably. While factional camps coalesced
behind Wiranto and Prabowo, this had no bearing on the regime's security forces' willingness to employ force to contain the student opposition.

Riots, Exit, and Endgame

The endgame for the New Order came in early May, when security forces
had their best opportunity to demonstrate their ability to protect the
regime. Just when ABRI had proved that it could maintain order,
Soeharto resigned. What changed were the calculations of ethnic Chinese
supporters of the regime, who were no longer willing to back it.

The decision that set in motion these events was the government's May 4
announcement that it would sharply decrease fuel and electricity subsidies. Price rises for these critical goods had the largest effects on poor
Indonesians, and their announcement caused sharp public outcry.[104] In the
days following the subsidy cuts, protest against the government spread
quickly from students and prodemocracy activists to regular Indonesians,
most notably the urban poor. Riots occurred in the cities of Medan, Solo,
and elsewhere across the archipelago as students and the urban poor voiced
their opposition.[105] By now, to many Indonesians the term *reformasi* came
to signify not just reform of the New Order political and economic system

[100] *Asiaweek*, May 1, 1998.
[101] *Jakarta Post*, April 13, 1998; *Jakarta Post*, May 5, 1998.
[102] *Jakarta Post*, April 8, 1998.
[103] Aspinall 1999, 215–16.
[104] *Jakarta Post*, May 5, 1998.
[105] O'Rourke 2002, 78–89; Pour 1998, 4.

but Soeharto's actual resignation. Nevertheless, Soeharto appeared unconcerned with the outbreak of mass protests against price raises, so much so that he left for a trip to Cairo on May 9.

While Soeharto was abroad, the tense political situation turned dramatically worse. Students at Trisakti University, a private university in Jakarta catering largely to the children of Indonesia's elites, organized a march from their campus to the DPR building. On the way, they met with police resistance, and a standoff ensued. Shortly after an apparently peaceful resolution to the standoff, violence broke out between security officials and students. While the police supposedly wielded only nonlethal weaponry – rubber bullets, tear gas, batons – during the melee unknown forces using live rounds shot dead four students.[106] Subsequent investigations have reached no firm conclusions regarding the groups responsible for the killings, but forces loyal to Prabowo likely orchestrated the murders, perhaps with Prabowo's knowledge. Prabowo's motive, it seems, was to frighten student demonstrators and their allies into quiescence.[107]

As students mourned their murdered comrades, Jakarta and several other cities succumbed to an orgy of violence. The events in Jakarta are best known. On May 13–14, rioters attacked citizens and business establishments in Jakarta's primarily ethnic Chinese neighborhoods. In addition to seemingly indiscriminate anti-Chinese violence, rioters targeted representatives of the New Order regime. Rioters torched Liem Sioe Liong's house and Tutut's office at the Ministry of Social Services, destroyed showrooms of Tommy Soeharto's Timor car company, and vandalized 122 branches of Bank Central Asia.[108] The Indonesian Human Rights Commission reported that the violence claimed 1,188 lives, many of them ethnic Chinese Indonesians but also rioters caught in burning buildings or killed as security forces restored order.[109] This figure does not include deaths in Solo, Surabaya, or other urban areas that witnessed violent anti-Chinese riots during this period. Beyond looting and killing, rioters raped hundreds of ethnic Chinese women in several areas of Jakarta. Precise figures, however, are unavailable, and later attempts to collect systematic data met with fierce political opposition.[110]

---

[106] See O'Rourke 2002, 89–94, for a detailed chronology of actors and events.
[107] See also Emmerson 1999a, 307; Hefner 2000, 206; Smith 2003, 118.
[108] *Asiaweek*, May 29, 1998; O'Rourke 2002, 97–102.
[109] *Kompas*, June 3, 1998.
[110] *Tempo*, October 12, 1998.

Observers have reached no consensus about what specifically caused the May 13–14 riots. The general conditions for riots of this type – ranked ethnic groups, declining economic conditions – certainly were present. Furthermore, ethnic violence in Indonesia had been common throughout the New Order. Yet never had rioting occurred on such a mass level, with such ferocity, or throughout so many parts of the country at once. These observations have led many researchers, as well as most Indonesians, to claim that some actor(s) had instigated the riots. Reports of agents provocateurs and military organizational support for riots filtered through the media in the weeks following the crisis. Many citizens of Jakarta report having seen individuals in military fatigues watching the riots unfold and claim that these agents had sparked the riots that later went beyond their control.[111] Many Indonesians may also believe that someone instigated the riots because the alternative – that the rapes and murders were simply ordinary Indonesians run amok – is too unsettling a prospect.[112]

Evidence for such specific charges in the case of the May 13–14 riots, in contrast to the case of Prabowo's role in the Trisakti killings, is inconclusive. Almost no Indonesians believe that the riots were purely spontaneous, but who among the military instigated the violence remains unknown. It is instructive that while several businesses connected to Soeharto's close ethnic Chinese cronies and his family burned, businesses connected to ABRI and the *pribumi* entrepreneurs escaped harm.[113] One perspective alleges that the riots were "no doubt centrally planned and provoked," likely by Prabowo loyalists, to discredit Wiranto and give Soeharto an excuse to impose martial law.[114] Evidence in favor of this argument is that security forces were slow to stop the rioting. Still, the slow response of the security forces may have been a result of the explosive spread of the riots.[115] Wiranto quickly restored order to Jakarta after calling in reserve units stationed in Semarang. Another view suggests that Wiranto, not Prabowo, had masterminded the violence, with Prabowo playing at best an auxiliary role. Fomenting conflict but immediately

---

[111] Interview with a newspaper editor, March 2006; interview with a Chinese Indonesian academic, February 2006; interview with Thung Ju Lan, social scientist at Lembaga Ilmu Pengetahuan Indonesia, March 13, 2006.

[112] Siegel 2001, 96–103.

[113] Interview with a newspaper editor, March 2006; interview with a Chinese Indonesian political observer, February 2006.

[114] Shiraishi 2001, 183–84.

[115] Emmerson 1999a, 309–10.

suppressing it would nudge Soeharto from power, leaving an opportunity for Wiranto and others to stake their own claims to power.[116] An investigation from an ad hoc committee from the National Human Rights Commission suggested that Major General Sjafrie Sjamsuddin was responsible.[117] This leaves open the question of why Wiranto did not then grab power from Habibie, Soeharto's vulnerable and inexperienced successor.

Whatever the trigger of the riots, the horrific scenes of violence in Jakarta and elsewhere led many Chinese Indonesians with sufficient means to flee the country. For some months already, Chinese-*pribumi* tensions had raised the specter of mass violence, and many Chinese had planned to escape if ethnic relations took a turn for the worse. By May 14, fleeing Chinese Indonesians packed flights to Singapore, Hong Kong, Australia, and elsewhere.[118] A common figure cited for the total number of Chinese Indonesians who fled the country is 100,000, and others put the total as high as 150,000,[119] but these are probably high – a more credible estimate is closer to 50,000.[120] This is a small percentage of all ethnic Chinese Indonesians, revealing that most Chinese Indonesians simply had no means to exit. Still, this figure included the wealthiest Chinese supporters of the regime and does not include the more widespread practice of internal migration of vulnerable ethnic Chinese to safer cities such as Pontianak in West Kalimantan.[121]

This mass exodus was decisive in bringing down the New Order regime. For the *konglomerat*, heretofore willing to trade economic benefits for physical security, the regime's loss of control indicated a new set of choices. Before, the Soeharto regime had protected them from anti-Chinese prejudice, entrusting them to help direct economic growth and simultaneously enrich other members of the regime. The regime's repressive machinery suppressed any potential opposition to wealth concentration in the hands of the *konglomerat*. But now the repressive arms of the regime had turned against them. This was the culmination of the growing antagonism between ABRI and *pribumi* owners of fixed capital, on one hand, and ethnic Chinese mobile capitalists, on the other, that

[116] O'Rourke 2002, 111–17.

[117] Interview with a figure in the Chinese Indonesian community, March 2006; interview with Wahyu Effendi, cofounder of Gerakan Anti-Diskriminasi Indonesia, February 28, 2006.

[118] *Jakarta Post*, May 14, 1998; *Straits Times*, May 15, 1998; *Weekend Australian*, May 16, 1998.

[119] *Jakarta Post*, June 9, 1998.

[120] Wibowo 2001, 136.

[121] Interview with a Chinese Indonesian political observer, February 2006.

Indonesia's twin crises had activated. To Chinese Indonesians who had supported the New Order, their benefit to supporting the regime – the provision of physical protection – was no longer available.[122] Seeing this, and witnessing the consequences of the breakdown of social relations in Jakarta, ethnic Chinese Indonesians voted with their feet and fled the country. They took with them their support for the regime. Those who did not physically flee began to agitate for Soeharto's resignation. For them, a political transition was now the best of many poor options.

With the support of mobile capital gone, the coalition supporting the New Order regime had fractured. Most other elites now began to abandon Soeharto, and those who remained gave him a sobering picture of what he needed to accomplish to retain power. From the true collapse of Soeharto's support coalition of fixed and mobile capital to his resignation, a rapid series of events ensued.[123] Soeharto returned from Cairo on May 15 to a city on edge. On May 16 he announced a reversal of subsidy price cuts, saying that price rises were the sources of the masses' anger. This was of course correct, but reversal was no longer a feasible strategy for retaining political support. On the same day, Harmoko and Syarwan Hamid met with Soeharto to tell him that the social climate had changed and that they now wanted him to resign. Harmoko and Hamid, along with Ismael Matareum of PPP and Fatimah Achmad of PDI, the next day reported that Soeharto had agreed to shuffle the cabinet.[124]

Golkar and ABRI figures now moved to protect their own economic interests in a post-Soeharto Indonesia by aligning themselves against Soeharto and his family. On May 18 Harmoko upped the ante by becoming the first member of the regime's inner core of supporters to call publicly on Soeharto to resign. Other MPR and Golkar members joined Harmoko in this demand. Wiranto hit back against Harmoko and the protestors, declaring that the call for resignation was inappropriate and that only an MPR session held under constitutional procedures could force Soeharto to resign.[125] Meanwhile, on May 19 students occupied the DPR building and refused to leave. Soeharto then tried to bring Muslim leaders together in a last ditch attempt to enlist a new coalition of supporters among highly placed Muslims with widespread grass-roots support. Soeharto also tried to bide his time by announcing early elections

---

[122] Interview with Benny Gatot Setiono, head of Perhimpunan Indonesia Tionghoa, March 16, 2006; interview with Emil Salim.

[123] Forrester 1998; Luhulima 2001; O'Rourke 2002, 118–35; Sulastomo 2001.

[124] *Jakarta Post*, May 17, 1998.

[125] *Jakarta Post*, May 19, 1998.

and political reforms in the coming months. He appeared on television flanked by members of the Muslim elite, but this overture did not satisfy protestors.[126] Behind the scenes, his support continued to crumble.

Amien Rais and other opposition leaders had scheduled a massive prodemocracy rally in Jakarta for May 20. As that day approached, Prabowo, Tutut, Wiranto, and Soeharto discussed plans to repress it, and Wiranto dispatched troops in advance to forestall any more mass protests.[127] In the end, Amien Rais called off the demonstrations, a seeming victory for Soeharto, but high-level negotiations to preserve the regime still proved fruitless. On the evening of May 20, the reformist Muslim intellectual Nurcholish Madjid (Cak Nur) told Soeharto that he refused to head a proposed Komite Reformasi (Reform Committee) and reported that only three out of forty-five individuals contacted had agreed to serve in it.[128] At the same time, defections from fixed capital became clear as Ginandjar reported that fourteen current ministers also refused to serve on a *reformasi* cabinet or on a reshuffled Seventh Development Cabinet.[129] At this news from Ginandjar and Cak Nur, Soeharto decided to resign. Before doing so, though, he met with Wiranto. He first checked to see if Wiranto could restore order; Wiranto told him that he could, but that it would be costly.[130] The pair considered this option seriously enough to draft a notice of martial law.[131] Soeharto then asked Wiranto if the general would guarantee his personal safety. Wiranto agreed. The next morning Soeharto handed over the presidency to Habibie.

Conclusion

In retrospect, the collapse of the New Order amid Indonesia's economic collapse seems inevitable. But I have argued in this chapter that despite the many accounts for the breakdown of the New Order, there has been no attempt to sort out precisely why the New Order collapsed when it did, and the way that it did. In this chapter, I have shown that the path from economic crisis to political transition followed the struggles over adjustment policy within the regime, which split along the fault line of mobile capital versus fixed capital. It is no accident that the charges leveled

---

[126] Loveard 1998, 28–29.
[127] Hefner 2000, 207; Luhulima 2001, 135–36.
[128] Pour 1998, 153.
[129] Luhulima 2001, 17.
[130] Shiraishi 1999, 82.
[131] Vatikiotis and Schwarz 1998, 65.

against ethnic Chinese Indonesians stressed economic sabotage and currency manipulation, and that those making them were both high-level indigenous capital holders and ordinary Indonesians. When the masses rioted and ABRI failed – either by design or through incompetence – to protect its ethnic Chinese Indonesian allies, ethnic Chinese allies fled the country and took their mobile capital assets with them. Only when ethnic Chinese Indonesians withdrew their support from Soeharto did the New Order collapse. The final week of Soeharto's rule was merely an attempt to cobble together a new coalition.

This account fulfills the conditions that I set out earlier in the chapter by explaining facts that other accounts have left unresolved. ABRI remained unified before and after Soeharto's collapse because its factional divisions were far less serious than previously thought. The relevant political cleavage during Indonesia's crisis was not Islamist versus nationalist in the military but rather mobile versus fixed capital, and ABRI fell into the latter group. Soeharto remained strong after his resignation because he was not irrational but rather quite calculating in managing the economic crisis to minimize the adjustment costs paid by his political supporters. A lack of legitimacy did not cause Soeharto to resign because he did not particularly care about legitimacy. However much the New Order's institutions may have ossified in the final years of Soeharto's rule, institutional failure does not explain the specific axis of political conflict between mobile and fixed capital that we observe. Soeharto resigned on May 21, 1998, rather than at some other time during the crisis because only at that point had his supporters withdrawn their support.

One alternative reading of fracture between Chinese Indonesians and *pribumis* in the military and business community is simply one of ethnic scapegoating. In this reading, the interests and actions of the *konglomerat* are immaterial; they suffered because in conditions of economic decline, Chinese Indonesians are a convenient "other" upon whom vulnerable groups can heap their frustrations. This would mean that I have identified the correct trigger of the regime's collapse (coalitional fracture) but the wrong causal mechanism (conflict over adjustment). Some amount of simple prejudice was doubtless at play. But other evidence reinforces that economic motivations drove the New Order coalition's fracture. One piece of evidence is the choice of scapegoat. *Konglomerat* are not the only potential target of popular frustration in Indonesia. At various points in New Order history, both Christians and communists have been blamed for the economic troubles that the country periodically faced. For instance, the "latent danger of communism" (*balatkom*) served as a frequent rallying cry for the New Order's assaults against organized labor, yet it found no place in Soeharto's final months. Just any scapegoat would not do.

Likewise, the rhetoric that accompanied targeting of ethnic Chinese Indonesians specifically referenced the issue of capital flight. Even instances of what appear to be pure prejudice against ordinary ethnic Chinese – such as the February 16 meeting in Surabaya – are packaged in the language of economic patriotism. This is important because there are many ways in which anti-Chinese prejudice is articulated in Indonesia: Chinese are accused of being a communist fifth column, of failing to convert to Islam, of harboring a secretive culture, of not contributing to rural development, and so forth. Were simple prejudice the dominant concern, we would expect any number of these issues to emerge, yet discursive attacks against *konglomerat* were remarkably consistent in their emphasis on capital flight. Rioters destroyed Bank Central Asia branches but not symbols of Bob Hasan's forestry concessions. At the same time, we know that the *konglomerat* lobbied the regime to maintain capital account openness and that influential *pribumis* lobbied otherwise (see Chapter 4), which underscores how different interests translated into the policy demands that drove the regime's collapse. Together, the nature of the scapegoating of Chinese Indonesians and the policy conflict surrounding it reinforce the political conflict between *konglomerat* and *pribumi* as not simply a matter of prejudice but a reflection of the division of fixed versus mobile capital.

Postscript: From Authoritarian Breakdown to Democratization

My coalitional explanation for the New Order's collapse does not deny the importance of mass preferences for *reformasi* in the wake of Soeharto's resignation. Nor does it deny the influence of mass preferences for a transition to democracy rather than simply to a new authoritarian regime. Others have traced Indonesian politics from the resignation of Soeharto to the election of Gus Dur with great success.[132] Without minimizing the importance of Indonesia's prodemocracy opposition movement, on the antecedent question of authoritarian breakdown, contradictory preferences over adjustment policy were decisive.

---

[132] See, e.g., O'Rourke 2002.

The theory, though, does yield some insights on democratization's path in Indonesia. We should observe a new attempt by fixed capital to forge a coalition with labor, their natural allies during the twin crises. But as noted in Chapter 2, new potential coalition partners such as labor should resist overtures made during crises, for these overtures alone lack credibility. Democratization – vesting ordinary Indonesian citizens with real political power – is one way to increase the credibility of any new coalition.[133]

By late May 1998, Habibie found himself in a difficult position. With mobile capital having abandoned the regime, the New Order's coalition simply no longer existed. Yet the New Order's institutions – Golkar, ABRI, the bureaucracy – remained intact, with Habibie overseeing them in an uncertain political environment. Continued economic deterioration kept the stakes high for any political settlement, but without mobile capital, the choices Habibie faced were limited. Holders of fixed capital could attempt to rule alone, or they could look to the Indonesian masses to form a new political coalition, much as Soeharto had attempted by calling together Islamists in his final days in office.

Habibie certainly would have preferred to rule alone, using his nationalist and Islamist credentials to head a New Order regime supported by fixed capital but without concessions to *reformasi* protestors. Indeed, the Seventh Development Cabinet included key representatives of fixed capital, and when the New Order coalition collapsed, these figures united to push Soeharto from office (and to marginalize Soeharto's greedy children) with an eye toward protecting the interests of fixed capital. But continued economic collapse and factionalism among *pribumi* business groups, Golkar leaders, and ABRI forced Habibie to seek allies in the Indonesian masses, which ranged from middle-class conservatives who had so enjoyed political stability under the New Order to radical student protestors energized by incipient political liberalization. Habibie thus resorted to economic populism, attempting to cobble together a new coalition between fixed capital and Indonesian labor under the New Order's institutional structure, achieving regime continuity and political succession without democratization or even any meaningful political liberalization. In the weeks following Soeharto's resignation, Habibie spoke of a new "People's Economy" that would empower *pribumi* entrepreneurs and end corruption. This did buy Habibie some time, as it was consistent with rhetoric from popular reformist leaders such as Amien Rais, who refused to lament the

---

[133] Acemoglu and Robinson 2006.

loss of the "parasites" who had forsaken their country for economic gain.[134]

Yet the promise of a new, populist New Order could not placate Habibie's opponents who continued to demand *reformasi*, nor could it co-opt elite opposition leaders who sought an independent road to power. Soeharto's resignation had marked a turning point in Indonesian politics. Now, although Habibie remained president, a formerly quiescent domestic media hit politicians and generals with tough questions, while activists marched and the regime's opponents made their pleas for democracy in a political environment that, while far from open, was already more liberal than Indonesia had seen in four decades. Those demanding incorporation included not only the protestors but also workers, farmers, and Islamists – in short, all Indonesians for whom meaningful politics had been closed since 1966. Of course, these groups were hardly united behind a common set of demands. Students and NGOs divided along secular-Islamist and radical-moderate lines, while opposition elites formed new parties and began in earnest to organize their supporters. But containing *reformasi* was no longer feasible, for even moderates sympathetic to Golkar were unwilling to trust the regime's promises of reform. Habibie and other Golkar leaders surveyed the political scene and decided that, to survive politically, they would need to burnish their own *reformasi* credentials. Only democratic elections would accomplish this. Accordingly, new electoral laws were introduced in November 1998, and DPR elections scheduled for June of that year. Golkar contested these as just one of many parties, ultimately finishing second. Thus ended the New Order.

The 1999 general elections marked the end point of Indonesia's transition to democracy. Yet it would be a mistake to view this as the end of fixed capital's political influence in Indonesia. Even with democratization – and decentralization two years later – money politics remains rampant in Indonesia. The corporate interests of *pribumi* entrepreneurs still played a central role in shaping economic reform under the IMF.[135] New political institutions have not ended corruption or shielded electoral politics from the interests of big business; rather, they have transformed the political economy from a single, centralized, hierarchical system of bribery and corruption into multiple diffuse networks of patronage and influence peddling.[136] And holders of mobile capital – in particular those

---

[134] Chua 2008, 77–78.
[135] Robison and Hadiz 2004, 187–217.
[136] Pepinsky 2008b, 235–43.

konglomerat who sent such vast sums of investment capital overseas –
still retain substantial structural power.[137] In 2005 the Indonesian press
reported that following a meeting with several *konglomerat* in Beijing,
one promised that the *konglomerat* would "repatriate . . . foreign exchanges but under the condition that the government is willing to create
economic certainty in the country."[138] Mobile capital abandoned the
New Order in order to protect its interests, and its return remains conditional on the establishment of a political environment that coincides with
those interests.

So while the collapse of the New Order coalition and Soeharto's resignation left fixed capital to struggle through the remainder of Indonesia's
economic crisis, neither the military nor Habibie and his nationalist allies
were able to contain the *reformasi* movement. My argument does suggest
that owners of fixed capital would begin a new effort after Soeharto's
resignation to steer economic policy in their favor, searching for new
coalition partners while minimizing any threats to the special position that
they enjoyed in the Indonesian economy. Combined with the insight that
potential new coalition partners – in this case, the Indonesian masses –
require a commitment mechanism to guarantee their allegiance to any
political leaders, we should observe democratization on the impetus of
the incumbents. This is what occurred. Still, while the collapse of Soeharto's system meant that holders of fixed capital could not succeed in imposing the nationalist policy response that Malaysia's regime implemented in
August 1998, new democratic institutions have served them well.

There are some exceptions. Bob Hasan, an ethnic Chinese crony who
did not flee the country because he owned timber concessions, was found
guilty of misusing Ministry of Forestry funds in 2001 and sentenced to a
short jail sentence, which he completed in 2004.[139] Prajogo Pangestu,
another ethnic Chinese timber baron, has fared better, but still faced
investigations for alleged misuse of forestry funds in 2001.[140] Also in
2001, Tommy Soeharto ordered the murder of the presiding judge in
his trial, M. Syafiuddin Kartasasmita. Another court found him guilty
and sentenced him to fifteen years in prison in 2002, reduced to ten years
upon appeal. He served time not for his actions under his father's rule but
for his subsequent crimes. On November 28, 2005, a court in Jakarta

[137] Chua 2008, 86–113.
[138] Dow Jones International News, August 31, 2005.
[139] *Kompas*, February 20, 2004.
[140] *Jakarta Post*, June 12, 2001.

sentenced Probosutedjo to four years in prison on corruption charges.[141] These examples show how under the new democratic regime, some of the New Order's biggest cronies have been punished. Still, Soeharto's other family members have largely escaped prosecution for their political corruption and economic abuses. The new *pribumi* business groups have persisted through the democratic period as well, represented perhaps most notably by Aburizal Bakrie – appointed as coordinating minister for people's welfare in 2005.[142]

ABRI leaders have fared the best after Soeharto. Initial reforms undertaken during the democratic period were successful, ending the military's official sociopolitical function and decoupling the national police force from the military (now renamed TNI or National Army of Indonesia). But deeper reforms – privatization of military businesses and cooperatives, and full subordination of the military to civilian authorities – have yet to occur.[143] Military personalities also figure prominently in democratic politics. In October 2005 Wiranto finished third in a presidential contest ultimately won by Susilo Bambang Yudhoyono, another former subordinate.

Democratization has not ended the influence of the military or big business on Indonesian politics. But it has changed the terms of this influence, in ways that the New Order's supporters fiercely resisted as long as they could. I now turn to Malaysia, which did not experience a political transition, to demonstrate how support coalitions remained united as a result of the country's adoption of a fixed exchange rate and capital controls.

[141] *Kompas*, November 29, 2005.
[142] Pepinsky 2008b.
[143] Mietzner 2006.

7

Authoritarian Stability in Malaysia

Malaysia's authoritarian regime survived the severe economic crisis that brought down Indonesia's New Order. Mahathir Mohamad retained firm control over Malaysia's political machine throughout Malaysia's crisis, even as contestation over Malaysia's political future rocked Malaysian society. In addition to implementing Malaysia's controversial capital controls and ringgit peg, Mahathir oversaw the arrest and conviction of his erstwhile deputy Anwar Ibrahim, as well as the regime's clampdown on a Malaysian *reformasi* movement. By December 1999 the BN had won its seventh election since 1969, easily retaining a two-thirds majority in the Dewan Rakyat (DR). Economic recovery through 1999 and 2000 reaffirmed UMNO's position at the top of Malaysia's political hierarchy. With the loyal and famously clean deputy prime minister Abdullah Ahmad Badawi prepared to succeed Mahathir on Mahathir's own terms, the stability of Malaysia's authoritarian regime was assured.

There are many existing explanations for the Malaysian regime's ability to withstand pressure for democratization. In this chapter, I argue that this political stability is the product of the regime's adjustment policies, which fulfilled the demands of each of its political supporters, poor Malays and the new Malay business class. Capital controls enabled expansionary policies, fulfilling the demands of fixed capital and the Malay masses. The effect of this radical adjustment measure for Malaysia's political opposition was striking. Having received their preferred adjustment policies, the regime's coalition of supporters had no incentive to withdraw support. So Malaysia's regime survived the crisis, despite the BN's most significant political challenge since the racial riots of 1969.

Of course, newly galvanized by economic stagnation and the regime's excesses, opposition parties for the first time formed a coalition, the Barisan Alternatif (Alternative Front, BA), in order to contest elections. But protest alone was no match for UMNO's firm control over the state's extensive security apparatus, and calls for justice and reform could not compete with the BN's adjustment policies that delivered the goods that its supporters demanded. Mahathir and his allies had no intention of losing the 1999 election – and might have declared a state of emergency had they not retained a two-thirds majority in the DR[1] – but successful adjustment allowed the regime to prevail.

As was the case with the breakdown of Indonesia's New Order, there are three primary benefits of my account. First, my account explains how the political crisis unfolded in Malaysia better than alternative explanations. I am able to highlight certain aspects of Malaysia's political crisis that have received little attention from area specialists, especially the question of why the BN remained so united in the face of widespread antiregime protests. I also need not assume a fundamental change in the nature of Malaysia's ruling authoritarian regime. The regime concentrated on the interests of the same coalition of regime supporters in adjusting to Malaysia's economic crisis as it had always done in making economic policy since the creation of the New Economic Policy in 1971. Finally, I continue to assume that all actors behaved rationally, given the new constraints imposed by Malaysia's economic crisis. Observers today rarely consider Mahathir to have been irrational in dealing with Anwar, but many during late 1997 and early 1998 were quick to label Mahathir's anti-Western outbursts as revealing an increasingly unhinged autocrat. My account uncovers the purposive logic behind political maneuvers that kept the regime in power.

"The Tragedy That Didn't Happen"

Researchers have struggled to explain Malaysia's political continuity, as many of the explanations used in the study of Indonesia would predict a breakdown of the Malaysian regime as well. The Malaysian regime faced severe economic contraction, a public factional squabble at the apex of the ruling party, and a large opposition movement that campaigned openly for regime change. If the opposition movement had succeeded in

---

[1] Interview with an anonymous reserve officer in the Malaysian army, July 2006; Milne and Mauzy 1999, 188.

TABLE 7.1. *Families of Explanations for Malaysia's Stability*

Cause	Explanation	Hypothesis
Impact	The crisis in Malaysia was not serious enough to unseat the BN.	Mild Crisis
Legitimacy	The ruling party offered a coherent ideology of governance.	Mahathirism vs. Anarchy
Institutions	The regime's political structure contained opposition.	Party System
Interests	The regime's policies satisfied the demands of its supporters.	Coalitional Unity

toppling Malaysia's government, any one of these factors could have served as an explanation. But, in the words of one pro-BN source, Malaysia's crisis was "the tragedy that didn't happen."[2] Table 7.1 lists the families of explanations for Malaysia's stability. All accounts focus on the interactions between ruling elites and the opposition. My argument falls into the category of "coalitional unity," where regimes remain stable if they fulfill the interests of their supporters.

Mild Crisis

Looking in comparison to Indonesia, many authors have focused on the idea that the crisis was "not so bad" in Malaysia as an explanation for the regime's stability.[3] Authors who make such comparisons invoke the case of the New Order's breakdown as a comparison, observing that a more serious economic contraction in Indonesia coincided with Soeharto's resignation. But data in Chapter 6 (Figure 6.1) show that economic contraction was actually more severe in Malaysia until *after* Soeharto's resignation. This contradicts the simple explanation for regime stability in Malaysia as resulting from a shallower economic crisis. And, after all, even the comparatively mild crisis in the Philippines – with GDP contraction of about 1 percent from 1997 to 1998 – contributed to mass popular unrest that allowed Joseph Estrada's National People's Coalition to defeat the incumbent Lakas Party.

---

[2] Tourres 2003.
[3] Case 2002, 135–36; Emmerson 1999b, 47–48; Rasiah and Shari 2001, 75; M. Weiss 1999, 440.

Even without considering Indonesia, the claim that Malaysia's economic downturn was insufficient to unseat the authoritarian regime seems odd. GDP contracted by more than 7 percent between 1997 and 1998, and the regime's struggle to combat the crisis and minimize its impact on business and ordinary Malays was a constant theme in Malaysian politics for two years. Mahathir and his political allies within UMNO and the BN certainly viewed the economic crisis as a deep threat to the regime's hold on power, even forbidding the Malaysian media from using the word "crisis" until well after the crisis had passed.[4] To observe that the regime was successful in managing this opposition simply pushes back the analysis a step further. What allowed the Malaysian regime to be so successful in containing political opposition?

Mahathirism versus Anarchy

The hypothesis of Mahathirism versus Anarchy emphasizes Mahathir's intelligence and devotion to the Malaysian people. This view is popular among many BN politicians,[5] as well as among other regime apologists.[6] Mahathirism, in this story, proved attractive enough to Malaysians that they continued to support their leader as he steered the country through difficult times. By contrast, Anwar had proved himself to be a power-hungry politician rather than a committed reformist, whose appeal to justice and reform after his dismissal from UMNO smacked of insincerity and sour grapes.[7]

A more nuanced view suggests that Mahathir's personality was less important than the regime's ideology. In this view, the regime continued to champion Malay rights and privileges, highlighting its developmental successes and economic recovery while reinforcing values of racial harmony and social stability.[8] Alternatively, the BN survived because of the lack of a coherent ideology among the regime's domestic opponents.[9] The BA consisted of three large parties, each of which advocated a different vision of Malaysian society. The DAP had for years emphasized social democratic policies that protected the rights of non-*bumiputras*, whereas

---

[4] Lim 1998a, xv.
[5] Interview with an anonymous Malaysian academic, June 2006.
[6] E.g., Tourres 2003, 3.
[7] Gomez 2004b, 6; Weiss 2000, 420–21.
[8] Emmerson 1999b, 52; Lee and Heng 2000, 222; Loh 2002, 48–49.
[9] Biro Analisis Politik 2000, 5–6; Case 2002, 248–49; Gomez 2004b, 6; Hilley 2001, 157; Liow 1999, 48–50; Saravanamuttu 2001, 116–18.

PAS advocated the imposition of *syariah* (Islamic law) across Malaysia. Wan Azizah's National JUSTice Party (KeADILan) emphasized multiculturalism, justice, and reform, but many accused it of lacking a coherent plan of rule.

The argument suggests that, had the BN regime lost its popular legitimacy, it would have collapsed. It is easy to dismiss this argument in light of Malaysia's political history and the strategies employed by UMNO and its coalition partners to retain political power in the face of earlier crises of legitimacy. In 1969, when ethnic riots followed a general election in which the ruling coalition won less than a two-thirds majority in the DR, the regime suspended democracy and retooled the political system to give UMNO greater advantages. In the late 1980s Tengku Razaleigh challenged Mahathir from within UMNO, eventually leading a splinter party that succumbed to political manipulation and no small amount of repression. In both instances, the ruling coalition faced crises of legitimacy but employed strong-arm tactics to preserve its rule. During the crisis, even if legitimacy helped the regime to preserve its authority, it did so only with drastic restrictions on opposition party campaigning and a credible (if largely unspoken) threat of repression.[10]

The Party System

Arguments about legitimacy beg the question of what allowed the regime such a free hand to manipulate political symbols during the crisis. Malaysia's political institutions are one possible answer. Focusing on Malaysia as an example of what he calls a "semi-democracy (or at times a "pseudo-democracy"), William Case argues that this distinct regime type has inherent institutional advantages that allow elites in power to retain control over their political opponents while allowing some dissent.[11] Alternatively, control over political institutions gave the ruling coalition free reign to crack down on the *reformasi* movement after Anwar's dismissal, or enabled the country's elites to forge a stable long-term bargain to survive short-term challenges and defections from within the ruling elite.[12] Moreover, the BN's entrenched system of money politics allowed the government to channel development funds to its supporters. Outside of the "Malay belt" in the northern part of the Malay Peninsula, where

---

[10] Case 2004, 36–37; Hilley 2001, 157.
[11] Two works (Case 2001a; 2002, ch. 4) use the term "semi-democracy." The alternative "pseudodemocracy" appears in Case 2001b.
[12] Brownlee 2007; Slater 2005, 321–45.

sympathetic religious leaders in local mosques facilitated effective distribution of ideas and limited patronage from PAS, BA parties had negligible financial resources with which to reward potential voters and lacked a patronage apparatus through which to disburse what funds that they did possess.[13]

The two party-system arguments differ in important respects: one argues that opportunities to vent grievances placate dissatisfied opponents, and the other that institutions confer overwhelming advantages to the incumbent BN. Yet each mechanism should have worked in Indonesia as well. In terms of containing political opposition, Golkar's penetration of nearly every facet of Indonesian political and social life, combined with ABRI's territorial presence throughout the archipelago, would seem to give the Indonesian regime *more* of an institutional advantage than the Malaysian regime.

Even looking within Malaysia, Chapter 5 details how political institutions specifically did not contain political conflict over adjustment, as institutional arguments predict they should have. Mobile capital strongly opposed the move by the regime to ban capital outflows, and non-Malay opposition parties decried the regime's retreat toward political favoritism in economic policy and development planning. All campaigned for regime change. Moreover, examining political institutions alone ignores the preferences of the regime's supporters. As in Indonesia, loyalty and quiescence of Malaysia's security apparatus were paramount for maintaining order. In contesting the 1999 general elections, each component party of the BN had incentives to preserve the existing system, keeping the BN's component parties unified, whereas in the 1990 general elections, a large proportion of UMNO members defected to form Semangat '46, which forged two electoral alliances, one with the DAP and the other with PAS. In 1999 the elites that unified behind the regime did so because they supported its policies, *not* in spite of the short-term costs they faced. Those elites who refused to unite behind the regime had clear gripes and were not dissuaded by the overwhelming advantage of the dominant coalition. This fact points to an incomplete understanding of what kept the regime's supporters united behind it.

Successful Adjustment
Coalitional unity lay behind the regime's successful manipulation of ideology and its exploitation of institutional advantages to preserve

---

[13] Gomez 2002, 107; Liow 1999, 50.

power. Of course, others do note that UMNO continued to protect the interests of the Malay masses and politically connected Malay business elites. Many middle-class Malays remained loyal to the regime that continued to give them favorable treatment.[14] The regime's supporters in the Malay corporate world enjoyed expansionary macroeconomic policies and remained loyal UMNO supporters.[15] The cohesiveness of the regime's supporters was the singular precondition for it to withstand political opposition. These works still fail to explain why the regime's support coalition remained unified while Indonesia's did not – if a regime can retain power by protecting its supporters, why do all regimes not adopt such policies? The answer lies in complementary preferences for economic adjustment among fixed capital and the Malay masses.

Mahathir's Malaysia in 1997

Malaysian politics at the beginning of 1997 looked as stable as Indonesian politics looked before its economic crisis. The most recent general elections had taken place in 1995, with the BN garnering almost two-thirds of all popular votes, giving it 162 out of 192 seats in the DR. It was even more successful in state elections. Outside of the states of Kelantan and Terengganu, where UMNO historically has never had the influence that it enjoyed elsewhere in the peninsula, the BN carried more than 85 percent of contested seats. In Terengganu and Kelantan, the BN's success was mixed. PAS won an outright majority of seats in Kelantan, retaining its control over the state legislature that it had previously gained in 1990. In Terengganu, PAS succeeded in winning a substantial minority of seats, but these were not enough to unseat the UMNO-dominated government.

Further developments between the 1995 elections and the onset of currency problems reflected Mahathir's continued authority. Semangat '46 folded shortly after the party's disappointing finish in the 1995 elections, its members quietly filing back to UMNO. By June 1997 every former Semangat '46 parliamentarian had returned to UMNO.[16] Thus, on the eve of the crisis, PAS was the only Malay party capable of challenging UMNO for Malay support. Even then, the vast majority of both urban and rural Malays outside of northeast Malaya remained loyal to the UMNO, and PAS had no support in East Malaysia.

---

[14] Abdul Rahman 2002, 200–1; Saravanamuttu 2003, 15.
[15] Case 2004, 38; Rasiah 2001a 60; H. Singh 2000, 543–44.
[16] *Utusan Malaysia*, June 25, 1997.

Other opposition parties were similarly weak. Aside from PAS, the DAP was the only party with significant representation in the DR, yet it found its leadership under attack from the Malaysian judiciary. The issue revolved around Rahim Tamby Chik, the chief minister for Melaka and head of UMNO Youth accused in 1994 of impregnating a fifteen-year-old girl. A dozen other men were convicted of improper sexual relations with the girl, yet Rahim remained free. Lim Guan Eng, a deputy secretary-general for DAP and the son of its secretary-general Lim Kit Siang, helped to distribute pamphlets lambasting the prosecution's handling of Rahim. In response, he was convicted of sedition for criticizing the judiciary – without tangible evidence to support this charge – and for making false publications. Even as Lim Guan Eng appealed his sentence, Attorney-General Mohtar Abdullah appealed the decision as too lenient.[17] These attacks left the DAP disorganized and preoccupied with legal maneuvering.

Mahathir Mohamad had by 1997 spent sixteen years as prime minister and UMNO president, and had given no signal of any intent to resign either post – indeed, UMNO banned contestation of the posts of president and deputy president in the 1996 UMNO party congress. Yet political succession remained a topic of speculation. Most attention centered on Anwar Ibrahim's rapid rise through the UMNO party ranks. Anwar became deputy president of UMNO in 1993 after defeating Ghafar Baba in party elections. With that post came the office of deputy prime minister, meaning that Anwar could expect to succeed Mahathir, barring any other challenges from within UMNO. Anwar had for years carefully crafted a network of connections with the Malaysian corporate world, and Anwar's corporate allies controlled several influential media outlets.[18] Anwar also held the finance portfolio, making him the public face of the regime's economic team. But his rapid ascent raised questions about his willingness to wait patiently for Mahathir to retire. Personal differences between the two politicians contributed to such speculation. In an interview given in May 1997, just months before Thailand's currency crisis spread to Malaysia, Mahathir spelled out the often difficult relationship between the two leaders.[19] Mahathir suggested that differences in their public demeanors were superficial, more reflections of personal

---

[17] *New Straits Times*, May 1, 1997; *Asiaweek*, May 16, 1997.
[18] Interview with an anonymous Malaysian economist, April 2005; Gomez 1994, 155–56; 2002, 98; 2004a, 162–63; Gomez and Jomo 1999b, 124–25.
[19] *Asiaweek*, May 9, 1997.

leadership styles than fundamental political visions for UMNO or Malaysia. He indicated no reluctance to hand over authority to Anwar eventually, but he also gave the impression that he had no intention of retiring in the near future.

By mid-1997 the BN faced no serious challenge from outside of the regime. Within the BN, UMNO remained *primus inter pares*, and within UMNO, Mahathir's position seemed secure. Questions about political succession were hardly new, having been common throughout his tenure as prime minister. Even the personal differences between Anwar and Mahathir had long been the subject of rumor. UMNO and especially Mahathir continued to enjoy widespread political support for their pro-Malay policies from the Malay masses, as well as political and financial support from their allies within the Malay corporate world. Similar to the case of Soeharto in Indonesia, the greatest political concern for the ruling coalition was Mahathir's willingness to hand over power smoothly to his chosen successor.

From Economic to Political Crisis
Upon the onset of Malaysia's crisis, Mahathir's repeated outbursts against currency speculators and an international Jewish conspiracy led many observers to question his erratic leadership. On the domestic front, Mahathir moved immediately to preempt demands for a political shake-up – even before BNM floated the ringgit, Mahathir stressed that political stability was the best incentive to attract investment.[20] Repeatedly throughout the summer of 1997, the regime insisted that currency depreciation and stock market weaknesses were only temporary disruptions in an otherwise healthy economy. The BN projected a united front, with Deputy Finance Minister Affifudin Omar and Minister of International Trade Rafidah Aziz exhorting Malaysians not to criticize the regime.[21] In the ensuing months, other UMNO leaders joined Mahathir and his cabinet members in supporting the regime's policies.[22] Moreover, the media throughout the fall of 1997 painted UMNO as the only party capable of protecting the economic well-being of *bumiputras*.[23]

At the same time, the regime also began to project more seriously its resolve to prevent political criticism. Anwar, as acting prime minister

[20] *Utusan Malaysia*, June 19, 1997.
[21] *Utusan Malaysia*, July 18, 1997; July 19; 1997.
[22] *Utusan Malaysia*, July 28, 1997; October 20, 1997.
[23] *Mingguan Malaysia*, October 5, 1997.

while Mahathir traveled abroad on a working vacation, defended the police forces' responsibility for detaining anyone accused of questioning the country's security forces.[24] Upon returning, Mahathir gave an interview in which he reiterated the importance of maintaining political continuity in order to foster economic development.[25] Mahathir also began to play off of nationalist sentiments with veiled threats against mobile capital. By late August, he began to criticize domestic finance companies, blaming them for sabotaging the country's economy and threatening to pull their licenses if they lent money for speculative purposes. These criticisms had strong anti-Chinese overtones, made evident later in the regime's special announcements placed in Chinese dailies to fight speculation.[26] In September, Inspector-General of the Police Abdul Rahim Noor vowed to use the draconian Internal Security Act against any Malaysians acting as economic saboteurs.[27] Already, the axis of political conflict in Malaysia mirrored that which ultimately drove the breakdown of Indonesia's New Order.

During the fall of 1997, condemnation of external actors moved from charges of an international conspiracy to harm Muslim nations to an international conspiracy to overthrow Mahathir.[28] UMNO leaders rallied around him, condemning the foreign press for suggesting a crisis of confidence in Mahathir's leadership and fomenting instability within the country.[29] Several days later, Mahathir revealed that the regime was considering banning foreign publications held to be excessively critical of the government. At the same time, Deputy Finance Minister Affifudin reassured Malaysians that Mahathir's commentary in the foreign press did not harm the Malaysian economy.[30]

The repeated statements concerning foreign plots and domestic disloyalty reveal that the regime viewed the country's economic crisis as a threat. The BN accordingly redoubled its efforts to demonstrate its broad-based support among holders of fixed capital and the Malay masses. Several key by-elections became focal points for the regime to project its populist, developmentalist, pro-Malay image. In the mid-August by-election in Semarak, Kelantan, it campaigned heavily on the

[24] *Utusan Malaysia*, July 18, 1997.
[25] *Mingguan Malaysia*, August 3, 1997.
[26] *Berita Harian*, August 30, 1997; *Utusan Malaysia*, September 4, 1997.
[27] Gill 1998, 62.
[28] *Berita Harian*, October 4, 1997.
[29] *Mingguan Malaysia*, October 5, 1997.
[30] *New Straits Times*, October 12, 1998; *Utusan Malaysia*, October 16, 1998.

theme that PAS's Islamist ideology was incompatible with Malaysian development.[31] In the run-up to two by-elections on November 8, the Malay media focused almost exclusively on the BN's developmentalist vision for all Malaysians, especially in the bitter campaign in the majority-Chinese constituency of Sungai Bakap on Penang. The BN won all three of these by-elections, handily defeating PAS in Changkap Jering, Perak, edging by the DAP in a tight three-way race in Sungai Bakap, and even wrestling the Semarak seat away from PAS.

As the crisis continued unabated through the end of November, BN politicians remained loyal to the cabinet. After each of Mahathir's anti-Western outbursts, Anwar reassured foreign investors that Mahathir's views were not as radical as they appeared.[32] In response to rumors that their different demeanors masked more serious policy differences, Anwar himself claimed that he was merely giving explanations of Mahathir's ideas rather than gainsaying them.[33] Following Mahathir's anti-Jewish statements in mid-October, and a draft motion of censure by thirty-four U.S. senators in response, Anwar led a vote of confidence on November 19 that received unanimous support from BN politicians. Anwar himself also began to warn the domestic opposition not to overstep its bounds in criticizing the BN.[34] When Mahathir announced the formation of the National Economic Action Council (NEAC) on November 20, observers considered it yet another signal of Mahathir's authority over economy policy making. Reacting to the observation that every time he spoke in public the ringgit depreciated further against the U.S. dollar, Mahathir announced with characteristic aplomb that every time *Time* and *Newsweek* published negative stories about him, his domestic position strengthened.[35]

Anwar versus Mahathir

Behind the regime's public face of unity lurked the political struggle between Anwar, increasingly identified with the IMF's adjustment recommendations, and Mahathir, still vocally disparaging the global financial system. As their relationship had long been the subject of speculation, policy differences initially appeared relatively insignificant. Later events would prove suspicions of a deep political rift to be accurate.

[31] *Utusan Malaysia*, August 6, 1997; *Berita Harian*, August 10, 1997.
[32] See Athukorala 2001, 65; Jomo 1998, 185–86.
[33] *Utusan Malaysia*, October 5, 1997.
[34] *Utusan Malaysia*, November 20, 1997.
[35] *New Straits Times*, November 12, 1997.

Anwar's position within UMNO and the BN was far from secure. He had earlier been accused in a sex scandal, the details of which circulated in several *surat layang* (literally, "flying letters") among BN politicians. Mahathir commented frequently on these rumors in the summer and fall of 1997, calling them baseless, politically motivated rumors.[36] Several weeks later, Malaysian police arrested several individuals in connection with these rumors. It emerged in late October that Anwar had instructed police officers to investigate the matter, an event that would prove crucial in the following year in investigations of Anwar's alleged misuse of power. While the Malaysian media dropped the subject of Anwar's alleged sexual improprieties beginning in November, these rumors continued to circulate throughout political circles.

Mahathir publicly defended Anwar on the subject of sexual misconduct, but in economic management he began to move against Anwar. The NEAC, created out of the Economic Planning Unit within the Prime Minister's Department but inviting the participation of private business interests and social groups, was the first move to neutralize Anwar's independence in economic matters. Shortly thereafter, in December 1997, the first real policy rifts emerged between Anwar and Mahathir, with Anwar supporting fiscal cutbacks and pledging to maintain an open capital account with a floating ringgit. The tone of the policy debate also began to change, with Mahathir continuing to blame foreign conspiracies and Anwar focusing on domestic cronyism and inefficiency. Two factions had coalesced by April 1998. On one side, Mahathir, Daim, and members of the NEAC advocated an expansionary and protectionist economic recovery through lower interest rates and bailouts of troubled banks and firms. On the other side, Anwar and technocrats such as BNM governor Ahmad Mohd. Don continued to advocate macroeconomic tightening and liberalization.[37]

Mahathir's rhetorical attacks against westerners, the foreign media, Jews, and currency traders continued through the beginning of 1998, with comments now also directed at domestic audiences. In his Aidil Fitri (Eid ul-Fitr) radio address on January 30, 1998, he lashed out against foreign criticisms of the BN by calling international markets undemocratic.[38] Later that spring Mahathir would claim that "freedom to the poor is not freedom at all. It is inconsiderate to deprive people of their livelihood

---

[36] *Utusan Malaysia*, August 25, 1997.
[37] Case 2002, 132–33; Khoo 1998b, 6; Liow 1999, 46.
[38] Mahathir 1999, 14.

because we want them to be free from their allegedly corrupt or oppressive Government."[39] By contrast, Anwar blamed Malaysia's economic problems largely on the country's own political and economic weaknesses. Much more than Mahathir – and much more than he admitted in the domestic press – Anwar's reform agenda called for a widespread shake-up of the Malaysian corporate world. This would include especially fixed capital holders such as the new Malay entrepreneurs and ethnic Chinese associates of UMNO,[40] although it remains unclear whether Anwar felt that the same tough medicine should apply to his own corporate circle. Still, Anwar's own statements in the Malaysian media remained pro-Malay, focusing on rural development, controls on price rises, and continued affirmative action for *bumiputra* small businesses.

So while Anwar retained his ideological commitment to pro-Malay policies, his acceptance of many IMF-style reforms and hostility toward the new Malay entrepreneurs put him increasingly at odds with Mahathir. So while Mahathir remained firmly allied with fixed capital and Malay labor, Anwar's allegiance to the former began to wane. Mahathir threw his weight behind fixed capital in spite of the excesses of Malay entrepreneurs and ethnic Chinese UMNO allies that came to light during this period. In Anwar's own recounting of the events, he claims that while he confronted Mahathir regarding several corporate scandals taking place throughout these months, Mahathir refused to listen. Anwar also claims that Mahathir became increasingly "egotistical" and "megalomaniacal" as the crisis deepened through 1997 and 1998.[41] For his own part, Mahathir claims to have repeatedly warned Anwar that following the IMF would bankrupt the economy.[42] As the crisis worsened, the relationship between Mahathir and his deputy worsened as well.

Containing Domestic Opposition

As Mahathir and Anwar struggled over adjustment policy measures during the early months of 1998, they assiduously tried to forestall an opposition movement. Their main targets were DAP and PAS, whose criticisms mounted in early 1998. Lim Kit Siang spoke out against the NEAC, declaring this supraconstitutional body to be undemocratic and calling

---

[39] Mahathir 1998a, 18–19.
[40] *Asiaweek*, December 12, 1998.
[41] Interview with Anwar Ibrahim; Anwar 1998a.
[42] Mahani 2002, 272.

on all cabinet ministers to resign in January 1998.[43] Lim also commented on the possibility of racial violence if economic conditions did not improve, forcing Anwar to once again defend the BN's record on creating stable race relations.[44] In March 1998 Lim also publicly demanded an investigation into the corporate scandals involving the politically linked Perwaja Steel and UEM. In response, the regime stepped up its attacks on the DAP. On April 1 the court of appeals increased Lim Guan Eng's sentence for charges of sedition and making false publications. Mahathir maintained that the judiciary reached its decision without political interference and was merely following the law.[45] Kit Siang's defense of his son occasioned a split within the DAP, as several members questioned the propriety of defending Guan Eng amid the more significant economic problems facing the country.[46] This intraparty squabble contributed to the DAP's ineffectiveness as a viable critic of the BN during the spring and summer of 1998. Mahathir especially capitalized on the political implications of the Guan Eng affair, declaring it to be proof that the DAP was plagued with corruption and nepotism.[47]

Criticisms of mobile capital in general, and Chinese Malaysians in particular, grew as the crisis deepened in 1998. Already by late 1997, the chief minister of the southern Malayan state of Johor, Abdul Ghani Othman, warned citizens not to transfer their currency holdings to Singapore.[48] In May the president of Gerakan, Lim Keng Yaik, alleged that Chinese millionaires were parking their funds in Singapore, totaling as much as RM20 billion – approximately U.S.$5 billion at the prevailing exchange rate.[49] Using a Chinese member of the BN as a mouthpiece for the regime's concerns about mobile capital helped to soften these accusations of unpatriotic behavior, but the reaction within the Chinese community and from opposition parties was strongly negative. Guan Eng, already facing imprisonment, rejected these allegations as baseless and demanded proof. Nevertheless, grumbles about wealthy Chinese transferring funds to Singapore and elsewhere persisted, with UMNO Youth president Ahmad Zahid Hamidi complaining that wealthy individuals had repatriated only RM3.5 billion of that sum and Daim Zainuddin

[43] Lim 1998a, 3–4.
[44] *Utusan Malaysia*, January 12, 1998; Lim 1998a, 43.
[45] *Utusan Malaysia*, April 7, 1998.
[46] *New Straits Times*, June 8, 1998.
[47] *Utusan Malaysia*, June 6, 1998, Kua 1998.
[48] *New Straits Times*, December 30, 1997.
[49] *Utusan Malaysia*, May 9, 1998.

imploring mobile capitalists to strengthen the economy by repatriating funds.[50] In an attempt to ease public tensions, several prominent Chinese Malaysian hoteliers sold their assets abroad.[51] MCA president Ling Liong Sik subsequently joined Lim Keng Yaik in urging Chinese millionaires to bring money back into Malaysia, taking pains to note that some Malay and Indian Malaysian businessmen were guilty of moving their funds overseas as well.[52] Nevertheless, at a subsequent meeting with MCA Youth and MCA Women, Mahathir again emphasized the possibility that unpatriotic business practices could cause racial violence.

These invectives against mobile capital reflect the regime's fealty to fixed capital and the Malay masses. PAS, whose constituents are primarily ordinary Malays, presented a somewhat different problem. As a party with strong Islamist credentials and a reputation for criticizing UMNO cronyism, PAS attracted increasing sympathy from rural Malays in the Malay belt. In Kelantan, still under PAS control, the state government planned public-sector wage raises in May 1998. Although UMNO was in the process of studying an identical move, Minister of Entrepreneurial Development Mustapa Mohamed called the PAS plan "propaganda."[53] In July PAS stunned UMNO by winning in a by-election in Arau, Perlis – a traditional UMNO stronghold.[54] UMNO later alleged that PAS had won the vote fraudulently by employing phantom voters, a tactic more often associated with UMNO. Thus, despite media disparagement throughout this period, PAS was able to attract new supporters in the Malay heartland, a fact that increasingly worried the BN.

NGOs also faced intimidation. On May 3 Mahathir revealed that an unnamed NGO had spread false rumors that prison detainees had been poisoned and killed. Members of the regime responded by demanding public disclosure of the NGO's identity and warned that treasonous NGOs would be disbanded under the Societies Act.[55] Along similar lines, after Malaysian Trade Union Congress chairman G. Raja Sekaran alleged that 500,000 workers might be retrenched before the end of 1998, the Ministry of Human Resources demanded that he either offer firm proof or face legal action.[56] To ward off student activism, which was still illegal

[50] *Utusan Malaysia*, May 11, 1998; May 15, 1998.
[51] *Utusan Malaysia*, May 13, 1998.
[52] *Straits Times*, May 31, 1998.
[53] *Utusan Malaysia*, May 22, 1998.
[54] *Mingguan Malaysia*, July 5, 1998.
[55] *New Straits Times*, May 4, 1998; *Utusan Malaysia*, May 13, 1998.
[56] *Berita Harian*, May 5, 1998.

under Malaysian law, the regime also warned students to employ only the proper channels in voicing their frustrations with the government.[57]

While adopting policies to cripple domestic opponents, both Mahathir and Anwar also fought to secure their party position in the face of the upcoming UMNO General Assembly, scheduled for June 1998. In March 1998 Mahathir remarked that the party should delay turnover in party leadership positions as long as the country faced economic problems.[58] Anwar heartily supported this proposal, echoing Mahathir's arguments that with a stable government, politicians could concentrate on economic issues.[59] Anwar likewise suggested that UMNO members should consult with (*bermusyawarah*) and advise the party leadership, rather than using the excuse of democracy to justify criticism.

While Anwar supported these no-contest restrictions, they did have negative consequences for many of his allies within UMNO, many of whom wished to challenge the entrenched allies of Mahathir at the higher levels of the party hierarchy.[60] In response, Anwar's allies within UMNO's youth wing made a similar decision that prevented challengers from contesting the positions of head and deputy head of UMNO Youth.[61] Several weeks later, for reasons that remain unclear but which may reflect an early indication of upcoming factional realignments, UMNO Youth reversed this decision.

By May 1998 tensions between Mahathir and Anwar were clear enough to warrant repeated denials in the mainstream media that such tensions existed. Allegations of corruption, collusion, and nepotism (KKN) in government bailouts and financial sector dealings were increasingly employed by regime critics to discredit its economic management. As these scandals continued, Anwar's allies within UMNO Youth moved against Mahathir and his allies. Their apparent strategy was to use the 1998 UMNO party congress, taking place June 19–22, for their assault.[62] UMNO Youth president Ahmad Zahid Hamidi announced in early June that corruption in UMNO and the BN had reached unheralded proportions and that UMNO Youth would name all sources of nepotism within UMNO at the party congress.[63] The allegations by Ahmad Zahid, a well-known

---

[57] *Utusan Malaysia*, July 13, 1998.
[58] *Utusan Malaysia*, March 15, 1998.
[59] *Utusan Malaysia*, March 16, 1998.
[60] *Asiaweek*, April 24, 1998.
[61] *New Straits Times*, May 1, 1998.
[62] Case 2003, 120; Khoo 1998b.
[63] *Utusan Malaysia*, June 8, 1998; June 10, 1998.

Anwar ally and the head of the party's influential youth wing, were the first open, internal threat to Mahathir's position.

The threat, however, spurred Mahathir's allies into action and led to fierce condemnation of UMNO Youth members for disloyalty. Mahathir's allies, moreover, directly tied this disloyalty to economic conditions. Senator Zainuddin Maidin and others condemned UMNO Youth's plan, saying it would destabilize Malaysia's political structure and could cause racial violence. In particular, Zainuddin alleged that criticism of Mahathir from within UMNO would destroy party unity and damage international confidence in the Malaysian economy.[64] UMNO's women's arm pledged not to discuss the issue of corruption at the general assembly, maintaining that its members would instead focus on positive solutions to the country's economic crisis.[65] Defense Minister Najib Abdul Razak and Foreign Minister Abdullah Ahmad Badawi, both UMNO vice presidents, voiced their frustration not at corruption in UMNO's ranks but at complaints about corruption from within UMNO.[66] Ahmad Zahid quickly backtracked, claiming not to have any particular UMNO politicians in mind when making his allegations,[67] but the damage was done.

During the UMNO General Assembly itself, unknown groups circulated an inflammatory pamphlet entitled *50 Reasons Why Anwar Cannot Become Prime Minister*, by Khalid Jafri, an author long rumored to have links with Mahathir and other UMNO politicians. The pamphlet attacked Anwar's character, focusing on his alleged hypocrisy, his past as an Islamist and student activist, rumors of sexual misconduct, allegations of corruption and nepotism, his lack of vision for Malaysia's development, and so on.[68] It also claimed that UMNO party stalwarts – and allies of Mahathir – such as Kedah chief minister Sanusi Junid, Abdullah, and Rahim Tamby Chik thought poorly of Anwar and his "vengeful temperament." The allegations in the pamphlet were themselves nothing new, but its circulation during the UMNO party congress was inflammatory. In the media, the pamphlet received constant attention, even though Anwar had obtained an injunction barring its publication even before the UMNO congress began.[69] Mahathir promised to investigate how the pamphlet came to be circulated but, tellingly, also promised to

---

[64] *Utusan Malaysia*, June 14, 1998.
[65] *Utusan Malaysia*, June 15, 1998.
[66] *Utusan Malaysia*, June 16, 1998.
[67] *Utusan Malaysia*, June 17, 1998.
[68] Khalid 1998.
[69] *New Straits Times*, June 18, 1998, Hilley 2001, 106; Hwang 2003, 290.

investigate the allegations contained within the pamphlet, in particular those concerned with sexual impropriety.[70] On August 12 the attorney-general charged Khalid Jafri on one count of libel, but almost eight years passed before Khalid faced these charges in court.[71] Meanwhile, Khalid himself sued PAS and the publishers of its newsletter *Harakah* for defamation, winning a settlement of RM200,000 in 2001.[72]

The circulation of the inflammatory pamphlet was only the opening salvo against Anwar. Mahathir also responded by tying the BN's rule to the economic fortunes of the regime's supporters among fixed capital. The day before the UMNO party congress opened, Mahathir warned UMNO members that they should not make accusations of KKN without firm evidence.[73] Mahathir then made allegations of his own, publicizing the names of all groups and individuals who had profited from government tenders.[74] In the following days, newspapers carried the full list of beneficiaries that Mahathir had released, making it clear that KKN within UMNO and the BN extended far beyond Mahathir and his corporate circle.[75] This accomplished two things: it deflected the spotlight from Mahathir and back onto Anwar's own corporate connections; and it communicated to holders of fixed capital, and in particular the new Malay entrepreneurs, the benefits that they enjoyed through their allegiance to UMNO. Furthermore, during the party congress, Mahathir reiterated his personal support for Anwar but added that he would no longer object if any UMNO member sought to challenge Anwar in his position as deputy president.[76]

Their apparent plan to challenge Mahathir having failed, Anwar, Ahmad Zahid, and their associates threw their support behind him again. Ahmad Zahid advocated reform but stipulated that no policy should cause a rift in UMNO party unity. Other UMNO Youth members distanced themselves from Ahmad Zahid's earlier comments.[77] Anwar himself pledged loyalty to Mahathir and, by the end of the congress, appeared solidly behind him. Mahathir's own supporters, meanwhile, voiced their allegiance to him in ever stronger terms. UMNO Women chief Siti

[70] *New Straits Times*, June 21, 1998.
[71] *Berita Harian*, July 9, 2005.
[72] *New Straits Times*, August 14, 2001.
[73] *Utusan Malaysia*, June 18, 1998.
[74] Felker 2000, 52; M. Weiss 1999, 427.
[75] *Mingguan Malaysia*, June 21, 1998.
[76] *Berita Harian*, June 20, 1998.
[77] *Utusan Malaysia*, June 19, 1998.

Zaharah Sulaiman warned party members not to engage in personal agendas.[78] Echoing this sentiment, Sanusi Junid revealed "five agendas" to bring down Mahathir during the UMNO party congress, each being masterminded by an unnamed UMNO member dissatisfied with Mahathir.[79] In the same speech, Sanusi promised to protect Mahathir from Anwar or any other challenger, a statement that received thunderous applause from the assembly.[80]

International Retreat and Domestic Offensive

Throughout this period, despite intense factional conflict within UMNO, the regime maintained a firm commitment to adopting policies that would benefit its Malay supporters. Mahathir's offensive against Anwar and his associates increased in intensity in the wake of the UMNO General Assembly and once again mirrored adjustment policy developments that privileged fixed capital and the Malay masses. Mahathir's first move, on June 24, was to appoint his longtime ally Daim Zainuddin to the post of minister with special functions in the Prime Minister's Department. The regime explained this decision through Daim's continuing role as executive director of the NEAC, arguing that Daim's new position would facilitate communication between the NEAC and the cabinet.[81] Given Daim's past service as minister of finance under Mahathir and the growing adjustment policy rift between Mahathir and Anwar, observers understood Daim's appointment to be a direct assault on Anwar's Finance portfolio. Mahathir on several occasions denied that Daim was replacing Anwar; Anwar as well denied that Daim's appointment affected his position as minister of finance.[82] Indeed, Anwar did continue to direct the regime's economic management in the month following Daim's appointment, now criticizing the IMF for giving inconsistent advice and, ever more loudly, vowing not to cut development expenditures for Malays.[83] But now, Daim, a longtime representative of Malay fixed capital, emerged as a competing champion of the regime's policies.

Mahathir also moved against the Malay-language mass media. In July, Johan Jaafar and Ahmad Nazri Abdullah, the editors of *Utusan Malaysia*

[78] *New Straits Times*, June 19, 1998.
[79] *Utusan Malaysia*, June 22, 1998.
[80] *New Straits Times*, June 22, 1998.
[81] *Berita Harian*, June 25, 1998.
[82] *Utusan Malaysia*, July 1, 1998.
[83] *Utusan Malaysia*, July 8, 1998; July 21, 1998.

and *Berita Harian*, the two Malay-language dailies with the broadest circulation, were dismissed. These editors were close to Anwar, as was Yunus Said of TV3, the leading Malaysian television station, who was also dismissed.[84] The regime exhorted the new editors of Malay-language dailies to support Mahathir and the BN, and accordingly, critics such as columnist Rustam A. Sani lost their positions.[85] The dismissal of these pro-Anwar media figures gave Mahathir an even freer hand to manipulate the public face of the BN regime.

In August an UMNO committee convened to reexamine the party's constitution. First on the agenda was the existing practice of awarding ten extra votes to any candidate for president or deputy president who received a division nomination, a practice that had allowed Anwar to unseat former deputy prime minister Ghafar Baba in 1993.[86] Anwar denied furiously swirling rumors that he had resigned his cabinet posts, while simultaneously pledging loyalty to Mahathir and promising not to contest Mahathir for the UMNO presidency.[87] Other UMNO leaders continued to rally around Mahathir: Ghafar Baba reiterated the importance of the BN's leadership for reviving the Malaysian economy, while Abdullah Ahmad Badawi insisted that UMNO should have only one "general."[88]

Capital Controls and Crackdown

On September 1 Mahathir announced Malaysia's controversial adjustment package of selective controls on capital outflows, a hard peg of the ringgit at RM3.80 to the U.S. dollar, and expansionary monetary and fiscal policies. Having conferred the desired policies on fixed capital and Malay labor, and shielded from the threat of capital outflows, Mahathir now embarked on his final offensive against Anwar. On the same day that Mahathir announced the ringgit peg, he offered to accept Anwar's resignation from the positions of deputy prime minister and minister of finance. When Anwar refused to resign, Mahathir sacked him and, on September 3, expelled him from UMNO. Anwar's sacking followed only days after the resignation of BNM governor Ahmad Mohd. Don and deputy governor Fong Weng Phak, both of whom had opposed capital

[84] Anwar 1998a; Gomez and Jomo 1999b, 200; Hilley 2001, 106; Mustafa 2002, 162; Zaharom 1998.
[85] Rustam 2004, ix, 376–80.
[86] *Utusan Malaysia*, August 19, 1998.
[87] *Utusan Malaysia*, August 12, 1998.
[88] *New Straits Times*, August 22; *Utusan Malaysia*, August 26.

controls and the exchange rate peg, and both of whom were close to Anwar while he was minister of finance. On September 7 Mahathir appointed himself to the new cabinet post of first finance minister and appointed Mustapa Mohamed – at that time the minister of entrepreneurial development – to hold the new post of second finance minister. Former managing director of the Economic Planning Unit within the Prime Minister's Department, Ali Abul Hassan Sulaiman, became the new governor of BNM, while former BNM adviser Zeti Akhtar Aziz became the new deputy governor of BNM.

With Anwar sacked, Mahathir's control over the reins of economic decision making was secure. Television and print media swiftly rallied behind Mahathir – beginning here and continuing throughout the subsequent months, the onslaught of anti-Anwar and pro-Mahathir stories makes it impossible to gauge public sentiment from local media sources. It is clear, though, that the highest levels of UMNO party leadership remained united behind Mahathir. The foreign media was much less supportive of Mahathir's radical adjustment plan and Anwar's sacking, as the *Asian Wall Street Journal* showed in an editorial:

It is far from clear that Mr. Anwar's loss is a gain for anyone else. The most optimistic scenario is only a short-term one in which pump priming and capital controls and the like will produce an illusion of economic well-being that lasts just long enough for Dr. Mahathir to declare victory, call an election, and eventually leave the inevitable mess for an unlucky successor. By that time – if they are wise enough not to follow Malaysia's current example – regional neighbors will be on the road to a lasting recovery.[89]

The editors' view of the Malaysian regime's new adjustment package reflects its economic logic, even if their pessimism about the package's efficacy now seems misguided. Anwar, however, did not fade quietly into the political background, as Mahathir and his allies expected. Instead, he launched his own *reformasi* campaign against Mahathir. His attempt to form an alternative coalition depended not on a Malay-based alliance between fixed capital and the Malay masses but on multiethnic reformist principles.

Anwar appears to have been aware of the impending moves against him. Anwar claims to have heard from Daim Zainuddin that Attorney-General Mohtar Abdullah had prepared charges against him and that Mohtar, Abdul Rahim Noor, and Chief Justice of the Malaysian Supreme

[89] *Asian Wall Street Journal*, September 4, 1998.

Court Eusoff Chin met repeatedly during the month of August to discuss these charges.[90] After Anwar's expulsion from UMNO, Rahim announced that the police would investigate several of the charges contained in the inflammatory *50 Reasons* pamphlet, in particular those related to Anwar's alleged homosexuality.[91] Facing the prospect of criminal investigations and effectively banned from formal politics, Anwar traveled throughout the country in the company of his wife and other supporters, issuing vitriolic condemnations of Mahathir's regime as corrupt, autocratic, and immoral.[92] Anwar found supporters among a number of prodemocracy Malaysians, including some young middle-class Malays, who supported his message of justice and political reform. Mahathir allowed these events to continue until September 20, the date of a large pro-*reformasi* rally in Kuala Lumpur. That evening, Anwar was arrested under the ISA. While in detention, he suffered humiliating treatment, in addition to a savage beating from Rahim himself.[93]

The arrests did not stop with Anwar. On September 14 the police arrested Anwar's personal secretary, Munawar Ahmad Anees, and Anwar's adopted brother, Sukma Darmawan. Munawar was charged with having committed sodomy with Anwar, and Sukma with having committed sodomy with Azizan Abu Bakar, Anwar's personal driver. Both Munawar and Sukma confessed to these charges after having been beaten and tortured.[94] After Anwar's arrest, the regime continued by detaining under the ISA a number of Anwar's associates. These included the UMNO Youth chief Ahmad Zahid Hamidi, several UMNO division heads known to be close to Anwar, officials in several affiliated organizations such as the Malaysian Muslim Youth Movement (ABIM), and even Anwar's lawyer Zulkifli Nordin.[95] Aside from Anwar, these individuals' detentions under the ISA were for the most part brief. Most were released within two weeks, and upon their release, most swore allegiance to Mahathir and to UMNO. For example, Kamaruddin Jaafar, chairman of the Anwar-affiliated Institute for Policy Research, claimed that *reformasi* was an anti-UMNO movement, initiated by Anwar, which he could not support.[96] Ahmad Zahid

[90] Interview with Anwar Ibrahim; Anwar 1998a.
[91] *Utusan Malaysia*, September 3, 1998.
[92] Hwang 2003, 307; Liow 1999, 46.
[93] Interview with Anwar Ibrahim; Hilley 2001, 154; Netto 2004, 87–88; M. Weiss 1999, 428.
[94] Case 2003, 127; Munawar 1998.
[95] *Berita Harian, Utusan Malaysia*, and *New Straits Times*, various dates.
[96] *Straits Times*, October 12, 1998.

resigned as head of UMNO Youth after his release but vowed to continue to support party unity.[97] On October 14 the Ministry of Internal Security changed Anwar's detention from one under the ISA to a standard criminal detention under charges of corruption and sodomy. He remained in prison without bail as the prosecution prepared the charges against him.

Anwar's detention did not deter most *reformasi* protestors, who continued to demonstrate in the following months. On October 17 the police's Federal Reserve Unit arrested 133 protestors for illegally demonstrating, using fire hoses to disperse crowds and truncheons to beat the peaceful protestors into submission.[98] Throughout late 1998 and 1999 as well, in the wake of Anwar's trials and convictions, *reformasi* activists led additional massive demonstrations against what many deemed Mahathir's unjust treatment of Anwar. In arresting existing protestors and intimidating other potential protestors, the regime deployed the legal instruments at its disposal, including the Official Secrets Act, the Universities and University Colleges Act, and the Sedition Act.[99] Anwar's trial on corruption charges – specifically, for improperly influencing the police Special Branch in its investigations of his alleged sexual misconduct – ended in a conviction.[100] The trial was hardly fair: Anwar's lawyer Zainur Zakaria was at one point jailed for contempt, and the opposition media was forbidden to comment on the case.[101] In this way, the regime was able to clamp down successfully on the *reformasi* movement, while neutralizing Anwar and allowing its reflationary macroeconomic policies to stimulate the economy.

Even though Anwar's treatment galvanized the opposition against the BN, it would be a mistake to overestimate its importance. Many dedicated opposition figures who had witnessed Anwar's rise within UMNO, his obsequious pro-Mahathir stance for more than a decade, and his increasing involvement in the Malay corporate world viewed Anwar as little more than an opportunist.[102] In the words of one activist, Anwar was a "seasoned political *gajah* [elephant] who played for the highest stakes in the power game, and lost."[103] Instead, Anwar attracted such widespread support within the opposition movement because leaders saw

---

[97] *Utusan Malaysia*, October 3, 1998.
[98] *Utusan Malaysia*, October 18, 1998; Aliran Executive Committee 1998.
[99] Liow 1999, 52–53.
[100] Case 2003.
[101] Netto 1998.
[102] Interview with an anonymous Malaysian academic, April 2005.
[103] Khoo 1998a, 6.

an opportunity to promote anti-Mahathir sentiment. Many middle-class Malays, supporters of *reformasi* or at least greater political openness, viewed Mahathir's public assault on Anwar to be excessive.[104] Opposition politicians who had had little use for Anwar began at least to support his opposition to Mahathir. Anwar's conviction on April 14, 1999, for corruption only reinforced the demand for *reformasi* among opposition supporters, as did the launching of his second trial, this time for having committed sodomy.

So even as capital controls eased the costs of adjustment for the regime's key supporters, opposition politicians took the lead in attempting to form a civil society *reformasi* movement with political teeth. Anwar's wife, Wan Azizah, played a prominent role, founding with veteran social activist Chandra Muzaffar the Movement for Social Justice (Pergerakan Keadilan Sosial) in December 1998. This group served as an umbrella organization to unite several competing NGOs and social movement organizations agitating for *reformasi*.[105] In April 1999, shortly before Anwar's conviction on corruption charges, Wan Azizah used this organization to form the KeADILan. In early May, KeADILan joined with the DAP, PAS, and the small opposition Parti Rakyat Malaysia (PRM, Malaysian People's Party), announcing Malaysia's first united opposition coalition, the BA, to heavy media derision.[106]

Meanwhile, the regime used the media and the courts to harass the opposition. Among others, Chandra Muzaffar was a popular target. He was removed from his position as director of the Centre for Civilisational Dialogue at the University of Malaya on February 24 without explanation.[107] Regime leaders wasted no time in lambasting him for using his role as a public intellectual to fan the opposition, referring to him as another "pseudo-opportunistic intellectual" with crony links to Anwar.[108] During the summer of 1999, the attorney-general pursued charges of contempt of court for Muzaffar for criticizing the Malaysian judiciary branch in its handling of Anwar's case, using for evidence a statement of dubious provenance downloaded from the Internet.[109] Later accusations held that Muzaffar and the frequently critical opposition

---

[104] Funston 2004, 171; Khoo 1998a, 6; Netto 1998; Welsh 2004, 133.
[105] M. Weiss 1999, 430–32.
[106] See, e.g., *New Straits Times*, May 16, 1998.
[107] Doss 1999.
[108] Interview with Chandra Muzaffar, former deputy chairman of Parti KeADILan Nasional, July 5, 2006; *New Straits Times*, March 16, 1999.
[109] *New Straits Times*, August 3, 1999.

organization Aliran had received around RM5 million in illegal payments
from Anwar between 1992 and 1997.[110]

Within UMNO, Mahathir's allies worked assiduously to rid the party
of Anwar's former allies, including several who had been detained earlier
under the ISA. Kamaruddin Jaafar, for instance, was expelled along with
several of his division colleagues on July 6, 1999, for having worked with
the opposition.[111] During the winter of 1998, UMNO leaders had forced
Kamaruddin to sell his stake in several major print media outlets, which
he held in trust for the party.[112] Many other corporate figures associated
with Anwar found themselves under heavy pressure to sell their stakes in
UMNO-linked companies, and still others were removed from corporate
directorships.[113] By autumn of 1999, around four hundred suspected
Anwar sympathizers had been removed from their positions in UMNO,
with particular attention paid to suspected Anwar loyalists in the party's
divisional leaderships.[114] Some joined opposition parties, such as Ruslan
Kassim, who became the information chief of KeADILan after his expulsion. Most, however, faded into the political background.

The 1999 General Elections

While the Malaysian economy continued to recover in 1999, and the
regime used the media and courts to attack *reformasi* supporters, opposition politicians set their sights on the upcoming parliamentary elections
as their best chance to unseat the regime. Economic recovery was by this
point clear. Targeting their constituencies among the Malay masses,
Mahathir and other BN politicians emphasized this point throughout
the year. Far in advance of the official campaign period and in clear
violation of electoral regulations, BN politicians stumped on related
themes of interracial harmony and pro-*bumiputra* development. Meanwhile, on October 23, 1999, KeADILan, PAS, DAP, and PRM unveiled
the BA's joint manifesto, calling for justice, fairness, and democracy.[115] It
is instructive that the document made no criticism of capital controls or
expansionary macroeconomic policies.

Elections were due sometime in 2000, but Mahathir called snap elections on November 29, 1999. By calling elections on this early date, the

[110] *New Straits Times*, October 29, 1999; Pillay 1999.
[111] *New Straits Times*, July 7, 1999.
[112] *Asian Wall Street Journal*, November 20, 1998.
[113] Liow 1999, 52–53.
[114] Hilley 2001, 110; Hwang 2003, 308.
[115] *New Straits Times*, October 24, 1999.

BN capitalized on several opportunities to minimize the impact of potential opposition voters. Approximately 680,000 newly registered voters, the majority of whom would likely vote for the BA, were disenfranchised because their registrations had not yet received approval.[116] Moreover, the elections took place just before the Muslim fasting month of Ramadan, during which many urban Malays return to their rural home villages. In holding the elections before Ramadan, the BN hoped to avoid the possibility that local religious leaders who supported PAS would spread their ideas to urban Malays. The monsoon season also worked in the BN's favor, discouraging voters from attending outdoor opposition rallies.[117] The official campaign period before the elections was the shortest in Malaysian history, only eight days. This hampered the ability of BA candidates to campaign, whereas BN candidates had campaigned unofficially for months.

The BN's campaign strategy played to its strengths. It emphasized economic recovery, focusing on social development, pro-*bumiputra* economic policies, and the beneficial effects of capital controls.[118] The regime also criticized the BA as self-contradictory, questioning the political viability of a coalition that included the democratic socialist and largely Chinese DAP along with PAS, which continued to advocate the formation of an Islamic state.[119] As noted, economic recovery made it difficult to campaign on promises of economic prosperity, so the BA's campaign strategy focused on *reformasi*, justice, and equality.[120] Both coalitions focused on corruption: the BN highlighted Anwar's corrupt practices, and the BA attacked Mahathir. As had been the case since Anwar's dismissal from UMNO, the BN's control of the Malaysian media gave it a crucial advantage in spreading its message, both before and during the formal campaign period. Tellingly, throughout 1999, the mainstream Malay, English, Chinese, and Tamil presses did not print a single pro-BA editorial, letter, or opinion, while these same newspapers published multiple pro-BN pieces daily.[121]

---

[116] Biro Analisis Politik 2000, 4; Weiss 2000, 421.

[117] *Asiaweek*, December 3, 1999.

[118] See, e.g., *Business Times*, November 16, 1999; interview with Patricia Martinez, Malaysian political scientist, July 18, 2006; interview with Zakaria Haji Ahmad, Malaysian political scientist and reserve colonel in the Malaysian armed forces, July 6, 2006; interview with an anonymous Malaysian economist, July 2006.

[119] See, e.g., *New Straits Times*, October 25, 1999.

[120] Interview with Chandra Muzaffar; interview with KJ John, columnist and former government employee, July 14, 2006; Case 2002, 136–40; Weiss 2000, 421–23; Welsh 2004.

[121] Mustafa 2003, 55.

The regime also targeted Anwar himself in the media, describing in graphic detail the charges against him and publishing pictures of him dancing with unknown women.[122] To control opposition media, the regime limited the distribution of party publications such as PAS's newsletter *Harakah* to official party members only and restricted the circulation of the opposition group Aliran's long-running monthly journal.[123]

The BN's criticism of an alliance between the DAP and PAS represented a larger campaign to frighten Chinese Malaysian voters into supporting the BN. This campaign is itself unrelated to considerations of capital specificity, but is important nevertheless. By emphasizing PAS's demand for an Islamic state and its support of *syariah* law, UMNO played off of fears held by many non-Muslims that they would face even more discrimination in the event of an opposition victory.[124] The BN also emphasized the threat of racial violence. Press releases throughout late 1998 and 1999 raised the specter of anti-Chinese violence, using images from the May 1998 anti-Chinese riots in Indonesia and discussing the potential disastrous consequences of a society without the BN to contain Malay displeasure with Chinese wealth.[125] It compounded the threat by highlighting what it deemed violent protests by (mostly Malay) *reformasi* supporters.[126] Opposition politicians played down the threat of racial violence by arguing that Malays' improved economic situation would prevent them from rioting.

The regime's final strategy before the election was to increase its redistributive efforts targeting the Malay masses. The media had concentrated on the 2000 budget since August 1999, anticipating the mix of growth-enhancing policies along with redistributive efforts. Released on October 29, the expansionary 2000 budget included dozens of giveaways, including housing credits, bonuses, and pay raises to the largely Malay public service; special two-year Islamic savings bonds for retirees, offering returns well in excess of market rates; new infrastructure investments; and tax cuts of 1 percent across the board.[127] Opposition

---

[122] Interview with Chandra Muzaffar; Case 2002, 140; Mustafa 2002, 163.

[123] Committee to Protect Journalists 1999; Mustafa 2002, 163.

[124] Hilley 2001, 261; Weiss 2000, 430.

[125] Interview with Chandra Muzaffar; interview with Lim Kit Siang; interview with Patricia Martinez; Derichs 2004, 110; Felker 2000, 53; Gomez 2002, 107; Hefner 2001, 33; Liow 1999, 57; Mustafa 2003, 58.

[126] Gomez 2002, 107; Mustafa 2002, 162.

[127] *Business Times* (Malaysia), October 30, 1999; *New Straits Times*, October 30, 1999; *New Sunday Times*, October 31, 1999.

parliamentarians labeled the BN's 2000 budget an "election budget," whereas Daim termed it a "people's budget."[128] On October 27, Jomo K. S., a PRM member and respected economist, introduced the BA's shadow budget. This mirrored the BN's budget in many ways, although it called for more extensive and more transparent privatization efforts to weed out government cronyism.[129] This demonstrates how the BA could not campaign on the regime's lack of economic recovery and focused instead on reform of current practices to ensure transparency. It also makes clear the threat that a BA government represented to politically connected holders of fixed capital. By contrast, the BN ramped up its targeting of Malay entrepreneurs. On November 20–21, Daim chaired a meeting with 1,200 young *bumiputra* professionals, introducing them to the government's business policies and reminding them of their benefits under the New Economic Policy.[130] In the week before the election, ASB announced 12 percent returns for 1999, comprised of an 8.5 percent regular dividend, a 2 percent "new millennium dividend," and a 1.5 percent bonus dividend.[131] The media commended ASB's parent company PNB for prudently managing *bumiputra* equity and reported widespread satisfaction among Malays.[132]

The conduct of the 1999 election was similar to previous Malaysian elections, marked by extensive money politics and voting irregularities. The Malaysian police and armed forces oversaw polling, leading to some complaints of voter intimidation. Many voters found themselves moved to new constituencies on polling day, presumably to shore up potential losses. Spoiled ballots were common, especially in tight races where the number of spoiled ballots certainly made a difference in the vote's outcome. Allegations of phantom voters mysteriously appearing on electoral rolls were extensive.[133] Lim Kit Siang alleged that there were up to forty voters listed at one address in his constituency of Bukit Bendera, Penang, and DAP candidate D. Jeyakumar claimed there were 250 phantom voters in the Sungai Siput, Perak,

---

[128] *Business Times* (Malaysia), October 30, 1999; *New Straits Times*, October 31, 1999.
[129] *New Straits Times*, October 28, 1999.
[130] *New Straits Times*, November 11, 1999.
[131] Interview with an anonymous Malaysian economist, April 2005; interview with an anonymous Malaysian journalist, July 2006; interview with an anonymous Chinese Malaysian opposition party worker, July 2006; *New Straits Times*, November 25, 1999.
[132] See, e.g., *Business Times* (Malaysia), November 25, 1999.
[133] Interview with Anwar Ibrahim; interview with Lim Kit Siang.

TABLE 7.2. *Malaysia's 1999 General Election Results*

	Seats		Vote Share	
Party/Coalition	1999 Results	Change from 1995	1999 Results	Change from 1995
BN	148	−12	56.53	−8.62
DAP	10	+1	12.50	0.44
KeADILan	5	n.a.	11.67	n.a.
PAS	27	+19	15.00	7.69
PBS	3	0	2.16	−1.15

Source: Suruhanjaya Pilihan Raya Malaysia 1999.

parliamentary constituency where he challenged MIC president S. Samy Vellu.[134] Charges of vote buying were similarly prevalent.[135]

The results of the election saw the BN retain its two-thirds majority in the DR, albeit with a smaller margin of victory than in the 1995 general elections (Table 7.2). The BN lost 12 total seats, winning 148 out of 193 seats in the DR. While the DAP and KeADILan each made small inroads, PAS experienced the greatest increase in support, both in the percentage of total votes cast and in parliamentary representation. In Sabah, the opposition United Sabah Party (PBS), which did not join the BA, fared the same as it had previously.

Some observers have interpreted these results as evidence that Malays fled UMNO en masse in favor of parties such as PAS and KeADILan. Also marshaled in evidence of this conclusion is the fact that, for the first time in Malaysia's electoral history, UMNO seats made up less than half of all BN seats. But this conclusion misses key points about the election results. Broken down by state, there is clear regional variation in the parties that voted for PAS (Table 7.3).

The northern states of Kelantan and Terengganu, PAS's longtime strongholds, did indeed vote overwhelmingly for PAS. PAS took almost every parliamentary seat in these states, and even made a strong showing in Mahathir's home state of Kedah. But in the western and southern states of the Malay Peninsula, UMNO was far more successful. It won every seat that it contested in Johor, Melaka, Negeri Sembilan, Pahang, Selangor, and Kuala Lumpur, with additional big wins in Penang and Perak. UMNO also picked up every seat it contested in Sabah and Labuan in

[134] Interview with Lim Kit Siang; *New Straits Times*, November 24, 1999; December 3, 1999.
[135] Weiss 2000, 433.

TABLE 7.3. *Malaysia's Parliamentary Election Results, by Component Party and State*

State	DAP		KeADILan		PAS		PRM		UMNO		MCA		MIC		Gerakan		Sarawak BN Parties[a]		Sabah BN Parties[b]	
	C	W	C	W	C	W	C	W	C	W	C	W	C	W	C	W	C	W	C	W
Johor	6		7		5		2		13	13	6	6	1	1						
Kedah	1		4		10	8			13	5	2	2								
Kelantan			3	3	11	10			14	1										
Kuala Lumpur	5	4	3		1				3	3	4	1			3	2				
Labuan					1				1	1										
Melaka	1	1	2		2				3	3	2	1								
Negeri Sembilan	3		3		2				4	4	2	2	1	1						
Pahang	2		2		6				8	8	3	3								
Penang	7	4	3	1	1				4	3	3	1			3	3				
Perak	9	1	7		7	2			11	9	7	6	2	2	4	2				
Perlis			1		2				3	3										
Sabah	2		3		2				11	11									8	5
Sarawak	7		13		1												25	25		
Selangor	4		7	1	5		1		8	8	6	6	3	3						
Terengganu			1	1	7	7			8											
TOTAL	47	10	59	5	63	27	1	0	104	72	35	28	7	7	10	7	25	25	8	5

Note: C = contested; W = won.

[a] Parti Bansa Dayak Sarawak, Parti Pesaka Bumiputera Bersatu, Sarawak United People's Party.

[b] Parti Bersatu Rakyat, Sabah Progressive Party, United Pasokmomogun Kadazandusun Murut Organisation.

Source: Bernama Library and Infolink Service 1999.

East Malaysia. Only 51 percent of Chinese Malaysians who voted chose the BN, and of the 61 seats with no large racial majority, the BN captured sixty.[136] DAP's chairman Lim Kit Siang and deputy chairman Karpal Singh both lost their parliamentary seats in races where vote margins were far smaller than the number of spoiled ballots. Lim lost the Bukit Bendera, Penang, seat to Chia Kwang Chye (Gerakan) by a margin of 34.9 to 34.7 percent, a difference of 104 votes (1,051 votes spoiled). Singh lost the Jerutong, Penang, seat to Lee Kah Choon (Gerakan) by a margin of 36.2 to 34.9 percent, a difference of 775 votes (1,012 votes spoiled).

State Assembly elections yielded similar results. PAS retained control of the Kelantan state legislature and gained the Terengganu state legislature, but fared much worse in most southern and western states on the Malay Peninsula. In southern states (Johor, Melaka, and Negeri Sembilan) and Penang, Malay state constituencies remained firmly within UMNO's grasp. In western states aside from Penang, PAS picked up several seats per state, but its inroads in Malay state constituencies were small. Mirroring their performance in parliamentary elections, the DAP and KeADILan had very limited success across Peninsular Malaysia.

The 1999 general elections marked the conclusion of Malaysia's political crisis. By now, Mahathir's rule was secure – and Malaysia was just as clearly as ever an authoritarian regime. In the months after the elections, the regime shut down several opposition newspapers, arresting several of their editors for sedition.[137] When a KeADILan candidate won a parliamentary by-election in Mahathir's home state of Kedah in 2000, police arrested several KeADILan party leaders under the ISA.[138] In the 2001 UMNO General Assembly, Mahathir attacked UMNO's opponents within the Malay community for having forgotten UMNO's generosity.[139] Mahathir retired in October 2003, turning over power to Abdullah Ahmad Badawi, his own chosen political successor. The crisis having passed, Malaysian politics under Mahathir returned to its usual state of UMNO dominance.

Conclusion

By November 1999, most observers agreed that the BN would win a majority of seats in the parliamentary and state elections; the real

---

[136] Loh 2003, 103.
[137] Committee to Protect Journalists 1999; Funston 2004, 172; Netto 1999.
[138] Hwang 2004, 75.
[139] Mahathir 2001.

question was whether the BN would retain its two-thirds majority. Why, given the dramatic economic crisis of 1998, and the difficult process of economic recovery, were so many Malaysians still willing to support Mahathir, UMNO, and the BN at large? Why did so few BN politicians defect in favor of opposition parties? Why did the opposition BA campaign so heavily on abstract issues of justice and reform, instead of attacking the BN for mismanaging the economy enough to cause an economic contraction of almost 8 percent of GDP in 1998? As in Indonesia, it is no accident that the fault lines of political conflict centered on currency manipulation and economic sabotage, with persistent threats toward Chinese Malaysians and foreigners. But Malaysia's regime was fundamentally different from Indonesia's. It was a coalition between fixed capital and the Malay masses, one that excluded those Malaysians who would demand capital account openness as a condition for political support. The regime's economic adjustment policies, given the crisis, fulfilled the interests of both new Malay entrepreneurs and ordinary Malays, the two groups that had for decades constituted the BN's support coalition. This allowed Mahathir to use favorable adjustment policies as a campaign tool and removed adjustment policies from the opposition's ideological arsenal. Before his sacking, even Anwar Ibrahim vociferously championed the BN's adjustment policies – indeed, Anwar struggled to portray himself as a staunch advocate of Malay economic rights through heterodox policies, and Mahathir strove to paint him as the opposite. In contrast to the institutionalist argument that elites support dominant parties during crises because dominant parties enable short-term sacrifice for long-term gain, the BN's supporters, elites and masses alike, stood behind the regime *because they faced no short-term sacrifice.*

Once Malaysia's regime adopted its controversial policy choices, Malaysian politics returned to the familiar patterns of BN domination. Still, it is important not to overemphasize the regime's success. As common intuition suggests, economic crises such as those that hit Malaysia from 1997 to 1998 threaten the very foundations of authoritarian regimes. Measured in terms of electoral returns, one of the few methods we have to measure an authoritarian regime's control, the Malaysian regime suffered a setback. What remains to be explained is why the Malaysian regime survived this political crisis – why just a relatively minor setback, not a transition? I have shown that, given that Mahathir and his allies enacted policies that shifted the burden of adjustment away from the Malay masses and holders of fixed capital, these supporters continued to stand behind Mahathir.

The theory accordingly helps make sense of Malaysia's political land-scape at the turn of the millennium. In areas where Malay support of UMNO had never been particularly strong – the rural heartland states of Kelantan and Terengganu – the BN lost votes. In areas where Malay support of UMNO had customarily been highest and where the impact of the crisis was most acutely felt, along the southern and western states on the Malay Peninsula, the UMNO and other BN parties were strikingly successful.[140] In Malaysia's historical context, the BN did not even fare as poorly as it had in 1990 after an UMNO party split, when the BN won only 71 percent of seats in the DR. Non-*bumiputra* voters did contribute to the BN's success in the 1999 elections, but their support for the BN was hardly unequivocal. Unlike in Indonesia, where economic crisis spun out of control, with Soeharto and other New Order leaders unable to adopt policies that protected their key political supporters, in Malaysia the BN government responded with a radical set of adjustment measures that fulfilled the interests of the regime's supporters. These policies not only helped to spur economic recovery but also kept the regime in power.

---

[140] Interview with Shahrir Abdul Samad, MP for Johore Bahru and former chairman of the Barisan Nasional Backbenchers Club, July 10, 2006.

8

Cross-National Perspectives

In Chapter 2 of this book, I noted that the twin crises in Indonesia and Malaysia are examples of a phenomenon that has become common as emerging market economies have opened their borders to capital flows and privatized their financial sectors. Nothing in my theory, however, is specific to Southeast Asia during the Asian Financial Crisis. Can this theory help us to make sense of financial crises, economic adjustment, and regime survival elsewhere in the world?

In this chapter, I show that it can. My theory uncovers two fundamental regularities in the politics of twin crises. First, coalitional politics determines adjustment policy. By taking seriously the preferences of supporters of autocratic regimes across the world, we can understand adjustment policies in a wide range of authoritarian regimes. Second, preferences for adjustment are at the heart of political conflict over autocratic regime survival. I demonstrate empirically that regimes that impose capital account restrictions during twin crises are more likely to survive these crises than regimes that do not. This finding holds up across countries and when controlling for alternative explanations for regime breakdown. These findings each lend crucial support to the theory that I derived from the experiences of Indonesia and Malaysia, and they reassure us that their experiences are indicative of a larger trend across the world, one that until now has escaped the notice of political scientists.

The methodology employed in this chapter differs from that used elsewhere in this book. Here, I focus on large-n quantitative analyses complemented by briefer case studies. In demonstrating that capital account restrictions increase the likelihood of regime survival, I am able to collect data on all countries within the sample using a variety of sources. In the case of my antecedent claim, that coalitional politics determines adjustment policy, comparable and reliable quantitative data on the coalitional bases of autocratic rule do not exist – recall that this was the main reason for the field research and historical analysis to measure this concept in Chapter 3. So again, case studies are instrumental for investigating causal relations between support coalitions and economic adjustment. I rely here on secondary sources and, where applicable, statistical indexes to measure key variables in the cases that I choose.

I have chosen cases according to several criteria. The first is *representativeness*: multiple cases from Latin America complement my analysis of two Southeast Asian states. Consistent findings in very different countries reinforce that my theory is not specific to Southeast Asia in the late 1990s. The second criterion is *within-country variation over time*: Mexico experienced twin crises twice (once in the 1980s and once in the 1990s), the first of which the regime survived, the second of which the regime did not. By exploiting this variation, I control by construction for country-specific factors, allowing me to focus on political differences between the first and the second twin crises. The third criterion is *clustering*: twin crises have historically come in groups, from the Latin American debt crisis to the collapse of the European Exchange Rate Mechanism to the Asian Financial Crisis. By selecting the four Latin American authoritarian regimes that experienced twin crises in the early 1980s, I control for time-specific factors. Each of these case selection methods has its distinct benefits and drawbacks, but together they give me powerful tools to check that my theory is applicable across time and space.

Capital Account Restrictions and Regime Survival

A key implication of my argument is that when the supporters of an autocratic regime can agree on capital account restrictions as a method for adjusting to twin crises, the regime should survive. Mobile capital will demand capital openness as a condition for its political support during a crisis. Even when regimes dependent in part on mobile capital are on the verge of collapse, they should still err on the side of mobile capital, for its ability to diversify overseas gives it a stronger bargaining position in a contest for political influence. Only regimes without mobile capital as a coalition partner will impose capital controls, and doing so will allow them to survive crises.

Indeed, we observe that, across the developing world, regimes that impose capital account restrictions are more likely to survive twin crises than their counterparts that do not. Table 2.2 contained a sample of thirty-six twin crises under autocratic regimes, nine of which resulted in democratic transitions. Data from Menzie Chinn and Hiro Ito measure regulations on international financial transactions and provide a good measure for capital account policy.[1] In the years following the onset of twin crises, their index *KAOPEN decreases* on average by .225 in autocracies that survive their twin crises, whereas it *increases* on average by .073 in autocracies that experienced democratic transitions. This is rough initial evidence that capital controls are associated with regime survival during financial crises.

To probe this relationship further, I estimate a series of regressions that model the probability of an authoritarian breakdown as a function of both capital account restrictions and other potential determinants of regime survival. In the first series of models, I restrict the analysis to instances of twin crises, so the unit of analysis is the crisis. The functional form of the probit estimator employed through the analysis is given in equation (1).

$$\Pr(trans = 1 | \Delta k_i, \mathbf{x}_i) = \Phi(\gamma k_i + \mathbf{x}_i{}'\boldsymbol{\beta}) \qquad (1)$$

In this model, *trans* is a binary variable coded 1 if the country experiences a transition during crisis i, and 0 otherwise. The variable of theoretical interest is k_i, the change in capital account openness. My theory predicts that the parameter γ is positive, where increasing capital account openness increases the probability of autocratic regime breakdown. I measure k_i in two different ways. The first is the value of *KAOPEN* at the onset of the currency or banking crisis that led to the twin crises (*KAOPENONS*). The second is the difference between *KAOPENONS* and the value of *KAOPEN* at the end of the twin crises (*DKAOPEN*). Because my theory argues that increases in capital account restrictions during crises increase the likelihood of regime survival, *DKAOPEN* is the main theoretical variable. But including *KAOPENONS* in regressions allows me to control for the fact that countries that already have substantial capital account restrictions at the onset of the crisis have few additional restrictions that they can implement.

---

[1] Chinn and Ito 2008.

Control variables enter the equation in x_i, with the associated parameters β, to test the alternative explanations against which I argued earlier in the book. These alternative explanations are both economic and political in nature. The variable *GDPPC* measures per capita gross domestic product of each country at the onset of the currency or banking crisis that led to the twin crises, testing the modernization hypothesis that economic development encourages democratization. The variable ΔGDP measures the greatest percentage change in the country's gross domestic product between the onset of the currency or banking crisis that led to the twin crises and the end of the twin crises. This captures the argument that more severe economic crises are more likely to lead to regime transitions. Comparable data on GDP contraction do not exist for the country of Laos, which experienced two twin crises in the 1990s. For this reason, my sample size shrinks to thirty-four observations for all cross-national estimations. The variable *AGE* tests whether more entrenched regimes are more likely to withstand economic crises. Two dummy variables, *CIVILIAN* and *MILITARY*, test the argument that military dictatorships are more likely to experience democratic transitions during economic crises than civilian authoritarian regimes or monarchies, the omitted category.[2] The variable *POLITYONS* is the Polity IV score for each regime at the onset of the currency or banking crisis that led to the twin crises. It allows me to control for the possibility that more "democratic" authoritarian regimes are more likely to withstand pressures for democratization. To check for regional patterns of authoritarian breakdowns, I also include in some models dummy variables that code for the region of the world in which each country is located (sub-Saharan Africa, the Middle East and North Africa, Asia, and Latin America). Table 8.1 lists the independent variables, their definitions, and their sources, and Table 8.2 presents their descriptive statistics.

In all estimations, I include Indonesia and Malaysia during the Asian Financial Crisis. If, contrary to my expectations, capital account changes are idiosyncratic while institutional or economic factors are the true determinants of autocratic breakdowns, it would be misleading to exclude these cases where confounding variables have values consistent with their alternative hypotheses. If I do drop Indonesia and Malaysia from the analysis to construct a true "out-of-sample test," the findings remain virtually identical.

---

[2] Geddes 2003, 44–86.

TABLE 8.1. *Authoritarian Breakdowns: Variables, Definitions, and Sources*

Variable Name	Concept/Description	Source
AGE	The age of the current regime, in years	Cheibub and Gandhi (2004)
CIVILIAN	Dummy variable = 1 if a civilian autocratic regime, 0 otherwise	Cheibub and Gandhi (2004)
DKAOPEN	Maximum change in *DKAOPEN* during the crisis	Calculated from Chinn and Ito (2008)
GDPPC	GDP per capita at the onset of the banking or currency crisis preceding the twin crises	Heston, Summers, and Aten (2006)
KAOPENONS	Capital openness at the onset of the banking or currency crisis preceding the twin crises	Chinn and Ito (2008)
MILITARY	Dummy variable = 1 if a military autocratic regime, 0 otherwise	Cheibub and Gandhi (2004)
POLITYONS	The Polity IV combined score	Polity IV Project (2006)
ΔGDP	The maximum percentage one-year change in GDP during the crisis	Heston, Summers, and Aten (2006)

TABLE 8.2. *Authoritarian Breakdowns: Descriptive Statistics*

Variable Name	Mean	Standard Deviation	Minimum	Maximum
AGE	22.324	13.832	1	44
CIVILIAN	0.412	0.450	0	1
DKAOPEN	−0.190	1.014	−3.335	2.996
GDPPC	0.450	0.839	0.008	4.044
KAOPENONS	−0.518	1.317	−1.753	2.623
MILITARY	0.471	0.507	0	1
POLITYONS	−3.118	4.715	−9	8
TRANS	0.265	0.448	0	1
ΔGDP	−5.413	5.229	−15.727	3.048

TABLE 8.3. *Determinants of Autocratic Breakdowns during Twin Crises*

Variable	Model 1	Model 2	Model 3	Model 4	Model 5	Model 6
POLITY	−0.348**	−0.348***	−0.378**	−0.346***	−0.342***	−0.032
	(0.168)	(0.132)	(0.173)	(0.132)	(0.126)	(0.021)
MILITARY	−2.693	−2.693	−2.951	−2.515	−2.849	0.227
	(1.995)	(1.969)	(1.995)	(1.766)	(1.910)	(0.339)
CIVILIAN	−3.311*	−3.311**	−4.064**	−3.230***	−3.427***	0.130
	(1.881)	(1.348)	(1.933)	(1.239)	(1.260)	(0.313)
GDPPC	−1.610	−1.610**	−2.672**	−1.523**	−1.855***	0.078
	(1.020)	(0.629)	(1.207)	(0.651)	(0.620)	(0.096)
ΔGDP	−0.052	−0.052	−0.215*	−0.049	−0.057	−0.007
	(0.104)	(0.082)	(0.118)	(0.081)	(0.082)	(0.020)
AGE	−0.092*	−0.092	−0.129**	−0.087	−0.094*	−0.005
	(0.056)	(0.057)	(0.065)	(0.055)	(0.055)	(0.008)
KAOPENONS	1.687**	1.687***	2.023**	1.644***	1.669***	0.028
	(0.700)	(0.481)	(0.814)	(0.489)	(0.459)	(0.101)
DKAOPEN	1.840**	1.840***	2.624**	1.871***	2.041***	0.173*
	(0.799)	(0.557)	(1.034)	(0.552)	(0.638)	(0.094)
Africa			−2.221**			−0.561*
			(1.081)			(0.271)
Middle East				−0.250		−0.615*
				(1.196)		(0.305)
Latin America					1.073	−0.254
					(0.668)	(0.292)
East Asia						(omitted)
Constant	3.244	3.244	4.239	3.062	3.343	0.495
	(2.407)	(2.367)	(2.585)	(2.226)	(2.325)	(0.419)
(Pseudo) R-squared	0.509	0.509	0.603	0.510	0.524	0.460
Model	Probit	Probit	Probit	Probit	Probit	Linear probability
Residuals clustered within country?	No	Yes	Yes	Yes	Yes	No

Note: Cells contain parameter estimates and standard errors. * = statistically significant at $\alpha < .1$, ** = statistically significant at $\alpha < .05$. *** = statistically significant at $\alpha < .01$. Probit model does not converge with an East Asia dummy.

Evidence presented in Table 8.3 is consistent with the hypothesis that governments that restrict cross-border capital flows are more likely to survive twin crises. In five out of six specifications, the estimate of γ is positive, as hypothesized, and statistically significant at the $\alpha < .05$ level. In Models 2–5, where I relax the assumption that errors are distributed

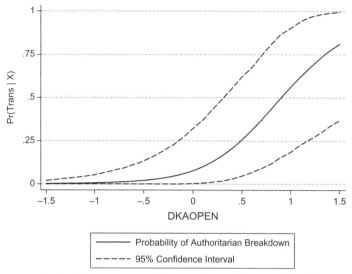

FIGURE 8.1. Capital Account Restrictions and Transition Probabilities.

independently across twin crises in the same countries, the significance is well beyond the $\alpha < .01$ level.

To interpret parameter estimates substantively, we can evaluate changes in predicted probabilities of transition given a change in capital account openness with all other variables held at their means.[3] To fix the example in the real world, consider an increase in the change in capital account openness from −1 (approximately Cameroon from 1994 to 1996) to 1 (approximately the Philippines from 1983 to 1987). I estimate that such a change leads to a 56 percent increase in the expected probability of regime breakdown (estimate = .556, standard error = .200). To see this graphically, Figure 8.1 displays the results from Model 2, plotting the simulated expected probability of autocratic breakdown given values of *DKAOPEN* ranging from −1.5 to 1.5. As Figure 8.1 shows, the probability of transition increases as *DKAOPEN* increases. Although it is difficult to tell from the graph, the 95 percent confidence interval never includes zero.

Results for alternative hypotheses are likewise encouraging. Civilian authoritarian regimes appear more likely to survive twin crises than military or monarchical regimes, although robustness tests presented here show this result to be quite fragile. I cannot reject the null hypothesis

---

[3] Geddes 2003, 44–86; King, Tomz, and Wittenberg 2000.

that severe economic contraction during twin crises does not increase the probability of autocratic breakdowns during twin crises. On the basis of Indonesia's and Malaysia's historical experiences, I argued that the severity of economic contraction varied across the two countries but had no causal effect on regime stability. The cross-national findings show that this argument holds up more broadly. Note that I did not make any correction for the portion of yearly economic contraction in the wake of the breakdown of an autocratic regime, even though I argued in the case of Indonesia that yearly data may lead us to mistakenly attribute economic contraction in the wake of autocratic breakdown to the previous regime.

Several robustness tests increase our confidence in these findings despite a small sample size ($n = 34$). I note here two, each based on a linear probability model that gives nearly identical results to Model 1. The "Cook's D" statistic measures the leverage that particular observations have on overall findings. Observations for which the statistic exceeds the standard critical value of $4/n$ (in my case .118)[4] are held to warrant further investigation. Only one observation truly stands out: Botswana's 1996 twin crises in the linear probability model are associated with a Cook's D of .227, which is almost twice the critical value. This might be expected, given that many analysts dispute the coding of Botswana as an authoritarian regime.[5] Reestimating the linear probability model as well as Model 2, excluding the observation from Botswana, the results remain virtually unchanged. Four other observations have Cook's D statistics that just barely exceed the critical value. Their serial exclusion also has no influence for *KAOPENONS* and *DKAOPEN*, but results for other variables appear more fragile. In many models, *CIVILIAN* loses significance, and even becomes significant and positive, while *MILITARY* is occasionally significant and negative. In other estimations, *POLITYONS* and *GDPPC* lose their significance. This indicates that findings about authoritarian institutions are *not* robust to influential points in the data, which is consistent with my argument throughout this book that authoritarian institutions had no causal impact on regime survival during twin crises in Indonesia and Malaysia. It is also consistent with research that argues that links from ruling parties to authoritarian regime survival depend on the heavy weight placed on a few very durable

---

[4] Bollen and Jackman 1985. *n* here is the number of observations.
[5] See, e.g., Robinson and Parsons 2006.

regimes.[6] As a final robustness check, I estimated a bootstrap regression model. Treating the sample as the population of cases, I estimated a linear probability model on a virtual dataset created by drawing with replacement from the sample. The results again remain substantively identical, although most parameters are estimated with less precision.

A broader test of my argument turns to the entire population of authoritarian regimes in Glick and Hutchison's dataset of crises to estimate a model of authoritarian breakdowns, both during financial crises and during normal times.[7] Now, the unit of analysis is the country-year. The panel setup takes all country-years in the dataset between 1975 and 1997, coding the variable $CRISIS = 1$ for all years coded as twin crises in Table 2.2, and 0 otherwise. $KAOPEN$ measures capital account restrictions, and the interaction between $CRISIS$ and $KAOPEN$ tests the argument that capital account restrictions decrease the probability of authoritarian breakdowns during twin crises. My interest is in modeling the probability that an authoritarian regimes collapses, conditional on covariates, in a particular year. Because the data likely feature considerable temporal dependence, I estimate grouped duration models,[8] using (2) as the baseline specification.

$$\begin{aligned} \Pr(TRANS_{it} = 1 | KAOPEN_{it-1}, CRISIS_{it-1}, \mathbf{x}_{it-1}) \\ = h(t | KAOPEN_{it-1}, CRISIS_{it-1}, \mathbf{x}_{it-1}) \\ = \Phi(\gamma_1 KAOPEN_{it-1} + \gamma_2 CRISIS_{it-1} \qquad (2) \\ + \gamma_3 KAOPEN * CRISIS_{it-1} + \mathbf{x}_{it-1}'\boldsymbol{\beta} \\ + \kappa_{t-t0}'\varphi) \end{aligned}$$

Similar to the previous models, $TRANS = 1$ if country i experiences a transition during year t. Now, $h(t|\cdot)$ is the hazard rate of a regime breakdown in year t conditional on the covariates, and κ_{t-to} are dummy variables measuring the age of the regime from onset (to) to the current year (t).[9] The theory predicts γ_3 to be positive (as $KAOPEN$ increases, the effect of $CRISIS$ increases), implying that countries with more open capital accounts during financial crises are more likely to experience authoritarian regime breakdowns. To evaluate this argument that the effect of crises is conditional on capital openness, I use (3):[10]

[6] Smith 2005.
[7] Glick and Hutchison 1999.
[8] Beck, Katz, and Tucker 1998.
[9] See also Box-Steffensmeier and Jones 2004.
[10] See Berry, Esarey, and Rubin 2007, 5.

TABLE 8.4. *Descriptive Statistics for the Panel Analysis of Authoritarian Breakdowns*

Variable	Observations	Mean	Standard Deviation	Minimum	Maximum
AGE	964	19.170	14.111	1	128
CIVILIAN	964	0.455	0.498	0	1
CRISIS	964	0.080	0.271	0	1
GDPPC	924	3598.367	3310.919	365.182	28361.03
KAOPEN	906	−0.612	1.227	−1.753	2.623
MILITARY	964	0.456	0.498	0	1
POLITY	919	−4.267	5.121	−10	10
TRANS	963	0.044	0.204	0	1
ΔGDP	924	1.783	7.764	−39.256	125.96

$$\frac{\partial CRISIS}{\partial TRANS} = [\Phi(\mathbf{x}_{it-1}'\boldsymbol{\beta} + \kappa_{t-t0}'\varphi)](\gamma_1 + \gamma_3 KAOPEN) \qquad (3)$$

All other variables are from the same sources as previously and capture the same alternative hypotheses. Their descriptive statistics for the panel analysis are in Table 8.4.

My baseline grouped duration probit model pools all observations in the sample. Because regional dummy variables are time invariant, fixed effects models are inappropriate for models that include them. Institutional variables, which are highly persistent but not time invariant, prevent a regional variable model from converging when they are included. Nevertheless, to check that country-specific factors do not dominate the effects of crises and capital account openness, I also estimate three additional models: a random effects probit model, a random effects probit model with regional dummies that drops the institutional variables, and a grouped duration logistic regression model with fixed effects that drops both institutional and regional dummies.[11]

Table 8.5 presents the results of the panel analysis, suppressing the temporal dummies κ for ease of interpretation. While the interaction terms make interpretation of such regression tables more difficult, the results once again confirm that capital controls decrease the probability that authoritarian regimes break down during financial crises.

To evaluate my argument, Figure 8.2 uses the results from Model 7 to plot the marginal effect of a financial crisis on the probability of an authoritarian breakdown for different levels of capital account

[11] In the logistic model, $\Pr(y = 1|\mathbf{x}_{it}) = h(t|\mathbf{x}_{it}) = \dfrac{1}{1 + e^{-(\mathbf{x}_{it}'\boldsymbol{\beta} + \kappa_{t-t0})}}$

TABLE 8.5. *Grouped Duration Results of the Panel Analysis*

Variable	Model 7	Model 8	Model 9	Model 10
POLITY	0.073***	0.147***	0.093**	0.632***
	(0.018)	(0.051)	(0.043)	(0.173)
MILITARY	<0.001	<0.001	<0.001	0.003***
	(<0.001)	(<0.001)	(<0.001)	(0.001)
CIVILIAN	−0.018	−0.017	−0.011	−0.054
	(0.014)	(0.019)	(0.017)	(0.068)
GDPPC	−0.009	−0.012	−0.02	0.09
	(0.009)	(0.015)	(0.013)	(0.091)
ΔGDP	0.709	1.328		
	(0.529)	(1.029)		
AGE	0.007	0.259		
	(0.527)	(0.964)		
CRISIS	0.653**	0.793**	0.838**	11.068***
	(0.291)	(0.402)	(0.372)	(4.039)
KAOPEN	−0.098	−0.165	−0.14	−1.388
	(0.088)	(0.148)	(0.137)	(1.169)
CRISIS*KAOPEN	0.375*	0.541*	0.459*	6.208**
	(0.198)	(0.280)	(0.263)	(2.796)
Africa			−1.514**	
			(0.764)	
Middle East			−1.817**	
			(0.905)	
Latin America			−0.478	
			(0.635)	
East Asia			−1.397*	
			(0.738)	
Constant	−2.233***	−2.485*	0.048	
	(0.820)	(1.303)	(1.133)	
Observations	699	820	820	402
Log-L	−122.823	−120.445	−120.411	−20.389
Model	Probit	Probit, random effects	Probit, random effects	Logit, fixed effects

Note: Cells contain parameter estimates and standard errors. * = statistically significant at α < .1, ** = statistically significant at α < .05. *** = statistically significant at α < .01.

openness.[12] Probabilities were calculated using equation (3) with *POLITY, GDPPC, ΔGDP,* and *AGE* at their sample means, and the temporal dummies all set at 0 except for κ_{10} (set at 1). I estimate plots for both military and civilian regimes; the plot appearing on the left

[12] Brambor, Clark, and Golder 2006.

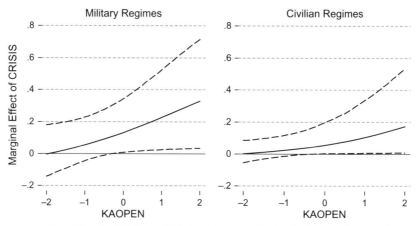

FIGURE 8.2. Marginal Effect of Twin Crises on the Probability of an Authoritarian Breakdown, by Capital Openness and Regime Type.

captures military regimes by setting $MILITARY = 1$ and $CIVILIAN = 0$, and the plot appearing on the right captures civilian regimes by setting $MILITARY = 0$ and $CIVILIAN = 1$.[13]

At low levels of capital account openness, twin crises have no impact on the probability that a regime experiences an authoritarian breakdown. But, consistent with my argument, as openness increases past approximately zero (around the mean of the $KAOPEN$ index), twin crises have a significant positive relationship on the probability that an authoritarian regime breaks down. This effect is present in both military and civilian regimes. Plots created from Models 8–10 are substantively identical.

Results from such grouped duration models may be fragile – either inefficient as a result of the large number of parameters κ_{t-t_0} or, more seriously, dependent on atheoretical assumptions about the functional form of baseline hazard rate. In results that I do not report here, I explored the sensitivity of results of Models 7–10 to the choice of estimators. Findings are substantively identical in replications that use linear splines in place of the temporal dummies. Results are also consistent when estimated via the semiparametric Cox proportional hazards model, which makes no assumptions of the distribution of the baseline hazard rate.[14] Among the family of

---

[13] I do this because marginal probabilities derived from interactive models with binary dependent variables depend on the values of *all* variables in the model, not just the interacted variables. See Berry, Esarey, and Rubin 2007.

[14] Cox 1972.

duration models, though, Cox's model does assume that whatever the hazard rate's distribution, all hazards are proportional – so that independent variables have constant effects across time. If this assumption does not hold, parameter estimates are biased.[15] I test this assumption through a global proportionality test of the Schoenfeld residuals,[16] and find no evidence to reject the null hypothesis of proportional hazards. Together these tests confirm that the findings reported are not an artifact of the estimation strategy.

Results from other variables are interesting and consistent in robustness tests as well. The coefficient on *KAOPEN* (γ_2) is insignificant, indicating that during normal times (*CRISIS* = 0) capital account openness has no impact on authoritarian regime survival. This confirms that authoritarian regimes such as Indonesia and Malaysia can thrive with open capital accounts during fat times, even as China and many Middle Eastern dictatorships place heavy restrictions on capital flows. Capital openness influences regime survival only during financial turmoil. No other variables except for *POLITY* are consistently significant, reinforcing the results from the preceding sensitivity analyses. *POLITY*, though, has the opposite sign: now more "democratic" authoritarian regimes are *more* likely to succumb to democratic pressures. This suggests that the effect of regime liberalism is conditional on the existence of an economic crisis.

The results of these cross-national analyses are encouraging for my theory. Both in a restricted sample of countries experiencing twin crises and in the broader panel approach, capital account restrictions allow authoritarian regimes to survive financial crises. I find no consistent effects for crisis severity or authoritarian institutions. The results are highly robust to estimation technique. But as mentioned previously, the difficulty in interpreting these quantitative analyses is that they obscure the causal mechanisms. My theory holds that coalitional politics within autocratic regimes determines adjustment policies to twin crises, yet the cross-national tests that I present here are incapable of determining why countries vary in the adjustment policies that they impose. Four case studies from Latin America demonstrate that, consistent with my theory, coalitional politics within autocratic regimes determines these adjustment policies outside of Southeast Asia.

---

[15] Box-Steffensmeier and Zorn 2001.
[16] Grambsch and Therneau 1994.

Debt Crises in the Southern Cone

The Latin American debt crisis, separated from the Asian Financial Crisis by a continent and more than a decade, offers the clearest regional parallel to Indonesia and Malaysia. Four authoritarian regimes entered the 1980s with highly leveraged financial sectors (Argentina, Chile, Mexico, and Uruguay), and by the mid-1980s, two of these regimes had collapsed amid financial panic (Argentina and Uruguay), while two others steered through the crisis by employing capital controls. Table 8.6 summarizes the arguments in this section about the coalitional origins of adjustment measures.

In analyzing these four cases, I begin with the Southern Cone, discussing Chile first and then comparing it to Argentina and Uruguay. I save the Mexican case until the end, setting the stage for a within-country comparison between Mexico's debt crisis of the 1980s and the Tequila Crisis of the mid-1990s.

Chile, 1981–1985

Chile in 1980 was in many ways similar to Indonesia in 1996. Its regime was rightist, antilabor, probusiness, and headed by a personalist dictator with a strong military pedigree. The regime based many of its policies on the advice of a clique of U.S.-trained technocrats with strong promarket ideological orientations. It encouraged international overborrowing through lax financial regulation under a pegged exchange rate and sought IMF assistance in adjusting to a subsequent financial crash. But Chile veered sharply away from the Indonesian crisis management strategy: like

TABLE 8.6. *Coalitions, Adjustment, and Breakdown in the Latin American Debt Crisis*

	Coalition	Capital Controls	Macroeconomic Policy	Outcome
Argentina	Fixed and mobile capital	No (imposed post-fracture)	Varies between tight and loose	Breakdown
Chile	Fixed capital	Yes	Moderately loose	Survival
Mexico	Fixed capital and labor (populist)	Yes	Moderately loose	Survival
Uruguay	Fixed and mobile capital	No	Varies between tight and loose	Breakdown

Malaysia, it closed its capital account, repegged its exchange rate, adopted reflationary macroeconomic policies, and punished financial conglomerates. And, also like Malaysia, its regime survived widespread political protest. The specific interests of the regime's political supporters are the key to explaining Chile's adjustment strategy and, by extension, the regime's survival.

By 1980 General Augusto Pinochet had consolidated his rule over a regime that was openly hostile to labor and, in particular, to organized labor.[17] In the coup of 1973 that ousted the socialist government of Salvador Allende, Pinochet's greatest support lay in the business community, with additional support coming from conservative and middle-class Chileans. After cracking down on organized labor and leftist elements, Pinochet embarked on a program of privatization and economic liberalization that had been previously unparalleled in Latin America. Neoliberal reforms were not neutral among the business community: losers included most notably the previously protected import-competing industrial enterprises, but the immediate beneficiaries were internationally competitive export sectors such as mining and agriculture.[18] After two years, the regime stepped up the pace of economic reform under the consultation of the Chicago Boys, a group of technocrats educated under the monetary economists Milton Friedman and Arnold Harberger.[19] The Chicago Boys directed further rounds of privatization, this time of the country's domestic financial sector, in order to encourage foreign capital investment and efficient credit allocation. By 1980 Chile had seen the rise of an important new group of conglomerates, the *grupos*, based around new domestic financial institutions. The largest of these, with names such as Vial and Cruzat-Larraín and personal connections to the Chicago Boys, diversified into areas such as property speculation and into the more traditional export-oriented sectors.[20]

Yet extensive controls on capital inflows remained. From 1979 until 1982, at the very height of the Chicago Boys' influence, the Chilean government banned all inflows of capital with maturities of less than twenty-four months. For capital inflows with maturities of between twenty-four and fifty-five months, the regime required owners to deposit a percentage in noninterest bearing accounts (*encaje*) at Banco Central de Chile. This had profound effects on the maturity structure of Chilean

---

[17] Drake 1996, 117–48; Vergara 1986, 96–106; Winn 2004.
[18] Muñoz Goma 1989, 174–75; Silva 1996, 65–95.
[19] Foxley 1983; Valdés 1995.
[20] Foxley 1986; Valdés 1995, 218–40; Vergara 1986, 93–96.

capital inflows.[21] Accordingly, while the regime opened itself to trade rather quickly, openness to capital flows was much lower in the 1970s and early 1980s.

The open hostility of Pinochet's government to labor masks the complex sectoral politics among Chilean capital owners under Pinochet. Indeed, Jeffry Frieden has described Pinochet's Chile as the ultimate expression of class conflict unfettered by sectoral divisions.[22] Yet whatever alliance between fixed or industrial capital and mobile or financial capital existed was the product of convergent interests under a generally business-oriented stabilization program. The rise of mobile capital (the *grupos*) as a pressure group began after Pinochet had secured his rule and lasted only until 1982.[23] Evidence that the *grupos'* membership in the regime's support coalition was at best tenuous comes from a variety of sources. The adoption of strict monetarism in economic planning was slow and halting rather than immediate, and the *grupos* who later exploited lax financial regulation did not yet exist when the Chicago Boys first turned toward monetarism and financial deregulation.[24] The state retained control over key industries rooted in Chile, including the country's lucrative copper industry in addition to petroleum, other mining industries, and transportation sectors.[25] Moreover, military elites never sat on the boards of directors of *grupos*, yet they did sit on the boards of various state-owned enterprises.[26] The *grupos* rose to exploit the newly deregulated financial sector, but while mobile capital was instrumental in shaping Chile's economic transformation from 1973 to 1982 under Pinochet's regime, it never became part of the regime's support coalition. Facing the failure of strict monetarism in the face of severe currency and banking distress, the Chicago Boys' policies and the *grupos* that they had nurtured were dismantled in favor of policies that protected the interests of Chile's traditional business class.

The antecedents to Chile's twin crises were in many ways analogous to those experienced by Indonesia before 1997. Chile had since 1979 a fixed peso-dollar exchange rate regime designed to anchor expectations over future prices. With a largely open capital account, despite short-term restrictions on inflows, macroeconomic policy was ineffective. Lagging

[21] Edwards 1999.
[22] Frieden 1991a.
[23] Silva 1996.
[24] Kurtz 1999.
[25] Biglaiser 2002, 120–27; Fortin 1985, 174.
[26] Biglaiser 2002, 120–27; Frieden 1991a, 167; Remmer 1989, 126–27.

export performance resulted in a current account deficit financed by extensive capital inflows – despite the restrictions placed upon them. With capital inflows came a boom in the underregulated domestic financial sector. Speculative activities from foreign investors and domestic actors alike contributed to an unsustainable financial bubble. When the price of copper, Chile's main export commodity, tumbled in 1981 along with an increase in global interest rates, capital inflows slowed. When this decrease in the availability of foreign funds exposed financial sector weaknesses, capital inflows nearly ceased, leading to a domestic banking crunch and increasing downward pressure on the peso.[27]

Initially, the regime made little attempt to use policy levers at its disposal to minimize the impact of capital outflows on the economy. With a fixed exchange rate and capital outflow, domestic interest rates rose sharply, to the detriment of business and employment alike. But, predictably, the ensuing credit crunch led to protests from industrial elites. Chilean labor suffered as well, as a result of retrenchment from cash-strapped businesses. After several months business pressures began to bear fruit.[28] Throughout January, the Central Bank allowed a series of devaluations of the peso. The effects were clear for the indebted *grupos*, and especially for their in-house *financieras* (lightly regulated nonbank financial institutions), which found that their effective debt burden had nearly doubled. In September 1982, in a major break with Chicago Boys' monetarist principles, the government announced selective bans on capital outflows as it simultaneously began to actively target domestic interest rates. Exchange controls on capital outflows included strict quotas on currency held by domestic travelers, forcing speedy import payments and lowering the limit on foreign exchange held by exporters. As was the case with Malaysia's capital controls, the regime did not restrict capital outflows that paid down foreign debt, nor did it restrict the repatriation of profits from foreign direct investment.[29]

The retreat from monetarism and the imposition of capital account restrictions were indicative of the Pinochet regime's strategy of protecting the interests of export-oriented domestic business.[30] Expansionary monetary policies helped to ease the impact of the previous banking crunch for domestic business, and, as in Malaysia, the government took possession of troubled financial institutions and nationalized their debt while

[27] Ffrench-Davis 2002, 29–146; Foxley 1986, 27–30.
[28] Meller 2000, 102–29.
[29] Corbo and Fischer 1993, 14.
[30] García Hurtado 1983, 35–36; Kurtz 1999, 420–22; Muñoz Goma 1989, 179–80; Silva 1996, 151–82.

dismantling the corporate empires based around them. Meanwhile, the heretofore vaunted Chicago Boys became something of a pariah. Owing to agitation from the domestic business community, between 1982 and 1986 the country saw six different ministers of finance, with the Chicago Boys increasingly marginalized. Holders of mobile capital suffered under the regime's adjustment measures, as the regime identified with export-oriented industrial capitalists, domestic business, and landowners, even going as far as to imprison Javier Vial (head of the *grupo* Vial) and Rolf Lüders (a former bi-minister of finance and the economy) for financial crimes. Observers called this marked change toward active political intervention in the economy the "Chicago Road to Socialism," recalling the earlier dictum that Allende's nationalization of private enterprises constituted "Chile's Road to Socialism." Not all *grupos* suffered, though: those with more fixed capital investments than financial market involvement such as the Angelini group did not collapse but survived and expanded.[31]

While Chile serves as a nice foil to Indonesia in showing how even rightist, probusiness military regimes can vary in their support coalitions, Chile's adjustment strategies also differ in predictable ways from Malaysia's. Recall that in Malaysia, Malay labor was an integral partner with fixed capital, whereas the Pinochet regime froze out labor. While adjustment policies adopted after the retreat from monetarism and capital account openness were expansionary, their distributional impacts were ultimately regressive. Unemployment exceeded 24 percent from 1982 to 1985, with declines in both real wages and statutory minimum wages. Pensions, indexed to inflation, were cut, as was public spending on housing and other social programs.[32] These distributional costs fostered the most sustained open opposition to Pinochet since 1973. But with fixed capital solidly behind the regime, the regime turned its repressive arm against labor groups and the unorganized, dissatisfied urban poor. Large-scale protests that some believed would bring the regime to its knees were put down violently, and the regime survived.[33] Pinochet's regime survived the debt crisis of the early 1980s by retreating from financial openness, enabling it to enact the targeted reflationary policies that its supporters demanded while crushing domestic opposition.

---

[31] Remmer 1989, 168–69.
[32] Foxley 1986, 26–27; Meller 2000, 133–38.
[33] Chavkin 1989, 248–78; Constable and Valenzuela 1991, 261–67; Martínez and Díaz 1996, 18–19.

Argentina, 1981–1983

The case of Argentina differs sharply from Chile, and contrasting the two cases allows us to observe why two regimes that were similar in many respects diverged so dramatically. Like Chile, Argentina was a rightist, military-led dictatorship that oppressed labor and nurtured industrial and financial growth. Substantial inflows of foreign capital during the five years preceding the country's economic collapse led to reckless and ultimately unsustainable financial expansion. But unlike Chile's, Argentina's regime could not contain the popular discontent that its financial crisis unleashed. Mirroring Indonesia, the regime veered sharply between orthodox and heterodox policies, refused to curtail outflows of hot money, and ultimately succumbed to pressures for regime change. To be sure, Argentina's path to regime collapse differed from Indonesia's: it launched the fateful Falklands/Malvinas War with the United Kingdom in a desperate attempt to unite the populace, and its defeat sealed the regime's fate. Still, we find that struggles between holders of fixed and mobile capital struck at the heart of the strategy that the regime had employed to encourage growth after decades of economic stagnation. Faced with irreconcilable preferences among pressure groups with deep ties to the regime, struggles over Argentina's adjustment policy directly contributed to the regime's breakdown.

Argentina's military regime under General Jorge Videla had close links to both mobile capital and domestic heavy industry. Videla seized power in the wake of the disastrous second Peronist government (1973–76), which espoused populist ideologies but was never stable amid factional infighting. In an effort to stabilize the country, the military regime continued the "Dirty War" that had begun under the previous government, accompanying it with El Proceso de Reorganización Nacional, which sought to transform Argentine society through ideological indoctrination.[34] Under the military regime, labor faced restrictions on collective bargaining, the right to strike, and the right to participate in politics; the regime also appointed military overseers of existing unions and maintained wage controls.[35] Adjustment measures pursued under the military junta had a profoundly regressive impact on labor, with sharp rises in unemployment and stagnating real wages.

[34] Marchak 1999.
[35] Drake 1996, 149–80; Munck 1998, 65–93; Pozzi 1988.

Unlike in Chile, in Argentina capital faced almost no restrictions on its ability to move across borders. Under Minister of the Economy José Martínez de Hoz, most restrictions on capital flows were abolished by 1977, and all were dismantled by 1980.[36] Like the Chicago Boys, Martínez de Hoz had personal and business links to international financial circles, and the policies that he enacted had a clear affinity with orthodox monetarist principles.[37] These encouraged massive capital inflows with no parallel in Chile: as occurred in Chile, the financial boom amid orthodox stabilization policies encouraged the growth of *financieras*, but in Argentina they forged close links with the highest levels of the regime's leadership, allowing short-term capital inflows to grow to unprecedented sums.[38]

Argentina's openness to capital flows was partially the result of the economic climate that the military regime inherited, one already marked by heavy annual inflation. The challenge – as had been the case in Indonesia in the 1960s – was to encourage investment. Inflows of foreign capital helped to finance the country's budget deficit, while open borders allowed domestic holders of liquid assets to protect themselves against peso inflation by converting assets into foreign currency as a store of value. Significant real appreciation of the exchange rate under a system of preannounced devaluations (*tablita*) only encouraged this practice.[39] Estimates of foreign currency holdings by Argentine citizens reached U.S.\$20–30 billion in the early 1980s, increasing annually by approximately U.S.\$3 billion.[40] Additionally, large inflows of hot money led to skyrocketing foreign debt. Domestic borrowers sought dollar loans, and then directed them toward short-term domestic deposits with high interest rates, or toward the booming stock market. From 1975 to 1982, private-sector financial debt increased from U.S.\$2,413 million to U.S.\$13,099 million, while public-sector debt jumped from U.S. \$4,021 million to U.S.\$28,616 million.[41] Among the investors were military figures in the Videla regime, who used their positions to obtain loans to engage in these activities.[42] The use of foreign loans to speculate

---

[36] Calvo 1986, 518–19; Nogués 1986, 16–18.

[37] Manzetti 1991, 94–98.

[38] Calvo 1986, 514–18; Flichman 1990, 19–20; Frieden 1991a, 207–9; Peralta-Ramos 1987, 50–51.

[39] Calvo 1986, 520–29; Nogués 1986, 18–19; Sjaastad 1989, 265–67.

[40] Fischer, Hiemenz, and Trapp 1985, 61.

[41] World Bank 1987, 94.

[42] Lewis 1990, 462–63; Peralta-Ramos 1987, 54.

in the domestic market during this period became known as the "bicycle" (*bicicleta*), which would remain upright so long as one kept pedaling.

Meanwhile, despite financial opening to an unprecedented scale, military links to domestic big business remained tight. The military regime retained much of the state's earlier involvement in the economy through state-run enterprises.[43] Holders of fixed capital hence exerted strong pressures on the regime. In many cases, military-linked firms successfully lobbied the regime to increase investment in their industries[44] and enjoyed corporate protectionism.[45] As occurred in Chile, the regime's trade position moved from ISI to a more fundamentally outward orientation, to the detriment of many import-competing industries. Yet this outward orientation did not eliminate the strong links between mobile capital, fixed capital, and the regime.

How can we be sure that Argentina's regime depended on both mobile and fixed capital, when Chile's regime adopted similar orthodox measures without depending on mobile capital? Domestic critics are one source, albeit an imperfect one. Leftist critics especially noted the clear affinity between the military's industrial base and increasingly mobile capital flowing into the country for investment purposes and out of the country as a store of value against inflation.[46] Also, Argentina abolished restrictions on capital outflows because of political pressure from holders of mobile assets who desired to move currency assets overseas. Finally, as noted by authors cited earlier, a number of the military government's members participated directly in speculative financial activities and cross-border capital movements. This alliance between mobile capitalists allied with orthodox monetarists and economic nationalists demanding heterodox adjustment policies had dire consequences for crisis management.[47]

Argentina's debt crisis began in March 1980 with the collapse of Banco Intercambio Regional, a heavily leveraged financial institution with extensive foreign liabilities. This signaled to domestic deposit holders and foreign currency traders alike that the *bicicleta* had finally tipped, and in the ensuing banking panic most of the big *financieras* that had risen under the military regime (such as Sasetru, Oddone, Grecco, and others) collapsed as well.[48]

[43] Biglaiser 2002, 127–32.
[44] Flichman 1990, 20–22; Frieden 1991a, 211, 14–15; Lewis 1990, 450–57.
[45] Biglaiser 2002, 104–6; Nogués 1986, 43–45.
[46] See, e.g., Dabat and Lorenzano 1984, 33–38.
[47] Pion-Berlin 1985.
[48] Lewis 1990, 462–69; Pion-Berlin 1985, 60.

Through 1981–82, capital outflows grew, driven by 100 percent annual inflation rates along with fragile domestic financial institutions. The regime attempted to defend the peg as capital outflows exerted downward pressure, but by 1981 outflows forced the regime to allow a sharp devaluation. With the devaluation came an interest rate hike designed to draw foreign capital back into the financial system, yet this was unsuccessful.[49]

With continued downward currency pressure and systemic banking fragility, political conflict over adjustment worsened.[50] Paralleling the Indonesia case, Argentine adjustment measures between 1981 and the collapse of the regime in 1983 vacillated between orthodox and heterodox policies. Indebted industrial groups that found that tight monetary policies had eroded their profitability demanded bailouts. When these were not forthcoming, they eventually turned against the regime.[51] Mirroring the statements of key military personnel in Indonesia, prominent Argentine military figures such as Admiral Armando Lambruschini (commander in chief of the Argentine navy) claimed publicly that "speculation [is] the greatest enemy of economic freedom in the realm of production."[52] After Videla's long-planned retirement, a new government under General Roberto Viola backtracked to a degree on the earlier policy of macroeconomic tightening and then repegged the peso with two parallel exchange rates – a full float for financial transactions and a crawling peg for commercial transactions. At the same time, the regime guaranteed all foreign currency debt held in the domestic financial sector, and liquidity support further contributed to increased spending and looser macroeconomic policies.[53]

Because the regime was divided by adjustment policy pressures, a military coup by General Leopoldo Galtieri ousted Viola. The new military government abolished Viola's dual exchange rate system and adopted a "dirty" float of the peso, which continued to depreciate because of capital flight. Galtieri's minister of the economy, Roberto Alemann, was a fierce proponent of orthodox adjustment measures, as were other members of Galtieri's inner circle. Yet orthodox adjustment measures could not placate the demands of industrialists and other holders of fixed capital assets, and the effects of the crisis on Argentine labor and the middle class continued to worsen. In a dramatic bid to unite the populace, Galtieri

[49] Dornbusch 1989, 296–97.
[50] See especially Munck 1998; Pion-Berlin 1985.
[51] Maxfield 1989, 82–83.
[52] Quoted in Pion-Berlin 1985, 61.
[53] Fischer, Hiemenz, and Trapp 1985, 12; Frieden 1991a, 224–25.

launched the disastrous Malvinas War against the United Kingdom, but economic management remained critically divisive.[54] Uncertainty amid the war led to further depreciation, which further increased financial sector debt burdens and led to military grumblings about orthodox policies.[55]

Galtieri's regime did not survive the loss of the Malvinas War. After General Reynaldo Bignone assumed the Argentine presidency, there were new steps to reform the financial sector. These were ineffective, and with no restrictions on capital outflows, mass conversions of liquid peso assets to fixed assets and foreign currency continued. In the face of mass opposition and a political coalition that had crumbled, the military leadership agreed to hold elections in October 1983. Anticipating a future victory by populist-nationalist political groups, the regime by mid-1983 began to adopt a host of exchange controls and protectionist policies to shield domestic business from international markets.[56]

The loss of the Malvinas War directly foreshadowed the end of authoritarian rule in Argentina, yet, as many have argued, the war itself was a symptom of the larger collapse of the coalition of capitalist interests in the midst of twin crises.[57] Opposition mobilization, as in Indonesia, became impossible to ignore as successive governments desperately sought to contain the country's economic meltdown. But the regime broke down ultimately because of divergent interests between holders of mobile and fixed capital.[58] The democratic government under Raúl Alfonsín that came to power in December 1983 was, in fact, much more closely aligned with populist elements of both business and labor. Among its nationalist stabilization attempts was the ill-fated Austral Plan, which froze wages and prices while fixing the exchange rate under a new currency, the Austral.[59] Argentina's experience in the early 1980s mirrors Indonesia's, demonstrating the impact of a coalition between mobile and fixed capital during a financial crisis. As in Indonesia, preferences for adjustment cleaved mobile capitalists from holders of fixed assets, leading to dramatic vacillation in adjustment measures and ultimately to the regime's collapse.

---

[54] Dabat and Lorenzano 1984, 83–109.
[55] Fischer, Hiemenz, and Trapp 1985, 12–13; Pion-Berlin 1985, 70; Sjaastad 1989, 267.
[56] Fischer, Hiemenz, and Trapp 1985, 20–32; Peralta-Ramos 1987, 60.
[57] Munck 1998, 139–44.
[58] Dabat and Lorenzano 1984, 125–68; Pion-Berlin 1985.
[59] Lewis 1990, 484–93; Manzetti 1991, 139–87; Manzetti and Dell'Aquila 1988.

Uruguay, 1981–1985

Like both Chile and Argentina, Uruguay was a rightist military regime that oppressed labor and, like Argentina, Uruguay welcomed mass capital inflows during the decade before the crisis of the early 1980s. In another respect, Uruguay parallels Indonesia even more closely than does Argentina: very early during the period of military rule, the regime rapidly abolished nearly all capital account restrictions, while moving very slowly in liberalizing the current account and dismantling military-owned industrial concerns. Under the military, Uruguay regained its reputation as the "Switzerland of Latin America," owing as much to its high financial openness as to its size and location between regional powers. The contours of Uruguay's transition amid financial panic differs from the other two Southern Cone military regimes, as Uruguay had taken halting steps toward the restoration of civilian rule since 1980, before crisis onset.[60] Yet the ensuing struggles over adjustment measures revealed contradictory preferences between owners of mobile and fixed capital, both of whom had the ear of the military regime, and hastened the regime's ultimate collapse.

Uruguay's military regime followed economic stagnation and conflict between an urban leftist guerrilla movement, the Tupamaros, and counterguerrillas supported by the military and a weak civilian president, Juan María Bordaberry. Facing a deeply hostile legislature, the military and Bordaberry suspended democratic rule in 1973, with Bordaberry later removed from office in 1976.[61] Following a brief interlude, the military installed Aparicio Méndez, who had the approval of armed forces' head General Julio César Vadora in addition to support between the civilian-military consultative group, the Council of the Nations. Similar to the other Southern Cone military regimes, labor activists and leftists were systematically repressed.[62] This complemented the regime's push for orthodox stabilization policies under a new coalition between holders of mobile and fixed capital.

Economic policy under the Uruguayan military regime balanced the interests of both military-linked industrial firms and private businesses in the corporate and financial sectors. Before 1973, Bordaberry's coalition of supporters included landowners and firms in the industrial sector as well as the nascent financial sector.[63] Following the installation of Méndez, rightist

[60] Gillespie 1991.
[61] Gillespie 1991, 33–49; Handelman 1981; Kaufman 1979, 21–54.
[62] Drake 1996, 91–116; Kaufman 1979, 77–82.
[63] Kaufman 1979, 43.

factions within the military gained the upper hand in economic policy making.[64] The regime abolished currency transactions by residents in September 1974 and implemented Uruguay's own *tablita* of preannounced exchange rate depreciations in October 1978. Domestically, the regime lifted regulations on nonbank financial institutions (*casas bacarias*) in 1977, leading to their rapid growth in number from just one in 1976 to twenty-three in 1981.[65] Under Minister of the Economy Alejandro Végh Villegas, the regime also made some concerted efforts to eliminate protectionism and reverse import-substitution policies while combating inflation with strict monetarist policies.[66] Yet these efforts were less successful, owing primarily to opposition from powerful domestic business lobbies.

Coalition politics in Uruguay thus resembled coalitional politics in Argentina, despite the more bureaucratic military apparatus in Uruguay. As in Argentina, industrialists who feared that deregulation would harm their interests sought and obtained backing from the military. Yet Végh had a free hand in financial matters, about which the military and its industrial allies cared little. These interest group pressures resisting domestic industrial reforms and trade liberalization continued under Végh's successor, Valentín Arismendi. Aside from Végh and Arismendi, though, few economists manned economic ministries under the military regime. Consequently, neoliberal ideas had few champions, and orthodox economic policies were promoted only gradually or, in the case of privatization, hardly at all.[67] Survey evidence from Charles Gillespie confirms that the two social groups closest to the military regime were mobile and fixed capital, which Gillespie glosses as "big business" and "bankers."[68] Excluded from the regime's coalition were labor and the poor, who suffered under the regime's policies.

Financial liberalization in the mid- to late 1970s, as elsewhere, encouraged rapid capital inflows. Foreign debt grew from U.S.$515 million to U.S.$4 billion between 1976 and 1982, with most of these loans feeding a booming property market.[69] The collapse of the Argentine peso, exacerbated by the substantial overvaluation of the Uruguayan peso, fed a speculative attack against the Uruguayan peso. Unable to defend the currency,

[64] Gillespie 1991, 54–55; Kaufman 1979, 56–60.
[65] Hanson and de Melo 1985, 919–20; Laens, Lorenzo, and Osimani 1993, 160–62.
[66] Biglaiser 2002, 39–40; Hanson and de Melo 1983, 481–88; Ramos 1986, 28–29.
[67] Biglaiser 2002, 106–9, 132–34.
[68] Gillespie 1991, 60–62. See also Handelman 1981, 377, who refers to "industrial leaders" and "spokesmen for the banking and commercial sector."
[69] Hanson and de Melo 1985, 922–23; Weinstein 1988, 63–64.

the regime abandoned the *tablita* at the end of November 1982. Thereafter, the peso fell precipitously, and large numbers of domestic investors who had counted on a steady devaluation under the *tablita* went bankrupt. Seeking to minimize the impact of the crisis, the regime attempted to renegotiate the country's foreign debt and received IMF loans on the condition that it adopt a strongly orthodox set of adjustment measures. Resistance from powerful industrial firms and the military, though, ensured that the regime actually completed very few privatization or deregulation exercises.[70] Between 1982 and 1985, as much as U.S.$2 billion fled overseas because of worsening economic conditions.[71] Despite this substantial conversion of pesos to dollars, capital openness remained a key part of the regime's economic policy program because of the political influence of mobile capital; this policy continued after the regime brought back Végh as minister of the economy in 1983 as a last-ditch effort to find a solution to the crisis. But predictably, amid economic collapse and high interest rates, holders of fixed capital in the industrial sector became estranged from the regime, creating a fundamental conflict among the regime's backers.[72] Within three years, the military regime had given way to a populist democratic government under Julio María Sanguinetti.

Uruguay's protracted democratization complicates the parallel between the breakdown of its authoritarian regime and authoritarian breakdowns in Indonesia and Argentina. Méndez was succeeded by General Gregorio Conrado Álvarez Armelino in 1981 following a national plebiscite that supported the restoration of democracy. Álvarez allowed free democratic elections in 1984, which Sanguinetti won as the candidate from the Colorado Party; Álvarez then stepped down in favor of a caretaker administration, until Sanguinetti took office in March 1985. So the process leading to democratization had already begun before the crisis hit in 1981. Nonetheless, intracoalition conflict between mobile and fixed capital hastened the breakdown of the regime and prevented the two capitalist groups from retrenching their positions in favor of the authoritarian status quo when confronting a mass-based prodemocracy movement.

Mexico: 1980s and 1990s

Mexico has fallen victim to twin crises twice in recent history, once during the Latin American debt crises and again during the mid-1990s. In broad

[70] Biglaiser 2002, 41; Weinstein 1988, 62.
[71] Weinstein 1988, 97.
[72] Gillespie 1991, 107–8.

strokes, Mexico's experiences conform nicely to the theory's predictions. Mexico's initial response to the Latin American debt crisis was proudly heterodox, as evident in the comment of President José López Portillo on September 1, 1982:

This financial plague creates misery wherever it spreads. As in medieval times, it devastates country after country. It is transmitted by rats, and its remains are unemployment and misery, industrial ruin and speculators' enrichment. The remedy for these is to deprive the patient of food, to subjugate him by force. . . . There is a group of Mexicans . . . led, advised, and supported by private bankers, who have plundered our country of more money than the imperialists who have exploited us since the beginning of our history.[73]

Sixteen years to the day before Malaysia imposed capital controls, López Portillo nationalized Mexico's banking sector, imposed strict capital controls, and embarked on economic expansion through moderately loose macroeconomic policies and a range of redistributive subsidies. Just over a decade later, facing the Tequila Crisis, President Ernesto Zedillo Ponce de León maintained an open capital account and stood by an orthodox adjustment policy response that contributed directly to the eventual end of seven decades of authoritarian rule under the Institutional Revolutionary Party (PRI). Yet my theory can make little sense of these two divergent outcomes under the same regime unless the coalitional basis of authoritarian rule in Mexico somehow changed between 1982 and 1994. This coalitional shift – which took place under López Portillo's successor Miguel de la Madrid Hurtado – muddies the analysis somewhat. But the findings still lend crucial support to the theory. After de la Madrid broke with the PRI's traditional constituency among organized labor and national industry, the regime settled on a new internationalist coalition involving externally oriented domestic industry and mobile financiers at home and abroad. The Tequila Crisis broke this coalition, leading to popular resistance from workers, peasants, and industrialists to orthodox adjustment strategies. Unable to contain this mass pressure, the regime succumbed to democracy at the ballot box in 1997 and 2000.

The Latin American Debt Crisis in Mexico

Mexico's political system under the PRI arose in the wake of the Mexican Revolution of 1910, first consolidating into a tentative populist alliance around 1917 and ultimately culminating in a labor-capital alliance under

---

[73] López Portillo 1982.

Lázaro Cárdenas (1934–40). Until the mid-1980s, and despite occasional challenges to PRI hegemony from radical unionists, labor enjoyed tight links with the regime through Mexican unions.[74] At the same time, the private sector forged close informal links to the PRI government as well, despite formal exclusion from political life under the PRI. Under López Portillo's rule (1976–82), political ties between the PRI and domestic businesses grew especially prominent.[75] At the same time, public enterprises and state-controlled firms flourished. The PRI thus served as a bridge between organized labor and business interests, serving the former by facilitating wage bargaining and the latter by containing labor unrest and militancy.

In cementing this coalition between organized labor and the private sector, Mexico under the PRI paralleled Malaysia, with a few notable exceptions. The absence of politicized ethnicity in Mexico is but one. In Malaysia labor unionism has always been restrained because of the government's fear of a panethnic, class-based challenge to its rule, but in Mexico state-linked labor unions were a key political ally. Moreover, the Mexican peasantry increasingly languished under the PRI,[76] whereas rural Malays have continually benefited from the favoritism of the ruling United Malays National Organisation. The tenuous political position afforded mobile capital in Mexico, though, parallels the Malaysian case. Sylvia Maxfield details the "bankers' alliance" that pushed for international financial openness in Mexico and competed for political influence with the "Cárdenas coalition."[77] Like Malaysia under Mahathir until 1998, under the presidencies of Luis Echeverría Álvarez and López Portillo, the Mexican regime maintained an open capital account and welcomed capital inflows. Also like Malaysia, these policies beneficial to the bankers' alliance – mobile capital – existed despite its inability to penetrate the PRI's coalition.

Mexico's experience with the Latin American debt crises is familiar. Fueled by high petroleum prices in the 1970s, López Portillo's government embarked on an imprudent fiscal expansion under an overvalued exchange rate. Foreign capital inflows, in the form of private bank and corporate debt as well as public-sector debt, grew rapidly. When petroleum prices collapsed in late 1980 and 1981, the regime continued its

---

[74] Collier 1992, 43–64; Middlebrook 1995; Samstad and Collier 1995, 10–12.
[75] Bazdresch and Levy 1991, 246–52; Camp 1989, 27–29; Luna 1995, 78–79.
[76] Foley 1991.
[77] Maxfield 1990. See also White 1992.

heavy public spending while defending the peso against devaluation. Still, capital flight – reaching a total of U.S.$11.6 billion in 1981 alone – forced a devaluation in February 1982.[78] The currency crisis, then, exposed the fragility of Mexico's banking sector, leading to sharp distributional conflicts over the course of economic adjustment.[79]

The need to shield the regime's constituents from the costs of adjustment was particularly acute in early 1982, as the PRI faced a July presidential election that would be a natural rallying point for dissatisfied citizens. To head off opposition from the private sector, López Portillo's government maintained expansionary fiscal policies, including several bailouts of government-connected firms and state-owned enterprises, such as Mexicana Airlines.[80] It complemented these fiscal measures with a relatively lax monetary stance designed to forestall a credit crunch.[81] Meanwhile, to placate labor, the government mandated a series of wage increases, beginning with a 30 percent increase for the country's lowest-paid workers and progressively smaller percentage increases at higher wage levels.[82] These measures managed to forestall temporarily popular discontent with the PRI's economic governance, allowing it to easily prevail in July 1982 elections, but capital flight continued in the subsequent months. In his final moves to regain control over the financial sector, in August 1982 López Portillo froze dollar-denominated accounts held in Mexican financial institutions, subsequently mandating their forced conversion to pesos at well below the market exchange rate.[83] A month later, he nationalized the entire domestic financial sector, placing full controls on capital account transactions. As expected, such measures were immediately popular among organized labor and holders of fixed capital alike, while deeply criticized by the financial sector and by other holders of mobile capital.[84] Shielded from the pressure of capital outflows and with firm control over the domestic financial sector, López Portillo maintained relatively expansionary policies and rode out the remainder of his term.

In December 1982 de la Madrid assumed the Mexican presidency. Unlike López Portillo, he had a reputation as a technocrat, willing to

---

[78] Lustig 1998, 24.
[79] Collier 1992, 79–111; Hamilton 1984.
[80] Collier 1992, 79.
[81] Looney 1985, 112; White 1992, 107–8.
[82] Bailey 1988, 54; Lustig 1998, 25.
[83] Lustig 1998, 25.
[84] Hamilton 1984, 17–23; Maxfield 1990, 142–53; 1992; Santín Quiroz 2001, 92; White 1992, 106–23.

accept short-term austerity in the interest of long-term recovery. The IMF bailout negotiated in the final weeks of López Portillo's presidency suggested a future turn to orthodoxy. Yet policy outcomes reveal that at least for the first two years of de la Madrid's presidency, adjustment policies remained remarkably close to the previous administration. To be sure, the country experienced a recession that hit labor especially hard with retrenchment and real wage decreases. But these first two years also saw notable *increases* in many public spending programs, with targets such as worker training and housing programs, as well as new food subsidies and government-decreed increases in profit sharing.[85] Public employment during this period rose, and the public enterprise share of employment in sectors such as manufacturing remained high until the late 1980s.[86] Moreover, there were continued rhetorical commitments after de la Madrid's election that the government redistribution would support social welfare. Throughout this period, labor actively pressured the regime for favorable treatment, and the regime responded accordingly.[87]

From the perspective of Mexican capital owners, de la Madrid's initial policies were also consistent with López Portillo's. In fact, López Portillo's capital account restrictions remained in effect for three more years. As reflected in the Chinn and Ito index, capital account reliberalization did not even begin until 1987. Meanwhile, domestic real interest rates remained low, and until July 1985 the regime maintained a complex system of dual exchange rates – one fixed and appreciated for financial transactions and the other quasi-pegged for other transactions.[88] Likewise, during this period there was no real movement on privatization of government enterprises or divestiture, largely because of political opposition from within the party, from affected business interests, and from labor groups.[89] Heavy protection of domestic industry through tariffs, nontariff barriers, and a wide range of limits on foreign direct investment complemented these policies.

Despite having accepted IMF loans mandating an orthodox austerity package, the de la Madrid administration's adjustment policies during the first several years closely matched the heterodox adjustment package in Malaysia. Industrial groups benefited from Mexican adjustment policies in the immediate aftermath of the crisis, through subsidized loans and

[85] Collier 1992, 83; Middlebrook 1989, 209; Teichman 1992, 92.
[86] Rogozinski 1998, 138.
[87] Collier 1992, 81–83; Hamilton 1984, 25–27.
[88] Ros 1987, 87–92.
[89] Schneider 1989, 101; Teichman 1995, 79–82, 130–31.

artificially high exchange rates for foreign loan repayment. The losers from these policies were holders of mobile capital. In response, financial sector organizations began to organize in 1983 to push for reliberalization. This organization continued apace in the subsequent years, with many holders of mobile capital assets throwing their political support behind the National Action Party (PAN).[90] Conflict between mobile and fixed capital, in fact, dominated conflict between capital and labor, despite the losses that labor faced under de la Madrid's first several years in office.[91]

If Mexico's economic troubles had ended there, the story would be a simple confirmation of the theory. Yet, unlike events in Chile and Malaysia, economic turmoil in Mexico did not end in the mid-1980s. By 1985 a series of additional external shocks led the PRI to forgo its traditional cross-class alliance in favor of a new political coalition, one that brought together holders of mobile and fixed capital with increasing hostility toward Mexican labor.

From Orthodoxy to the Tequila Crisis to Authoritarian Breakdown

Ruth Collier dates the onset of the coalitional shift in Mexico to 1985.[92] She argues that four distinct shocks hit the Mexican political economy in that year, the combination of which led the PRI to forgo its traditional alliance with labor. The first shock was truly exogenous: the devastating Mexico City earthquake exposed a state whose incompetent response to mass devastation alienated many of the urban poor.[93] The second was international delegitimation as a result of widespread accusations of fraud at midterm elections. The third came from the suspension of IMF loan disbursements for noncompliance with loan conditions, the result of the regime's return to expansionary policies in 1984.[94] The final shock was the second petroleum crisis of the 1980s.[95] In the wake of these shocks, economic policy veered sharply from populism toward neoliberal orthodoxy, from nationalism, state intervention, and import-substitution industrialization to export-oriented industrialization.

These new policies greatly hastened the limited steps toward liberalization that de la Madrid's regime had taken in its first two years in office.

---

[90] Maxfield 1992, 89–90; Valdés Ugalde 1994, 220–27.
[91] Davis 1993, 64–66.
[92] Collier 1992, 86–89.
[93] See also Bailey 1988, 141; Cornelius 1986, 35–37; Whitehead 1998, 192.
[94] See also Lustig 1998, 34–36.
[95] See also Cornelius 1986, 5–7; Ros 1993, 313; Teichman 1995, 83.

Most notable from the perspective of urban wage laborers was price liberalization.[96] The regime also accelerated the process of privatization that had stalled in the previous years, dismantling hundreds of state-run firms.[97] On the external sector, the regime liberalized trade, beginning with its accession to the General Agreement on Trades and Tariffs in 1986 and proceeding quickly thereafter. It also sought actively to attract capital flows back into the country by liberalizing investment regulations and the financial sector.[98] With the shift to economic orthodoxy came the break-down of the existing populist coalition. The traditional alliance between the PRI and organized labor fractured, spawning resistance from more traditional PRI members and a range of state-linked business groups that had previously enjoyed government favoritism.[99] In remaking the PRI's support coalition as a reformist coalition of fixed and mobile capital, the regime thus abandoned its traditional support base.

To be clear, this coalitional shift lies outside of my theory. But a wide range of sources have noted this coalitional shift and explained it as a function of several factors unique to the Mexican political system. Mexico's *sexenio*, the single six-year term that a Mexican president serves, entails continual executive turnover, meaning that new economic ideologies can rise in prominence quickly. In replacing López Portillo, de la Madrid brought his own ideas about proper economic management. By contrast, in Southeast Asia and elsewhere in Latin America during the 1970s and early 1980s, authoritarian leaders ruled until they retired voluntarily or were ousted. It is also possible that regimes can withstand economic crises only so long, so that adjustment policies that protect short-term interests but fail to spur satisfactory recovery in the medium to long run frustrate policy makers, leading them to attempt radically new policies. Either of these possibilities, or both, could explain why de la Madrid's regime in 1985 chose to embark on a far more orthodox adjustment package in response to the additional shocks of 1985. The subsequent rise of leftist and labor opponents to the regime, however, confirms that, as expected, constituents who do not obtain their preferred policies from the regime withdraw political support from their former patrons.

---

[96] Collier 1992, 91; Lustig 1998, 111.

[97] Lustig 1998, 103–07; Rogozinski 1998; Schneider 1989, 102–5; Teichman 1995, 130–40.

[98] Lustig 1998, 128–29; Pastor and Wise 1997, 433–34.

[99] Baer 1993, 53–56; Collier 1992, 103–11, 124–125; Gibson 1997; Middlebrook 1995, 293–99; Morris 1995, 27–28; Samstad and Collier 1995, 13–18; Teichman 1992, 96–99.

The 1988 elections evinced the new hostility between the PRI regime and Mexican labor. Many factions of labor for the first time united not with the PRI but with the opposition under the National Democratic Front (FDN), whose members even included some former PRI stalwarts. The Front's presidential candidate, Cuauhtémoc Cárdenas, evoked the PRI's former alliance with labor (his father was Lázaro Cárdenas) and hence support from peasants and laborers who suffered under de la Madrid's new economic policies. A new rise in social movements agitating for reform and justice reflected the unprecedented new popular opposition to the PRI.[100] Only through unprecedented electoral fraud was Carlos Salinas de Gortari able to prevail over Cárdenas.

Salinas furthered the liberalization of de la Madrid's last three years in office. Domestically, he initiated new agricultural reforms and ramped up privatization. Internationally, he signed the North American Free Trade Agreement in 1993, which relied on a new externally oriented business coalition.[101] With trade liberalization came capital account liberalization to encourage the Mexican financial sector to rejoin international capital markets.[102]

These reforms were a direct product of the regime's new coalition among holders of mobile and fixed capital. Throughout this period, business groups of all types sought closer relations with the Salinas government, both through individual connections and through the creation and expansion of business and trade organizations.[103] Salinas's reforms were popular among large industrial firms as well as the newly ascendant and internationally linked financial sector, although small enterprise and statist business groups lost out.[104] Politically, Salinas linked this newly ascendant business coalition to the rising Mexican middle class, whose fortunes improved under new economic growth.[105] At the same time, the regime reverted to more authoritarian methods of control, including coercion, media manipulation, and more open electoral fraud. In this way, Mexico's new support coalition grew to resemble late New Order Indonesia.

The parallel with Indonesia also extends to the regime's management of labor relations and social policy. Many developmentalist programs and

---

[100] Grindle 1996, 156–61; Tamayo 1990.
[101] Thacker 1999.
[102] Santín Quiroz 2001, 93–109.
[103] Luna 1995, 82–84; Valdés Ugalde 1994, 231–38.
[104] Grindle 1996, 83–85; Morris 1995, 80–84; Teichman 1995, 152–58, 83–91.
[105] Baer 1993, 56–58.

labor relations organizations continued to exist, as the state's corporatist heritage persisted in new forms under Salinas – Indonesia too had numerous official corporatist bodies that contained labor opposition. Salinas's administration settled on concepts of "New Unionism" and "New Syndicalism," ideas that would remake traditional state-labor relations. Many members of the labor movement, correctly interpreting these as moves to weaken organized labor's political voice, heartily if unsuccessfully resisted.[106] At the same time, the regime attempted to forge collaborative relations between the state and civil society through *concertación*, although this process was ultimately unsuccessful. The regime's most important step to reconnect with the Mexican poor was the National Solidarity Program (PRONASOL), but the program suffered from extensive political interference, with performance suffering accordingly.[107] As in Indonesia throughout the late 1980s and 1990s, renewed growth in Mexico during the early 1990s was able to placate temporarily workers and peasants who now found themselves outside of the regime's coalition. This afforded the regime a measure of stability until the 1994 crisis struck.

Under Salinas, financial liberalization encouraged mass inflows of portfolio capital, supplemented by a boom in the domestic financial sector that resulted in real peso appreciation.[108] But a series of economic and political events near the end of Salinas's term spelled the end of easy foreign credit. Among these were the country's large current account deficit; a rise in foreign interest rates; and political instability surrounding the murders of PRI presidential candidate Luis Donaldo Colosio and PRI secretary-general José Francisco Ruiz Massieu and the Zapatista uprising in Chiapas. As capital flows slowed, they exposed the massive accumulation of loans in the Mexican financial system.[109]

With capital outflows beginning in early 1994, the Salinas regime initially resisted monetary tightening in advance of another presidential election. In fact, monetary policy was actively expansionary during early 1994.[110] PRI candidate Ernesto Zedillo was able to prevail in the 1994 elections, but upon entering office he faced the legacy of his predecessor's

[106] Collier 1992, 133–41; Morris 1995, 84–88; Pastor and Wise 1997; Samstad 2002; Samstad and Collier 1995, 18–31.
[107] Cornelius, Craig, and Fox 1994.
[108] Edwards 1997, 105–10; Lustig 1998, 147–57; Pastor and Wise 1997, 424; Santín Quiroz 2001, 199–207.
[109] Calvo and Mendoza 1996.
[110] González Gómez 1998, 47–49.

economic policies: financial fragility, capital flight, and a severely over-valued exchange rate. On December 20, 1994, the regime floated the peso, which depreciated severely amid the accompanying massive capital outflows.[111] The ensuing credit crunch put adjustment policy back on the table.

Recalling López Portillo's bank nationalization and capital account restrictions, many in the financial sector feared that Zedillo would impose capital controls, harming not only the many foreign owners of *tesobonos* (dollar-denominated swap instruments) but also Mexican financial conglomerates, which moved cash to safer holdings overseas.[112] But, despite popular pressures from labor, small businesses, and industrial groups, the regime did not break its links to international capital markets. As in Indonesia, the regime's new reliance on mobile capital led it to protect mobile capital's interests during the crisis, hence constraining its adjustment policy responses and putting it into direct conflict with fixed capital and labor.

Adjustment measures under Zedillo accordingly followed IMF orthodoxy. To draw capital back into the country, the regime raised interest rates to above 40 percent and sharply contracted the supply of money.[113] Fiscal spending was cut 10 percent, and the regime mandated extensive price rises for basic goods such as petroleum, electricity, and tolls.[114] Meanwhile, the United States, Canada, several other industrial countries, and the IMF made available substantial funds upon which the regime could draw.[115] The impact of these austerity measures was, of course, predictable: massive labor retrenchment, eroded business profitability, and industrial hardship because of tight credit conditions.

The political fallout from orthodox adjustment measures brought the PRI to its knees. The idiosyncrasies of Mexican presidential turnover may have affected the official response to this loss of popularity, for Zedillo, despite the massive shift of public opinion against the PRI in the wake of the peso devaluation, showed no desire to repress emerging opposition movements.[116] In this willingness to tolerate the opposition even as it threatened the PRI's rule, he differed from his predecessors. Business

---

[111] Edwards 1997, 118; Lustig 1998, 161–67; Pastor and Wise 1997, 425.
[112] Lustig 1998, 176–77.
[113] Edwards 1997, 119–20; González Gómez 1998, 51; Ramírez de la O 1996, 26; Springer and Molina 1995, 67.
[114] González Gómez 1998, 51; Springer and Molina 1995, 67.
[115] Lustig 1998, 172–86.
[116] Cornelius 1996, 36–37, 115–19; Rubio 1998, 13–18.

associations and industrial forms demanded the relaxation of fiscal austerity measures and an end to high interest rates.[117] Mass social movements united indebted firms and business-minded small businesses with
leftist social movements – one illustrative example was the Civil Association Representing the National Union of Agricultural and Livestock
Producers, Businesspeople, Industrialists, and Service Providers (the
Barzón).[118] Altogether, the public apportioned blame for economic hardship largely among Salinas, Zedillo, and Mexican speculators.[119] This is
the precise type of distributive conflict – labor and fixed capital against
mobile capital – that adjustment policy during twin crises unleashes.

But, unlike in 1982, when the regime faced similar problems, in 1994
the PRI's support coalition now included both mobile and fixed capital.
Zedillo's decision to adhere to orthodoxy led to the coalition's fracture, as
economic performance both alienated holders of fixed capital and encouraged worker and peasant activism.[120] In the first national elections following the peso crisis, in 1997, the PRI for the first time failed to attain a
majority of seats in the Chamber of Deputies, Mexico's lower house. In a
victory fraught with political symbolism, Cuauhtémoc Cárdenas trounced
the PRI's candidate to become the first opposition mayor of Mexico City
under the PRI. By the 2000 elections, the fracture of the PRI's network of
support and patronage meant that the PRI was no longer able to turn out
its traditional voters and that opposition voters were far more likely to
turn out than they had been in the 1970s and early 1980s.[121] It was clear
that the political struggle in Mexico was no longer over authoritarian
survival but rather over how liberal Mexico's new democracy would be.

Conclusion: Cross-National Perspectives on Crises, Coalitions, and Change

During the Latin American debt crises, distributional conflicts over
adjustment policy drove the Argentine regime's collapse, hastened the
democratic transition in Uruguay, and severely tested regimes in Mexico
and Chile. As suggested in Chapter 2, formative moments had created
four very different support coalitions underlying these regimes. In Argentina and Uruguay, militaries with personal links to financial sector players

---

[117] Morris and Passe-Smith 2001, 135–37.
[118] Williams 2001a; 2001b.
[119] Davis and Bartilow 2002; Magaloni 2006, 151–74, 93–226; Smith 1997, 45–49.
[120] Dresser 1997, 70–71; Whitehead 1998, 194–97.
[121] Klesner and Lawson 2001.

overthrew incumbent regimes and established coalitions between mobile and fixed capital in response to inflationary crises. In Chile, a similar crisis and a military without links to the financial sector spawned a regime that embraced export-competitive fixed capital, allowing mobile capital only limited influence on policy making, conditional on good economic conditions. Mexico's populist regime formed absent inflationary pressures or an interventionist military.

In contrast to the work of Frieden, whose analysis of debt crises and political conflict in Latin America is the standard by which all analyses should be judged,[122] I argue that political conflict is not determined ex ante, but develops according to the nature of the financial crises facing regimes. In all cases, holders of fixed capital came into direct conflict with mobile capital, and, in all but rightist Chile, fixed capital allied explicitly with labor to demand favorable adjustment policies. Coalitional alignments are therefore critical for understanding final policy choices. Regimes in Argentina and Uruguay sought desperately to find acceptable adjustment policies, vacillating between tight and loose macroeconomic policies and adopting an ever-changing set of exchange rate policies. Neither regime could forestall eventual regime breakdown. In Chile, a rightist regime with links to fixed capital but not mobile capital settled upon capital controls and expansionary macroeconomic policy to steer through the crisis. In Mexico, a populist authoritarian regime adopted strict capital controls, nationalized banks, and expanded the economy. In 1994, facing another financial crisis but now supported by a very different coalition, the Mexican regime did none of these things and succumbed to pressure for regime change. Consistent with this argument, across the world authoritarian regimes that adopt capital controls during financial crises are more likely to survive them than their counterparts that do not.

It is worth noting how the focus on distributional struggles among labor, fixed capital, and mobile capital differs from existing explanations of adjustment and breakdown during financial crises in modern Latin America. Most obviously different from other works is my insistence that adjustment and regime survival during economic crises are fundamentally intertwined. Many authors study the politics of economic adjustment without considering conflict over regime survival, or regime trajectories without seriously addressing economic adjustment. A few works consider economic adjustment and regime collapse together for particular countries.[123] But

[122] Frieden 1991a.
[123] The best example is Pion-Berlin 1985.

none bring to bear cross-national evidence, and hence they do not offer theoretical accounts that are general enough to explain variation, or specific enough to be falsifiable. My approach in this regard is unique.

On a basic level, I differ with several authors in my coding of adjustment strategies in Latin America. Some argue that Mexico and Chile adopted orthodox policy responses to the Latin American debt crises of the early 1980s.[124] So far as the imposition of capital controls and Keynesian demand stimuli are the hallmarks of heterodox adjustment policies, I simply disagree. Chile's adjustment was consistently *regressive*, but this is distinct from its orthodoxy. Years later, regimes embarked upon more orthodox recovery policies. But the immediate response to both countries' crises was profoundly heterodox until the point when the crisis had abated (Chile) or when a series of additional shocks ruptured the existing coalition (Mexico). Mexico and Chile parallel Malaysia on this count as well. After all, once financial turmoil ceased in Malaysia, capital controls were removed – within a year, the heaviest restrictions on capital outflows were lifted. This return to orthodoxy does not mean that Malaysia's adjustment strategy had never been heterodox, but rather that the heterodox solution was applied only as a short-term solution to financial sector weaknesses rather than a long-term development strategy.

Until recently, Latin America dominated the literature on authoritarianism in the developing world. I argue against the concept of state autonomy that was so prevalent in this older literature. Regime behavior and political conflict clearly demonstrate that regimes found economic crises to be deeply troubling. If authoritarian states were really autonomous, then why would they care about economic crises? Moreover, adjustment policy would vary only according to neutral economic calculations and national economic characteristics. Yet we observe that, when confronting four very similar crises, the countries adopted very different responses. Country experiences also challenge the independent effect of economic ideology on policy choice, which has long been a prized explanation for economic policy in Latin America. Chile, the dictatorship most identified with neoconservative orthodoxy, broke most decisively from it during its crisis.

My approach also leads me to engage in a bit of trespassing. Subtypes of "military" or "bureaucratic authoritarian" or "populist authoritarian" regimes are widely employed in the comparative analysis of Latin American authoritarianism. Within categories, regimes are more or less similar. Across

---

[124] Kaufman and Stallings 1989.

categories, differences in regime behavior are identified with the differences between the categories. Hence, similar patterns of rule in Brazil, Chile, Argentina, Uruguay, and other countries are held to be determined by the nature of bureaucratic authoritarianism, and the patterns are different in Mexico and Venezuela because neither was a bureaucratic authoritarian regime. My coalitional approach encourages analysts to look for similarities across categories and differences within categories, and not simply to attribute patterns of action to a loosely specified logic of military or bureaucratic authoritarian rule. This trespassing flies in the face of most of the literature on crisis, adjustment, and transitions in Latin America, but it is a fruitful avenue of inquiry.

9

Conclusions

This book has investigated how authoritarian regimes grapple with financial crises. I argue that different coalitions of regime supporters yield predictably different adjustment policy responses, which in turn have powerful impacts on regime survival. Coalitions vary according to their economic profiles. I study the preferences of three types of economic actors that can support nondemocratic regimes – mobile capital, fixed capital, and labor – and argue that the twin pressures of an insolvent banking sector and currency depreciation put the interests of mobile capital at odds with fixed capital and labor. The key is mobile capital's ability to redeploy assets abroad in response to poor economic conditions or unfavorable economic policies at home. Both fixed capital and labor, unable to divest and move overseas, will welcome capital account restrictions to facilitate expansionary macroeconomic policies. Accordingly, mobile capital prefers an open capital account with neutral macroeconomic policy (orthodoxy), whereas fixed capital and labor prefer a closed capital account with interventionist macroeconomic policy (heterodoxy). Across financial crises in emerging markets, we observe struggles over adjustment policy that follow this split between holders of fixed capital – often in alliance with labor, or strategically forming "nationalist" or "populist" alliances – and mobile capital, usually painted as disloyal, manipulative, or unpatriotic.

When authoritarian regimes have support coalitions that include both mobile and fixed capital, they face mutually incompatible adjustment policy pressures. Adjustment policy conflict in such regimes ultimately brings them down, with the support coalition fracturing across the cleavage of mobile capital versus fixed capital. Regimes supported by coalitions of fixed capital and labor face complementary pressure for heterodox adjustment strategies. Because adjustment policy pressures do not conflict with one another, the regime can adopt these heterodox adjustment strategies and survive the crisis intact. During financial crises, coalitions explain adjustment policy choices, and adjustment policy conflict explains regime survival.

This theory solves with one set of tools two enduring puzzles from the Asian Financial Crisis. Why did adjustment policy vary so substantially between Indonesia and Malaysia? And why did Indonesia's regime break down as a consequence of the crisis, whereas Malaysia's survived? Indonesia's coalition between ethnic Chinese holders of mobile capital and holders of fixed capital in the military prevented the regime from adopting coherent adjustment measures, and this conflict caused the New Order's collapse. By contrast, Malaysia's coalition between Malay fixed capitalists and the Malay masses led the regime to adopt heterodox adjustment strategies, which protected the interests of both and allowed the regime to survive. Moreover, this unified explanation of adjustment policy and regime survival surpasses alternative explanations – which focus on crisis severity, economic fundamentals, international pressure, technocratic competence, irrationality, and political institutions – in its parsimony and empirical accuracy. These alternative explanations ignore the very politics at the heart of struggles over regime survival. Coalitions mediate the link between economic interests and the policies that can keep authoritarian regimes in power.

This theory was vital for guiding the empirical work, leading me to seek evidence that existing studies of crisis politics in Southeast Asia have ignored. The theory guided me, when interviewing Anwar Ibrahim, to seek information not only about his assault by Malaysia's inspector-general of police and his imprisonment on trumped-up charges but also about his strategy for economic adjustment amid financial turmoil. Likewise, the theory guided me, when interviewing the former Indonesian minister of finance, Fuad Bawazier, to seek information not only on the groups pressuring President Soeharto to adopt capital controls but also on the political consequences of Soeharto's eventual refusal. Theory and fieldwork informed one another, yielding new insights and shaping the argument in ways that other accounts have missed.

My argument also explains political conflict and regime trajectories during financial crises in other emerging markets. Focusing on twin crises in Latin America, I show that coalitional politics played a powerful role in determining adjustment policies under authoritarian regimes in Argentina, Chile, Mexico, and Uruguay during the Latin American debt crises of the early 1980s. Cross-nationally, I use data on capital account openness to demonstrate that capital account restrictions during twin crises systematically increase the durability of authoritarian rule, controlling for alternative explanations for regime survival. These additional case studies and quantitative tests show that the experiences of Indonesia and Malaysia in the 1990s have parallels from across the developing world.

Implications for Social Science

My argument has consequences for three literatures that span the fields of international relations and comparative politics: theories of authoritarianism, the politics of open economies, and the political economy of regime transitions.

Theories of Authoritarianism

How do nondemocratic regimes maintain power, and how do nondemocratic regimes vary? The practice of distinguishing among types of nondemocratic regimes began with distinctions between authoritarianism and totalitarianism.[1] In the 1970s and 1980s, the experiences of newly independent states in Africa, the Middle East, and Asia – in concert with the return to authoritarianism in Latin America – led to further classifications of regimes as military or praetorian regimes,[2] patrimonial regimes,[3] bureaucratic authoritarian regimes,[4] and many others. Recent work on typologies of authoritarianism looks at parties, legislatures, and electoral systems in nondemocratic regimes, distinguishing regimes that possess such institutions from those that lack them.[5] Other approaches conceive of autocracy and democracy as two poles on a continuum and examine gradations of "authoritarian-ness."

All of these are ways to think about how authoritarian regimes can vary. I focus on the economic foundations of durable authoritarian rule, which I show to vary across regimes according to the stable coalitions underlying them. This suggests intuitive hypotheses about the economic

---

[1] Friedrich and Brzezinski 1965; Linz 2000.
[2] Nordlinger 1970; Perlmutter 1969; 1980; Stepan 1988.
[3] Eisenstadt 1972; Theobald 1982; Weber [1912] 1968.
[4] O'Donnell 1973; 1988.
[5] Brownlee 2007; Gandhi and Przeworski 2006; Geddes 2003, 44–86; Levitsky and Way 2002; Smith 2005.

behavior of different kinds of authoritarian regimes that rest on different coalitional foundations. Regimes adopt policies that fulfill the interests of their constituents, and different kinds of constituents have different economic interests. My theory also draws attention to the "informal" sources of regime durability in these countries, which is a sharp contrast to recent studies of institutions under authoritarianism. The cases of Indonesia and Malaysia are notable both for the extreme prominence of their authoritarian institutions (Golkar and UMNO, the DPR and the Dewan Rakyat) *and* for the malleability of these institutions. Throughout the discussions of Indonesia and Malaysia, I referred to behaviors outside of formal institutions and channels of authority – the sacking of uncooperative officials, the instantaneous creation of competing policy-making bodies, the private lobbying of decision makers by interested parties, and the rapid reversals of unpopular or ineffective policies. Even in the highly institutionalized authoritarian regimes of Indonesia and Malaysia, informal channels of influence dominate formal channels of influence. Particular institutions in such settings may, in fact, be endogenous to exchange relations rather than independently constraining them. And even if we allow for effective, constraining institutions under authoritarian regimes such as Malaysia and Mexico, interests are instrumental for constructing any model of policy choice.

To uncover economic interests, I distinguish among three groups on the basis of two economic dimensions: whether individuals rent labor or own capital; and, for owners of capital, whether they enjoy cross-border mobility of their assets. These are certainly not the only dimensions across which economic interests of regime supporters can vary, and for other questions, other dimensions will certainly play a much larger role in determining regime behavior. For example, import competitiveness had little role to play in this analysis of a financial sector crisis, with the exception of several firms in each country who resisted foreign loan conditions stipulating trade liberalization. For other types of questions – on why authoritarian regimes switch from import-competition industrialization to outward-oriented industrialization, for example – a firm's import competitiveness will play a dominant role, with cross-border asset mobility playing a much smaller role. More broadly, outside of the economic policy realm, economic profiles may have little impact on policy choice. But coalitions will nevertheless matter. The fact that Malaysia's coalition is ethnically constituted, for instance, helps to explain the adoption of Islam as the state religion in Malaysia, whereas the coalition between disparate capitalist elements and the military under the New Order had no inherent interest in supplanting the five official state religions in Indonesia – whose Muslim majority is far larger than Malaysia's – with Islam alone.

Even though coalitions are complex and difficult to observe, they are central to understanding the behavior of authoritarian regimes. Interests matter, and coalitions translate interests into political outcomes. Some classics of comparative politics and political economy implicitly followed this approach. Prime examples include works by Gregory Luebbert and Barrington Moore, who each considered dictatorships alongside liberal democracies, but who largely confined their analysis to advanced industrial societies.[6] Recently, David Stasavage has argued that seventeenth-century France's weak public finances were caused by social cleavages and coalitional alignments, not by political centralization that prevented credible commitments.[7] David Waldner places coalitions at the very center of the economic development trajectories of newly industrializing countries: different kinds of coalitions prompt authoritarian rulers to create different kinds of institutions, which in turn can produce either high- or low-growth developmental trajectories.[8] Eva Bellin shows how a cross-class coalition among elements of Tunisian society favored by the state has produced a regime that is responsive to the demands of its constituents, who accordingly have little interest in further political liberalization.[9] My approach joins this body of scholarship on comparative authoritarianism, which takes seriously the social forces that constitute politics in authoritarian regimes, and shows their implications for a new class of political outcomes.

My approach and theirs sharply contrast with the most recent articulations of an interest-based theory of authoritarian rule, for which authoritarian regime supporters are always and everywhere "the rich," broadly construed.[10] In a world of sectors and coalitions, it is unlikely to capture more than the broadest contours of authoritarian politics. Instead of assuming who the supporters of a regime are, my approach stresses the importance of uncovering who they are. Another recent contribution by Bruce Bueno de Mesquita and coauthors classifies authoritarian regimes as those where the *size* of the ruling coalition (the "winning coalition") is small relative to the country's population.[11] This, too, is elegant – and

---

[6] Luebbert 1991; Moore 1966.
[7] Stasavage 2003.
[8] Waldner 1999.
[9] Bellin 2002.
[10] See most notably Acemoglu and Robinson 2006.
[11] Bueno de Mesquita et al. 2003.

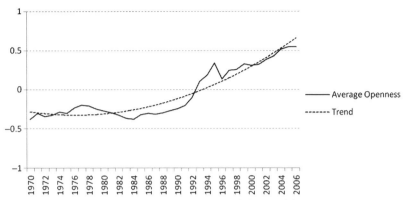

FIGURE 9.1. Average Capital Openness Around the World, 1970–2006. *Source:* Chinn and Ito 2008.

makes no assumptions about the economic interests of a country's rulers – but, in focusing purely on institutions, it cannot predict actual policies. To do this, the composition of the coalition matters, not just its size.

Open Economy Politics

Most recent scholarship on the link between domestic politics and the global economy has focused on the causes of increasing economic openness and globalization and on the consequences of this openness for national politics. Students of capital mobility in particular have developed a rigorous understanding of the consequences of international financial integration for national policy making[12] and have studied whether capital mobility has led to policy convergence across countries.[13] More than any other substantive area, this is where researchers have bridged the gap between the subfields of comparative politics and international relations.

In this book, I study behavior that political economists rarely study: strategic decisions by governments to *retreat* from international economic openness. International financial integration is not inexorable. The reason lies in demands for domestic economic policy. A simple average of capital openness scores from Chinn and Ito's index brings this observation to light (Figure 9.1).

The Chinn-Ito index ranges from −1.79 to 2.54, but despite a clear upward trend since the mid-1980s, average capital openness around the world is only around 0.55 today. Notable also is the sharp dip coinciding

[12] Cohen 1996; 2006; Frieden 1991b.
[13] Garrett 1995; Mosley 2000; Oatley 1999.

with the Asian Financial Crisis in 1997. This same drop is visible in OECD and non-OECD subsamples as well. Clearly, states occasionally retreat from international financial integration during periods of international economic turmoil, much as they did in the wake of the global depression of the 1930s and (as the figure shows) during the Latin American debt crises. I have explained why Malaysia did retreat whereas Indonesia did not, but the pattern of decreases in capital openness across the world calls out for attention as well.

This insight means that financial integration should not be taken as exogenous when studying macroeconomic policy choice. In addition to negotiating policies given particular levels of financial integration, politicians negotiate the level of financial integration itself in order to make possible new kinds of politics. Rather than taking financial openness as given, the Malaysian regime changed its level of financial openness. Doing so created new policy options. Models of policy choice that analyze capital account restrictions given macroeconomic conditions and models that analyze macroeconomic policy given capital account restrictions have missed the critical dynamics by which politicians jointly determine the two policies.

Many studies of open economy politics have recognized that coalitions of interests coalesce around particular economic policy areas. Standard models of trade policy predict varying degrees of conflict among factors and sectors depending on both the relative abundance of the factor and its sector specificity.[14] Financial internationalization spawns new conflicts, and so long as capital moves unimpeded across borders, conflict over interest rates becomes conflict over exchange rates, with coalitions depending on the type of international competition a sector faces.[15] By bringing in an analysis of the consequences of banking sector fragility, I have uncovered new policy cleavages between holders of mobile and fixed capital. Such conflict between groups with names such as "international finance" and "domestic industry" has been noted in other studies,[16] but my argument concludes that *the level of conflict between mobile and fixed capital varies according to financial market conditions.* During good times domestic industrial groups benefit not only from capital inflows but also from easy credit from domestic financiers, while holders of mobile assets profit from excellent rates of return. With the onset of

[14] Hiscox 2002.
[15] Frieden 1991b.
[16] Gourevitch 1986; Helleiner 1994; Maxfield 1990.

currency depreciation that exposes banking sector fragility, mobile and fixed capital part ways. With the recognition that mobile capital's size and market penetration do not necessarily correspond to its political power, this insight illuminates new axes of political conflict in the modern global economy.

Authoritarian Breakdowns

Students of authoritarian regime survival have long suspected that economic crises should be a key factor in driving authoritarian regimes out of power. Despite the intuitive appeal of this hypothesis, though, there is surprisingly little systematic cross-national evidence that links economic crises to regime breakdowns.[17] Too many regimes in countries like Malaysia, Zimbabwe, and Egypt survive their crises. Yet in Indonesia in 1998, an economic crisis clearly hastened the breakdown of an authoritarian regime. Other cases under consideration seem to match the Indonesian case, in particular Argentina in 1983 and Mexico in the 1990s. How can we reconcile these seemingly disparate findings?

The answer lies in additional sources of variation within nondemocratic countries facing crises. Institutionalists argue that the institutional basis of the regime matters: party-based regimes survive crises, whereas military regimes succumb to coups during crises.[18] Others argue that the type of crisis matters. Oil crises rarely lead to authoritarian breakdowns, and then only when regimes began to develop while receiving windfall oil rents rather than before receiving them;[19] only inflationary crises led to autocratic breakdowns in the 1980s.[20] The coalitional theory focuses on another source of variation, that of *endogenous adjustment policy*: some regimes adopt adjustment policies that decrease the likelihood of regime breakdown during twin crises, whereas others do not. The coalitional bases of authoritarian rule explain why some regimes are able to adopt policies that preserve their rule. In this way, the coalitional theory deepens the causal chain from crises to transitions by probing the circumstances under which regime supporters will forgo their patrons during economic meltdowns.

This point deserves further attention. Mobile capital is a dangerous coalition partner for authoritarian regimes because it can easily redeploy

---

[17] Gasiorowski 1995; Smith 2004.
[18] Geddes 2003, 44–86. See also Brownlee 2007.
[19] Smith 2006.
[20] Gasiorowski 1995.

overseas. Industrialists and laborers facing tight credit and labor markets can only hope to lobby regimes for favorable policies. But again, mobile capital's relations with fixed capital are not fundamentally contradictory, only situationally so.[21] Robert Bates and Carles Boix have each argued that capital mobility facilitates the rise of representative government, for only by giving mobile capital owners political voice is it possible for regimes credibly to commit not to expropriate from them. These authors, though, have less to say about regimes like New Order Indonesia, which survived for decades with a mutually beneficial partnership between mobile and fixed capital. Here, political voice was granted mobile capital under an authoritarian regime and made credible, as Andrew MacIntyre has argued, through a policy of capital account openness.[22] Only when a currency crisis exposed banking sector fragility did this coalition fracture. Likewise, whereas Bellin observes that capital and labor may both support an authoritarian status quo because of the substantial benefits they receive from it,[23] the Indonesian case (for capital) and the Malaysian case (for capital and labor) both demonstrate how conditional this support is on whether the policies enacted preserve these benefits.

My argument confronts recent institutionalist scholarship on the links between strong ruling parties and authoritarian regime survival. While the experiences of Indonesia and Malaysia are compelling, the benefit of coalitional preferences becomes even clearer when studying regimes in Latin America. Recent research on authoritarian political institutions makes a powerful case that hegemonic party systems and inclusive legislative institutions can promote regime durability during economic crises. But such approaches cannot explain variation in policy choice and regime survival during the Latin American debt crisis in the Southern Cone, for no authoritarian regimes there created the sort of mass party organizations often held to promote regime durability. This remaining unexplained variation demands attention and shows the powerful influence that coalitional politics has on the manner in which authoritarian regimes persist and collapse. The finding that similar patterns hold in an empirical context where ruling parties *cannot* have affected outcomes is valuable support for this coalitional story.

My approach suggests a more nuanced political economy of regime transitions than that adopted by most correlational studies. Regimes and

---

[21] Contrast to Bates and Lien 1985; Boix 2003.
[22] MacIntyre 2003a.
[23] Bellin 2002.

TABLE 9.1. *Probability of Autocratic Breakdown, by Crisis and Coalition Type*

	Support Coalition	
	Country A: Labor–Fixed Capital	Country B: Mobile Capital–Fixed Capital
Economic crisis		
Twin crises	Low	High
Commodity shock	High	Low

their constituents respond strategically to rapidly changing economic conditions with new behaviors that seek to protect their interests. Groups agitate for adjustment policies during crises, and their ability to obtain such policies conditions their willingness to support the regime. Politicians in authoritarian regimes are fundamentally vulnerable to factors that enable them to deliver the goods to their constituents. This idea has strong links to Michael Bratton and Nicolas van de Walle's dictum that "neopatrimonial elites fracture over access to patronage,"[24] with a few caveats – I make no claim that the fracture lies between insiders and outsiders in the struggle for patronage, nor do I locate the impetus for fracture in struggles over regime personnel management, nor do I restrict the explanatory scope of such elite maneuvering to regimes that are identifiably "neopatrimonial." As the cases of Indonesia and Malaysia show, struggles over patronage are common in highly institutionalized authoritarian regimes as well.

This approach implies that there are likely multiple paths leading from crises to authoritarian breakdowns.[25] My argument theorizes about how financial sector crises lead to regime transitions. Other crises should yield different probabilities of regime survival given the same type of crisis. Generally, during crises, the likelihood of regime breakdown depends on two variables: the identity of the regime's supporters, and the type of crisis. Table 9.1 gives the example of two regimes, one a labor–fixed capital coalition (A) and the other a mobile capital–fixed capital coalition (B), facing two types of crisis, twin crises and a commodity shock.

This book shows that the probability of authoritarian breakdown during twin crises is low for country A, and high for country B. In a country

[24] Bratton and van de Walle 1994, 462.
[25] Cf. Collier 1999 on "paths towards democracy"; Haggard and Kaufman 1995 on "crisis" and "noncrisis" transitions.

facing a commodity crisis that has an immediate negative effect on industries employing large quantities of labor, we should find the opposite. Industrial enterprises often respond to decreased demand through retrenchment. Labor and fixed capital will have contradictory adjustment interests during a commodity crisis, as labor resists retrenchment to protect employment. Mobile capital and fixed capital face no such contradiction, because each favors retrenchment. The likelihood of an autocratic breakdown during a commodity crisis in country A will therefore be higher than in country B.

This extension of my argument remains speculative, and only further research that is beyond the scope of this book can confirm its applicability. But it illustrates how my approach to authoritarian breakdown can inform future studies. If all authoritarian regimes are essentially identical, or differ only in their institutions or their wealth, the type of economic crisis should have no impact on the probability of authoritarian breakdown. Allowing the economic interests of nondemocratic regimes to vary, and focusing tightly on the distributional implications of economic crises as well as the endogenous policy responses adopted by self-interested politicians, makes this result intuitive.

This book also contributes to the study of modern Southeast Asian politics in its analysis of the determinants of authoritarian breakdown in Indonesia. The survey of existing explanations in Chapter 6 revealed a number of problems with existing approaches to the breakdown of the New Order. These include the *post hoc ergo propter hoc* fallacy linking events (especially protest) to outcomes; poor measurement of variables of interest; failure to trace out causal logics; and researchers' interests in democratic transitions leading to neglect of the ancillary process of authoritarian breakdown. For all of these reasons, careful study of precisely why the New Order collapsed has been rare – May 1998 in Indonesia, for most political scientists, is but a data point in a regression. This book provides an explanation for the timing and nature of the New Order's collapse that both addresses the specialist literature on Indonesian politics and contributes to general social scientific approaches to regime survival and transitions.

Normative Implications

Positivist social scientists are often hesitant to speculate on the normative implications of their findings. But, like most other social research, this book is guided by normative questions. How can oppressed oppositions overthrow entrenched incumbents? What are the political costs of economic recovery? My findings are disheartening on some counts, encouraging on others.

I argue that sustained mass opposition was not sufficient to push the New Order from power. Rather, mass opposition emerged as a response to adjustment policies pursued by a political coalition that was fundamentally unsustainable given banking and currency panics. The New Order broke down because the coalition sustaining it fractured, not because *reformasi* protestors forced democratization. The mistake is to interpret mass protest as causing regime change when the two co-occur, while brushing aside the real threat of large-scale repression, which in the Indonesian case was indeed a possibility. In Malaysia, the regime survived despite significant mass opposition because the regime's supporters demanded complementary policies, enabling it to deliver the goods to its supporters while repressing its opponents. These experiences of *reformasi* in Indonesia and Malaysia both suggest that mass opposition does not itself cause regime breakdown or democratization. The People's Power movement in the Philippines is a powerful image, yet likely not a successful model of regime transition without fundamental contradictions that prevent an incumbent regime from simply oppressing its challengers.[26] Popular opponents to entrenched autocrats still require an opening in the regime if their opposition is to be successful.

None of the preceding analysis should minimize the value of *reformasi* movements in either country. Indeed, *reformasi* protests in Indonesia represented an unprecedented outpouring of democratic emotion from groups across Indonesian society demanding real political change. In the wake of Soeharto's resignation, a mass opposition movement fundamentally committed to reform and democratization, was instrumental in ensuring that Indonesia's autocratic breakdown was followed by a democratic transition rather than another authoritarian regime. Today, critics charge that parties, courts, and other institutions in Indonesia are weak, corrupt, and ineffectual; and that reforms have yielded neither a true people's economy nor meaningful economic recovery. All of this is true. But democracy is inherently valuable, and Indonesia is a democracy today. The *reformasi* movement in Malaysia was also a unique democratic moment for that country, where for the first time in Malaysia's history a panethnic social movement united behind the causes of

---

[26] O'Donnell and Schmitter 1986.

democracy and justice, forming the BA, a truly representative opposition coalition.[27] That it was unsuccessful does not obviate its worth, or the sacrifices made by regime protestors and reform leaders who confronted the hostile regime.

A special, further note on ethnic Chinese Indonesians is warranted. None of this book should be construed as ignoring or excusing the long-standing discrimination that ethnic Chinese Indonesians have faced. The Chinese who directly supported Soeharto were only a small fraction of all ethnic Chinese Indonesians. The overwhelming majority of ethnic Chinese Indonesians did not benefit from personal connections with Soeharto and other leaders but rather lived under continued discrimination and fear of violence under the New Order. The bargain under Soeharto that allowed a small coterie of cronies to amass stunning wealth ensured that ordinary ethnic Chinese Indonesians suffered. The continued reproduction of Chinese stereotypes and continued reification of Chinese Indonesians as non-*pribumi* served the regime well, even as the alliance between the military and ethnic Chinese business groups sowed the seeds of the regime's demise during financial upheaval.

Coincident with the debate about how to spur democratic openings in Indonesia and Malaysia was the debate about economic adjustment. Few economic policy debates are as unsettled as the economic consequences of unrestricted capital mobility. Proponents customarily argue that any barrier to the movement of foreign capital across borders constitutes a politically induced market imperfection, whereas skeptics argue that, in a second-best world, temporary barriers to the unimpeded flow of capital across borders can often shield vulnerable economies from the vagaries of international financial volatility.[28] Empirical evidence in favor of either position is mixed.[29] Reviewing a large body of econometric literature, Michael Dooley finds that capital controls are effective in giving countries the policy autonomy to implement interest rates that differ from world rates, but he sees no evidence that this autonomy translates to higher growth.[30] Responding to the orthodox view that capital controls, as a form of financial repression, are actually harmful for long-term economic growth, a much-cited subsequent essay by Dani Rodrik finds no relationship between controls and growth.[31] Recent research argues that the

---

[27] Weiss 2005.
[28] See, e.g., Bhagwati 1998; Dornbusch 1998; Tobin 1978.
[29] Henry 2006.
[30] Dooley 1996.
[31] Rodrik 1998.

effect of capital controls depends on the economic context – during periods of expansion, capital controls hinder growth, but during periods of financial turmoil, they promote growth.[32] Unlike the case of trade, which nearly all mainstream economists hold to be welfare-enhancing on both good economic theory and extensive empirical evidence, there remains no consensus on the long-term welfare consequences of unimpeded capital mobility.

This book investigates a different question: the political consequences of adjustment policies. I have argued that capital controls in particular were a key component of an adjustment strategy that allowed an authoritarian regime in Malaysia to remain in power. The implications of this finding are unsettling for proponents of capital account restrictions to combat financial sector turmoil. There is convincing evidence that capital controls promoted Malaysia's economic recovery,[33] yet I showed that in nondemocratic regimes this economic recovery can come at the expense of basic political rights and civil liberties, which may flourish in the wake of a crisis that unseats an entrenched authoritarian regime. The trade-off is stark: in advocating an adjustment policy that may protect a country's short-term economic fortunes, policy makers may be advocating policies that consign citizens of a nondemocratic regime to further years of nondemocratic rule.

Recent work that finds that the long-term welfare consequences of capital controls depend on a country's level of democracy may help to resolve this dilemma.[34] In established democracies, capital controls are associated with higher growth; in authoritarian regimes, capital controls are associated with lower growth. The combination of these findings about the economic consequences of capital controls in nondemocratic regimes, with this book's findings about the political consequences of capital controls in authoritarian regimes, yields a pair of powerful arguments against capital controls in authoritarian contexts. Despite the manifest imperfections of international capital markets, and the populist arguments that support their imposition during periods of financial turmoil, capital controls in nondemocratic regimes have real political costs.

So long as research on the economic consequences of capital controls remains settled, then so do the final implications of this book. If authoritarian regimes indeed suffer from capital account restrictions during

---

[32] Eichengreen and Leblang 2003.
[33] Kaplan and Rodrik 2001.
[34] Satyanath and Berger 2007.

crises, then Malaysia is an outlier as an authoritarian regime that employed capital controls and escaped the worst of Asia's crisis. Facing financial crises in other authoritarian regimes, countries should not adopt capital controls as an adjustment strategy, both in the interest of economic recovery and in order to promote democratization. But if capital controls do promote economic recovery, it may come at the expense of democratization. The cost of growth may be freedom. The findings in this book bring the terms of this uncomfortable dilemma to light.

References

Abdul Aziz Abdul Rahman. 1994. Agricultural Development. In *Malaysia's Economy in the Nineties*, edited by Jomo K. S., 63–107. Petaling Jaya: Pelanduk Publications (M) Sdn. Bhd.

Abdul Gafur. 2000. *Hari-Hari Terakhir Seorang Presiden*. Jakarta: Pustaka Sinar Harapan.

Abdul Rahman Embong. 2002. *State-Led Modernization and the New Middle Class in Malaysia*. Houndmills: Palgrave.

Abraham, Collin E. R. 1997. *Divide and Rule: The Roots of Race Relations in Malaysia*. Kuala Lumpur: INSAN.

Acemoglu, Daron, and James A. Robinson. 2006. *Economic Origins of Dictatorship and Democracy*. Cambridge: Cambridge University Press.

Alagappa, Muthiah. 1988. Military Professionalism and the Development Role of the Military in Southeast Asia. In *Soldiers and Stability in Southeast Asia*, edited by J. Soedjati Djiwandono and Yong Mun Cheong, 15–48. Singapore: Institute of Southeast Asian Studies.

Alesina, Alberto, and Allan Drazen. 1991. Why Are Stabilizations Delayed? *American Economic Review* 81(5): 1170–88.

Ali, Fachry, Bahtiar Effendy, Umar Juoro, and Musfihin Dahlan. 2003. *Politik Bank Sentral: Posisi Gubernur Bank Indonesia Dalam Mempertahankan Independensi*. Jakarta: LSPEU Indonesia.

Aliran Executive Committee. 1998. Current Concerns. *Aliran Monthly* 18(10): 24–27.

Allen, Franklin, and Douglas Gale. 2000. Financial Contagion. *Journal of Political Economy* 108(1): 1–33.

Alt, James E., Jeffry A. Frieden, Michael Gilligan, Dani Rodrik, and Ronald Rogowski. 1996. The Political Economy of International Trade: Enduring Puzzles and an Agenda for Inquiry. *Comparative Political Studies* 29(6): 689–717.

Alt, James, and Michael Gilligan. 1994. The Political Economy of Trading States: Factor Specificity, Collective Action Problems and Domestic Political Institutions. *Journal of Political Philosophy* 2(2): 165–92.

Anderson, Benedict R. O'G. 1983. Old State, New Society: Indonesia's New Order in Comparative Historical Perspective. *Journal of Asian Studies* 42(3): 477–96.

Anderson, Benedict R. O'G., and Ruth T. McVey. 1971. *A Preliminary Analysis of the October 1, 1965 Coup in Indonesia*. Ithaca: Modern Indonesia Project, Southeast Asia Program, Cornell University.

Anwar Ibrahim. 1998a. From the Halls of Power to the Labyrinths of Incarceration. Available online at http://www.jamaat.org/digest/anwar.html [accessed December 15, 2007].

Anwar Ibrahim. 1998b. Penerangan Menteri Mengenai Langkah-Langkah Bagi Mengukuhkan Kestabilan Ekonomi Negara Di Dewan Rakyat Pada 24 Mac 1998. Available online at http://www.treasury.gov.my/index.php?ch=36&; pg=126&ac=561 [accessed December 15, 2007].

Arasaratnam, Sinnappah. 1979. *Indians in Malaysia and Singapore*. Rev. ed. Kuala Lumpur: Oxford University Press.

Asian Development Bank. 1999. Country Assistance Plans –Malaysia. Available online at http://www.adb.org/Documents/CAPs/MAL/default.asp?p=ctrymal [accessed December 15, 2007].

Aspinall, Edward. 1995. Students and the Military: Regime Friction and Civilian Dissent in the Late Suharto Period in Indonesia. *Indonesia* 59: 21–44.

   1998. Opposition and Elite Conflict in the Fall of Soeharto. In *The Fall of Soeharto*, edited by Geoff Forrester and R. J. May, 130–53. Bathurst, NSW: Crawford House.

   1999. The Indonesian Student Uprising of 1998. In *Reformasi: Crisis and Change in Indonesia*, edited by Arief Budiman, Barbara Hatley, and Damien Kingsbury, 212–37. Clayton: Monash Asia Institute, Monash University.

   2005. *Opposing Suharto: Compromise, Resistance, and Regime Change in Indonesia*. Stanford: Stanford University Press.

Aspinall, Edward, and Mark T. Berger. 2001. The Break-up of Indonesia? Nationalisms after Decolonisation and the Limits of the Nation-State in Post-Cold War Southeast Asia. *Third World Quarterly* 22(6): 1003–24.

Athukorala, Prema-chandra. 1998a. Malaysia. In *East Asia in Crisis: From Being a Miracle to Needing One?*, edited by Ross H. McLeod and Ross Garnaut, 85–101. London: Routledge.

   1998b. Swimming against the Tide: Crisis Management in Malaysia. *ASEAN Economic Bulletin* 15(3): 281–89.

   2001. *Crisis and Recovery in Malaysia: The Role of Capital Controls*. Cheltenham: Edward Elgar Publishing Limited.

Badan Pusat Statistik. 1998. *Buletin Ringkas: Juli 1998*. Jakarta: Percetakan BPS.

   1999. *Indikator Ekonomi: Mei 1999*. Jakarta: Badan Pusat Statistik.

Baer, M. Delal. 1993. Mexico's Second Revolution: Pathways to Liberalization. In *Political and Economic Liberalization in Mexico: At a Critical Juncture?*, edited by Riordan Roett, 51–68. Boulder: Lynne Rienner Publishers.

Bailey, John J. 1988. *Governing Mexico: The Statecraft of Crisis Management*. New York: St. Martin's Press.

Bank Negara Malaysia. 1999. *The Central Bank and the Financial System in Malaysia: A Decade of Change*. Kuala Lumpur: Bank Negara Malaysia.

Barr, Christopher M. 1998. Bob Hasan, the Rise of Apkindo, and the Shifting Dynamics of Control in Indonesia's Timber Sector. *Indonesia* 65: 1–36.

Barraclough, Simon. 1984. Political Participation and Its Regulation in Malaysia: Opposition to the Societies (Amendment) Act 1981. *Pacific Affairs* 57(3): 450–61.

Bates, Robert H., and Anne O. Krueger, eds. 1993. *Political and Economic Interactions in Economic Policy Reform: Evidence from Eight Countries.* Cambridge: Blackwell Publishers.

Bates, Robert H., and Da-Hsiang Donald Lien. 1985. A Note on Taxation, Development, and Representative Government. *Politics and Society* 14(1): 53–70.

Bazdresch, Carlos, and Santiago Levy. 1991. Populism and Economic Policy in Mexico, 1970–1982. In *The Macroeconomics of Populism in Latin America,* edited by Rudiger Dornbusch and Sebastian Edwards, 223–59. Chicago: University of Chicago Press.

Beck, Nathaniel, Jonathan N. Katz, and Richard Tucker. 1998. Taking Time Seriously: Time-Series-Cross-Section Analysis with a Binary Dependent Variable. *American Journal of Political Science* 42(4): 1260–88.

Bellin, Eva. 2002. *Stalled Democracy: Capital, Labor, and the Paradox of State-Sponsored Development.* Ithaca: Cornell University Press.

Berg, Andrew. 1999. The Asian Crisis: Causes, Policy Responses, and Outcomes. IMF Working Paper WP/99/138.

Bernama Library and Infolink Service. 1999. 1999 Election > Parlimen. Available online at http://blisdemo.bernama.com/section.phtml?SN=3e08365d8ca5 99fa5222079041683761&s=2&p=2806&SN=3e08365d8ca599fa5222079 041683761 [accessed December 15, 2007].

Berry, William D., Justin Esarey, and Jacqueline H. Rubin. 2007. Testing for Interaction in Binary Logit and Probit Models: Is a Product Term Essential? Working Paper, Department of Political Science, Florida State University.

Bertocchi, Graziella, and Michael Spagat. 2001. The Politics of Co-Optation. *Journal of Comparative Economics* 29(4): 591–607.

Bertrand, Jacques. 1996. False Starts, Succession Crises, and Regime Transition: Flirting with Openness in Indonesia. *Pacific Affairs* 69(3): 319–40.

Bhagwati, Jagdish N. 1998. The Capital Myth: The Difference between Trade in Widgets and Dollars. *Foreign Affairs* 77(3): 7–12.

Biglaiser, Glen. 2002. *Guardians of the Nation? Economics, Generals, and Economic Reform in Latin America.* South Bend: University of Notre Dame Press.

Bird, Graham, and Alistair Milne. 1999. From Miracle to Meltdown: A Pathology of the East Asian Financial Crisis. *Third World Quarterly* 20(2): 421–37.

Biro Analisis Politik. 2000. *Dilema UMNO: Analisis Pilihanraya Umum 1999* (UMNO in Trouble). Petaling Jaya, Malaysia: Strategic Info Research Development.

Boix, Carles. 2003. *Democracy and Redistribution.* Cambridge: Cambridge University Press.

Bollen, Kenneth, and Robert Jackman. 1985. Regression Diagnostics: An Expository Treatment of Outliers and Influential Cases. *Sociological Methods & Research* 13(4): 510–42.

Boorman, Jack, Timothy Lane, Marianne Schulze-Ghattas, Aleš Bulíř, Atish R. Ghosh, Javier Hamann, Alexandros Mourmouras, and Steven Phillips. 2000. Managing Financial Crises: The Experience in East Asia. IMF Working Paper WP/00/107.

Booth, Anne. 2000. The Impact of the Indonesian Crisis on Welfare: What Do We Know Two Years On? In *Indonesia in Transition: Social Aspects of Reformasi and Crisis*, edited by Chris Manning and Peter van Diermen, 145–62. Singapore: Institute of Southeast Asian Studies.

Bowen, John R. 1986. On the Political Construction of Tradition: Gotong Royong in Indonesia. *Journal of Asian Studies* 45(3): 545–61.

Bowie, Alasdair. 1991. *Crossing the Industrial Divide: State, Society, and the Politics of Economic Transformation in Malaysia*. New York: Columbia University Press.

Box-Steffensmeier, Janet M., and Bradford S. Jones. 2004. *Event History Modeling: A Guide for Social Scientists*. Cambridge: Cambridge University Press.

Box-Steffensmeier, Janet M., and Christopher J. W. Zorn. 2001. Duration Models and Proportional Hazards in Political Science. *American Journal of Political Science* 45(4): 972–88.

Brambor, Thomas, William Roberts Clark, and Matt Golder. 2006. Understanding Interaction Models: Improving Empirical Analyses. *Political Analysis* 14(1): 63–82.

Bratton, Michael, and Nicolas van de Walle. 1994. Neopatrimonial Regimes and Political Transitions in Africa. *World Politics* 46(4): 453–89.

Bresnan, John. 1993. *Managing Indonesia: The Modern Political Economy*. New York: Columbia University Press.

Brownlee, Jason. 2007. *Authoritarianism in an Age of Democratization*. Cambridge: Cambridge University Press.

Broz, J. Lawrence, and Jeffry A. Frieden. 2001. The Political Economy of International Monetary Relations. *Annual Review of Political Science* 4: 317–43.

Budisusilo, Arief. 2001. *Menggugat IMF: Pergulatan Indonesia Bangkit Dari Krisis*. Jakarta: Bina Rena Pariwara.

Bueno de Mesquita, Bruce, Alastair Smith, Randolph Siverson, and James Morrow. 2003. *The Logic of Political Survival*. Cambridge, MA: MIT Press.

Bullard, Nicola, Walden Bello, and Kamal Malhotra. 1998. Taming the Tigers: The IMF and the Asian Crisis. In *Tigers in Trouble: Financial Governance and the Crises in East Asia*, edited by Jomo K. S., 85–136. London: Zed Books.

Calvo, Guillermo A. 1986. Fractured Liberalism: Argentina under Martínez De Hoz. *Economic Development and Cultural Change* 34(3): 511–33.

Calvo, Guillermo A., and Enrique G. Mendoza. 1996. Mexico's Balance-of-Payments Crisis: A Chronicle of a Death Foretold. *Journal of International Economics* 41(3–4): 235–64.

Camp, Roderic Ai. 1989. *Entrepreneurs and Politics in Twentieth-Century Mexico*. New York: Oxford University Press.

Camroux, David. 1996. State Responses to Islamic Resurgence in Malaysia: Accommodation, Co-Option, and Confrontation. *Asian Survey* 36(9): 852–68.

Case, William. 1996. *Elites and Regimes in Malaysia: Revisiting a Consociational Democracy*. Clayton: Monash Asia Institute, Monash University.

———. 2001a. Malaysia's General Elections in 1999: A Consolidated and High Quality Semi-Democracy. *Asian Studies Review* 25(1): 35–55.

———. 2001b. Malaysia's Resilient Pseudodemocracy. *Journal of Democracy* 12(1): 43–57.

———. 2002. *Politics in Southeast Asia: Democracy or Less*. Richmond, Surrey: Curzon Press.

———. 2003. The Anwar Trial and Its Wider Implications. In *Malaysian Economics and Politics in the New Century*, edited by Colin Barlow and Francis Loh Kok Wah, 119–31. Cheltenham: Edward Elgar.

———. 2004. Testing Malaysia's Pseudo-Democracy. In *The State of Malaysia: Ethnicity, Equity and Reform*, edited by Edmund Terence Gomez, 29–48. London: RoutledgeCurzon.

Chavkin, Samuel. 1989. *Storm over Chile: The Junta under Siege*. Chicago: L. Hill.

Chee, Stephen. 1991. Consociational Political Leadership and Conflict Regulation in Malaysia. In *Leadership and Security in Southeast Asia: Institutional Aspects*, edited by Stephen Chee, 53–86. Singapore: Institute of Southeast Asian Studies.

Cheibub, José Antonio, and Jennifer Gandhi. 2004. Classifying Political Regimes: A Six-Fold Classification of Democracies and Dictatorships. Paper presented at the 100th Annual Meeting of the American Political Science Association, Chicago.

Chen, Yehning. 1999. Banking Panics: The Role of the First-Come, First-Served Rule and Information Externalities. *Journal of Political Economy* 107(5): 946–68.

Cheong, Sally. 1993. *Bumiputera Controlled Companies in the KLSE*. 2nd ed. Petaling Jaya: Corporate Research Services Sdn Bhd.

Chin Kok Fay, and Jomo K. S. 2001. Financial Liberalisation and System Vulnerability. In *Malaysian Eclipse: Economic Crisis and Recovery*, edited by Jomo K. S., 90–134. London: Zed Books.

Chin Ung-Ho. 1997. *Chinese Politics in Sarawak: A Study of the Sarawak United People's Party*. Kuala Lumpur: Oxford University Press.

Chinn, Menzie, and Hiro Ito. 2008. A New Measure of Financial Openness. *Journal of Comparative Policy Analysis* 10(3): 309–22.

Chinn, Menzie, and Kenneth Kletzer. 2000. International Capital Inflows, Domestic Financial Intermediation and Financial Crises under Imperfect Information. NBER Working Paper No. 7902.

Chua, Christian. 2004. Defining Indonesian Chineseness under the New Order. *Journal of Contemporary Asia* 34(4): 465–79.

———. 2008. *Chinese Big Business in Indonesia: The State of Capital*. New York: Routledge.

Cohen, Benjamin J. 1996. Phoenix Risen: The Resurrection of Global Finance. *World Politics* 48(2): 268–96.

———. 2006. Monetary Governance and Capital Mobility in Historical Perspective. In *The Regulation of International Financial Markets: Perspectives for Reform,* edited by Rainer Grote and Thilo Marauhn, 27–53. Cambridge: Cambridge University Press.

Cole, David C., and Betty F. Slade. 1998. Why Has Indonesia's Financial Crisis Been So Bad?*Bulletin of Indonesian Economic Studies* 34(2): 61–66.

Collier, Ruth Berins. 1992. *The Contradictory Alliance: State-Labor Relations and Regime Change in Mexico.* Berkeley: International and Area Studies, University of California at Berkeley.

    1999. *Paths toward Democracy: The Working Class and Elites in Western Europe and South America.* Cambridge: Cambridge University Press.

Comber, Leon. 1983. *13 May 1969: A Historical Survey of Sino-Malay Relations.* Kuala Lumpur: Heinemann Asia.

Committee Against Repression in the Pacific and Asia. 1988. *Tangled Web: Dissent, Deterrence and the 27th October 1987 Crackdown.* Haymarket: Committee Against Repression in the Pacific and Asia.

Committee to Protect Journalists. 1999. Malaysia. Available online at http://www.cpj.org/attacks99/asia99/Malaysia.html [accessed May 1, 2006].

Constable, Pamela, and Arturo Valenzuela. 1991. *A Nation of Enemies: Chile under Pinochet.* New York: W. W. Norton.

Coppel, Charles A. 1983. *Indonesian Chinese in Crisis.* Kuala Lumpur: Oxford University Press.

Corbett, Jenny, and David Vines. 1999. Asian Currency and Financial Crises: Lessons from Vulnerability, Crisis, and Collapse. *World Economy* 22(2): 155–77.

Corbo, Vittorio, and Stanley Fischer. 1993. Lessons from the Chilean Stabilization and Recovery. Working Paper No. 158. Santiago: Institute of Economics, Pontificia Universidad Católica de Chile.

Corden, W. Max. 1999. *The Asian Crisis: Is There a Way Out?* Singapore: Institute for Southeast Asian Studies.

    2001. The World Financial Crisis: Are the IMF Prescriptions Right? *The Political Economy of International Financial Crisis: Interest Groups, Ideologies, and Institutions*, edited by Shale Horowitz and Uk Heo, 41–61. Singapore: Institute of Southeast Asian Studies.

Cornelius, Wayne. 1986. *The Political Economy of Mexico under De La Madrid: The Crisis Deepens, 1985–1986.* La Jolla: Center for U.S.-Mexican Studies, University of California, San Diego.

    1996. *Mexican Politics in Transition: The Breakdown of a One-Party-Dominant Regime.* La Jolla: Center for U.S.-Mexican Studies, University of California, San Diego.

Cornelius, Wayne, Ann L. Craig, and Jonathan Fox, eds. 1994. *Transforming State-Society Relations in Mexico: The National Solidarity Strategy.* La Jolla: Center for U.S.-Mexican Studies, Institute of Americas, University of California, San Diego.

Corsetti, Giancarlo, Paolo Pesenti, and Nouriel Roubini. 1998. What Caused the Asian Currency and Financial Crisis? Part I: A Macroeconomic Overview. NBER Working Paper No. 6833.

    1999. Paper Tigers? A Model of the Asian Crisis. *European Economic Review* 43: 1211–36.

Cox, D. R. 1972. Regression Models and Life-Tables. *Journal of the Royal Statistical Society. Series B (Methodological)* 34(2): 187–220.

Cribb, Robert, ed. 1990. *The Indonesian Killings of 1965–1966: Studies from Java and Bali*. Clayton: Centre for Southeast Asian Studies, Monash University.

Crouch, Harold. 1975–76. Generals and Business in Indonesia. *Pacific Affairs* 48(4): 519–40.

———. 1978. *The Army and Politics in Indonesia*. Ithaca: Cornell University Press.

———. 1979. Patrimonialism and Military Rule in Indonesia. *World Politics* 31(4): 571–87.

———. 1994. Industrialization and Political Change. In *Transformation with Industrialization in Peninsular Malaysia*, edited by Harold Brookfield, 14–34. Kuala Lumpur: Oxford University Press.

———. 1996. *Government and Society in Malaysia*. Ithaca: Cornell University Press.

———. 2001a. Establishing Civilian Supremacy in Southeast Asia. In *Democratic Transitions in Asia*, edited by Uwe Johannen and James Gomez, 173–84. Singapore: Select Publishing.

———. 2001b. The Perils of Prediction: Understanding the Indonesian Transition, 1998–99. In *Southeast Asian Middle Classes: Prospects for Social Change and Democratisation*, edited by Abdul Rahman Embong, 139–57. Bangi: Penerbit Universiti Kebangsaan Malaysia.

Dabat, Alejandro, and Luis Lorenzano. 1984. *Argentina: The Malvinas and the End of Military Rule*. Translated by Ralph Johnstone. London: Verso.

Dahl, Robert A. 1971. *Polyarchy: Participation and Opposition*. New Haven: Yale University Press.

Danaharta. 2005. Final Report. Available online at http://www.bnm.gov.my/websites/danaharta.com.my/main/index.html [accessed December 15, 2007].

Davis, Charles L., and Horace A. Bartilow. 2002. Attribution of Blame in the Global Economy: The Case of the Mexican Public and the Peso Devaluation Crisis. *Mexican Studies* 18(1): 133–58.

Davis, Diane E. 1993. The Dialectic of Autonomy: State, Class, and Economic Crisis in Mexico, 1958–1982. *Latin American Perspectives* 20(3): 46–75.

de Brouwer, Gordon. 2003. "Towards Improved Monetary Policy in Indonesia": A Comment. *Bulletin of Indonesian Economic Studies* 39(3): 325–28.

Derichs, Claudia. 2004. Political Crisis and Reform in Malaysia. In *The State of Malaysia: Ethnicity, Equity and Reform*, edited by Edmund Terence Gomez, 105–29. London: RoutledgeCurzon.

Djiwandono, J. Soedjati. 1988. The Military and National Development in Indonesia. In *Soldiers and Stability in Southeast Asia*, edited by J. Soedjati Djiwandono and Yong Mun Cheong, 75–91. Singapore: Institute of Southeast Asian Studies.

Djiwandono, J. Soedradjad. 2000. Bank Indonesia and the Recent Crisis. *Bulletin of Indonesian Economic Studies* 36(1): 47–72.

———. 2001a. *Bergulat Dengan Krisis Dan Pemulihan Ekonomi Indonesia*. Jakarta: Pustaka Sinar Harapan.

———. 2001b. *Mengelola Bank Indonesia Dalam Masa Krisis*. Jakarta: Pustaka LP3ES Indonesia.

2004. Liquidity Support to Banks during Indonesia's Financial Crisis. *Bulletin of Indonesian Economic Studies* 40(2): 59–75.

Dooley, Michael P. 1996. A Survey of Literature on Controls over International Capital Transactions. *IMF Staff Papers* 43(4): 639–87.

Dornbusch, Rudiger. 1989. Argentina after Martínez De Hoz, 1981–1983. In *The Political Economy of Argentina, 1946–1983*, edited by Guido Di Tella and Rudiger Dornbusch, 286–315. Pittsburgh: University of Pittsburgh Press.

1998. Capital Controls: An Idea Whose Time Is Past. *Princeton Essays in International Finance* 207: 20–27.

Doss, Stephen. 1999. Standing up and Speaking Out. *Aliran Monthly* 19(3): 9–10.

Drake, Paul W. 1996. *Labor Movements and Dictatorships: The Southern Cone in Comparative Perspective*. Baltimore: Johns Hopkins University Press.

Dresser, Denise. 1997. Falling from the Tightrope: The Political Economy of the Mexican Crisis. In *Mexico 1994: Anatomy of an Emerging-Market Crash*, edited by Sebastian Edwards and Moisés Naím, 55–79. New York: Carnegie Endowment for International Peace.

Editors. 1982. Current Data on the Indonesian Military Elite. *Indonesia* 33(1): 129–48.

1994. Current Data on the Indonesian Military Elite, September 1, 1993–August 31, 1994. *Indonesia* 58: 83–101.

1997. Indonesian Military in the Mid-1990s: Political Maneuvering or Structural Change? *Indonesia* 63: 91–105.

1999. Current Data on the Indonesian Military Elite, January 1 1998–January 31 1999. *Indonesia* 67: 133–62.

Edwards, Sebastian. 1997. Bad Luck or Bad Policies? An Economic Analysis of the Crisis. In *Mexico 1994: An Anatomy of an Emerging-Market Crash*, edited by Sebastian Edwards and Moisés Naím, 95–124. New York: Carnegie Endowment for International Peace.

1999. How Effective Are Capital Controls? *Journal of Economic Perspectives* 13(4): 65–84.

Edwards, Sebastian, and Carlos A. Végh. 1997. Banks and Macroeconomic Disturbances under Predetermined Exchange Rates. *Journal of Monetary Economics* 40(2): 239–78.

Eichengreen, Barry, and David Leblang. 2003. Capital Account Liberalization and Growth: Was Mr. Mahathir Right? *International Journal of Finance and Economics* 8(1): 205–24.

Eisenstadt, Samuel N. 1972. *Traditional Patrimonialism and Modern Neopatrimonialism*. London: Sage Publications.

Eklöf, Stefan. 1997. The 1997 General Election in Indonesia. *Asian Survey* 37(12): 1181–96.

2002. Politics, Business, and Democratization in Indonesia. In *Political Business in East Asia*, edited by Edmund Terence Gomez, 216–49. London: Routledge.

Election Watch. 1995. The 1990 General Elections: The Election Watch Report. Excerpted in "Will History Repeat Itself." *Aliran Monthly* 15(1): 6–10.

Elson, R. E. 2001. *Suharto: A Political Biography*. Cambridge: Cambridge University Press.

Emmerson, Donald K. 1999a. Exit and Aftermath: The Crisis of 1997–98. In *Indonesia Beyond Suharto: Polity, Economy, Society, Transition*, edited by Donald K. Emmerson, 295–343. Armonk: M. E. Sharpe.

——— 1999b. A Tale of Three Countries. *Journal of Democracy* 10(4): 35–53.

Enloe, Cynthia H. 1978. The Issue-Saliency of the Military-Ethnic Connection: Some Thoughts on Malaysia. *Comparative Politics* 10(2): 267–85.

Enoch, Charles, Olivier Frécaut, and Arto Kovanen. 2003. Indonesia's Banking Crisis: What Happened and What Did We Learn? *Bulletin of Indonesian Economic Studies* 39(1): 75–92.

Faaland, Just, Jack Parkinson, and Rais Saniman. 2003. *Growth and Ethnic Inequality: Malaysia's New Economic Policy*. 2nd ed. Kuala Lumpur: Utusan Publications & Distributors Sdn Bhd.

Fane, George. 2000. Indonesian Monetary Policy during the 1997–98 Crisis: A Monetarist Perspective. *Bulletin of Indonesian Economic Studies* 36(3): 49–64.

Fatah, Eep Saefulloh. 2000. *Zaman Kesempatan: Agenda-Agenda Besar Demokratisasi Pasca-Orde Baru*. Bandung: Penerbit Mizan.

Felker, Greg. 2000. Malaysia in 1999: Mahathir's Pyrrhic Deliverance. *Asian Survey* 40(1): 49–60.

Feridhanusetyawan, Tubagus. 1997. Survey of Recent Developments. *Bulletin of Indonesian Economic Studies* 33(2): 3–39.

Ffrench-Davis, Ricardo. 2002. *Economic Reforms in Chile: From Dictatorship to Democracy*. Ann Arbor: University of Michigan Press.

Fischer, Bernhard, Ulrich Hiemenz, and Peter Trapp. 1985. *Argentina: The Economic Crisis in the 1980s*. Tübingen: J. C. B. Mohr (Paul Siebeck).

Fisk, E. K. 1982. Development in Malaysia. In *The Political Economy of Malaysia*, edited by E. K. Fisk and H. Osman-Rani, 1–23. Kuala Lumpur: Oxford University Press.

Flichman, Guillermo. 1990. The State and Capital Accumulation in Argentina. In *The State and Capital Accumulation in Latin America*, vol. 2: *Argentina, Bolivia, Colombia, Ecuador, Peru, Uruguay, Venezuela*, edited by Christian Anglade and Carlos Fortin, 1–31. Pittsburgh: University of Pittsburgh Press.

Foley, Michael W. 1991. Agenda for Mobilization: The Agrarian Question and Popular Mobilization in Contemporary Mexico. *Latin American Research Review* 26(1): 39–74.

Fortin, Carlos. 1985. The Political Economy of Repressive Monetarism: The State and Capital Accumulation in Post-1973 Chile. In *The State and Capital Accumulation in Latin America*, vol. 1: *Brazil, Chile, and Mexico*, edited by Christian Anglade and Carlos Fortin, 139–209. Pittsburgh: University of Pittsburgh Press.

Forrester, Geoffrey. 1998. A Jakarta Diary, May 1998. In *The Fall of Soeharto*, edited by Geoff Forrester and R. J. May, 24–69. Bathurst, NSW: Crawford House.

Foxley, Alejandro. 1983. *Latin American Experiments in Neo-Conservative Economics*. Berkeley: University of California Press.

——— 1986. The Neoconservative Economic Experiment in Chile. In *Military Rule in Chile: Dictatorship and Oppositions*, edited by J. Samuel Valenzuela and Arturo Valenzuela, 13–50. Baltimore: Johns Hopkins University Press.

Frankel, Jeffrey A. 2004. Contractionary Currency Crashes in Developing Countries. The 5th Mundell-Fleming Lecture, IMF Annual Research Conference, Washington, DC.

Frécaut, Olivier. 2004. Indonesia's Banking Crisis: A New Perspective on $50 Billion of Losses. *Bulletin of Indonesian Economic Studies* 40(2): 37–57.

Freedom House. 2006. *Freedom in the World 2006: The Annual Survey of Political Rights and Civil Liberties*. Lanham: Rowman & Littlefield.

Frieden, Jeffry A. 1991a. *Debt, Development, and Democracy: Modern Political Economy and Latin America, 1965–1985*. Princeton: Princeton University Press.

1991b. Invested Interests: The Politics of National Economic Policies in a World of Global Finance. *International Organization* 45(4): 425–51.

Friedman, Jed, and James Levinsohn. 2002. The Distributional Impacts of Indonesia's Financial Crisis on Household Welfare: A "Rapid Response" Methodology. *World Bank Economic Review* 16(3): 397–423.

Friedrich, Carl J., and Zbigniew K. Brzezinski. 1965. *Totalitarian Dictatorship and Autocracy*. New York: Praeger.

Funston, N. J. 1980. *Malay Politics in Malaysia: A Study of the United Malays National Organisation and Party Islam*. Kuala Lumpur: Heinemann Educational Books (Asia) Ltd.

2004. The Mahathir Years: The Rural Malay Heartland. In *Reflections: The Mahathir Years*, edited by Bridget Welsh, 168–76. Washington, DC: Southeast Asia Studies Program, Paul H. Nitze School of Advanced International Studies (SAIS), Johns Hopkins University.

Gale, Bruce. 1981. *Politics and Public Enterprise in Malaysia*. Petaling Jaya: Eastern Universities Press Sdn. Bhd.

1985. *Politics & Business: A Study of Multi-Purpose Holdings Berhad*. Petaling Jaya: Eastern Universities Press (M) Sdn Bhd.

Gandhi, Jennifer, and Adam Przeworski. 2006. Cooperation, Cooptation, and Rebellion under Dictatorships. *Economics and Politics* 18(1): 1–26.

García Hurtado, Alvaro. 1983. The Political Economy of the Rise and Fall of the Chicago Boys. Working Paper No. 38. Cambridge: Centre of Latin American Studies, University of Cambridge.

Garnaut, Ross. 1998. The Financial Crisis: A Watershed in Economic Thought about East Asia. *Asian-Pacific Economic Literature* 12(1): 1–11.

Garrett, Geoffrey. 1995. Trade, Capital Mobility, and the Domestic Politics of Economic Policy. *International Organization* 49(4): 657–87.

Gasiorowski, Mark J. 1995. Economic Crisis and Political Regime Change: An Event-History Analysis. *American Political Science Review* 89(4): 882–97.

Geddes, Barbara. 2003. *Paradigms and Sand Castles: Theory Building and Research Design in Comparative Politics*. Ann Arbor: University of Michigan Press.

Gibson, Edward L. 1997. The Populist Road to Market Reform: Policy and Electoral Coalitions in Mexico and Argentina. *World Politics* 49(3): 339–70.

Gill, Ranjit. 1998. *Asia under Siege: How the Asian Miracle Went Wrong*. Singapore: Epic Management Services.

Gillespie, Charles Guy. 1991. *Negotiating Democracy: Politicians and Generals in Uruguay*. Cambridge: Cambridge University Press.

Girling, John L. S. 1981. *The Bureaucratic Polity in Modernizing Societies: Similarities, Differences, and Prospects in the ASEAN Region*. Singapore: Institute of Southeast Asian Studies.

Glassburner, Bruce. 1976. In the Wake of General Ibnu: Crisis in the Indonesian Oil Industry. *Asian Survey* 16(12): 1099–1112.

Glick, Reuven, and Michael Hutchison. 1999. Banking and Currency Crises: How Common Are Twins? Working Paper, Department of Economics, University of California-Santa Cruz.

Goh Cheng Teik. 1971. *The May Thirteenth Incident and Democracy in Malaysia*. Kuala Lumpur: Oxford University Press.

Goldfajn, Ilan, and Rodrigo O. Valdés. 1997. Capital Flows and the Twin Crises: The Role of Liquidity. IMF Working Paper WP/97/87.

Goldstein, Morris. 1998. *The Asian Financial Crisis: Causes, Cures, and Systemic Implications*. Washington, DC: Institute for International Economics.

Gomez, Edmund Terence. 1990. *Politics in Business: UMNO's Corporate Investments*. Kuala Lumpur: Forum.

1991. *Money Politics in the Barisan Nasional*. Kuala Lumpur: Forum.

1994. *Political Business: Corporate Involvement of Malaysian Political Parties*. Townsville: Centre for South-East Asian Studies, James Cook University of North Queensland.

1996. Electoral Funding of General, State and Party Elections in Malaysia. *Journal of Contemporary Asia* 26(1): 81–99.

1998. Malaysia. In *Political Party Systems and Democratic Development in East and Southeast Asia*, vol. 1: *Southeast Asia*, edited by Wolfgang Sachsenröder and Ulrike E. Frings, 226–88. Aldershot: Ashgate.

2002. Political Business in Malaysia: Party Factionalism, Corporate Development, and Economic Crisis. In *Political Business in East Asia*, edited by Edmund Terence Gomez, 82–114. London: Routledge.

2004a. Governance, Affirmative Action and Enterprise Development: Ownership and Control of Corporate Malaysia. In *The State of Malaysia: Ethnicity, Equity and Reform*, edited by Edmund Terence Gomez, 157–93. London: RoutledgeCurzon.

2004b. Introduction: Politics, Business and Ethnicity in Malaysia: A State in Transition? In *The State of Malaysia: Ethnicity, Equity and Reform*, edited by Edmund Terence Gomez, 1–28. London: RoutledgeCurzon.

Gomez, Edmund Terence, and Jomo K. S. 1999a. Malaysia. In *Democracy, Governance, and Economic Performance: East and Southeast Asia*, edited by Ian Marsh, Jean Blondel and Takashi Inoguchi, 230–60. New York: United Nations University Press.

1999b. *Malaysia's Political Economy: Politics, Patronage and Profits*. 2nd ed. Cambridge: Cambridge University Press.

González Gómez, Mauricio A. 1998. Crisis and Economic Change in Mexico. In *Mexico under Zedillo*, edited by Susan Kaufman Purcell and Luis Rubio, 37–65. Boulder: Lynne Rienner Publishers.

Gourevitch, Peter. 1986. *Politics in Hard Times: Comparative Responses to International Economic Crises*. Ithaca: Cornell University Press.

Government of Indonesia. 1997. IMF Letter of Intent, October 31, 1997. Available online at http://www.imf.org/external/np/loi/103197.htm [accessed December 15, 2007].

———. 1998a. Memorandum of Economic and Financial Policies, April 10, 1998. Seven Appendices. Available online at http://www.imf.org/external/np/loi/041098.htm [accessed December 15, 2007].

———. 1998b. Memorandum of Economic and Financial Policies, January 15, 1998. Available online at http://www.imf.org/external/np/loi/011598.htm [accessed December 15, 2007].

Grambsch, Patricia M., and Terry M. Therneau. 1994. Proportional Hazards Tests and Diagnostics Based on Weighted Residuals. *Biometrika* 81(3): 515–26.

Greene, Kenneth. 2007. *Why Dominant Parties Lose: Mexico's Democratization in Comparative Perspective*. Cambridge: Cambridge University Press.

Grenville, Stephen. 2000. Monetary Policy and the Exchange Rate during the Crisis. *Bulletin of Indonesian Economic Studies* 36(2): 43–60.

Grindle, Merilee S. 1996. *Challenging the State: Crisis and Innovation in Latin America and Africa*. Cambridge: Cambridge University Press.

Habibie, B. J. 1995. Liberalisasi Ekonomi, Pemerataan, Dan Iptek. In *Liberalisasi Ekonomi, Pemerataan, Dan Kemiskinan*, edited by Loekman Soetrisno and Faraz Umaya, 3–7. Yogyakarta: Tiara Wacana Yogya.

Haggard, Stephan. 2000a. Interests, Institutions, and Policy Reform. In *Economic Policy Reform: The Second Stage*, edited by Anne O. Krueger, 21–57. Chicago: University of Chicago Press.

———. 2000b. *The Political Economy of the Asian Financial Crisis*. Washington, DC: Institute for International Economics.

Haggard, Stephan, and Robert R. Kaufman. 1992. The Political Economy of Inflation and Stabilization in Middle-Income Countries. In *The Politics of Economic Adjustment: International Constraints, Distributive Conflicts, and the State*, edited by Stephan Haggard and Robert R. Kaufman, 270–315. Princeton: Princeton University Press.

———. 1995. *The Political Economy of Democratic Transitions*. Princeton: Princeton University Press.

Haggard, Stephan, Jean-Dominique Lafay, and Christian Morrisson. 1995. *The Political Feasibility of Adjustment in Developing Countries*. Paris: OECD.

Haggard, Stephan, and Steven B. Webb, eds. 1994. *Voting for Reform: Democracy, Political Liberalization, and Economic Adjustment*. New York: Oxford University Press.

Hamilton, Nora. 1984. State-Class Alliances and Conflicts: Issues and Actors in the Mexican Economic Crisis. *Latin American Perspectives* 11(4): 6–32.

Handelman, Howard. 1981. Labor-Industrial Conflict and the Collapse of Uruguayan Democracy. *Journal of Interamerican Studies and World Affairs* 23(4): 371–94.

Hansen, Gary. 1975. Indonesia 1974: A Momentous Year. *Asian Survey* 15(2): 148–56.

Hanson, James, and Jaime de Melo. 1983. The Uruguayan Experience with Liberalization and Stabilization, 1974–1981. *Journal of Interamerican Studies and World Affairs* 25(4): 477–508.

  1985. External Shocks, Financial Reforms, and Stabilization Attempts in Uruguay during 1974–83. *World Development* 13(8): 917–39.

Haseman, John B. 1986. The Dynamics of Change: Regeneration of the Indonesian Army. *Asian Survey* 26(8): 883–96.

Hefner, Robert W. 2000. *Civil Islam: Muslims and Democratization in Indonesia.* Princeton: Princeton University Press.

  2001. Introduction: Multiculturalism and Citizenship in Malaysia, Singapore, and Indonesia. In *The Politics of Multiculturalism: Pluralism and Citizenship in Malaysia, Singapore, and Indonesia*, edited by Robert W. Hefner, 1–58. Honolulu: University of Hawai'i Press.

Helleiner, Eric. 1994. *States and the Reemergence of Global Finance: From Bretton Woods to the 1990s.* Ithaca: Cornell University Press.

Hellman, Joel. 1998. Winners Take All: The Politics of Partial Reform in Postcommunist Transitions. *World Politics* 50(2): 203–34.

Heng Pek Koon. 1988. *Chinese Politics in Malaysia: A History of the Malaysian Chinese Association.* Singapore: Oxford University Press.

  1992. The Chinese Business Elite of Malaysia. In *Southeast Asian Capitalists*, edited by Ruth McVey, 127–44. Ithaca: Southeast Asia Program, Cornell University.

Henry, Peter Blair. 2006. Capital Account Liberalization: Theory, Evidence, and Speculation. NBER Working Paper No. 12698.

Heryanto, Ariel. 1998. Ethnic Identities and Erasure: Chinese Indonesians in Public Culture. In *Southeast Asian Identities: Culture and the Politics of Representation in Indonesia, Malaysia, Singapore and Thailand*, edited by Joel S. Kahn, 95–114. Singapore: Institute of Southeast Asian Studies.

Heston, Alan, Robert Summers, and Bettina Aten. 2006. Penn World Table Version 6.2, Center for International Comparisons of Production, Income and Prices at the University of Pennsylvania.

Hicken, Allen, Shanker Satyanath, and Ernest Sergenti. 2005. Political Institutions and Economic Performance: The Effects of Accountability and Obstacles to Policy Change. *American Journal of Political Science* 49(4): 897–907.

Higley, John, and Michael G. Burton. 1989. The Elite Variable in Democratic Transitions and Breakdowns. *American Sociological Review* 54(1): 17–32.

Hill, Hal. 1998. The Indonesian Economy: The Strange and Sudden Death of a Tiger. In *The Fall of Soeharto*, edited by Geoff Forrester and R. J. May, 93–103. Bathurst, NSW: Crawford House.

  1999. *The Indonesian Economy in Crisis: Causes, Consequences, and Lessons.* Singapore: Institute of Southeast Asian Studies.

  2000. Indonesia: The Strange and Sudden Death of a Tiger Economy. *Oxford Development Studies* 28(2): 117–39.

Hilley, John. 2001. *Malaysia: Mahathirism, Hegemony and the New Opposition.* London: Zed Books.

Hinich, Melvin, and Michael C. Munger. 1994. *Ideology and the Theory of Political Choice*. Ann Arbor: University of Michigan Press.

Hirschman, Albert O. 1970. *Exit, Voice, and Loyalty: Responses to Decline in Firms, Organizations, and States*. Cambridge, MA: Harvard University Press.

Hiscox, Michael J. 2002. *International Trade and Political Conflict: Commerce, Coalitions, and Mobility*. Princeton: Princeton University Press.

Honna, Jun. 1999. Military Ideology in Response to Democratic Pressure during the Late Suharto Era: Political and Institutional Contexts. *Indonesia* 67: 77–126.

Hua Wu Yin. 1983. *Class and Communalism in Malaysia: Politics in a Dependent Capitalist State*. London: Zed Books.

Hughes, Helen. 1999. Crony Capitalism and the East Asian Currency and Financial "Crises." *Policy* 1999 (Spring): 3–9.

Hwang In-Won. 2003. *Personalized Politics: The Malaysian State under Mahathir*. Singapore: Institute of Southeast Asian Studies.

2004. Malaysia's "Presidential Premier": Explaining Mahathir's Dominance. In *Reflections: The Mahathir Years*, edited by Bridget Welsh, 67–76. Washington, DC: Southeast Asia Studies Program, Paul H. Nitze School of Advanced International Studies (SAIS), Johns Hopkins University.

Imawan, Riswandha. 1991. Konglomerat Dan Tuan Tanah: Apa Bedanya? *Prisma* 20(8): 57–59.

International Monetary Fund. 2007. International Financial Statistics. Available online at http://www.imfstatistics.org/imf/ [accessed December 15, 2007].

Irwin, Gregor, and David Vines. 1999. *A Krugman-Dooley-Sachs Third Generation Model of the Asian Financial Crisis*. Centre for International Economic Studies Discussion Paper No. 99/15, University of Adelaide.

Ishak Shari. 2003. The Financial Crisis and Its Social Implications. In *Malaysian Economics and Politics in the New Century*, edited by Colin Barlow and Francis Loh Kok Wah, 62–74. Cheltenham: Edward Elgar.

Jabatan Perangkaan Malaysia. 1999. *Buku Tahunan Perangkaan Malaysia 1999*. Kuala Lumpur: Jabatan Perangkaan.

Jackson, Karl D. 1978. Bureaucratic Polity: A Theoretical Framework for the Analysis of Power and Communications in Indonesia. In *Political Power and Communications in Indonesia*, edited by Karl D. Jackson and Lucian W. Pye, 3–22. Berkeley: University of California Press.

Jenkins, David. 1984. *Suharto and His Generals: Indonesian Military Politics, 1975–1983*. Ithaca: Modern Indonesia Project, Southeast Asia Program, Cornell University.

Jeshurun, Chandran. 1988. Development and Civil-Military Relations in Malaysia: The Evolution of the Officer Corps. In *Soldiers and Stability in Southeast Asia*, edited by J. Soedjati Djiwandono and Yong Mun Cheong, 255–78. Singapore: Institute of Southeast Asian Studies.

Jesudason, James V. 1990. *Ethnicity and the Economy: The State, Chinese Business, and Multinationals in Malaysia*. Singapore: Oxford University Press.

1997. Chinese Business and Ethnic Equilibrium in Malaysia. *Development and Change* 28(1): 119–41.

Johnson, Chalmers. 1998. Economic Crisis in East Asia: The Clash of Capitalisms. *Cambridge Journal of Economics* 22(6): 653–61.

Johnson, Colin. 1998. Survey of Recent Developments. *Bulletin of Indonesian Economic Studies* 34(2): 3–60.

Johnson, Simon, and Todd Mitton. 2003. Cronyism and Capital Controls: Evidence from Malaysia. *Journal of Financial Economics* 67(2): 351–82.

Jomo K. S. 1986. *A Question of Class: Capital, the State, and Uneven Development in Malaya.* Singapore: Oxford University Press.

——— ed. 1995. *Privatizing Malaysia: Rents, Rhetoric, and Reality.* Boulder: Westview Press.

——— 1998. Malaysia: From Miracle to Debacle. In *Tigers in Trouble: Financial Governance and the Crises in East Asia*, edited by Jomo K. S., 181–98. London: Zed Books.

——— 2001a. Capital Controls. In *Malaysian Eclipse: Economic Crisis and Recovery*, edited by Jomo K. S., 199–215. London: Zed Books.

——— 2001b. Capital Flows. In *Malaysian Eclipse: Economic Crisis and Recovery*, edited by Jomo K. S., 134–73. London: Zed Books.

——— 2001c. From Currency Crisis to Recession. In *Malaysian Eclipse: Economic Crisis and Recovery*, edited by Jomo K. S., 1–46. London: Zed Books.

——— 2003. *M Way: Mahathir's Economic Legacy.* Petaling Jaya: Forum.

Jomo K. S., and Edmund Terence Gomez. 1996. Rents and Development in Multiethnic Malaysia. In *The Role of Government in East Asian Economic Development: Comparative Institutional Analysis*, edited by Masahiko Aoki, Hyung-Ki Kim, and Masahiro Okuno-Fujiwara, 342–73. Oxford: Oxford University Press.

——— 2000. The Malaysian Development Dilemma. In *Rents, Rent-Seeking and Economic Development: Theory and Evidence in Asia*, edited by Mushtaq H. Khan and Jomo K. S., 274–303. Cambridge: Cambridge University Press.

Jomo K. S., and Natasha Hamilton-Hart. 2001. Financial Regulation, Crisis and Policy Response. In *Malaysian Eclipse: Economic Crisis and Recovery*, edited by Jomo K. S., 67–89. London: Zed Books.

Jomo K. S., and Hwok Aun Lee. 2001. Social Impacts. In *Malaysian Eclipse: Economic Crisis and Recovery*, edited by Jomo K. S., 216–55. London: Zed Books.

Jomo K. S., and Patricia Todd. 1994. *Trade Unions and the State in Peninsular Malaysia.* Kuala Lumpur: Oxford University Press.

Kadir, Suzaina. 1999. The Islamic Factor in Indonesia's Political Transition. *Asian Journal of Political Science* 7(2): 21–44.

Kaminsky, Graciela L., and Carmen M. Reinhart. 1999. The Twin Crises: The Causes of Banking and Balance-of-Payments Problems. *American Economic Review* 89(3): 473–500.

Kammen, Douglas, and Siddharth Chandra. 1999. *A Tour of Duty: Changing Patterns of Military Politics in Indonesia in the 1990s.* Ithaca: Southeast Asia Program, Cornell University.

Kaplan, Ethan, and Dani Rodrik. 2001. Did the Malaysian Capital Controls Work? NBER Working Paper No. 8142.

Kartasasmita, Ginandjar. 2000. Globalization and the Economic Crisis: The Indonesian Story. Lecture at the FASID/GSAPS/WIAPS Joint ADMP, Waseda University, October 26.

Kaufman, Edy. 1979. *Uruguay in Transition: From Civilian to Military Rule*. New Brunswick: Transaction Books.

Kaufman, Robert, and Barbara Stallings. 1989. Debt and Democracy in the 1980s: The Latin American Experience. In *Debt and Democracy in Latin America*, edited by Barbara Stallings and Robert Kaufman, 201–23. Boulder: Westview Press.

Kenward, Lloyd R. 1999. Assessing Vulnerability to Financial Crisis: Evidence from Indonesia. *Bulletin of Indonesian Economic Studies* 35(3): 71–95.

Khalid Jafri. 1998. 50 Dalil Mengapa Anwar Tidak Boleh Jadi PM. Available online at http://www.geocities.com/CapitolHill/Congress/3832/frame/50.html [accessed December 15, 2007].

Khong Cho Oon. 1986. *The Politics of Oil in Indonesia: Foreign Company-Host Government Relations*. Cambridge: Cambridge University Press.

Khong Kim Hoong. 1991. *Malaysia's General Election, 1990: Continuity, Change and Ethnic Politics*, Research Notes and Discussions Paper No. 74. Singapore: Institute of Southeast Asian Studies.

Khoo Boo Teik. 1998a. All Over? Or All over Again? *Aliran Monthly* 18(8): 6–8.

   1998b. Reflections on the UMNO General Assembly. *Aliran Monthly* 18(6): 2–7.

Khoo Boo Teik, and Francis Loh Kok Wah. 2002. Introduction. In *Democracy in Malaysia: Discourses and Practices*, edited by Francis Loh Kok Wah and Khoo Boo Teik, 1–16. Richmond, Surrey: Curzon Press.

Kindleberger, Charles P. 2000. *Manias, Panics, and Crashes: A History of Financial Crises*. 4th ed. New York: John Wiley & Sons.

King, Dwight Y. 1982. Indonesia's New Order as a Bureaucratic Polity, a Neo-patrimonial Regime or a Bureaucratic Authoritarian Regime: What Difference Does It Make? In *Interpreting Indonesian Politics: Thirteen Contributions to the Debate*, edited by Benedict Anderson and Audrey Kahin, 104–16. Ithaca: Southeast Asia Program, Cornell University.

   1995–96. Bureaucracy and Implementation of Complex Tasks in Rapidly Developing States. *Studies in Comparative and International Development* 30(4): 78–92.

   2000. Corruption in Indonesia: A Curable Cancer? *Journal of International Affairs* 53(2): 603–24.

King, Gary, Michael Tomz, and Jason Wittenberg. 2000. Making the Most of Statistical Analyses: Improving Interpretation and Presentation. *American Journal of Political Science* 44(2): 341–55.

Klesner, Joseph L., and Chappell Lawson. 2001. "Adios" to the PRI? Changing Voter Turnout in Mexico's Political Transition. *Mexican Studies* 17(1): 17–39.

Krueger, Anne O. 1993. *The Political Economy of Policy Reform in Developing Countries*. Cambridge, MA: MIT Press.

   ed. 2000. *Economic Policy Reform: The Second Stage*. Chicago: University of Chicago Press.

Krugman, Paul. 1998a. Malaysia's Opportunity? *Far Eastern Economic Review* 161(38): 32–33.

   1998b. Saving Asia: It's Time to Get Radical. *Fortune* 138(5): 74–80.

1998c. What Happened to Asia? Available online at http://web.mit.edu/krug-man/www/DISINTER.html [accessed December 15, 2007].

1999. Capital Control Freaks: How Malaysia Got Away with Economic Heresy. Available online at http://slate.msn.com/id/35534/ [accessed December 15, 2007].

Kua Kia Soong. 1998. DAP's Latest Purge: Another Rerun of a Bad Movie. *Aliran Monthly* 18(6): 33–34, 40.

Kurtz, Marcus J. 1999. Chile's Neo-Liberal Revolution: Incremental Decisions and Structural Transformation, 1973–1989. *Journal of Latin American Studies* 31(2): 399–427.

Laens, Silvia, Fernando Lorenzo, and Rosa Osimani. 1993. Macroeconomic Conditions and Trade Liberalization: The Case of Uruguay. In *Macroeconomic Conditions and Trade Liberalization*, edited by Adolfo Canitrot and Silva Junco, 159–205. Washington, DC: Inter-American Development Bank.

Lahiri, Amartya, and Carlos A. Végh. 2005. Output Costs, Currency Crises, and Interest Rate Defense of a Peg. NBER Working Paper No. 11791.

Lee Hwok Aun. 2003. Development Policies, Affirmative Action and the New Politics in Malaysia. In *The State Economic Development and Ethnic Co-Existence in Malaysia and New Zealand*, edited by Edmund Terence Gomez and Robert Stephens, 29–52. Kuala Lumpur: CEDER Secretariat, Faculty of Economics and Administration, University of Malaya.

Lee Kam Hing, and Heng Pek Koon. 2000. The Chinese in the Malaysian Political System. In *The Chinese in Malaysia*, edited by Lee Kam Hing and Tan Chee-Beng, 194–227. Kuala Lumpur: Oxford University Press.

Lee, Raymond L. M. 1988. Patterns of Religious Tension in Malaysia. *Asian Survey* 28(5): 400–18.

Levitsky, Steven, and Lucan A. Way. 2002. The Rise of Competitive Authoritarianism. *Journal of Democracy* 13(2): 51–65.

Lewis, Paul H. 1990. *The Crisis of Argentine Capitalism*. Chapel Hill: University of North Carolina Press.

Liddle, R. William. 1987. The Politics of Shared Growth: Some Indonesian Cases. *Comparative Politics* 19(2): 127–46.

1991. The Relative Autonomy of the Third World Politician: Soeharto and Indonesian Economic Development in Comparative Perspective. *International Studies Quarterly* 35(4): 403–27.

1996a. Indonesia: Suharto's Tightening Grip. *Journal of Democracy* 7(4): 58–72.

1996b. A Useful Fiction: Democratic Legitimation in New Order Indonesia. In *The Politics of Elections in Southeast Asia*, edited by R. H. Taylor, 34–60. New York: Woodrow Wilson Center Press and Cambridge University Press.

1999a. Indonesia's Unexpected Failure of Leadership. In *Politics of Post-Suharto Indonesia*, edited by Adam Schwarz and Jonathan Paris, 16–39. New York: Council on Foreign Relations.

1999b. Regime: The New Order. In *Indonesia beyond Suharto: Polity, Economy, Society, Transition*, edited by Donald K. Emmerson, 39–70. New York: M. E. Sharpe.

Liem, Yusiu. 2000. *Prasangka Terhadap Etnis Cina: Evaluasi 33 Tahun Di Bawah Rejim Soeharto*. Jakarta: Djambatan.

Lijphart, Arend. 1969. Consociational Democracy. *World Politics* 21(2): 207–25.

Lim Hong Hai. 2003. The Delineation of Peninsular Electoral Constituencies: Amplifying Malay and UMNO Power. In *New Politics in Malaysia*, edited by Francis Loh Kok Wah and Johan Saravanamuttu, 25–52. Singapore: Institute of Southeast Asian Studies.

Lim Kit Siang. 1986. *BMF: Scandal of Scandals*. Petaling Jaya: Democratic Action Party.

  1998a. *Economic & Financial Crisis*. Petaling Jaya: Democratic Action Party Economic Committee.

  1998b. EPF Funds Used to Save VIPs, Tycoons and Cronies. *Aliran Monthly* 18(4): 6–8.

  1998c. An Obstinate Silence: Trade Union Reps on EPF Board Should Exert Their Power. *Aliran Monthly* 18(3): 6–8.

Lim Mah Hui. 1983. *Ownership and Control of the One Hundred Largest Corporations in Malaysia*. Singapore: Oxford University Press.

Lindgren, Carl-Johan, Tomás J. T. Baliño, Charles Enoch, Anne-Marie Gulde, Marc Quintyn, and Leslie Teo. 1999. *Financial Sector Crisis and Restructuring: Lessons from Asia*. IMF Occasional Paper No. 188. Washington, DC: International Monetary Fund.

Linz, Juan J. 2000. *Totalitarian and Authoritarian Regimes*. Boulder: Lynne Rienner Publishers.

Liow, Joseph. 1999. Crisis, Choice and Change: Malaysian Electoral Politics at the End of the 20th Century. *Asian Journal of Political Science* 7(2): 45–74.

Loh Kok Wah, Francis. 2002. Developmentalism and the Limits of Democratic Discourse. In *Democracy in Malaysia: Discourses and Practices*, edited by Francis Loh Kok Wah and Khoo Boo Teik, 19–50. Richmond, Surrey: Curzon Press.

  2003. A New Politics in Malaysia: Ferment and Fragmentation. In *Malaysian Economics and Politics in the New Century*, edited by Colin Barlow and Francis Loh Kok Wah, 93–105. Cheltenham: Edward Elgar.

Looney, Robert E. 1985. *Economic Policymaking in Mexico: Factors Underlying the 1982 Crisis*. Durham: Duke University Press.

López Portillo, José. 1982. VI Informe de Gobierno del Presidente Constitucional de los Estados Unidos Mexicanos José López Portillo y Pacheco, 1 de septiembre de 1982. Dirección Servicio de Investigación y Análisis. Available online at http://www.diputados.gob.mx/cedia/sia/re/RE-ISS-09-06-15.pdf [accessed February 26, 2009].

Loveard, Dewi. 1998. People Power, Amuk Massa: Hari-Hari Terakhir Di Tampuk Kekuasaan. In *Soeharto Lengser: Perspektif Luar Negeri*, edited by Alas Gambiran, 16–34. Yogyakarta: LKiS.

Loveard, Keith. 1999. *Suharto: Indonesia's Last Sultan*. Singapore: Horizon Books.

Lowry, Robert. 1996. *The Armed Forces of Indonesia*. St Leonards: Allen & Unwin.

Luebbert, Gregory M. 1991. *Liberalism, Fascism, or Social Democracy: Social Classes and the Political Origins of Regimes in Interwar Europe.* New York: Oxford University Press.

Luhulima, James. 2001. *Hari-Hari Terpanjang: Menjelang Mundurnya Presiden Soeharto Dan Beberapa Peristiwa Terkait.* Jakarta: Penerbit Kompas.

Luna, Matilde. 1995. Entrepreneurial Interests and Political Action in Mexico: Facing the Demands of Economic Modernization. In *The Challenge of Institutional Reform in Mexico*, edited by Riordan Roett, 77–94. Boulder: Lynne Rienner Publishers.

Lustig, Nora. 1998. *Mexico: The Remaking of an Economy.* 2nd ed. Washington, DC: Brookings Institution Press.

MacIntyre, Andrew. 1991. *Business and Politics in Indonesia.* Sydney: Allen & Unwin.

———. 1994. Power, Prosperity and Patrimonialism: Business and Government in Indonesia. In *Business and Government in Industrializing Asia*, edited by Andrew MacIntyre, 244–67. Ithaca: Cornell University Press.

———. 1999a. Indonesia. In *Democracy, Governance, and Economic Performance: East and Southeast Asia*, edited by Ian Marsh, Jean Blondel, and Takashi Inoguchi, 261–86. New York: United Nations University Press.

———. 1999b. Political Institutions and the Economic Crisis in Thailand and Indonesia. In *Politics of the Asian Economic Crisis*, edited by T. J. Pempel, 143–62. Ithaca: Cornell University Press.

———. 2001. Institutions and Investors: The Politics of the Economic Crisis in Southeast Asia. *International Organization* 55(1): 81–122.

———. 2003a. Institutions and the Political Economy of Corruption in Developing Countries. Discussion paper, Workshop on Corruption, Stanford University, January 31–February 1, 2003.

———. 2003b. *The Power of Institutions: Political Architecture and Governance.* Ithaca: Cornell University Press.

MacIntyre, Andrew, and Sjahrir. 1993. Survey of Recent Developments. *Bulletin of Indonesian Economic Studies* 29(1): 5–33.

Mackie, J. A. C. 1990. Property and Power in Indonesia. In *The Politics of Middle Class Indonesia*, edited by Richard Tanter and Kenneth Young, 71–95. Clayton: Centre of Southeast Asian Studies, Monash University.

———. 1992. Changing Patterns of Chinese Big Business in Southeast Asia. In *Southeast Asian Capitalists*, edited by Ruth McVey, 161–90. Ithaca: Southeast Asia Program, Cornell University.

———. 1993. Indonesia: Economic Growth and Depoliticization. In *Driven by Growth: Political Change in the Asia-Pacific Region*, edited by James W. Morley, 69–96. Armonk: M. E. Sharpe.

———. 1999. Entrepreneurship and Institutions: The Southeast Asian Experience. In *Institutions and Economic Change in Southeast Asia: The Context of Development from the 1960s to the 1990s*, edited by Colin Barlow, 72–84. Cheltenham: Edward Elgar.

Mackie, Jamie, and Andrew MacIntyre. 1994. Politics. In *Indonesia's New Order: The Dynamics of Socio-Economic Transformation*, edited by Hal Hill, 1–53. Honolulu: University of Hawai'i Press.

Magaloni, Beatriz. 2006. *Voting for Autocracy: Hegemonic Party Survival and Its Demise in Mexico*. Cambridge: Cambridge University Press.

Mahani Zainal Abidin. 2002. *Rewriting the Rules: The Malaysian Crisis Management Model*. Petaling Jaya: Pearson Malaysia Sdn. Bhd.

Mahathir Mohamad. 1998a. *Currency Turmoil*. Petaling Jaya: Limkokwing Integrated.

———. 1998b. Ucapan Belanjawan 1999. Available online at http://www.treasury.gov.my/index.php?ch=10&pg=150&ac=168 [accessed December 15, 2007].

———. 1999. *Koleksi Ucapan Mahathir (Januari–Disember 1998)*. Edited by Razali Kidam and Amidah Hamim. Kuala Lumpur: Jabatan Penerangan Malaysia.

———. 2001. *Melayu Mudah Lupa*. Subang Jaya: Pelanduk Publications.

Malley, Michael. 1998. The 7th Development Cabinet: Loyal to a Fault? *Indonesia* 65: 155–78.

Mann, Richard. 1998. *Economic Crisis in Indonesia: The Full Story*. Bath: Gateway Books.

Manning, Chris, and Sisira Jayasuriya. 1996. Survey of Recent Developments. *Bulletin of Indonesian Economic Studies* 32(2): 3–43.

Manzetti, Luigi. 1991. *The International Monetary Fund and Economic Stabilization: The Argentine Case*. New York: Praeger.

———. 2003. Political Manipulations and Market Reforms Failures. *World Politics* 55(3): 315–60.

Manzetti, Luigi, and Marco Dell'Aquila. 1988. Economic Stabilisation in Argentina: The Austral Plan. *Journal of Latin American Studies* 20(1): 1–26.

Marchak, M. Patricia. 1999. *God's Assassins: State Terrorism in Argentina in the 1970s*. Montreal: McGill-Queen's University Press.

Martinelli, César, and Mariano Tommasi. 1997. Sequencing of Economic Reforms in the Presence of Political Constraints. *Economics and Politics* 9(2): 115–31.

Martínez, Javier, and Alvaro Díaz. 1996. *Chile: The Great Transformation*. Washington, DC: Brookings Institution.

Mauzy, Diane K. 1983. *Barisan Nasional: Coalition Government in Malaysia*. Kuala Lumpur: Marican & Sons (Malaysia) Sdn. Bhd.

Maxfield, Sylvia. 1989. National Business, Debt-Led Growth, and Political Transition in Latin America. In *Debt and Democracy in Latin America*, edited by Barbara Stallings and Robert Kaufman, 75–90. Boulder: Westview Press.

———. 1990. *Governing Capital: International Finance and Mexican Politics*. Ithaca: Cornell University Press.

———. 1992. The International Political Economy of Bank Nationalization: Mexico in Comparative Perspective. *Latin American Research Review* 27(1): 75–103.

May, R. J. 1998. The Fall of Soeharto in Comparative Perspective. In *The Fall of Soeharto*, edited by Geoff Forrester and R. J. May, 231–8. Bathurst, NSW: Crawford House.

McCawley, Peter. 1982. The Economics of Ekonomi Pancasila. *Bulletin of Indonesian Economic Studies* 18(1): 102–9.

McKinnon, Ronald I., and Huw Pill. 1997. Credible Economic Liberalizations and Overborrowing. *American Economic Review* 87(2): 189–203.

1998. International Overborrowing: A Decomposition of Credit and Currency Risks. *World Development* 26(7): 1267–82.

McLeod, Ross H. 1997. Survey of Recent Developments. *Bulletin of Indonesian Economic Studies* 33(1): 3–43.

1998a. From Crisis to Cataclysm? The Mismanagement of Indonesia's Economic Ailments. *World Economy* 21(7): 913–30.

1998b. Indonesia. In *East Asia in Crisis: From Being a Miracle to Needing One?*, edited by Ross H. McLeod and Ross Garnaut, 31–48. London: Routledge.

2000. Government-Business Relations in Soeharto's Indonesia. In *Reform and Recovery in East Asia: The Role of the State and Economic Enterprise*, edited by Peter Drysdale, 146–68. London: Routledge.

2004. Dealing with Bank System Failure: Indonesia, 1997–2003. *Bulletin of Indonesian Economic Studies* 40(2): 95–116.

McVey, Ruth T. 1982. The Beamtenstaat in Indonesia. In *Interpreting Indonesian Politics: Thirteen Contributions to the Debate*, edited by Benedict Anderson and Audrey Kahin, 84–91. Ithaca: Modern Indonesia Project, Southeast Asia Program, Cornell University.

Means, Gordon P. 1991. *Malaysian Politics: The Second Generation*. Singapore: Oxford University Press.

1996. Soft Authoritarianism in Malaysia and Singapore. *Journal of Democracy* 7(4): 103–17.

Meller, Patricio. 2000. *The Unidad Popular and the Pinochet Dictatorship: A Political Economy Analysis*. Translated by Tim Ennis. New York: St. Martin's Press.

Middlebrook, Kevin. 1989. The Sounds of Silence: Organised Labour's Response to Economic Crisis in Mexico. *Journal of Latin American Studies* 21(2): 195–220.

1995. *The Paradox of Revolution: Labor, the State, and Authoritarianism in Mexico*. Baltimore: Johns Hopkins University Press.

Mietzner, Marcus. 2006. *The Politics of Military Reform in Post-Suharto Indonesia: Elite Conflict, Nationalism, and Institutional Resistance*. Washington, DC: East-West Center.

Miller, Victoria. 1998. The Double Drain with a Cross-Border Twist: More on the Relationship between Banking and Currency Crises. *American Economic Review* 88(2): 439–43.

Milne, R. S., and Diane K. Mauzy. 1999. *Malaysian Politics under Mahathir*. London: Routledge.

Mohammad Agus Yusoff. 1992. *Consociational Politics: The Malaysian Experience*. Kuala Lumpur: Perikatan Pemuda Enterprise.

Montes, Manuel F. 1998. *The Currency Crisis in Southeast Asia*. Updated ed. Singapore: Institute for Southeast Asian Studies.

Montinola, Gabriella. 2003. Who Recovers First? Banking Crises Resolution in Developing Countries. *Comparative Political Studies* 36(5): 541–74.

Moore, Barrington. 1966. *Social Origins of Dictatorship and Democracy: Lord and Peasant in the Making of the Modern World*. Boston: Beacon Press.

Morris, Stephen D. 1995. *Political Reformism in Mexico: An Overview of Contemporary Mexican Politics*. Boulder: Lynne Rienner Publishers.

Morris, Stephen D., and John Passe-Smith. 2001. What a Difference a Crisis Makes: NAFTA, Mexico, and the United States. *Latin American Perspectives* 28(3): 124–49.

Mosley, Layna. 2000. Room to Move: International Financial Markets and National Welfare States. *International Organization* 54(4): 737–73.

Mubyarto. 1987. *Ekonomi Pancasila: Gagasan Dan Kemungkinan*. Jakarta: LP3ES.

Munawar Ahmad Anees. 1998. Dr. Munawar's Statutory Declaration (Excerpts). *Aliran Monthly* 18(11–12): 26–33.

Munck, Gerardo L. 1998. *Authoritarianism and Democratization: Soldiers and Workers in Argentina, 1976–1983*. University Park: Pennsylvania State University Press.

Mundell, R. A. 1963. Capital Mobility and Stabilization Policy under Fixed and Flexible Exchange Rates. *Canadian Journal of Economics and Political Science* 29(4): 475–85.

Muñoz Goma, Oscar. 1989. Crisis and Industrial Reorganization in Chile. *Journal of Interamerican Studies and World Affairs* 31(1–2): 169–92.

Munro-Kua, Anne. 1996. *Authoritarian Populism in Malaysia*. London: Macmillan.

Mustafa K. Anuar. 2002. Defining Democratic Discourses: The Mainstream Press. In *Democracy in Malaysia: Discourses and Practices*, edited by Francis Loh Kok Wah and Khoo Boo Teik, 138–64. Richmond, Surrey: Curzon Press.

———. 2003. The Role of Malaysia's Mainstream Press in the 1999 General Election. In *New Politics in Malaysia*, edited by Francis Loh Kok Wah and Johan Saravanamuttu, 53–65. Singapore: Institute of Southeast Asian Studies.

Muzaffar, Chandra. 1986. *Freedom in Fetters: An Analysis of the State of Democracy in Malaysia*. Penang: Aliran.

Nasution, Anwar. 1999. The Financial Crisis in Indonesia. In *East Asia's Financial Systems: Evolution and Crisis*, edited by Seiichi Masuyama, Donna Vandenbrink, and Chia Siow Yue, 74–108. Singapore: Institute of Southeast Asian Studies.

———. 2000. The Meltdown of the Indonesian Economy: Causes, Responses and Lessons. *ASEAN Economic Bulletin* 17(2): 148–62.

———. 2002. Economic Recovery from the Crisis in 1997–98. In *80 Tahun Mohamad Sadli: Ekonomi Indonesia Dalam Era Politik Baru*, edited by Mohamad Ikisan, Chris Manning, and Hadi Soesastro. Jakarta: Penerbit Buku Kompas.

National Economic Action Council. 1998. National Economic Recovery Plan: Agenda for Action. Kuala Lumpur: National Economic Action Council. Available online at http://www.neac.gov.my/view.php?ch=9&pg=140&ac=959&fname=file&dbIndex=0&ex=1166396362&md=%22q+%97M%F4%18%E7%AF%B2%A6%B9%A3%5C%F6%9B [accessed December 15, 2007].

Navaratnam, Ramon V. 1999. *Healing the Wounded Tiger: How the Turmoil Is Reshaping Malaysia*. Subang Jaya: Pelanduk Publications.

Nelson, Joan M., ed. 1989. *Fragile Coalitions: The Politics of Economic Adjustment.* New Brunswick: Transaction Books.

——— ed. 1990. *Economic Crisis and Policy Choice: The Politics of Adjustment in Developing Countries.* Princeton: Princeton University Press.

Netto, Anil. 1998. A Nation Awakens. *Aliran Monthly* 18(11–12): 2–5.

——— 1999. A Y2k Crackdown: Arrests of Critics a Sign of Nervousness Ahead of UMNO Polls. *Aliran Monthly* 19(11–12): 2–6.

——— 2004. A Black Eye for Human Rights. In *Reflections: The Mahathir Years,* edited by Bridget Welsh, 87–95. Washington, DC: Southeast Asia Studies Program, Paul H. Nitze School of Advanced International Studies (SAIS), Johns Hopkins University.

Ng Beoy Kui. 2001. Vulnerability and Party Capitalism: Malaysia's Encounter with the 1997 Financial Crisis. In *Mahathir's Administration: Performance and Crisis in Governance,* edited by Ho Khai Leong and James Chin, 161–87. Singapore: Times Books International.

Nogués, Julio J. 1986. *The Nature of Argentina's Policy Reforms during 1976–1981.* Washington, DC: World Bank Staff Working Papers number 765.

Nordlinger, Eric A. 1970. Soldiers in Mufti: The Impact of Military Rule upon Economic and Social Change in the Non-Western States. *American Political Science Review* 64(4): 1131–48.

Oatley, Thomas. 1999. How Constraining Is Capital Mobility: The Partisan Hypothesis in an Open Economy. *American Journal of Political Science* 43(4): 1003–27.

Ocorandi, Michael. 1998. An Anatomy of the Recent Anti Ethnic-Chinese Riots in Indonesia. Available online at http://www.fica.org/cs:analysis-mayriot-ocorandi [accessed December 15, 2007].

O'Donnell, Guillermo. 1973. *Modernization and Bureaucratic-Authoritarianism: Studies in South American Politics.* Berkeley: Institute for International Studies, University of California.

——— 1988. *Bureaucratic Authoritarianism: Argentina, 1966–1973, in Comparative Perspective.* Translated by James McGuire and Rae Flory. Berkeley and Los Angeles: University of California Press.

O'Donnell, Guillermo, and Philippe C. Schmitter. 1986. *Transitions from Authoritarian Rule: Tentative Conclusions about Uncertain Democracies.* Baltimore: Johns Hopkins University Press.

Ong Hong Cheong. 1998. Coping with Capital Flows and the Role of Monetary Policy: The Malaysian Experience, 1990–95. In *Coping with Capital Flows in East Asia,* edited by C. H. Kwan, Donna Vandenbrink, and Chia Siow Yue, 220–43. Singapore: Institute of Southeast Asian Studies.

——— 1999. Evolution of the Malaysian Financial System beyond the Financial Crisis. In *East Asia's Financial Systems: Evolution and Crisis,* edited by Seiichi Masuyama, Donna Vandenbrink, and Chia Siow Yue, 144–65. Singapore: Institute of Southeast Asian Studies.

O'Rourke, Kevin. 2002. *Reformasi: The Struggle for Power in Post-Soeharto Indonesia.* Sydney: Allen & Unwin.

Pangestu, Mari, and Iwan Jaya Azis. 1994. Survey of Recent Developments. *Bulletin of Indonesian Economic Studies* 20(3): 3–47.

Pangestu, Mari, and Manggi Habir. 2002. The Boom, Bust, and Restructuring of Indonesian Banks. IMF Working Paper WP/02/66.

Pastor, Manuel, and Carol Wise. 1997. State Policy, Distribution and Neoliberal Reform in Mexico. *Journal of Latin American Studies* 29(2): 419–56.

Peck, James, and Karl Shell. 2003. Equilibrium Bank Runs. *Journal of Political Economy* 111(1): 103–23.

Pepinsky, Thomas B. 2008a. Capital Mobility and Coalitional Politics: Authoritarian Regimes and Economic Adjustment in Southeast Asia. *World Politics* 60(3): 438–74.

    2008b. Institutions, Economic Recovery, and Macroeconomic Vulnerability in Indonesia and Malaysia. In *Crisis as Catalyst: Asia's Dynamic Political Economy*, edited by Andrew MacIntyre, T. J. Pempel, and John Ravenhill, 231–50. Ithaca: Cornell University Press.

Peralta-Ramos, Monica. 1987. Toward an Analysis of the Structural Basis of Coercion in Argentina: The Behavior of the Major Fractions of the Bourgeoisie, 1976–1983. In *From Military Rule to Liberal Democracy in Argentina*, edited by Monica Peralta-Ramos and Carlos H. Waisman, 39–67. Boulder: Westview Press.

Perkins, Dwight Heald, and Wing Thye Woo. 2000. Malaysia: Adjusting to Deep Integration with the World Economy. In *The Asian Financial Crisis: Lessons for a Resilient Asia*, edited by Wing Thye Woo, Jeffrey D. Sachs, and Claus Schwab, 227–55. Cambridge, MA: MIT Press.

Perlmutter, Amos. 1969. The Praetorian State and the Praetorian Army: Toward a Taxonomy of Civil-Military Relations in Developing Polities. *Comparative Politics* 1(3): 382–404.

    1980. The Comparative Analysis of Military Regimes: Formations, Aspirations, and Achievements. *World Politics* 33(1): 96–120.

Pillay, Subramaniam. 1997. The Currency Crisis: Part 2. *Aliran Monthly* 17(7): 8–11.

    1998. Bailout Blues: State Welfare for the Rich and Market Capitalism for the Poor. *Aliran Monthly* 18(3): 2–5.

    1999. A Total Lie. *Aliran Monthly* 19(9): 27–31.

Pincus, Jonathan, and Rizal Ramli. 1998. Indonesia: From Showcase to Basket Case. *Cambridge Journal of Economics* 22(6): 723–34.

Pion-Berlin, David. 1985. The Fall of Military Rule in Argentina: 1976–1983. *Journal of Interamerican Studies and World Affairs* 27(2): 55–76.

Polity IV Project. 2006. Political Regime Characteristics and Transitions, 1800–2004. Available online at http://www.cidcm.umd.edu/polity/ [accessed December 15, 2007].

Pour, Julius. 1998. *Jakarta Semasa Lengser Keprabon.* Jakarta: Penerbit PT Elex Media Komputindo.

Powell, Robert. 2004. The Inefficient Use of Power: Costly Conflict with Complete Information. *American Political Science Review* 98(2): 231–41.

Pozzi, Pablo A. 1988. Argentina 1976–1982: Labour Leadership and Military Government. *Journal of Latin American Studies* 20(1): 111–38.

Prawiro, Radius. 1998. *Indonesia's Struggle for Economic Development: Pragmatism in Action.* Kuala Lumpur: Oxford University Press.

Rachagan, S. Sothi. 1987. The Apportionment of Seats in the House of Representatives. In *Government and Politics of Malaysia*, edited by Zakaria Haji
Ahmad, 56–70. Singapore: Oxford University Press.

    1993. *Law and the Electoral Process in Malaysia*. Kuala Lumpur: University of
Malaya Press.

Radelet, Steven C., and Wing Thye Woo. 2000. Indonesia: A Troubled Beginning.
In *The Asian Financial Crisis: Lessons for a Resilient Asia*, edited by Wing
Thye Woo, Jeffrey D. Sachs, and Claus Schwab, 165–84. Cambridge, MA:
MIT Press.

Rahardjo, M. Dawam. 2000. *Independensi BI Dalam Kemelut Politik*. Jakarta:
Pustaka Cidesindo.

Raillon, François. 1993. The New Order and Islam, or the Imbroglio of Faith and
Politics. *Indonesia* 57: 197–217.

Rajan, Ramkishen S. 2002. Post-Crisis Southeast Asia: Is There a Case for Currency Baskets? *World Economy* 25(1): 137–63.

Rakindo, Adil. 1975. Chinese Scapegoat Politics in Suharto's "New Order." In
Ten Years' Military Terror in Indonesia, edited by Malcolm Gladwell, 125–
38. Nottingham: Spokesman Books.

Ram. 1997a. Dismal Reaction: Budget Fails to Restore Investors' Confidence.
Aliran Monthly 17(9): 2–6.

    1997b. Malaysia Inc. Falters: No Use Blaming Others for Own Mistakes.
Aliran Monthly 17(12): 2–7.

Ramasamy, P. 1994. *Plantation Labour, Unions, Capital, and the State in Peninsular Malaysia*. Kuala Lumpur: Oxford University Press.

Ramírez de la O, Rogelio. 1996. The Mexican Peso Crisis and Recession of 1994–
1995: Preventable Then, Avoidable in the Future? In *The Mexican Peso
Crisis: International Perspectives*, edited by Riordan Roett, 11–32. Boulder:
Lynne Rienner Publishers.

Ramos, Joseph. 1986. *Neoconservative Economics in the Southern Cone of Latin
America, 1973–1983*. Baltimore: Johns Hopkins University Press.

Rasiah, Rajah. 1998. The Malaysian Financial Crisis: Capital Expansion,
Cronyism and Contraction. *Journal of the Asia Pacific Economy* 3(3):
358–78.

    2001a. The Political Economy of the Southeast Asian Financial Crisis. In *South-
east Asian Middle Classes: Prospects for Social Change and Democratisation*,
edited by Abdul Rahman Embong, 46–79. Bangi: Penerbit Universiti Kebangsaan Malaysia.

    2001b. Pre-Crisis Economic Weaknesses and Vulnerabilities. In *Malaysian
Eclipse: Economic Crisis and Recovery*, edited by Jomo K. S., 47–66. London:
Zed Books.

Rasiah, Rajah, and Ishak Shari. 2001. Market, Government and Malaysia's New
Economic Policy. *Cambridge Journal of Economics* 25(1): 57–78.

Reeve, David. 1985. *Golkar of Indonesia: An Alternative to the Party System*.
Singapore: Oxford University Press.

Remmer, Karen L. 1986. The Politics of Economic Stabilization: IMF Standby
Programs in Latin America, 1954–1984. *Comparative Politics* 19(1): 1–24.

    1989. *Military Rule in Latin America*. Boston: Unwin Hyman.

Robinson, James A., and Q. Neil Parsons. 2006. State Formation and Governance in Botswana. *Journal of African Economies* 15(AERC Supplement): 100–40.

Robison, Richard. 1982. Culture, Politics, and Economy in the Political History of the New Order. In *Interpreting Indonesian Politics: Thirteen Contributions to the Debate*, edited by Benedict Anderson and Audrey Kahin, 131–48. Ithaca: Southeast Asia Program, Cornell University.

——— 1986. *Indonesia: The Rise of Capital*. North Sydney: Asian Studies Association of Australia in Association with Allen & Unwin.

——— 1988. Authoritarian States, Capital-Owning Classes, and the Politics of Newly Industrializing Countries: The Case of Indonesia. *World Politics* 41(1): 52–74.

Robison, Richard, and Vedi R. Hadiz. 2004. *Reorganizing Power in Indonesia: The Politics of Oligarchy in an Age of Markets*. London: RoutledgeCurzon.

Robison, Richard, and Andrew Rosser. 1998. Contesting Reform: Indonesia's New Order and the IMF. *World Development* 26(8): 1593–1609.

Rodrik, Dani. 1996. Understanding Economic Policy Reform. *Journal of Economic Literature* 34(1): 9–41.

——— 1998. Who Needs Capital Account Convertibility? *Princeton Essays in International Finance* 207: 55–65.

Rogozinski, Jacques. 1998. *High Price for Change: Privatization in Mexico*. Washington, DC: Inter-American Development Bank.

Ros, Jaime. 1987. Mexico from the Oil Boom to the Debt Crisis: An Analysis of Policy Responses to External Shocks. In *Latin American Debt and Adjustment Crisis*, edited by Rosemary Thorp and Laurence Whitehead, 68–116. Pittsburgh: University of Pittsburgh Press.

——— 1993. On the Political Economy of Market and State Reform in Mexico. In *Democracy, Markets, and Structural Reform in Latin America: Argentina, Bolivia, Brazil, Chile, and Mexico*, edited by William C. Smith, Carlos H. Acuña, and Eduardo A. Gamarra, 297–323. New Brunswick: Transaction Publishers.

Rosser, Andrew. 2002. *The Politics of Economic Liberalisation in Indonesia: State, Market, and Power*. Richmond, Surrey: Curzon Press.

Rubio, Luis. 1998. Coping with Political Change. In *Mexico under Zedillo*, edited by Susan Kaufman Purcell and Luis Rubio, 5–36. Boulder: Lynne Rienner Publishers.

Rustam A. Sani. 2001. Malaysia's Economic and Political Crisis since September 1998. In *Reinventing Malaysia: Reflections Its Past and Future*, edited by Jomo K. S., 84–99. Bangi: Penerbit Universiti Kebangsaan Malaysia.

——— 2004. *Menjelang Reformasi: Kumpulan Rencana-Rencana Akhbar 1997–1998*. Kuala Lumpur: R Publishing Services.

Said, Salim. 2001. *Militer Indonesia Dan Politik: Dulu, Kini Dan Kelak*. Jakarta: Pustaka Sinar Harapan.

——— 2002. *Tumbuh Dan Tumbangnya: Dwifungsi Perkembangan Pemikiran Politik Militer Indonesia 1958–2000*. Jakarta: Aksara Karunia.

Salazar, Lorraine Carlos. 2004. "First Come, First Served": Privatization under Mahathir. In *Reflections: The Mahathir Years*, edited by Bridget Welsh,

282–93. Washington, DC: Southeast Asia Studies Program, Paul H. Nitze School of Advanced International Studies (SAIS), Johns Hopkins University.

Samego, Indria, Ikrar Nusa Bhakti, Hermawan Sulistyo, Riza Sihbudi, M. Hamdan Basyar, Moch. Nurhasim, Nur Iman Subono, and Sri Yanuarti. 1998. *Bila ABRI Berbisnis: Buku Pertama yang Meningkap Data dan Kasus Penyimpangan dalam Praktik Bisnis Kalangan Militer.* Bandung: Penerbit Mizan.

Samstad, James G. 2002. Corporatism and Democratic Transition: State and Labor during the Salinas and Zedillo Administrations. *Latin American Politics and Society* 44(4): 1–28.

Samstad, James G., and Ruth Berins Collier. 1995. Mexican Labor and Structural Reform under Salinas: New Unionism or Old Stalemate? In *The Challenge of Institutional Reform in Mexico,* edited by Riordan Roett, 9–37. Boulder: Lynne Rienner Publishers.

Sandee, Henry, Roos Kities Andadari, and Sri Sulandjari. 2000. Small Firm Development during Good Times and Bad: The Jepara Furniture Industry. In *Indonesia in Transition: Social Aspects of Reformasi and Crisis,* edited by Chris Manning and Peter van Diermen, 184–98. Singapore: Institute of Southeast Asian Studies.

Santín Quiroz, Osvaldo. 2001. *The Political Economy of Mexico's Financial Reform.* Burlington: Ashgate.

Saravanamuttu, Johan. 2001. Is There a Politics of the Malaysian Middle Class? In *Southeast Asian Middle Classes: Prospects for Social Change and Democratisation,* edited by Abdul Rahman Embong, 103–18. Bangi: Penerbit Universiti Kebangsaan Malaysia.

Saravanamuttu, Johan. 2003. The Eve of the 1999 General Election: From the NEP to Reformasi. In *New Politics in Malaysia,* edited by Francis Loh Kok Wah and Johan Saravanamuttu, 1–22. Singapore: Institute of Southeast Asian Studies.

Sato, Yuri. 2003. Post-Crisis Economic Reform in Indonesia: Policy for Intervening in Ownership in Historical Perspective. Institute for Developing Economies, IDE Research Paper No. 4.

Satyanath, Shanker. 2006. *Globalization, Politics, and Financial Turmoil: Asia's Banking Crisis.* Cambridge: Cambridge University Press.

Satyanath, Shanker, and Daniel Berger. 2007. Capital Controls, Political Institutions and Economic Growth. *Quarterly Journal of Political Science* 2(4): 307–24.

Schambaugh, George E. 2004. The Power of Money: Global Capital and Policy Choices in Developing Countries. *American Journal of Political Science* 48(2): 281–95.

Schamis, Hector E. 1999. Distributional Coalitions and the Politics of Economic Reform in Latin America. *World Politics* 51(2): 236–68.

Schedler, Andreas. 2002. The Menu of Manipulation. *Journal of Democracy* 13(2): 36–50.

Schneider, Ben Ross. 1989. Partly for Sale: Privatization and State Strength in Brazil and Mexico. *Journal of Interamerican Studies and World Affairs* 30(4): 89–116.

Schneider, Martin, and Aaron Tornell. 2000. Balance Sheet Effects, Bailout Guarantees and Financial Crises. NBER Working Paper No. 8060.

Schwarz, Adam. 1994. *A Nation in Waiting: Indonesia in the 1990s*. St Leonards: Allen & Unwin.

——— 1999. Introduction: The Politics of Post-Suharto Indonesia. In *Politics of Post-Suharto Indonesia*, edited by Adam Schwarz and Jonathan Paris, 1–15. New York: Council on Foreign Relations.

Scott, James C. 1985. *Weapons of the Weak: Everyday Forms of Peasant Resistance*. New Haven: Yale University Press.

Searle, Peter. 1999. *The Riddle of Malaysian Capitalism: Rent-Seekers or Real Capitalists?* St Leonards: Allen & Unwin.

Setiono, Benny G. 2003. *Tionghoa Dalam Pusaran Politik*. Jakarta: Elkasa.

Sharma, Shalendra D. 2001. The Indonesian Financial Crisis: From Banking Crisis to Financial Sector Reforms, 1997–2000. *Indonesia* 71: 79–110.

Shidiq, Akhmad Rizal. 2003. Decentralization and Rent Seeking in Indonesia. *Ekonomi dan Keuangan Indonesia* 51(2): 177–207.

Shin Yoon Hwan. 1989. Demystifying the Capitalist State: Political Patronage, Bureaucratic Interests, and Capitalists-in-Formation in Soeharto's Indonesia. Ph.D. dissertation, Department of Political Science, Yale University.

Shiraishi, Takashi. 1999. The Indonesian Military in Politics. In *Politics of Post-Suharto Indonesia*, edited by Adam Schwarz and Jonathan Paris, 73–86. New York: Council on Foreign Relations.

——— 2001. Rethinking the Moral Foundation of the Indonesian State. In *Southeast Asian Middle Classes: Prospects for Social Change and Democratisation*, edited by Abdul Rahman Embong, 181–91. Bangi: Penerbit Universiti Kebangsaan Malaysia.

Shleifer, Andrei, and Robert Vishny. 1993. Corruption. *Quarterly Journal of Economics* 108(3): 599–617.

Sidel, John T. 1998. *Macet Total*: Logics of Circulation and Accumulation in the Demise of Indonesia's New Order. *Indonesia* 66: 159–94.

——— 2006. *Riots, Pogroms, and Jihad: Religious Violence in Indonesia*. Ithaca: Cornell University Press.

Siegel, James. 2001. Thoughts on the Violence of May 13 and 14, 1998, in Jakarta. In *Violence and the State in Suharto's Indonesia*, edited by Benedict R. O'G. Anderson, 90–123. Ithaca: Southeast Asia Program, Cornell University.

Sieh Lee Mei Ling. 1992. The Transformation of Malaysian Business Groups. In *Southeast Asian Capitalists*, edited by Ruth McVey, 103–26. Ithaca: Southeast Asia Program, Cornell University.

Silva, Eduardo. 1996. *State and Capital in Chile: Business Elites, Technocrats, and Market Economics*. Boulder: Westview Press.

Simandjuntak, Djisman S. 1999. An Inquiry into the Nature, Causes and Consequences of the Indonesian Crisis. *Journal of the Asia Pacific Economy* 4(1): 171–92.

Singh, Bilveer. 2000. *Succession Politics in Indonesia: The 1998 Presidential Elections and the Fall of Suharto*. Houndmills, Basingstoke, Hampshire: Macmillan.

Singh, Hari. 2000. Democratization or Oligarchic Restructuring? The Politics of Reform in Malaysia. *Government and Opposition* 35(4): 520–46.

Sjaastad, Larry A. 1989. Argentine Economic Policy, 1976–1981. In *The Political Economy of Argentina, 1946–1983*, edited by Guido Di Tella and Rudiger Dornbusch, 254–75. Pittsburgh: University of Pittsburgh Press.

Sjahrir. 1999. *Krisis Ekonomi Menuju Reformasi Total.* 2nd ed. Jakarta: Yayasan Obor Indonesia.

Slater, Dan. 2005. Ordering Power: Contentious Politics, State-Building, and Authoritarian Durability in Southeast Asia. Ph.D. dissertation, Department of Political Science, Emory University.

Smith, Benjamin B. 2003. "If I Do These Things, They Will Throw Me Out": Economic Reform and the Collapse of Indonesia's New Order. *Journal of International Affairs* 57(1): 113–28.

———. 2004. Oil Wealth and Regime Survival in the Developing World, 1960–1999. *American Journal of Political Science* 48(2): 232–46.

———. 2005. Life of the Party: The Origins of Regime Breakdown and Persistence under Single-Party Rule. *World Politics* 57(3): 421–51.

———. 2006. The Wrong Kind of Crisis: Why Oil Booms and Busts Rarely Lead to Authoritarian Breakdown. *Studies in Comparative International Development* 40(4): 55–76.

Smith, Peter. 1997. Political Dimensions of the Peso Crisis. In *Mexico 1994: Anatomy of an Emerging-Market Crash*, edited by Sebastian Edwards and Moisés Naím, 31–53. New York: Carnegie Endowment for International Peace.

Soebijono, A. S. S. Tambunan, Hidayat Mukmin, and Roekmani Koesoemo Astoeti. 1997. *Dwifungsi ABRI: Perkembangan Dan Peranannya Dalam Kehidupan Politik Di Indonesia.* Yogyakarta: Gadjah Mada University Press.

Soeharto. 1989. *Pikiran, Ucapan, Dan Tinkakan Saya: Otobiografi, Seperti Dipaparkan Kepada G. Dwipayana Dan Ramadhan K.H.* Jakarta: Citra Lamtoro Gung Persada.

Soesastro, Hadi. 2000. Governance and the Crisis in Indonesia. In *Reform and Recovery in East Asia: The Role of the State and Economic Enterprise*, edited by Peter Drysdale, 120–45. London: Routledge.

Soesastro, Hadi, and M. Chatib Basri. 1998. Survey of Recent Developments. *Bulletin of Indonesian Economic Studies* 34(1): 3–54.

Soesastro, M. Hadi, and Peter Drysdale. 1990. Survey of Recent Developments. *Bulletin of Indonesian Economic Studies* 26(3): 3–44.

Springer, Gary L., and Jorge L. Molina. 1995. The Mexican Financial Crisis: Genesis, Impact, and Implications. *Journal of Interamerican Studies and World Affairs* 37(2): 57–81.

Stasavage, David. 2003. *Public Debt and the Birth of the Democratic State: France and Great Britain, 1688–1789.* Cambridge: Cambridge University Press.

Stepan, Alfred. 1988. *Rethinking Military Politics: Brazil and the Southern Cone.* Princeton: Princeton University Press.

Stockwell, A. J. 1977. The Formation and First Years of the United Malays National Organization (U.M.N.O.), 1946–1948. *Modern Asian Studies* 11(4): 481–513.

Sulastomo. 2001. *Lengser Keprabon*. Jakarta: RajaGrafindo.

Sulistiyo, Hermawan. 2001. Greens in the Rainbow: Ethnoreligious Issues and the Indonesian Armed Forces. In *The Politics of Multiculturalism: Pluralism and Citizenship in Malaysia, Singapore, and Indonesia*, edited by Robert W. Hefner, 291–309. Honolulu: University of Hawai'i Press.

Sumarkidjo, Atmadji. 2001. The Rise and Fall of the Generals: The Indonesian Military at a Crossroads. In *Indonesia Today: Challenges of History*, edited by Grayson J. Lloyd and Shannon L. Smith, 136–45. Singapore: Institute of Southeast Asian Studies.

Sundhaussen, Ulf. 1982. *The Road to Power: Indonesian Military Politics, 1945–1967*. Kuala Lumpur: Oxford University Press.

Suruhanjaya Pilihan Raya Malaysia. 1999. Laporan Pilihan Raya Umum Malaysia 1999. Available online at http://www.spr.gov.my/laporan/1999/bm99.html [accessed April 25, 2006].

Suryadinata, Leo. 2002. *Elections and Politics in Indonesia*. Singapore: Institute of Southeast Asian Studies.

Syed Husin Ali. 1998. Economy in Crisis? Both External and Internal Factors to Blame. *Aliran Monthly* 18(3): 13–18.

Syed Hussein Alatas. 1977. *The Myth of the Lazy Native*. London: Frank Cass.

Tamayo, Jaime. 1990. Neoliberalism Encounters *Neocardenismo*. In *Popular Movements and Political Change in Mexico*, edited by Joe Fowaker and Ann L. Craig, 121–36. Boulder: Lynne Rienner Publishers.

Tan Chee-Beng. 2000. Socio-Cultural Diversities and Identities. In *The Chinese in Malaysia*, edited by Lee Kam Hing and Tan Chee-Beng, 37–70. Kuala Lumpur: Oxford University Press.

Tan Tat Wai. 2003. The Impact of the 1997 Financial Crisis on Malaysia's Corporate Sector and Its Response. In *Malaysian Economics and Politics in the New Century*, edited by Colin Barlow and Francis Loh Kok Wah, 29–45. Cheltenham: Edward Elgar.

Teichman, Judith. 1992. The Mexican State and the Political Implications of Economic Restructuring. *Latin American Perspectives* 19(2): 88–104.

——— 1995. *Privatization and Political Change in Mexico*. Pittsburgh: University of Pittsburgh Press.

Thacker, Strom C. 1999. NAFTA Coalitions and the Political Viability of Neoliberalism in Mexico. *Journal of Interamerican Studies and World Affairs* 41(2): 57–89.

Thee Kian Wie. 2003. The Indonesian Economic Crisis and the Long Road to Recovery. *Australian Economic History Review* 43(2): 183–96.

Theobald, Robin. 1982. Patrimonialism. *World Politics* 34(4): 548–59.

Thomson Datastream. 2006a. Indonesian Interbank Call – Middle Rate 1/1/1997 to 12/31/1998. Retrieved February 10, 2006, from Datastream database.

——— 2006b. Indonesian Rupiah to US $ (WMR) 1/1/1997 to 12/31/1998. Retrieved February 10, 2006, from Datastream database.

Timmer, C. Peter. 1993. Rural Bias in the East and South-East Asian Rice Economy: Indonesia in Comparative Perspective. *Journal of Development Studies* 29(4): 149–76.

Tobin, James. 1978. A Proposal for International Monetary Reform. *Eastern Economic Journal* 4(3–4): 153–59.

Tommasi, Mariano. 2005. Crisis, Political Institutions, and Policy Reform: The Good, the Bad, and the Ugly. Working Paper, Department of Economics, Yale University.

Tourres, Marie-Aimée. 2003. *The Tragedy That Didn't Happen: Malaysia's Crisis Management and Capital Controls*. Kuala Lumpur: Institute for Strategic and International Studies (Malaysia).

Toyoda, A. Maria. 2001. Malaysia: Ethnic Cleavages and Controlled Liberalization. In *The Political Economy of International Financial Crisis: Interest Groups, Ideologies, and Institutions*, edited by Shale Horowitz and Uk Heo, 91–109. Singapore: Institute of Southeast Asian Studies (ISEAS).

Usman, Marzuki. 1997. Peranan Kebijakan Ekonomi Makro (Pasar Modal) Dalam Mencapai Kemandirian Pembiayaan Pembangunan. In *Pembangunan Ekonomi Nasional: Suatu Pendekatan Pemerataan, Keadilan Dan Ekonomi Kerakyatan*, edited by M. Dawam Rahardjo, 81–96. Jakarta: PT Intermasa.

Valdés, Juan Gabriel. 1995. *Pinochet's Economists*. Cambridge: Cambridge University Press.

Valdés Ugalde, Francisco. 1994. From Bank Nationalization to State Reform: Business and the New Mexican Order. In *The Politics of Economic Restructuring: State-Society Relations and Regime Change in Mexico*, edited by Maria Lorena Cook, Kevin J. Middlebrook, and Juan Molinar Horcasitas, 219–42. La Jolla: Center for U.S.-Mexican Studies, University of California, San Diego.

van der Kroef, Justus M. 1971. Interpretations of the 1965 Indonesian Coup: A Review of the Literature. *Pacific Affairs* 43(4): 557–77.

Vatikiotis, Michael R. J. 1998. *Indonesian Politics under Suharto: The Rise and Fall of the New Order*. 3rd ed. London: Routledge.

Vatikiotis, Michael R. J., and Adam Schwarz. 1998. Kejatuhan Soeharto Dan Kebangkitan Rakyat Indonesia: Hari-Hari Terakhir Di Istana. In *Soeharto Lengser: Perspektif Luar Negeri*, edited by Alas Gambiran, 64–81. Yogyakarta: LKiS.

Vergara, Pilar. 1986. Changes in the Economic Functions of the Chilean State under the Military Regime. In *Military Rule in Chile: Dictatorship and Oppositions*, edited by J. Samuel Valenzuela and Arturo Valenzuela, 85–116. Baltimore: Johns Hopkins University Press.

von Vorys, Karl. 1975. *Democracy without Consensus: Communalism and Political Stability in Malaysia*. Princeton: Princeton University Press.

Vreeland, James R. 2003. *The IMF and Economic Development*. Cambridge: Cambridge University Press.

Waldner, David. 1999. *State Building and Late Development*. Ithaca: Cornell University Press.

Walter, Stefanie. 2008. A New Approach for Determining Exchange-Rate Level Preferences. *International Organization* 62(3): 405–38.

Wan Azizah Wan Ismail. 2001. Democracy in Asia: Riding the Wave. In *Democratic Transitions in Asia*, edited by Uwe Johannen and James Gomez, 51–555. Singapore: Select Publishing.

Wang Gungwu. 1970. Chinese Politics in Malaya. *China Quarterly* 43: 1–30.

Weber, Max. [1912] 1968. *Economy and Society: An Outline of Interpretive Sociology.* New York: Bedminster Press.

Weinstein, Martin. 1988. *Uruguay: Democracy at the Crossroads.* Boulder: Westview Press.

Weiss, Linda. 1999. State Power and the Asian Crisis. *New Political Economy* 4(3): 317–42.

Weiss, Meredith L. 1999. What Will Become of Reformasi? Ethnicity and Changing Political Norms in Malaysia. *Contemporary Southeast Asia* 21(3): 424–50.

———. 2000. The 1999 Malaysian General Elections: Issues, Insults, and Irregularities. *Asian Survey* 40(3): 413–35.

———. 2005. *Protest and Possibilities: Civil Society and Coalitions for Political Change in Malaysia.* Stanford: Stanford University Press.

Welsh, Bridget. 2004. Shifting Terrain: Elections in the Mahathir Era. In *Reflections: The Mahathir Years,* edited by Bridget Welsh, 119–33. Washington, DC: Southeast Asia Studies Program, Paul H. Nitze School of Advanced International Studies (SAIS), Johns Hopkins University.

Weyland, Kurt. 2002. *The Politics of Market Reform in Fragile Democracies: Argentina, Brazil, Peru, and Venezuela.* Princeton: Princeton University Press.

White, Russell N. 1992. *State, Class, and the Nationalization of the Mexican Banks.* New York: Crane Russak.

Whitehead, Laurence. 1998. Mexico's "Near Ungovernability" Revisited. In *Governing Mexico: Political Parties and Elections,* edited by Mónica Serrano, 185–204. London: Institute of Latin American Studies.

Wibowo, Ignatius. 2001. Exit, Voice, and Loyalty: Indonesian Chinese after the Fall of Soeharto. *Sojourn* 16(1): 125–46.

Williams, Heather. 2001a. Of Free Trade and Debt Bondage: Fighting Banks and the State in Mexico. *Latin American Perspectives* 28(4): 30–51.

———. 2001b. *Social Movements and Economic Transition: Markets and Distributive Conflict in Mexico.* Cambridge: Cambridge University Press.

Wilson, Dominic. 2000. Managing Capital Flows in East Asia. In *Reform and Recovery in East Asia: The Role of the State and Economic Enterprise,* edited by Peter Drysdale, 255–82. London: Routledge.

Winn, Peter, ed. 2004. *Victims of the Chilean Miracle: Workers and Neoliberalism in the Pinochet Era, 1973–2002.* Durham: Duke University Press.

Winters, Jeffrey A. 1994. Power and the Control of Capital. *World Politics* 46(3): 419–52.

———. 1996. *Power in Motion: Capital Mobility and the Indonesian State.* Ithaca: Cornell University Press.

Woodruff, David M. 2005. Boom, Gloom, Doom: Balance Sheets, Monetary Fragmentation, and the Politics of Financial Crisis in Argentina and Russia. *Politics and Society* 33(1): 3–45.

World Bank. 1987. *Argentina: Economic Recovery and Growth.* Washington, DC: World Bank.

———. 1998. *East Asia: The Road to Recovery.* Washington, DC: World Bank.

Yap Meow-Chung, Michael. 2001. The 1997 Currency Crisis and Subsequent Policy Response. In *Modern Malaysia in the Global Economy Political and Social Change into the 21st Century*, edited by Colin Barlow, 45–58. Cheltenham: Edward Elgar.

Young, Ken. 1998. The Crisis: Contexts and Prospects. In *The Fall of Soeharto*, edited by Geoff Forrester and R. J. May, 104–29. Bathurst, NSW: Crawford House.

Zaharom Nain. 1998. Pathetic Press: Journalism That Fits and (What Happens to) Journalists Who Don't. *Aliran Monthly* 18(7): 2–7.

　　2002. The Structure of the Media Industry: Implications for Democracy. In *Democracy in Malaysia: Discourses and Practices*, edited by Francis Loh Kok Wah and Khoo Boo Teik, 111–37. Richmond, Surrey: Curzon Press.

Zakaria Haji Ahmad. 1989. Malaysia: Quasi Democracy in a Divided Society. In *Democracy in Developing Countries: Asia*, edited by Larry Diamond, Juan J. Linz, and Seymour Martin Lipset, 347–81. Boulder: Lynne Rienner Publishers.

Index

MCP, 63
media
  foreign coverage, 179, 203
  in Indonesia
    post-Soeharto freedoms, 189
    proregime bias in, 112, 171
    restrictions on, 168
    targeting of Chinese in, 172, 176
  in Malaysia
    ownership of, 68, 199
    proregime bias in, 129, 200, 202,
      206, 208, 212, 215, 217–18, 219
    restrictions on, 68, 195, 210–11,
      214, 217–18, 222
Megawati Sukarnoputri. *See*
  Sukarnoputri, Megawati
Méndez, Aparicio, 248, 250
Mexico, 12, 16, 17, 18, 33, 226
  1982 crisis
    capital inflows and, 252
    policy response to, 252–55
    and regime survival, 253, 255
  1994 crisis
    capital inflows and, 258
    and democratization, 259–60
    policy response to, 258–59
MIC, 62, 63, 220
  1999 electoral results, 222
military
  in Indonesia. *See* ABRI
  in Malaysia, 66, 74
military regimes
  in Argentina, 243
  in Chile, 238–39
  and coalition formation, 17
  in Latin America, 261, 261–63
  and regime survival, 8, 19, 228–37,
    271
  in Uruguay, 248
Ministry of Finance (Indonesia), 91.
    See also Bawazier, Fuad;
    Muhammad, Mar'ie
  and bank closures, 100–2
  and bank restructuring. *See* IBRA
  personnel shakeups, 93
Ministry of Finance (Malaysia), 70, 75,
    76, 126, 138. *See also* Anwar

Ibrahim; Daim Zainuddin;
    Mustapha Mohamed; Tengku
    Razaleigh Hamzah
  and corporate bailouts, 137
Mirzan Mahathir, 74, 137
mobile capital. *See also* capital mobility
  in Argentina, 245, 247. *See also*
    Argentina, coalition structure
  in Chile, 241–42. *See also* Chile,
    coalition structure
  definition of. *See* capital mobility,
    definition of
  in Indonesia, 3, 40, 53–61. *See also*
    Chinese (ethnic group in
    Southeast Asia), in Indonesia
    and adjustment policy. *See*
    adjustment policy, in Indonesia
    and regime change. *See*
    authoritarian breakdowns, in
    Indonesia
  in Malaysia, 75. *See also*
    Chinese(ethnic group in Southeast
    Asia), in Malaysia, capital assets
    and adjustment policy. *See*
    adjustment policy, in Malaysia
  in Mexico, 252, 253, 255, 257
  preferences over adjustment policy,
    7, 14, 26–30, 31, 264
  in Uruguay, 249, 250. *See also*
    Uruguay, coalition structure
Mohd. Azlan Hashim, 148–49
Mohtar Abdullah, 199, 212
monetary policy. *See also* capital
    account policy; exchange rates;
    financial policy
  in Indonesia, 2, 91–94
  logic of, 22, 23, 26–30, 30, 31
  in Malaysia, 2, 130–133
Moore, Barrington, 268
MPR, March 1998 session, 160, 164,
    166, 170, 173, 174, 175, 177–
    79
Muhammad Hasan. *See* Hasan,
    Muhammad (Bob)
Muhammad, Mar'ie, 93, 100, 102, 112
Muhammadiyah, 160
Munawar Ahmad Anees, 213

Pinochet, Augusto, 14, 18, 239, 240, 241, 242
PKI, 42–43
PKR, 62. *See also* KeADILan
PNB, 66, 134, 219. *See also* ASB; ASN
populism
  in Argentina, 243, 247
  and authoritarian rule, 16, 262, 264
  in Indonesia, 159, 189
  in Malaysia, 79, 201. *See also* ˙ UMNO, targeting of Malay masses
  in Mexico, 17, 255, 256. *See also* PRI, populist origins of
portfolio investment, 25, 122–24, 147, 148, 154
PPP, 79, 115, 168, 169, 176, 184
Prabowo Subianto, 51, 101, 163, 174, 175, 177, 178, 179, 180, 182, 185
  and factionalism in ABRI. *See* ABRI, factionalism
  and student leaders' disappearances, 179
  involvement in May riots. *See* May 13–14 riots, responsibility for
  involvement in Trisakti massacre, 181
Prajogo Pangestu, 55, 59, 190
Prawirawata, Iwan, 102, 170, 177
PRI, 12, 16, 251
  changing coalition of, 255–58
  populist origins of, 17, 252
pribumi
  definition, 40
  entrepreneurs, 44, 52, 54, 60–61, 93, 112, 171, 172, 173, 182, 183, 188, 189, 191
Printing Presses and Publications Act, 68. *See also* media, in Malaysia, restrictions on
PRM, 215, 216, 219, 221
Probosutedjo, 100
Proton, 65, 69, 130, 139, 140

Raden Hartono, 51, 168, 178
Rahim Tamby Chik, 199, 208

Rashid Hussain Bank. *See* RHB Bank
red-and-white faction. *See* ABRI, factionalism
reformasi movement
  in Indonesia, 156, 160, 166, 174, 175, 180, 187, 188, 189, 275–76
  in Malaysia, 160, 192, 196, 212–15, 217, 218, 275–76
regime survival. *See* authoritarian breakdowns; democratization
Renong, 71, 136, 137, 139, 140
RHB Bank, 134, 136
Rodrik, Dani, 276

Salim Group, 55, 56, 97, 104
Salim, Anthony, 103
Salim, Sudono. *See* Liem Sioe Liong
Salinas de Gortari, Carlos, 257, 258
Samy Vellu, S., 128, 220
Sanusi Junid, 208, 210
Sarawak United People's Party, 76, 221
SBI, 91, 102
Sedition Act, 68, 214
Semangat '46, 197, 198
September 30 movement, 42
Seventh Development Cabinet, 177–78, 185, 188
Sime Bank, 135, 136, 138
Sime Darby, 130, 136, 142
Singapore Stock Exchange, 149
Siti Hardiyanti Rukmana. *See* Tutut
Siti Hartinah. *See* Tien Soeharto
Sixth Development Cabinet, 167
Sjafrie Sjamsuddin, 183
Sjahril Sabirin, 102, 113, 170, 177, 178
Societies Act, 68
Soedradjad Djiwandono, 92, 93, 99, 101–2, 106, 107, 111, 113, 170, 172, 177
Soeharto
  connections to ethnic Chinese cronies, 56, 276. *See also* Chinese (ethnic group in Southeast Asia), in Indonesia